Philosophical Perspectives, 2
Epistemology, 1988

Previously Published Volumes
Volume 1, Metaphysics—1987

Forthcoming Volumes
Volume 3, Philosophy of Mind and Action Theory—Fall 1989
Volume 4, Action Theory and Philosophy of Mind—Spring 1990
Additional Titles to be announced.

Philosophical Perspectives, 2
Epistemology, 1988

Edited by
JAMES E. TOMBERLIN
California State University, Northridge

Ridgeview Publishing Company ● Atascadero, California

Paper Text: ISBN 0-917930-47-9
Cloth Text: ISBN 0-917930-87-8

The typesetting and illustrations were done by the CSUN Graphics Department (Randall Tucker, Manager). The typesetter was Robert Olsen.

Published in the United States of America
by Ridgeview Publishing Company
P. O. Box 686
Atascadero, California 93423

Printed in the United States of America

CONTENTS

vi / Contents

PREFACE

The nature of knowledge and justification, perceptual evidence, coherentism and foundationalism, reliabilism, internalism versus externalism, epistemic obligation, self-knowledge, reason and deliberation, and naturalized epistemology—these are some of the central issues of epistemology addressed by nineteen leading philosophers in the present collection.

A new series of topical philosophy studies, *Philosophical Perspectives* aims to publish original essays by foremost thinkers in their fields, with each volume confined to a main area of philosophical research. The intention is to publish volumes annually.

Philosophical Perspectives could not have come to fruition without the precious encouragement it received from Administrative Officials at California State University, Northridge. I am particularly grateful to Dr. James W. Cleary, President of this institution, and Dr. Bob H. Suzuki, Vice President for Academic Affairs, who provided essential financial support through the Special Projects Fund of the California State University Foundation, Northridge. I also thank Dr. Jerome Richfield, Dean, School of Humanities, and Dr. Daniel Sedey, Chair, Department of Philosophy, for their consistent efforts in advancing this project. Pat Boles, Administrative Program Specialist, School of Humanitites, maintained logistical supervision and arranged for many valuable services. Dorothy Johnson, Betsy Leighton, Margie Martinez, and Susana Nugent contributed ever so many hours of invaluable clerical assistance and support.

I am pleased to conclude with some notes about several of the essays. First, the paper from Wilfrid Sellars was written during the sixties but never before published. This essay contains a remarkably deft presentation of his important view. Second, earlier versions of the papers by Hector-Neri Castañeda, Richard Feldman, Alvin Goldman, Jaegwon Kim, Keith Lehrer, John Pollock, and Marshall Swain were presented at the exhilarating Brown University Epistemology Conference in honor of Roderick M. Chisholm, November 1986.

May 1988   **JAMES E. TOMBERLIN**

Philosophical Perspectives, 2, Epistemology, 1988

POSITIVE EPISTEMIC STATUS AND PROPER FUNCTION

Alvin Plantinga
University of Notre Dame

Knowledge, so we thought for untold generations,[1] is justified true belief; and even in this enlightened post-Gettier era, we still think justification and knowledge intimately related. But what sort of thing is this alleged 'justification'? How shall we understand it? Contemporary epistemologists don't often focus attention on the *nature* of epistemic justification (although they often ask under what conditions a given belief has it); and when they do, they display deplorable diversity. Some claim that justification is a matter of epistemic dutifulness, others that it goes by coherence, and still others that it is conferred by reliability. In what follows I shall argue that none of the above is the correct answer, and suggest an alternative.

But how shall we initially locate this quality or quantity I mean to discuss; how shall we initially pin down epistemic justification? First 'justification', 'justified' and allied terms are terms of epistemic appraisal[2]; to say that a proposition is *justified* for a person is to say that it has what Roderick Chisholm calls 'positive epistemic status' for him; his holding that belief in his circumstances is *right*, or *proper*, or *acceptable*, or *approvable*, or *up to standard*. What we appraise are a person's *beliefs* (more exactly, his *believings*), as well as his skepticisms and (to use another Chisholmian term) his withholdings, his failings to believe. The evidentialist objector to theistic belief,[3] for example, claims that a theist who believes in God without sufficient evidence is so far forth unjustified in that belief; thus he offers a negative appraisal of the belief (when held without sufficient evidence) or of its holder—claiming, perhaps, that the believer in those circumstances has flouted some duty, or (more charitably) that she is suffering from a sort of neurosis or other cognitive dysfunction. In the same way we may appraise the belief that all contemporary flora and fauna arose by way of random genetic mutation and natural selection; and of course the less spectacular beliefs of everyday life are subject to similar evaluation and appraisal. Although Chisholm doesn't mention it, we also appraise the *degree* to which a person believes a proposition; if I believe that Homer was born before 800 B.C. with the same fervor that I believe that New York City is larger than Cleveland, then (given my epistemic circumstances) my degree of confidence in the former proposition is unjustified. We evaluate a person's beliefs and degrees of belief as warranted, or justified, or rational, or reasonable, contrasting them with beliefs that are unwarranted, unjustified, irrational, or unreasonable.

Secondly, epistemic justification or positive epistemic status comes in degrees. Some of my beliefs have more by way of positive epistemic status for me than others: for example, my belief that I live in Indiana has more by way of positive epistemic status or warrant, for me, than my belief that Homer was born before 800 B.C. (This is not to say that I am not equally *within my rights* in accepting these two beliefs to the *degrees* to which I do in fact accept them; I believe the former much more firmly than the latter.) But then we can distinguish degrees of positive epistemic status, at least for a given person.[4]

And thirdly, among the fundamental concepts of the theory of *knowledge* we find, naturally enough, the concept of knowledge. There is wide (though less than universal) agreement that true belief is necessary but not sufficient for knowledge. But then what more is required? What is this quantity enough of which (Gettier problems, perhaps, aside) epistemizes true belief? (We can't properly assume that it is a *simple* property or quantity; perhaps it is like a vector resultant of one or more others.) Whatever exactly this further element or quantity may be, it is either epistemic justification or something intimately connected with it. So perhaps the natural procedure would be just to *baptize* this element, whatever it is, 'epistemic justification'. But this would be misleading. The term 'justification' suggests duty, obligation, permission, and rights—the whole deontological stable. Furthermore, one of the main contending theories or pictures here (a theory or picture going back at least to Descartes) explicitly identifies the quantity in question with *aptness for epistemic duty fulfillment*; to use the term 'justification', then, as a name for the quantity in question would be to give this theory a confusing and unwarranted (if merely verbal) initial edge over its rivals. I shall therefore borrow Chisholm's more neutral term "positive epistemic status" as my official name for the quantity in question. Positive epistemic status, then, initially and to a first approximation, is a normative property that comes in degrees, enough of which is what epistemizes true belief. Now contemporary epistemology is dominated by three fundamentally different basic ideas as to what positive epistemic status is; after arguing that each of these three is deeply flawed, I shall go on to propose a more satisfactory alternative.

I. Chisholmian Internalism[5]

Over the past 25 years or so, Roderick Chisholm (clearly the dean of contemporary epistemologists) has presented a series of ever more refined and penetrating accounts of the central notions of the theory of knowledge. His work is surely as good a place to start as any. Chisholm belongs to an *internalist* tradition going back at least to Descartes. There is more than one important internalist tradition; but according to the dominant tradition, the Cartesian tradition, positive epistemic status is essentially connected with the fulfillment of epistemic duty, with the satisfaction of noetic obligation. This tradition is therefore the natural home of the use of term 'justification' for positive epistemic status, for according to this tradition what epistemizes true belief lies in the near neighborhood of epistemic duty fulfillment. Chisholm is an internalist; but the notion of internalism is less than wholly clear, and there is more than one variety of it.[6] But here I speak of Cartesian internalism, a whole system or congeries of ideas. Central to this system, I think, is the idea that (truth aside) whether a person has knowledge is *up to him* and within his control. More exactly, the central idea is that whether or not my beliefs *have positive epistemic* status for me is up to me and within my control. Perhaps I am the victim of a Cartesian demon or a subject in an Alpha Centaurian cognitive experiment, so that my beliefs are for the most part wildly wide of the mark; nevertheless I can still do my epistemic duty and thereby still achieve a state in which my beliefs have positive epistemic status for me. According to the internalist, we need give no hostages to fortune when it comes to justification or positive epistemic status; here our fate is in our own hands. Being justified in her beliefs (unlike, say, having a sunny disposition) is not something that just *happens* to a person; it is a result of her own efforts.

But if this is so, then something else must also be so—in fact three things must be so. First, our beliefs must be, at least to a large extent, within our voluntary control. The basic internalist idea is that it is up to me whether I adopt beliefs that are justified for me. But then which beliefs I adopt must be up to me; for any or most beliefs that suggest themselves, that come within my purview, it must be within my power to accept them and within my power to reject them. Second, if it is appropriately up to me whether my beliefs are justified, then I must be able to tell, somehow, whether a given belief *is* justified. Justification must be a property such that I can determine, with confidence and from the inside, so to speak, whether or not a belief or candidate for belief has it. The fates may conspire to deceive me; I could be wrong about whether there is an external world, or a past, or whether there are other persons; for all I can tell, I may be the victim of a malevolent Cartesian demon who delights in deception. Justification, however, is a different kettle of fish; whatever my problems with truth, at least I can determine whether my beliefs are justified. Thirdly, consider Chisholmian epistemic principles: non-contingent propositions stating the conditions under which a person's beliefs enjoy (one or another degree of) positive epistemic status with respect to her. Given the basic internalist idea and a couple of plausible assumptions, it follows that I can discover these principles, or at any rate can discover *some* of these principles *a priori*, just by reflection. I need not resort to a *posteriori* investigation (perhaps of a broadly psychological or anthropological sort); I need not know that my faculties are reliable or functioning properly. All three of these aspects of internalism are reflected in Chisholm's work.[7]

Chisholm presents his epistemology by way of stating and commenting upon epistemic principles: non-contingent conditionals whose antecedents specify a relation between a person **S**, a proposition **A**, and certain circumstances in which **S** finds himself, and whose consequents specify that **A** has a certain epistemic status for **S**—

certainty, perhaps, or *acceptability*, or *being evident*, or *being beyond reasonable doubt*. He begins by introducing an undefined technical locution: "**p** is more reasonable than **q** for **S** at **t**". Here the values for **p** and **q** will be *properties*: such properties, for example, as *believing that Albuquerque is in New Mexico* and *withholding the belief that Albuquerque is in New Mexico*—that is, believing neither that proposition nor its denial. (When one believes or withholds something, then, Chisholm assumes[8], there is indeed something one believes or withholds; call such things 'propositions'.) Given the notion of a proposition and 'is more reasonable than' as an undefined locution, Chisholm goes on to define a battery of "terms of epistemic appraisal" as he calls them: 'certain', 'beyond reasonable doubt', 'evident', 'acceptable', and so on. A proposition **A** is beyond reasonable doubt for a person at a time **t**, for example, if and only if it is more reasonable for him to accept that proposition then than to withhold it; **A** has some presumption in its favor for him at **t** just if accepting it then is more reasonable than accepting its negation. The epistemological principles Chisholm presents are formulated by way of these terms of epistemic appraisal; and the whole process culminates in a definition or analysis of knowledge.

Now Chisholm introduces 'is more reasonable than' as an undefined locution; nonetheless, of course, it has a sense, as he uses it, and a sense fairly close to the sense it has in English. The main thing to see is that as Chisholm uses it, this locution pertains to epistemic *duty* or *requirement* or *obligation*. In *Foundations of Knowing* (hereafter FK), his most recent full dress presentation of his epistemology, he says that "Epistemic reasonability could be understood in terms of the general requirement to try to have the largest possible set of logically independent beliefs that is such that the true beliefs outnumber the false beliefs. The principles of epistemic preferability are the principles one should follow if one is to fulfill this requirement." (7). In his earlier *Theory of Knowledge* (2nd edition (1976); hereafter TK) Chisholm puts it as follows: "We may assume," he says,

> that every person is subject to a purely intellectual
> requirement: that of trying his best to bring it about that for
> any proposition *p* he considers, he accepts *p* if and only if *p*
> is true (TK p. 14);

and he adds

> One might say that this is the person's responsibility *qua* intellectual being....One way, then of re-expressing the locution '*p* is more reasonable than *q* for **S** at *t*' is to say this: ' **S** is so situated at *t* that his intellectual requirement, his responsibility as an intellectual being, is better fulfilled by *p* than by *q*.'

Reasonability, therefore, is a *normative* concept. More precisely, it is a *deontological* concept; it pertains to requirement, duty, or obligation— *epistemic* duty or obligation. (Of course it doesn't follow that the normative character involved is strictly *moral*; perhaps an epistemic requirement is not a moral duty; perhaps it is a *sui generis* form of obligation.[9]) And Chisholm's fundamental contention here is that a certain requirement, or responsibility, or duty, or obligation lies at the basis of such epistemic notions as evidence, justification, positive epistemic status, and knowledge itself; for of course he analyzes knowledge in terms of positive epistemic status plus truth. To say, for example, that a proposition **p** is *acceptable* for a person at a time is to say that he is so situated, then, that it is not the case that he can better fulfill his epistemic duty by withholding than by accepting **p**; to say that **p** is *beyond reasonable doubt* for him is to say that he is so situated that he can better fulfill his intellectual responsibility by accepting **p** than by withholding **p**.

The suggestions made in FK and TK do not agree as to what our intellectual requirement is; neither, furthermore, is exactly right.[10] The basic idea, however, is that our epistemic duty or requirement is to try to achieve and maintain a certain condition—call it 'epistemic excellence'— which may be hard to specify in detail, but consists fundamentally in standing in an appropriate relation to truth. This is a duty I have "*qua* intellectual being"—that is, just by virtue of being the sort of creature that is capable of grasping and believing (or withholding) propositions. We must pay a price for our exalted status as intellectual beings; with ability comes responsibility. And the idea, presumably, is that *all* intellectual beings have this responsibility: angels, devils, Alpha Centaurians, what have you—all are subject to this requirement or obligation.

According to Chisholm, then, positive epistemic status is a matter of aptness for fulfillment of epistemic duty. A proposition has positive epistemic status for me, in certain circumstances, to the extent that I can fulfill my epistemic duty by accepting it in those circumstances.

This duty or obligation or requirement, furthermore, is one of *trying* to bring about a certain state of affairs. One's duty as an intellectual being is not that of *succeeding* in bringing it about that (say) one has a large set of beliefs, most of which are true; it is instead that of *trying* to bring about this state of affairs. My requirement is not to *succeed* in achieving and maintaining intellectual excellence; my requirement is only to try to do so. Presumably the reason is that it may not be within my power to succeed. Perhaps I don't know how to achieve intellectual excellence; or perhaps I do know how but simply can't do it. So my duty is only to *try* to achieve it.

But how shall I try to achieve epistemic excellence? What, more concretely, must I do? Chisholm's answer: follow the principles of epistemic preferability—the epistemic principles he has repeatedly tried to state. "The principles of epistemic preferability are the principles one should follow if one is to fulfill this requirement [i.e., the requirement to try to achieve epistemic excellence]" (FK p. 7). On several occasions and in several contexts Chisholm suggests that his epistemic principles are instances of the Reidian idea that we ought to trust our epistemic nature unless we have reason not to: "Our perceptual principles are instances of the more general truth: 'it is reasonable to trust the senses until one has positive reason for distrusting them'" (FK p. 23). How are we to understand this? As follows, I think. We human beings find ourselves with a battery of epistemic impulses, inclinations and dispositions. Upon being appeared to redly, for example, I find myself believing that I am appeared to in that way by some object, an object that is red. Upon considering an elementary truth of arithmetic or logic, I find myself believing that it is true; upon being asked what I had for breakfast this morning, I find myself believing that it was eggs on toast. Our natures are such that for each of a wide variety of circumstances there are certain beliefs we are strongly disposed or inclined to form; and when we find ourselves in these circumstances, we find ourselves with those beliefs. Now Chisholm's idea, I think, is that in these circumstances (given that we have no indication that our epistemic nature is flawed and misleading) it is reasonable to trust our epistemic nature—i.e., to believe as nature prompts us to. But of course 'reasonable' is, he says, to be understood in terms of epistemic duty or obligation: accordingly, in the circumstances in question, the dutiful thing to do is to fall in with our natural inclinations and accept the beliefs nature inclines us towards. In a nutshell, then: we have a duty to try to achieve epistemic excellence; in a wide variety of circumstances that duty can be best fulfilled by accepting the beliefs our nature inclines us to accept; and a belief or candidate for belief has positive epistemic status for me to the extent that in accepting it I can fulfill my epistemic duty.

This is a simple and attractive picture of the nature of justification and positive epistemic status. It is easy to see, however, that it can't be correct. The fundamental idea is that positive epistemic status is a matter of *aptness for the fulfillment of epistemic duty or obligation.* This may be an *element* or *moment* in positive epistemic status; but I think we can easily see that it cannot be the whole story. I shall give three examples to argue the point.[11]

First, suppose S knows that nine out of ten Frisians cannot swim and that Feike is a Frisian. He is aware of the fact that he knows these things, and that they disconfirm

(1) Feike can swim.

He has no evidence of any kind for (1); no perceptual evidence, no propositional evidence, no testimonial evidence—no evidence at all. Nevertheless, (1) seems overwhelmingly attractive to him; it seems wholly and obviously true; it has all the phenomenological *panache* of *modus ponens* itself. For S very much admires swimming and swimmers; and, due to a psychological malfunction (S is himself a very poor swimmer), he has a powerful tendency to assume, of anyone he likes or admires, that she is an excellent swimmer. S isn't aware of this malfunction and has no reason to think he suffers from it; and his lack of awareness is in no way due to epistemic malfeasance or lack of epistemic dutifulness. In fact S is extremely concerned with his epistemic duty. He is eager to achieve epistemic excellence, to bring it about that he is in the right relation to the truth. He is trying his level best to do so; indeed, he is nearly fanatic on the subject and devotes what many would consider an inordinate share of his energy to trying to achieve epistemic excellence.

Now what, under these conditions, would be the dutiful thing for S to do? Obviously, he should accept (1). Is he so situated that he can better fulfill his obligation to try to achieve epistemic excellence by *withholding* than by accepting (1)? Surely not. (l) seems utterly and obviously true to him; and while he knows that he knows some things that disconfirm it, the same holds for all sorts of propositions he knows to be true. (Thus, for example, he also knows that Tietje is a Frisian and has himself personally witnessed her winning the 100 meter freestyle at the Olympics.) It is true that his cognitive faculties are playing him false here, but he has no inkling of this fact, and his lack of this self-knowledge is in no way due to epistemic carelessness or other dereliction of epistemic duty. The way for him to try to achieve epistemic excellence in these circumstances, surely, is for him to act on what he nonculpably believes about how best to achieve this end. But (l) seems utterly and obviously true; so, naturally enough, he believes that the way to achieve the end in question is to accept (1). Indeed, there may be no other proposition such that **S** can better fulfill his duty to the truth by accepting it than by accepting (l); in that case, on Chisholm's official account of positive epistemic status, (1) would be *certain* for **S**. (1), therefore, is in these circumstances overwhelmingly apt for fulfillment of epistemic duty; if positive epistemic status were what Chisholm says it is, (l) would have positive epistemic status in *excelsis* for **S**. But surely it doesn't. Even if it is true, **S** certainly does not *know* that it is, and the idea that under these conditions it could have certainty, the maximal degree of positive epistemic status for him, seems wholly fantastic.

It is clear, therefore, that (l) has little by way of positive epistemic status for **S**; at any rate it has little or none of the sort of epistemic status enough of which confers knowledge. Still, it does seem to have *some* kind of positive status for him. We could certainly say that S is *permitted* to accept (l); he is violating no duty in accepting it; he is entirely within his epistemic rights in accepting it. He is *justified* in accepting it in the sense that he has a *right* to accept it; he is doing his epistemic best in accepting it, thus fulfilling his duty to the truth. Nevertheless the proposition in question doesn't have the sort of status for him enough of which (together with truth) constitutes knowledge. I don't mean merely that he doesn't know it (even if it turns out to be true); it is rather that the sort of status it has for him is not such that even if it had more or the maximal degree of *that* sort of status, then he *would* know it. To have the status for him required by *knowledge*, something quite different is demanded. We might say that he has **permissive** justification in accepting this proposition—using the term 'permissive' to indicate that the sort of justification he has is such that in accepting the proposition in question he is entirely within his epistemic rights and is flouting no epistemic duty. Nonetheless, the proposition has little by way of positive epistemic status for him.

A second example: according to Chisholm, something is *appearing* to someone, or appearing in a certain way to her, if (very roughly) it is appropriately causing her to be appeared to in that way (FK 16-17). Now suppose that, due to cerebral malfunction or the machinations of a Cartesian evil demon, I have a strong tendency or impulse to believe

(2) Nothing is appearing redly to me

whenever I am appeared to redly. This tendency is even stronger than the tendency normal people display, in the same circumstances, to believe the appropriate denial of (2); it seems to me utterly obvious, under these conditions, that there isn't anything appearing red to me. Furthermore, I have not the faintest inkling of this defect in my nature, and my failure to be aware of it is in no way due to lack of epistemic dutifulness. (Indeed, we may add in this case, as in the last, that doing my epistemic duty is the main passion of my life.) Then, surely, the dutiful thing for me to do, under those circumstances, would be to accept (2). But though I would be permissively justified in accepting that proposition, it would have little by way of positive epistemic status for me; surely it wouldn't have the sort of positive epistemic status, for me, enough of which is sufficient (with truth) for knowledge. The problem is that my cognitive faculties are not working properly. I display cognitive malfunction, so that no matter how magnificently I do my epistemic duty, no matter how hard I try, I won't have much by way of positive epistemic status. Or rather, I will have the justification that goes with doing my best to do my duty; I will be within my rights, not properly subject to blame or censure. I will have permissive justification. Indeed, I will have more than permissive justification; in trying as hard as I did to achieve epistemic excellence, I performed works of epistemic supererogation. But no amount of dutifulness or supererogatory effort is sufficient for the kind of positive epistemic status necessary for knowledge; for that an element of quite another kind is required.

A final example: Paul is so constructed (again, due to brain lesion or demon or mad Alpha Centaurian scientist) that when he is appeared to in one sense modality he forms beliefs appropriate to another. When he is aurally appeared to in the way in which one is appeared to upon hearing church bells, he has a nearly ineluctable tendency to believe that there is something that is appearing to him in that fashion, and that thing is orange—bright orange. He doesn't know about this defect in his epistemic equipment, and his lack of awareness is in no way due to indolence, or carelessness, or wishful thinking, or any other dereliction of epistemic duty. As a matter of fact, Paul is unusually dutiful, unusually concerned about doing his epistemic duty; fulfilling this duty is the main passion of his life. Add that those around him suffer from a similar epistemic deficiency. They have all been manipulated in this way by demons or Alpha Centaurians; or they live in Alaska and all suffer from similar lesions due to radioactive fallout from a Soviet missile test. Now suppose Paul is appeared to in the church bell fashion and forms the belief that he is being appeared to in that way by something that is orange. Surely, in these conditions, this proposition is such that accepting it is an appropriate way of doing his epistemic duty, of trying to achieve epistemic excellence. Nevertheless that proposition has next to nothing by way of positive epistemic status for him. Paul is beyond reproach; he has done his duty as he saw it; he is permissively justified, and more. Nevertheless there is a kind of quality this belief lacks—a kind crucial for knowledge. For *that* sort of status, it isn't sufficient to satisfy one's duty and do one's epistemic best. Paul can be ever so conscientious about his epistemic duties and still be such that his beliefs do not have positive epistemic status.

Clearly enough, we can vary the above sorts of examples. Perhaps you think that what goes with satisfying duty *in excelsis* is *effort*; perhaps (in a Kantian vein) you think that genuinely dutiful action demands acting contrary to inclination. Very well, alter the above cases accordingly. Suppose, for example, that Paul (due to lesion, demon or Alpha Centaurian) nonculpably believes that his nature is deeply misleading. Like the rest of us, he has an inclination, upon being appeared to redly, to believe that there is something red lurking in the neighborhood; unlike the rest of us, he believes that this natural inclination is misleading and that on those occasions there really isn't anything that is thus appearing to him. He undertakes a strenuous regimen to overcome this inclination; after intense and protracted effort he succeeds: upon being appeared to redly he no longer believes that something red is appearing to him. His devotion to duty costs him dearly. The enormous effort he expends takes its toll upon his health; he is subject to ridicule and disapprobation on the part of his fellows, who view his project as at best Quixotic; his wife protests his unusual behavior and finally leaves him for someone less epistemically nonstandard. Determined to do what is right, however, Paul heroically persists in doing what he is non-culpably convinced is his duty. It is obvious, I take it, that even though Paul is unusually dutiful in accepting, on a given occasion, the belief that nothing red is appearing to him, that belief has little by way of positive epistemic status for him.

What these examples show, I think, is that positive epistemic status is not or is not merely a matter of aptness for fulfillment of epistemic duty or obligation. That there *are* such duties or obligation seems eminently plausible, although tough problems attend this notion[12] and it isn't easy to say in any detail what our epistemic duties might be. Aptness for the fulfillment of such duties, however, is at most one aspect or moment of positive epistemic status.[13] It is obvious that a proposition can be maximal with respect to aptness for duty fulfillment for me, but nonetheless enjoy little by way of positive epistemic status.

II. Coherentism

A second suggestion as to the nature of positive epistemic status is made by the **coherentist**. There are, of course, many brands of coherentism and many ways to construe coherence;[14] I don't have the space to canvass them here. We can construe the coherentist in either of two ways: (1) she may agree with the Chisholmian that aptness for duty fulfillment is a moment in positive epistemic status, adding that the other element is provided or determined by coherence, or (2) she may hold that positive epistemic status is not complex and that it is determined solely by coherence. What she claims, taken the second way, is that a belief has positive epistemic status, for me, to the extent that it coheres with the appropriate system of beliefs. (She could then hold either that positive epistemic status *just is* coherence, or that it is instead a normative or axiological property that *supervenes* upon coherence.) I shall argue that coherentism is mistaken if taken the first way; but if mistaken that way, then it is also mistaken if taken the other.

An initial and important problem is that there are few serious attempts to *state* coherentism, few serious attempts to say what this alleged coherence relation is. Most coherentists are decently reticent about the nature of coherence; we are typically told that it is more than mere logical consistency but less than mutual entailment;

beyond this most coherentists maintain a decorous silence.[15] I think we can see, however, that on any plausible account of coherence, coherentism is unacceptable as an account either of warrant or of positive epistemic status. According to the weak version of coherentism, coherence is the source of one element or component of positive epistemic status, the other being aptness for epistemic duty fulfillment; on the strong version coherence just is or is the sole source of positive epistemic status. If the strong version is true, the weak follows trivially; I shall therefore argue that the weak version is false. The chief problem for coherentism, as I see it, is that coherence is thought of as a relation that obtains just among *beliefs*. But that means that one of my beliefs could have a great deal of positive epistemic status by virtue of standing in the coherence relation to the right body of beliefs or propositions, *no matter how it was related to my experience*; This, however, is clearly mistaken. Once again I shall proceed by way of examples. It is easy to see, I think, that a given belief could have next to nothing by way of positive epistemic status for a person, even though she was wholly dutiful in holding the belief, and even though the belief in question is coherent with the rest of her beliefs.

Consider, first, someone who suffers from a cognitive dysfunction: whenever he is appeared to redly (to use Chisholm's term), he forms the belief that no one is ever appeared to redly. It isn't that he believes, on these occasions, that *he* is not appeared to redly; perhaps that is impossible. Let us concede, for purposes of argument, that necessarily, if, at **t**, **S** is appeared to redly, then **S** does not at **t** believe that he is not appeared to redly. Let us also concede that if a person is appeared to redly and pays attention to his phenomenal field (perhaps asking himself whether and how he is being appeared to) then if he is being appeared to redly, he believes that he is. These concessions are consistent with **S**'s being such that whenever he is appeared to redly, he believes that no one is ever thus appeared to; for **S**, we may add, does not, on these occasions, pay any attention to his phenomenal field. He does not ask himself whether he is being appeared to redly, or, indeed, whether he is being appeared to at all. He simply finds himself, under these conditions, believing that no one is ever appeared to redly. Let us add both that **S** always does his best to fulfill his epistemic duty, and that this bizarre belief of his is coherent with the relevant body of beliefs, whatever that may be. And now suppose **S** is appeared to redly, on a given occasion, forming the belief that no one is ever appeared to redly. That belief satisfies the coherence requirement; furthermore, **S** is doing his epistemic duty in accepting it. Nevertheless the belief in question, clearly enough, has little by way of positive epistemic status for **S**. A second example: Timothy is a promising young artist with an intense, indeed, inordinate admiration for Picasso. Waiting at a supermarket checkout, he idly picks up a copy of *The National Inquirer*, reading therein that Picasso, contrary to what most of us have always thought, was really an alien from outer space. Due to nonculpable gullibility and his overwhelming admiration for Picasso, Timothy then forms the belief that he too is really an alien from outer space. The rest of his beliefs readjust themselves so as to form a coherent pattern; we may add that Timothy is wholly and nonculpably unaware of the psychological mechanisms at work in the formation of this belief, thus flouting no epistemic duties in believing as he does. The belief in question, then, satisfies the coherence condition; furthermore, it has permissive justification for him. Nevertheless it has little by way of positive epistemic status for him. Even if, *per impossibile*, it turned out that Timothy really *is* an alien from outer space, he certainly does not know that he is. And the reason, in this case as in the last, is clear: Timothy holds the belief in question because of cognitive malfunction, because of noetic deficiency.

A final example, suggested by Timothy's plight. Suppose at **t** I am in Oxford and know that I am; I am just outside the gates of Balliol College, idly observing a small but noisy flock of gowned undergraduates on their way to Examination Schools. I believe that the walls of Balliol are behind me, that Broad Street is before me, that I am standing upon a sidewalk, and so on. I am paying no attention to my phenomenal field, and hold no beliefs about my experience or how I am being appeared to. My beliefs at **t** form a coherent system; each is coherent with the rest. Now imagine that I leave Oxford, taking the train to London. My experience then changes in the normal way; my visual, auditory, and kinesthetic experience at **t***, when I am on the train bound for London, is just what one would expect. Furthermore, I am devoted to my epistemic duty, and am doing my level best to satisfy my obligation to try to bring it about that I am in the right relation to the truth. Due to a sudden burst of radiation as we pass a nuclear dump, however, I undergo a cerebral accident resulting in cognitive malfunction: my beliefs are no longer responsive to my experience and revert to what they were at **t**, when

I was in Oxford. Due to this cognitive dysfunction, at **t*** I believe just what I did at **t**: that I am in Oxford, that a flock of noisy undergraduates is passing by, that I am standing on a sidewalk just outside the walls of Balliol, and the like. My beliefs at **t*** are coherent, for they are the very beliefs I coherently held at **t**, which by hypothesis formed a coherent system of beliefs. I am also, of course, doing my epistemic duty. Nevertheless, the belief that I am then in Oxford has, obviously enough, very little by way of positive epistemic status for me. I conclude that coherence is not sufficient for positive epistemic status—either by itself or in conjunction with aptness for epistemic duty fulfillment.

III. Reliabilism

I turn thirdly to the *reliabilist* account of positive epistemic status. Here we are faced with an embarrassment of riches: there are many reliabilist accounts[16], and considerations that apply to some do not apply to others. For the sake of definiteness, I shall select three reliabilist accounts for brief consideration, although I believe that what I say applies to some of the others as well.

A. Robert Nozick

According to Nozick, **S** knows that **p** if and only if four conditions are satisfied: (l) **p** is true, (2) **S** believes **p**, (3) if **p** were not true, **S** would not believe **p**, and (4) if **p** were true, **S** would believe **p**.[17] The fourth condition may be initially a bit puzzling. The idea is approximately this: if **p** were true and things a bit different from what in fact they are, **S** would (still) believe **p**. In terms of possible worlds: in the nearby worlds in which **p** is true, **S** believes **p**. If conditions (3) and (4) hold, then, says Nozick, **S**'s belief "tracks the truth".

This account of knowledge has several interesting features. It turns out, for example, that while I know

(3) I am here in my study (on earth, back home in Indiana, nowhere near Alpha Centauri),

I do not know

(4) I am not a brain in a vat on Alpha Centauri, serving as a subject in an experiment in which the experimenters give me the very experiences and beliefs I do in fact have just now.

I don't know (4) because it does not meet the third condition: it is false that if (4) were not true, I wouldn't believe it. (If (4) were not true I would be a brain in a vat with the very experiences and beliefs I do in fact have and thus would believe (4).) I know (3) but don't know (4), despite the fact that I can clearly see that (3) entails (4); on the view in question, knowledge is not closed (or closeable) under known entailment. Nozick says he takes skepticism seriously (pp. 197ff); on his account, the skeptic is quite correct in claiming that I do not know that I am not a brain in a vat being given the very beliefs and experiences I would have under more normal circumstances; nor do I know that I am not being similarly deceived by a malicious Cartesian demon. But where the global skeptic typically goes wrong, says Nozick, is in concluding that I don't know that I am in my study; this latter belief meets the four conditions for knowledge, even if the former does not, and despite the fact that the latter entails the former.

I think Nozick's concession to the skeptic is more apparent than real. On his account, even if I don't know that I am not a brain in a vat, I do know that I am not a brain in a vat and am home in my study. (If that conjunction were true, I would believe it; if it were false, it would be false by virtue of the falsehood of its second conjunct, in which case I wouldn't believe the conjunction.)[18] Wherever the skeptic holds that I do not know the denial of some momentous proposition (such as **I am being systematically and massively deceived by a malicious Cartesian demon**), Nozick agrees; but on his view while indeed I do not know the denial of the momentous proposition in question, I do know the conjunction of its denial with some commonplace proposition. On his view the correct reply to the skeptic who claims you don't know that you are not a brain in a vat on Alpha Centauri is "Well yes, perhaps I don't know that, but I *do* know that I am here in my study and am not a brain in a vat on Alpha Centauri." We could hardly blame the skeptic for feeling that with friends like that....

More to the present point, however, I think we can easily see that the four conditions Nozick lays down as necessary and sufficient for knowledge are not sufficient either for knowledge or for positive epistemic status. I shall give three examples. First, suppose I am a brain in a vat on Alpha Centauri. My captors are running a cognitive experiment; they give me most of the experiences and beliefs I would have if I were at home carrying on my normal life, so that most of what I believe is absurdly false. Now a federally promulgated law for cognitive experiments, on Alpha Centauri, is that the subject must be given the true belief as to what the largest city on earth is; they therefore give me the belief that Mexico City is the largest city on earth. They also give me overwhelming evidence for the proposition that Mexico City is *not* the largest city on earth; I believe I have read many independent demographic surveys, many maps and atlases, all of which unite in declaring that *Cleveland* is the largest city on earth. I have no evidence at all for my belief that Mexico City is the largest. As things stand, then, the conditions for knowledge are met: where **M** is **Mexico city is the largest city on earth**, I believe **M**, **M** is true, in the nearby worlds where **M** is true I (still) believe **M**, and (because of that federally promulgated law) if **M** were not true I wouldn't have believed that it was. But surely I don't know **M**; in fact M has little if any positive epistemic status (beyond permissive justification) for me.

A second example: Our spaceship has landed on a small planet near Alpha Centauri. Tests indicate that the atmosphere, temperature and other conditions are propitious for human life; we confidently open the hatch and step out. We are immediately appeared to in the way that ordinarily (on earth) goes with perceiving a tiger at about 30 feet; naturally enough we form the belief that there is a tiger there. As it turns out, there is indeed a tiger (or an Alpha Centaurian tiger counterpart) there; but unbeknownst to us, Alpha Centaurian tigers emit a sort of radiation that makes them invisible to human beings. This planet's atmosphere, however, is suffused with a subtle sort of gas that causes earthlings to be appeared to in that characteristic tigerish fashion. Finally, tigers on this planet are attended by a certain parasite—one specific to tigers—that emits a kind of radiation in the absence of which, in the conditions that prevail on this planet, human beings are instantly rendered unconscious. Then Nozick's conditions for knowledge are met: our belief that there is a tiger there is true; in the nearby worlds where that proposition is true we believe it, and if it were not true we would not believe it (if it were not true we would have been rendered unconscious). But surely we don't know this proposition; indeed, it has little or no positive epistemic status for us. Nozick's conditions for knowledge are in fact met, but (so to speak) just by accident.

A final example: I suffer from a disease a symptom of which is the following condition. When a victim's retinas are irradiated with purple light, he is never appeared to visually but is instead appeared to aurally; he seems to hear a certain tune. The disease has a further symptom: whenever a victim seems to hear that tune, he forms the belief that there is something purple in the neighborhood. On a given occasion my retinas are thus irradiated and I form the belief that there is a purple object nearby. This belief meets Nozick's conditions for knowledge; but once more, surely, it does not constitute knowledge and it has little by way of positive epistemic status for me. I conclude that Nozick's suggested necessary and sufficient conditions for knowledge are not in fact sufficient. (If you think you can always increase your knowledge by deducing consequences of what you know, then you will think these conditions aren't necessary either). Something more must be added; below (section IV) I shall suggest a promising area in which to look for the missing element.

B. Dretske

A second style of reliabilism sees reliability as a matter of *probability*; on this sort of account a person is said to know a true proposition if he believes it, and the right probability relations hold between that proposition and its significant others. As an example I shall consider Fred Dretske's interesting "informational theoretic" analysis of knowledge in *Knowledge and the Flow of Information*.[19]
This analysis goes as follows:

> (D₁) **K** knows that **s** is **F** = **K**'s belief that **s** is **F** is caused
> (or causally sustained) by the information that **s** is **F** (p. 86).

Two preliminary comments: Dretske is concerned, here, primarily or exclusively with *perceptual* knowledge; in particular the account is not designed to apply to such items of **K**'s *a priori* knowledge as that, say, $7 + 5 = 12$. Secondly, the account is restricted to what Dretske calls "de re content" (p. 66); it is restricted, he says, to the kind of case where what **K** knows is a piece of information of or about **s**.

Now what sort of animal is this **information that s is F**? And what is it for a thing of that sort—presumably an abstract object or ensemble of abstract objects—to cause or causally sustain a belief? So far as I can see, Dretske says little by way of answer to the first question. What he does give are many examples of the sort **the information that s is F**. There is, for example, the information that Sam is happy, that the peanut is under shell number 3, that Susan is jogging. One might say that these are *bits* of information, except for the fact that the term "bit" has been pre-empted for a *measure* of information. We are to think of information as being generated by or associated with states of affairs; and the amount of information generated by a given state of affairs depends upon the number and probability of the possibilities that state of affairs excludes. Suppose I throw a fair 64 sided die. The information that the die came up on a side numbered from 1 to 32 reduces the possibilities by a half and carries one bit of information; the knowledge that the die came up on a side numbered from 1 to 16 reduces the possibilities by another half and accordingly carries two bits; the information that side 3 came up reduces the original 64 possibilities to 1 and carries six bits of information. As you can guess from the example, if a piece of news reduces **n** (equally probable) possibilities to 1, then the amount of information displayed by that piece of news is log (to base 2) **n**. In the general case, where the possibilities involved need not be equi-probable (and where P(**A**) is the probability that a given possibility **A** is true) the amount of information generated by **A** is given by

$$(\text{D}_2) \quad \text{I}(\mathbf{A}) = \log (1/P(\mathbf{A})), \text{ i.e., } -\log P(\mathbf{A}).$$

Now there are deep problems and deep unclarities here. What are the relevant alternative possibilities for, for example, **Paul is jogging**? D_2 is applicable only where the possibilities involved are finite in cardinality; is that so for a noncontrived real life possibility such as **Paul is now jogging**? Do these alternative possibilities *have* appropriate probabilities? These are pressing questions for an account of this kind, and I don't believe there are even reasonably satisfactory answers to them. I shall not stop to argue that here, however, because the notion of the *amount* of information doesn't enter crucially into Dretske's account of knowledge. Nor need we know, for Dretskian purposes, just what information *is*; all we really need to know is what it is for a piece of information to *cause* or *causally sustain* a belief. Here the answer is disarmingly straightforward:

> Suppose a signal *r* carries the information that *s* is *F* and carried this information in virtue of having the property *F'*. That is, it is *r's being F'* (not, say, its being *G*) that is responsible for *r's* carrying this specific piece of information. Not just any knock on the door tells the spy that the courier

has arrived. The signal is three quick knocks followed by a pause and another three quick knocks.... . It is the temporal pattern of knocks that constitutes the information-carrying feature (F') of the signal. The same is obviously true in telegraphic communication.

When, therefore, a signal carries the information that s is F *in virtue* of having property F', when it is the signal's *being F'* that carries the information, then (and only then) will we say that the information that s is F *causes* whatever the signal's *being F'* causes (87).

So far, then, what we have is that a person **K** knows that s is **F** if and only if **K** believes that **s** is **F** and there is a signal **r** such that **r** has some property **F'** in virtue of which it carries the information that **s** is **F**; and **r**'s having **F'** causes **K** to believe that **s** is **F**. To simplify matters, suppose we drop the reference to the property **F'** of the signal by virtue of which it carries the information that **S** is **F**. What the analysis then boils down to is that **K** knows that **s** is **F** if and only if **K** believes that **s** is **F** and this belief is caused by a signal that carries the information that **s** is **F**. What we still need to know, then, is what it is for a signal to carry the information that **s** is **F**. This is given by

> (D_3) A signal r carries the information that s is F = The conditional probability of s's being F, given r (and k) is 1 (but, given k alone, less than 1) (p. 65).

Now **k**, as Dretske explains, is the *background knowledge* of the receiver. D_3 must therefore be relativized to be accurate; a signal may carry the information that **s** is **F** relative to you but not to me. You already know that **s** is **F**; so the probability of **s**'s being **F** relative to your background knowledge is 1; no signal carries the information that **s** is **F** relative to you. I don't know that **s** is **F**; so any signal **r** which is such that the probability of s's being F on **r&k** (where **k** is my background information) equals 1 carries the information that **s** is **F** with respect to me. If you know that **s** is **F**, then no signal carries the information that **s** is **F** with respect to you; if I don't know that **s** is **F**, then any state of affairs carries that information with respect to me if its conjunction with what I do know entails that **s** is **F**. We can therefore rewrite D_3 as

(D$_4$) **r** carries the information that **s** is **F** relative to **K** iff P((**s** is
F) | (**r&k**)) = 1 and P((**s** is **F**) | **k**) < 1.

And now we can say that

(D$_5$) **K** knows that **s** is **F** if and only if **K** believes that **s** is **F**
and there is a state of affairs **r** such that (1) **r** causes **K**
to believe that **s** is **F** and (2) P((**s** is **F**) | (**r&k**)) = 1 and
P((**s** is **F**) | **k**) < 1.

We saw above that the problematic notion of the amount of information associated with a specific event or state of affairs can safely
be ignored, since that notion plays no role in Dretske's final account
of knowledge. But now we see that the same goes for any other
specifically information theoretic concept; this analysis of knowledge,
when spelled out, involves only the notions of probability, belief, and
causation. Nothing specifically information theoretic seems to be
involved.[20]

D$_5$, I think suffers from two sorts of deficiencies. In a way, the
deepest problem, I believe, is that there is no currently available conception of probability that will serve Dretske's purposes. The probabilities in question are to be *objective* (p.55); so personalist and subjective accounts of probability will not be relevant. That leaves frequency, propensity and logical accounts of probability. On frequency
accounts, however, there really isn't any such thing as the probability
of such a specific singular proposition as **Paul is jogging** on given
evidence; for on this conception a probability is a ratio between
classes. What we face here is the dreaded problem of the single case:
on frequency and propensity accounts, how can we go from genuine
probability statements (**the probability of a Frisian's being a
swimmer is .4**) to something like a probability for a singular proposition about some specific Frisian (who of course is a member of *many*
reference classes in which the frequency of the attribute **being a
swimmer** may differ wildly)? According to Reichenbach, such propositions have a "fictitious probability", which is to be arrived at by
"direct inference" and can be thought of as a kind of estimate or
posit. And the problem for Dretske's account here is that all of the
ways suggested for making such a direct inference refer to what we
know in such a way that the resulting 'probability' for a singular proposition is *relative to our knowledge*.[21] But then the 'probability' of
a singular proposition might be different for me than it is for you,

since your knowledge might significantly differ from mine.

Although I can't argue this here, the same result will follow on propensity accounts of probability. And here is the problem for Dretske: since the probability of singular propositions, on both these conceptions, is relative in this way to bodies of knowledge, the same will be true, on Dretske's account of knowledge, for propositions ascribing knowledge to a person: these propositions will inherit that relativity. But then we have, on Dretske's account, the distressing result that relative to *me*, it may be true that Paul knows that *s* is *F*, but relative to *you*, false that he does. So neither frequency nor propensity accounts will be of use to Dretske.

This leaves only the *logical* account of probability; but this account, from Dretske's point of view, suffers not only from its own intrinsic implausibility but from a difficulty specific to Dretske's theory: the logical account conjoined with what Dretske says about probability entails that causal laws are necessary in the broadly logical sense.

It therefore seems that there is no conception of probability that will serve Dretske's needs. But (as he points out) his theory really requires only the limiting case where the probability of one proposition on another is 1; and perhaps (as he suggests) that notion can be replaced by the notion of "a particular kind of lawful dependency between signal and source .".[22] In any event, I don't have the space here to detail these objections; let me instead turn to an objection more germane to our present interests. This objection is just that even if we had a relevant conception of probability, Dretske's conditions for knowledge would not be sufficient. I shall give three examples to make the point. First, suppose **K** suffers from a serious abnormality—a brain lesion, let's say. This lesion wreaks havoc with **K**'s noetic structure, causing him to believe an array of propositions most of which are absurdly false. It also causes him to believe, however, that he is suffering from a brain lesion. **K** hasn't the slightest shred of evidence for this belief; and he thinks of his other unusual beliefs as resulting from no more than an engagingly original turn of mind. According to D_5, however, it follows that **K** *knows* that he suffers from a brain lesion. His having this lesion causes him to believe that he is thus affected; furthermore the probability of his suffering from a brain lesion on his background information alone is less than 1, but of course its probability on **k** and **K** is **suffering from a brain lesion** is 1. But surely **K** does *not* know that he is suffering from a brain lesion. He has no evidence of any kind—sensory, memory, introspective, whatever—that he has such a lesion; his holding this belief is, from a cognitive point of view, no more than a lucky (or unlucky) accident. Indeed, we can add, if we wish, that **K** has powerful evidence for the conclusion that he is *not* thus suffering; he has just been examined by a trio of world famous experts from New York, who assure him that his brain is entirely normal. In this case, then, **K**'s belief that he has a brain lesion is not only such that he has no evidence for it; he has first rate evidence *against* it. In such a situation **K** clearly does not know that he has a brain lesion, despite the fact that this belief meets Dretske's conditions for knowledge. Examples of this kind can be multiplied; so let's multiply a couple. You have wronged me; you have stolen my Frisian flag. By way of exacting revenge I sneak into your house at night and implant in your dog a source of extremely high frequency radiation. This radiation has no effect upon either you or your dog, except to cause you to form the belief that aliens from Alpha Centauri have invaded your house and replaced your dog with a non-terrestrial look-alike that emits ultraviolet radiation. You christen this creature (who is in fact your dog) 'Spot'. Your belief that Spot emits ultraviolet radiation then satisfies Dretske's conditions for knowledge: Spot's emitting ultraviolet radiation causes you to believe that he does; relative to what you know this is not probable, but relative to the conjunction of what you know with **Spot emits ultraviolet radiation**, its probability is, of course, 1. But surely you don't know that Spot emits such radiation. Indeed, as in the previous case we can add that you have powerful (though misleading) evidence **against** that proposition. You have had Spot examined by a highly competent group of physicists based at the Stanford linear accelerator; I have corrupted them, bribing them to tell you that Spot is entirely normal; but you are nevertheless unable to divest yourself of the belief in question. Surely you don't know.[23]

A final example: you and I each hold a ticket for a valuable lottery; the winner gets an all-expenses-paid week in Philadelphia. I approach the official drawer and get him to agree to fix the lottery: I am to coat my ticket with a substance **S** and he is to coat his hand with a substance **S*** in virtue of which my ticket will stick to his hand. After I leave, you appear and offer him twice as much; he accepts. He then coats his hand with a substance **S**** that causes *your* ticket to stick to his hand, thus causing you to win the lottery. It also causes me, by virtue of a cerebral abnormality on my part which is otherwise undetectable, to believe that you will win. You and I witness the drawing; I suddenly and unaccountably find myself with the belief that you will win. On Dretske's account, I know that you will win, despite my knowledge that I have fixed the lottery. For (where T5 is your ticket) T5's being coated with **S**** causes me to believe that you will win; that you will win (let's suppose) has a probability of 1 on the conjunction of my background knowledge with **T5 has been coated with S**** but a vastly lower probability on my background knowledge alone. It is obvious, however, that under these conditions I don't know that you will win.

Clearly, there are as many examples of this sort as you please. One recipe for constructing them is just to consider some event **e** that causes **K** to believe that **e** occurs (or to believe some proposition entailed by **e**'s occurrence) where **e** causes **K** to form the belief in question by virtue of some pathological condition on **K**'s part—a brain lesion, let's say—and in such a way that it is a mere accident, from a cognitive point of view, that the belief is true. And what these examples show is that something further must be added to Dretske's account; the condition he suggests is not in fact sufficient. In section IV I shall make a suggestion as to what it is that must be added.

C. Goldman

Alvin Goldman suggests still another version of reliabilism, one that deserves that title *in excelsis*: "The justificational status of a belief", he initially says, "is a function of the reliability of the process or processes that cause it, where (as a first approximation) reliability consists in the tendency of a process to produce beliefs that are true rather than false" (10)[24]. After some interesting preliminary skirmishes, he gives his official account in a sort of recursive form:

(a) If S's belief in p results from a reliable cognitive process, and there is no reliable or conditionally reliable process available to S which, had it been used by S in addition to the process actually used, would have resulted in S's not believing p at t, then S's belief in p at t is justified.

(b) If S's belief in p at t results ("immediately") from a belief-dependent process that is (at least) conditionally reliable, and if the beliefs (if any) on which this process operates in producing S's belief in p at t are themselves justified, then S's belief in p at t is justified (13, 20).

He then adds an appropriate closure clause.

For present purposes we need not concern ourselves with (b); suppose instead we turn our attention to the base clause (a). It isn't easy to see exactly what (a) comes to. The notion of **resulting from** is imprecise enough to require a good deal of guesswork, as is the notion of a process's being available to **S**. And while Goldman concedes that the second condition in the antecedent ("there is no reliable or conditionally reliable...") isn't quite accurate, he doesn't tell us how to set things right. Furthermore, this condition is subject to some of the familiar problems often bedeviling analyses involving counterfactuals. As an example of what requires this condition, Goldman cites a case in which I accept a lot of memory beliefs dating from my boyhood, but also have a lot of testimonial evidence from my parents—fabricated evidence, in point of fact—that my ostensible memories from that period are for the most part false. If nonetheless I persist in accepting the memory beliefs, then, says Goldman, these beliefs are not justified for me. They fall under that second condition in the antecedent of (a): there is available to me the process of using one's evidence, which is such that if I were to use it "in addition" to my memory, then I would not accept the beliefs in question. But now suppose that this process—using one's available evidence—is the only process which is at all likely to inhibit the relevant memory beliefs; and suppose further that if I were to use this process, then I would become suspicious of my parents, begin to question their veracity, launch an investigation into the case, conclude that my memories are reliable after all, and continue to accept them. Then the antecedent of (a) is fulfilled, for these beliefs; but they would not, presumably, be justified.

Still another problem here is the fact that there may be more than one reliable process available to **S**; perhaps there is a reliable process **P** such that if he were to use it, then he would not believe **p**, but another reliable process **P*** such that if he were to use both **P** and **P*** then he would believe **p**, and no reliable process **P**** such that if he were to use all of **P, P*** and **P**** he would not believe **p**; then perhaps Goldman would want to say that **S**'s belief would be justified after all, despite the fact that there is a reliable process available to him which is such that if he were to use it then he would not believe **p**.

So there are problems of several sorts with (a); I want to concentrate on only one. (a) proclaims that if **S**'s belief in **p** results from reliable cognitive process (and meets that further condition), then S's belief is justified. But what are these "cognitive processes"? Here is Goldman's way of characterizing them:

> Let us mean by a 'process' a *functional operation* or procedure, ie., something that generates a *mapping* from certain states—'inputs'—into other states—'outputs'. The outputs in the present case are states of believing this or that proposition at a given moment. On this interpretation, a process is a *type* as opposed to a *token*. This is fully appropriate, since it is only types that have such statistical properties as producing truth 80% of the time; and it is precisely such statistical properties that determine the reliability of a process. Of course we also want to speak of a process as *causing* a belief, and it looks as if types are incapable of being causes. But when we say that a belief is caused by a given process, understood as a functional procedure, we may interpret this to mean that it is caused by the particular *inputs* to the process (and by the intervening events 'through which' the functional procedure carries the inputs into the output) on the occasion in question (11).

How, exactly, shall we understand this? A belief forming process, first of all, is a thing that "generates a mapping from certain states—'inputs'—into other states—'outputs'." Now a barometer or a thermometer generates such a mapping: a thermometer, for example, generates (among others) a mapping from the ambient temperature to the reading it displays. Goldman's processes, however, are not concrete instruments or mechanisms such as barometers, thermometers, anometers, sphygmomanometers and the like; he says they are *types*, and he says that these types themselves have inputs and outputs. That makes it sound very much as if the processes in question are *functions*—but if they were functions they would not merely *generate* mappings (as he says they do), they would *be* mappings. So what sort of types are these? What are their tokens like? You might think that the tokens of the relevant types would be such things as Paul's memory, or Paul's visual apparatus. These things would not be functions, or abstract objects of any kind, but specific and concrete belief producing mechanisms or faculties. Like functions, such mechanisms or faculties have an input and output; but they are analogous to barometers and altimeters rather than to functions from temperature or altitude to numbers. The problem with this plausible answer, however, is that according to Goldman it is only the relevant **types**, not their tokens, that are reliable or unreliable. I'm not sure why Goldman said this and I wish he hadn't; I should think a concrete instrument or mechanism—a barometer, for example—is quite properly said to be reliable or unreliable.

So how shall we think of these processes? What are their tokens like? Do their tokens also have inputs and outputs? What sorts of things are the inputs and outputs of these processes, or the inputs and outputs of their tokens (if their tokens have inputs and outputs)? It is clear, I think, that the *outputs* of these processes are beliefs; the inputs, apparently, are entities capable of *causing* the outputs. But then presumably the beliefs in question will not be *propositions* (propositions aren't caused by anything) but *events*: such events as **Paul's believing that all men are mortal**, for example. Presumably, then, the inputs will also be events, rather than such abstract objects as states of affairs or properties or types—such events, perhaps, as **Paul's mother telling him that all men are mortal**. Goldman gives some examples of the sorts of processes he has in mind:

> One example is reasoning processes, where the inputs include antecedent beliefs and entertained hypotheses. ... A third example is a memory process, which takes as input beliefs or experiences at an earlier time and generates as output beliefs at a later time. For example, a memory process might take as input a belief *at* t_1 that Lincoln was born in 1809 and generate as output the belief *at* t_n that Lincoln was born in 1809 (11-12).

Consider the memory process (the type) mentioned. The inputs for this process would be events consisting in a person **S**'s believing at a time **t** that Lincoln was born in 1809: **Paul's believing at t_1 that Lincoln was born in 1809, Sam's believing at t_2 that Lincoln was born in 1809**, etc.; the outputs for a given input will be an event consisting of **S**'s believing that same proposition at a later time: **Paul's believing at t_3 that Lincoln was born in 1809, Sam's believing at t_4 that Lincoln was born in 1809**, and the like. For any input or argument **x** of the process, furthermore, the value or output **x*** will be caused by **x**. Tokens of this type, furthermore, would be specific dateable sequences of concrete events—events taking place in Paul's brain, perhaps, but in any case events taking place somewhere in his cognitive apparatus. The types would be types of such tokens. Both tokens and types will have inputs and outputs; an input (for a token as well as a type) will be some event or state of the cognizing subject, and an output will be a specific concrete event of the sort consisting in Paul's believing at some time t that Lincoln was born in 1809. And a given input (whether token or type) will be causally involved in a relevant way with its corresponding output.

Plenty of problems about the ontology of these processes remain: for example, a given token of a process will be a sequence whose members are concrete events, and presumably concrete events in the cognitive apparatus of a single person. But what about the types? Will they too then be such items as **the type consisting in e_1, followed by e_2, ..., followed by e_n** (where 'e_1', 'e_2', etc. are *names* of specific concrete events)? Or would the types be such that their tokens were sequences of *types* rather than sequences of concrete events: $e^*_1, e^*_2, ..., e^*_n$, where each e^*_i is a relevant type of e_i? If the latter, would these types involve a reference to a particular person? Suppose we temporarily ignore these questions, saving them for a more propitious occasion. The main problem, as I see it, still remains. Note first that any particular token—any relevant sequence of concrete events—will be a token of many different types. Consider a specific visual process in Paul, where the input consists in retinal stimulation, let's say, and the output consists, for some particular scene **s** on his television, in his believing that he sees **s**. The process in question will presumably involve a large number of events; it will no doubt include an event consisting in Paul's being appeared to in a characteristic way. Now this sequence of events will be a token of many different types—**the cognitive process, the visual process, the cognitive process occurring on a Thursday, the visual process occurring in a middle aged man, the visual process occurring in a middle aged man under such and such lighting conditions, the visual process occurring in a middle aged man when his retinas are being stimulated by light of such and such a character**, and many more.

It is these types that are to be evaluated for reliability (since, as we recall, the degree of justification enjoyed by the belief in question is a function of the reliability of the process (type) causing it); but obviously the types may differ wildly among themselves with respect to reliability. Which is the relevant type? Which type is the one such that its reliability determines the justification Paul has for the belief in question? This is the *problem of generality*, noted by Goldman (12) and developed by Richard Feldman in "Reliability and Justification".[25] Now obviously we can't take the relevant type to be, say, **the cognitive process**, or **vision**; for the outputs of such processes will have many different degrees of justification. If the reliability of a given belief— Paul's belief that he is watching television, for example—is to be determined by the reliability of the relevant type of which it is an output, then the outputs of that type must be indistinguishable with respect to justification: they must have the same degree of justification, or, if we eschew degrees in favor of a comparative concept of justification, none must be more justified than any other. Furthermore, the relevant type must display the degree of reliability correlated with the (no doubt modest) degree of justification Paul's belief does in fact have. Still further, the type in question clearly couldn't be such a type as **cognitive process issuing in a true belief**; there can't be a specific degree of reliability such that it is a necessary truth that the type in question displays that degree of reliability.

These things mean that the relevant types must display a very considerable degree of specificity. Consider, for example, (to take a case like one of Goldman's) an occasion on which Paul sees a mountain goat. Here we have a sequence of concrete events, a sequence that takes something (retinal stimulation, e.g.) as input and as output yields the event of Paul's forming the belief: **that's a mountain goat**. Now what is the relevant type, the type whose reliability determines the degree of justification Paul has for this belief? Not, of course, **vision**, or **vision in the mountains**, or **vision on Mt. Shuksan** or **vision during daylight**, but something much more specific: **seeing a mountain goat at 350 yards under such and such light and atmospheric conditions**, perhaps, or **retinal stimulation of such and such a character under such and such lighting and atmospheric conditions**[26], (where it might be very hard to fill in the such and such's). Even this won't be specific enough, however; for people differ with respect to their familiarity with mountain goats, liability to buck fever, visual acuity at 350 yards, and the like. These process types, therefore, are of differing degrees of reliability for different people and hence yield differing degrees of justification for different people; we must add further parameters to the type in question.

Indeed, we might plausibly think that for any belief **B**, type **T** and specification **T*** of **T** (where, for example, the type **night vision** is a specification of the type **vision**) if **p** is in the output of both **T** and **T*** and **T** and **T*** differ with respect to reliability, then **T** will not be the type the reliability of which determines the justification of **B**. A type **T**, we might think, will be a relevant type for a belief **B** of Paul's—relevant in that its reliability determines the justification of **B**—only if it is **maximally specific with respect to reliability** ('max' for short), i.e., such that there is no specification of that type with a different degree of reliability. I say this is a plausible thought; but so far as I can see it does not follow from what Goldman says. (Of course it would be hard to see grounds for its rejection; on Goldman's view, what determines the degree of justification of a belief is the reliability of the relevant type generating it; and it is hard to see grounds for supposing that there might be a pair of types **T** and **T***—both, let us say, pertaining to psychological conditions alone— such that **T*** is a subtype, a specification of **T**, while it is **T** rather than **T*** the reliability of which determines the degree of justifica- tion of beliefs in the output of **T***.)

In any event, although it would be difficult to give an example of the types in question (i.e., the types the reliability of which deter- mine the justification of the beliefs in their outputs), it is easy to see that they will have to be types of very great specificity. And we can easily see further, I think, that the degree of justification of a belief issued by such a type and the degree of reliability enjoyed by that type will not nearly always be related in the way required by Goldman's theory. The cases that caused trouble for Dretske will also cause trouble, and similar trouble, for Goldman. Consider, for ex- ample, the person whose belief that he has a brain tumor is caused by his brain tumor. There is a rare but specific sort of brain tumor, we may suppose, such that associated with it are a number of cognitive processes of the relevant degree of specificity, most of which cause its victim to hold absurd beliefs. One of the processes associated with the tumor, however, causes the victim to believe that he has a brain tumor. Suppose, then, that **S** suffers from this sort of tumor and accordingly believes that he suffers from a brain tumor. Add that he has no evidence at all for this belief: no symptoms of which he is aware, no testimony on the part of doctors or other ex- pert witnesses, nothing. Then the relevant type, while it may be hard to specify in detail, will certainly be highly reliable; but surely it is not the case that this belief—the belief that he has a brain tumor—has much by way of positive epistemic status for **S**. Indeed, as in the Dretske case, we can add, if we like, that **S** has a great deal of evidence *against* the proposition that he has a brain tumor; he too has just been examined by that team of brilliant specialists from New York, who have given him a clean bill of health. This addition does not run afoul of the second clause of the antecedent of (a) above because **S** is such that if he were to use the "process" of consulting his available evidence (the only other reliable process available to him), he would become very much interested in the whole question of tumors, study the matter in considerable detail, make some new discoveries, and finally wind up concluding that he did indeed have a tumor. There is therefore no reliable process available to **S** which is such that if he had used it, then he would not have formed the belief that he has a tumor. The antecedent of (a) is then satisfied, for **S**[27]; but surely the belief in question has little positive epistemic status for him. Perhaps it has permissive justification; perhaps **S** is within his epistemic rights in holding the belief; indeed, perhaps it is not within **S**'s power *not* to accept this belief. But the belief in question has little or no positive epistemic status of any other sort for him; in particular, it is clear that it does not constitute *knowledge* for him, even though it is true and he is permissively justified in accepting it.

Obviously we can construct similar examples from the other cases that caused trouble for Dretske: the case where I implant a source of high energy radiation in your dog, for example, and the case of the doubly rigged Philadelphia lottery. As a result of cognitive malfunction, the degree of positive epistemic status enjoyed by a belief **B** does not, in these cases, match the reliability of the relevant process type that produces it. And obviously the general recipe for constructing such cases is to come up with an appropriately pathological process type of the right degree of generality which is in fact reliable, but (due to the pathology involved) does not confer much by way of positive epistemic status on the beliefs in its output. (Such types, we might say, are from a cognitive point of view *accidentally reliable*.[28]) Reliability, then, is not sufficient for positive epistemic status. A further condition must be added—a condition to which it is now time to turn.

IV. On Working Properly

A. The Basic Idea

In the above discussions there is a sort of recurring theme. We saw repeatedly that various proposed analyses of justification come to grief when we reflect on the variety of ways in which our noetic faculties can fail to function properly. Chisholm's dutiful epistemic agent who, whenever he is appeared to redly, always believes that nothing is appearing redly to him, Lehrer's coherent epistemic agent who believes that he is an alien from outer space, Dretske's and Goldman's epistemic agent whose belief that Spot emits ultraviolet radiation has been caused by the fact that Spot does indeed emit such radiation—all are such that their beliefs lack positive epistemic status for them. In each case the reason, I suggest, is *cognitive malfunction*, failure of the relevant cognitive faculties to function properly. Chisholm's agent believes as he does because of cognitive dysfunction due to a brain lesion, or the machinations of an Alpha Centaurian scientist, or perhaps the mischievous schemes of a Cartesian evil demon; and something similar can be said for the others. I therefore suggest that a necessary condition of positive epistemic status is that one's cognitive equipment, one's belief forming and belief sustaining apparatus, be free of such cognitive malfunction. A belief has positive epistemic status for me only if my cognitive apparatus is functioning properly, working the way it ought to work in producing and sustaining it.

It is important to see is that this condition—that of one's cognitive equipment functioning properly—is not the same thing as one's cognitive equipment functioning *normally* in the statistical sense. If I give way to wishful thinking, forming the belief that I will soon be awarded a Nobel Peace Prize, then my cognitive faculties are not working properly—even though wishful thinking may be widespread among (and in that sense normal for) human beings. It may be (and in fact is) the case that it is not at all unusual or abnormal for a person to form a belief out of jealousy, lust, contrariness, desire for fame, or wishful thinking; nevertheless when I form a belief in this way my cognitive equipment is not functioning properly; it is not functioning the way it ought to.

Suppose we initially and provisionally agree that a necessary condition of a belief's having positive epistemic status for me is that the relevant portion of my noetic equipment involved in its formation and sustenance be functioning properly. Still, your faculties' being in proper working order cannot be the whole story. You take a space trip to a planet revolving about a distant star—Alpha Centauri, say. Conditions there are much like they are on earth; indeed some of the inhabitants of the planet are (physiologically speaking) surprisingly similar to human beings. Conditions there are propitious for human life; still there are subtle epistemic differences. Cats (or their Alpha Centaurian counterparts) are invisible to human beings; but they emit a sort of radiation unknown on earth, a radiation which works directly on the appropriate portion of a human brain, causing its owner to form the belief that a dog is barking nearby. An Alpha Centaurian cat slinks by; you form the belief that a dog is barking nearby. There is nothing the matter with your noetic faculties, but the belief in question has very little positive epistemic status for you. The problem is not merely that the belief is false; even if a dog is barking nearby (but in a soundproof room, say, so that it is inaudible), you certainly don't know that it is. The problem is that your cognitive faculties and the environment in which you find yourself are not properly attuned. The problem is not with your cognitive faculties: they are in good working order; the problem is with the environment. In much the same way, your automobile might be in perfect working order, despite the fact that it will not run well at the top of Pike's Peak, let alone under water. So we must add another component to positive epistemic status; your faculties must be in good working order, and the environment must be appropriate for your particular repertoire of epistemic powers. (Cats are not invisible to the human like creatures native to the planet in question.)

We might think that a belief's having positive epistemic status just *is* its being produced by epistemic faculties that are functioning properly (in producing and sustaining that belief) in an epistemically appropriate environment; but this cannot be the whole story. For couldn't my cognitive faculties could be working properly (in an appropriate environment) in producing and sustaining a certain belief in me, while nonetheless that belief has little by way of positive epistemic status for me? Further, a pair of my beliefs could be **productively equivalent** (produced by faculties functioning properly to the same degree and in environments of equal appropriateness) but nonetheless such that one of them has vastly more by way of positive epistemic status than the other. *Modus ponens* (more exactly, its corresponding conditional) obviously has more by way of positive epistemic status for me than for the memory belief, now rather dim and indistinct, that forty years ago I owned a second hand 16 gauge shotgun and a red bicycle with balloon tires. So positive epistemic status can't be simply a matter of a belief's being produced by faculties working properly in an appropriate environment.

What more is required? Here, fortunately enough, there is an easy response. Not only does the first belief, the belief in the corresponding conditional of *modus ponens*, have more by way of positive epistemic status for me than the second, it is also one I accept much more firmly; I have a much stronger tendency or inclination to accept that proposition than to accept the other. Obviously another element of positive epistemic status is the degree to which I do or am inclined to accept the belief in question; I can't be said to *know* **p**, for example, unless I believe it very firmly indeed. If my faculties are working properly, the more strongly I believe (or am impelled or inclined to believe) **p** the more positive epistemic status **p** has for me. When our cognitive establishment is working properly, the strength of the impulse towards believing a given proposition (we may conjecture) will be proportional to the degree it has of positive epistemic status—or if the relationship isn't one of straightforward proportionality, the appropriate functional relationship will hold between positive epistemic status and this impulse. So when my faculties are functioning properly, a belief has positive epistemic status to the degree that I find myself inclined to accept it; and this (again, if my faculties are functioning properly) will be the degree to which I *do* accept it.

Initially and to a first approximation, therefore, we may put it like this (thus importing what is at this stage undoubtedly a spurious precision): a belief **B** has positive epistemic status for **S** if and only if that belief is produced in **S** by his epistemic faculties working properly; and **B** has more positive epistemic status than **B*** for **S** iff **B** has positive epistemic status for **S** and either **B*** does not or else **S** is more strongly inclined to believe **B** than **B***. (If we think degree of belief and degree of positive epistemic status are real valued functions, we can put the matter thus: where a person **S** accepts a proposition **P**, **S** has positive epistemic status to degree **r** for **P** if and only if his faculties are functioning properly in producing this belief and **S** accepts **P** to degree **r***, where **r*** is the value for **r** under the appropriate functional transformation.)

Now I mean to suggest that this or something like it is in fact how we think of positive epistemic status. But of course if that is so, then

something else must also be so: we must also think, as we do think, that (for the most part) when our faculties are functioning properly, the beliefs they produce—in particular the more confident beliefs they produce—are true, or at any rate *close* to the truth.
Of course so far this is merely programmatic, just a picture. Much must be said by way of clarification, articulation, qualification. Let me begin with a couple of obvious qualifications. First, I say that a belief has positive epistemic status for me only if my epistemic faculties are working properly in producing and sustaining it. But of course it isn't true that *all* of my cognitive faculties have to be functioning properly in order for a belief to have warrant for me. Suppose my memory plays me tricks; obviously that doesn't mean that I can't have warrant for such introspective propositions as that I am appeared to redly. What must be working properly are the faculties involved in the production of the particular belief in question. And even they need not be working properly over the entire range of their operation. Suppose I cannot properly hear high notes: I may still learn much by way of the hearing ability I do have. Furthermore, a faculty that doesn't function properly *without outside aid* can nonetheless furnish warrant; I can have warrant for visual propositions even if I need glasses and can see next to nothing without them. Still further, even if my corrected vision is very poor, I can still have warrant for visual propositions; even if I can't distinguish color at all, I can still have warrant for the proposition that I perceive something round. Still further, even if I can't perceive colors at all, I can still have visual warrant for the proposition that something is red; even if for me nothing appears redly (everything is merely black and white) I might still be able to see that something is red, in the way in which one can see, on a black and white television, which boxer is wearing the red trunks. Similar comments must be made, of course, about the environmental condition. There are problems here, but nothing that looks initially insurmountable.

Further, proper functioning, of course, *comes in degrees*; or if it does not, then approximation to proper functioning does. Clearly the faculties relevant with respect to a given belief need not be functioning *perfectly* for me to have warrant for my belief; how well, then, must they be functioning? And precisely how similar to the environment for which my faculties were designed, must my present environment be if I am to have warrant? Part of the answer here, of course, is that there is no answer; the ideas of warrant and knowledge are to some degree vague; there is therefore no precise answer to the question in question.

Still further, suppose I know that the environment is misleading; and suppose I know in just which ways it is misleading. (I'm on a planet where things that look square are really round.) Then, clearly enough, the fact that my environment is misleading need not deprive my beliefs of warrant. And of course the same must be said for the requirement that my faculties be in good working order. If I know, for example, that (as in Castaneda's fantasy) I suffer from a quirk of memory such that whenever I read a history book, I always misremember the dates, somehow adding ten years to the date as stated, I can still have warrant for beliefs—even beliefs about dates—formed by reading history books; I can compensate for my erroneous tendency. What counts here, of course, are uncorrected and uncompensated malfunctionings. Clearly there is here the need for a great deal of chisholming; let me postpone it, however, in order to turn to some other matters.

B. The Design Plan

A crucially important notion here is that of specifications, or blueprint, or *design plan*. We take it that when the organs (or organic systems) of a human being (or other organism) function properly, they function *in a particular way*. Such organs have a *function* or *purpose*; the purpose of the heart, for example, is to pump blood. Furthermore, such an organ, of course, functions in such a way as to fulfill its purpose; but it also functions to fulfill that purpose in just one of an indefinitely large number of possible ways. Here a comparison with artifacts is useful. A house is designed to produce shelter—but not in just any old way. There will be plans specifying the length and pitch of the rafters, what kind of shingles are to be applied, the kind and quantity of insulation to be used, and the like. Something similar holds in the case of us and our faculties; we seem to be constructed in accordance with a specific set of plans. Better (since this analogy is insufficiently dynamic) we seem to have been constructed in accordance with a set of specifications, in the way in which there are specifications for, for example, the 1983 GMC van. According to these specifications (here I am just guessing), after a cold start the engine runs at 1500 RPM until the engine temperature reaches 140 degrees F.; it then throttles back to 750 RPM.

In the same sort of way, there is something like a set of specifications for a well-formed, properly functioning human being—an extraordinarily complicated and highly articulated set of specifications, as any first year medical student could tell you. Suppose we call these specifications a 'design plan', leaving open the question whether human beings and other creatures have in fact been designed. Then of course the design plan will include specifications for our cognitive faculties (as well as for the rest of our powers and faculties). They too can work well or badly; they can misfunction or function properly. They too work in a certain way when they are functioning properly—and work in a certain way to accomplish their purpose. The purpose of the heart is to pump blood; that of our cognitive faculties is to supply us with reliable information— information about our environment, about the past, about the thoughts and feeling of others, and so on. But not just any old way of accomplishing this purpose in the case of a specific cognitive process is in accordance with our design plan. It is for this reason that it is possible for a belief to be produced by a cognitive process or belief producing mechanism that is *accidentally* reliable, as in the case of the processes cited as counterexamples to Goldman's version of reliabilism.[29] Although the belief producing processes in question are in fact reliable, their outputs have little by way of positive epistemic status; and the reason is that these processes are pathologically out of accord with the design plan for human beings.

Our design plan, of course, is such that our faculties are highly responsive to circumstances. Upon considering an instance of *modus ponens*, I find myself believing its corresponding conditional; upon being appeared to in the familiar way, I find myself holding the belief that there is a large tree before me; upon being asked what I had for breakfast, I reflect for a moment and then find myself with the belief that what I had was eggs on toast. In these and other cases I do not *decide* what to believe; I don't total up the evidence (I'm being appeared to redly; on most occasions when thus appeared to I am in the presence of something red; so most probably in this case I am) and make a decision as to what seems best supported; I simply find myself with the appropriate belief. Of course in some cases I may go through such a weighing of the evidence; I may be trying to decide, for example, whether the alleged evidence in favor of the theory that human life evolved by means of the mechanisms of random genetic mutation and natural selection from unicellular life (which itself arose by substantial similar mechanical processes from nonliving material) is in fact compelling; but in the typical case of belief formation nothing like this is involved.

According to our design plan, obviously enough, *experience* plays a crucial role in belief formation—both sensuous experience, such as **being appeared to greenly**, and the sort of experience involved in feeling impelled or disposed to accept a given belief. *A priori* beliefs, for example, are not, as this denomination mistakenly suggests, formed prior to or in the absence of experience. Thinking of the corresponding conditional of **modus ponens** *feels* different from thinking of, say, the corresponding conditional of **affirming the consequent**; and this difference in experience is crucially connected with our accepting the one and rejecting the other. Of course experience plays a different role here from the role it plays in the formation of perceptual beliefs; it plays a still different role in the formation of memory beliefs, moral beliefs, beliefs about the mental lives of other persons, beliefs we form on the basis of inductive evidence, and the like. Further, our design plan is such that under certain conditions we form one belief *on the evidential basis* of others; and of course if our faculties are functioning properly, we don't form just *any* belief on the evidential basis of just any other. I may form the belief that Sam was at the party on the evidential basis of other beliefs—perhaps I learn from you that Sam wasn't at the bar and from his wife that he was either at the bar or at the party. But if my faculties are functioning properly, I won't form the belief that Feike is a Catholic on the evidential basis of the propositions that nine out of ten Frisians are Protestants and Feike is a Frisian. And here too experience plays an important role. The belief about Sam *feels like* the right one; that belief about Feike (in those circumstances) feels strange, rejectable, inappropriate, not to be credited. Still further, the design plan dictates the appropriate *degree* or firmness of a given belief in given circumstances. You read in a relatively unreliable newspaper an account of a 53 car accident on a Los Angeles freeway; perhaps you then form the belief that there was a 53 car accident on the freeway. But if you hold that belief as firmly as, e.g., that $2 + 1 = 3$, then your faculties are not functioning as they ought to and the belief has little positive epistemic status for you. Again, experience obviously plays an important role. What we need is a full and appropriately subtle and sensitive description of the role of experience in the formation and maintenance of all these various types of beliefs; that project will have to await another occasion, as one says when one can't in fact deliver the goods.

Positive epistemic status, I said, is intimately related to proper function—so intimately related that a belief has positive epistemic status for me only if my cognitive faculties are functioning properly in forming and maintaining it. As I said above, a presupposition of our conception of positive epistemic status, clearly enough, is that beliefs formed by our faculties functioning properly in an appropriate environment will be for the most part close to the truth. We might put this by saying that a presupposition of our conception is that the purpose of our epistemic faculties is the production of beliefs that are mostly true or mostly nearly true. Still, there are cases in which our faculties are functioning perfectly properly, but where their working in that way does not seem to lead to truth—indeed, it may lead away from it. Someone may remember a painful experience as less painful than it was, as is sometimes said to be the case with childbirth. You may continue to believe in your friend's honesty long after evidence and objective judgment would have dictated a reluctant change of mind. I may believe that I will recover from a dread disease much more strongly than the statistics justify. In these cases, the relevant faculties may be functioning properly, functioning just as they ought to, but nevertheless not in a way that leads to truth, to the formation of true beliefs. But then how can I say that a belief has positive epistemic status if it is produced by one's faculties functioning properly?

The answer here is simplicity itself. Different parts or aspects of our cognitive apparatus could have different purposes; different parts or aspects of our design plan, could be aimed at different ends or goals. Not all aspects of the design of our cognitive faculties need be aimed at the production of true belief; some might be such as to conduce to survival, or relief from suffering, or the possibility of loyalty, or inclination to have more children, and the like. What confers positive epistemic status is one's cognitive faculties working properly, or working according to the design plan *insofar as that segment of the design plan is aimed at producing true beliefs.* But someone whose holding a certain belief is a result of an aspect of our cognitive design that is aimed not at truth but at something else won't properly be said to know the proposition in question, even if it turns out to be true (unless, of course, the same design would conduce both to truth and to the other state of affairs aimed at.)

Finally, our design plan obviously dictates change over time; our faculties and organs change and mature. Newborn babies are not able to walk; kittens are. Kittens are born blind; human beings are not, although there is maturation of human cognitive faculties just as of those of other organisms. Still further, the design plan of an organism may itself change over time, so that, conceivably, what is proper function at one time may not be at another. And of course the present view involves no specific or species chauvinism; it isn't necessary that a member of another species—an angel, for example, or an Alpha Centaurian—will have positive epistemic status for her beliefs only if her cognitive faculties function in accordance with *our* design plan.

C. Gettier Problems

I began this paper with a reference to Edmund Gettier and the salutary havoc his three page paper has introduced into contemporary epistemology. Gettier pointed out, of course, that belief, truth and justification are not sufficient for knowledge. Naturally enough, there have been many attempts to provide a "fourth condition", many attempts to add an epicycle or two to circumvent Gettier. Sadly, however, in most cases the quick response has been another Gettier problem that circumvents the circumvention. I don't mean at all to denigrate this often illuminating literature; but my aim here is not to enter the lists and try to produce a Gettier-proof analysis of knowledge. My aim instead is to see how the Gettier problem looks from the vantage point of the present conception of positive epistemic status. Gettier problems come in several forms. There is the original **Smith owns a Ford or Brown is in Barcelona** version: Smith comes into your office, bragging about his new Ford, shows you the bill of sale and title, takes you for a ride in it, and in general supplies you with a great deal of evidence for the proposition that he owns a Ford. Naturally enough you believe the proposition **Smith owns a Ford**; acting on the maxim that it is good to believe as many truths as possible, you infer from that proposition its disjunction with **Brown is in Barcelona**, where Brown is an acquaintance of yours about whose whereabouts you have no information. As it turns out, Smith is lying (he does not own a Ford) but Brown, by sheer coincidence, is indeed in Barcelona. So your belief **Smith owns a Ford or Brown is in Barcelona** is indeed both true and justified; but surely you can't properly be said to *know* it. A similar case, due to Lehrer: you see (at about 50 yards) what you think is a sheep in the field and (acting again on the above principle) infer that the field contains at least one sheep. As luck would have it, what you see is not a sheep (but a wolf in sheep's clothing); in a part of the field you can't see, however, there is indeed a sheep. Your belief that there is a sheep in the field is true and justified, but hardly a case of knowledge.

In these cases you infer the justified true belief from a justified false belief (that Smith owns a Ford, that *that* is a sheep); your justification, we might say, goes through a false belief. But of course this is not the key to Gettier problems. Consider the following case, due originally to Carl Ginet. You are driving through southern Wisconsin, near Waupun. In an effort to make themselves look more prosperous than they really are, the inhabitants have erected a large number of barn facades— three for each real barn. From the road, these facades are indistinguishable from real barns. You are unaware of this playful attempt at deception; looking at what is in fact a real barn you form the belief **that's a fine barn!** Again, the belief is true and it seems that you are justified in holding it; but surely it does not constitute knowledge. To continue the bucolic motif, one final case. The Park Service has just cleaned up a popular bridle trail in Yellowstone, in anticipation of a visit from a Department of the Interior bigwig. A wag with a perverse sense of humor comes along and scatters two bushels of horse manure on the trail. The official from the Department of the Interior arrives, goes for a walk on the trail, and forms the belief that horses have been on the trail recently. Once more, his belief is true and justified, but does not constitute knowledge.

But why not, precisely? What is going on in these cases? First, it seems that in each of these cases it is merely *by accident* that the justified true belief in question is true. It just happens that Brown is in Barcelona, that there is a sheep in another part of the field, that what you are looking at is a barn facade rather than a barn. In each of these cases, the belief in question could just as well have been false. (As a matter of fact, in some of these cases that's not putting it strongly enough; the belief could *better* have been false: there are so many other places Brown could have been, and wags don't often or ordinarily take the trouble to make the Park Service look bad.) But what is the force, here of saying that the beliefs are true by *accident*?

Here is a possibility. In each of these cases there is a sort of glitch in the cognitive situation, a minor infelicity due, we might say, to cognitive environmental pollution. We saw above that a necessary condition of my beliefs' having positive epistemic status is that the environment in which they are formed be appropriate for one with my repertoire of cognitive powers. If there is substantial lack of match between the cognitive environment and the sort of environment for which my powers are appropriate, then even if my belief happens to be true, it has little by way of positive epistemic status for me; the cognitive environment is deeply misleading, so that if I acquire a true belief, it is just by accident. Now in Gettier situations we have a sort of mild version of what goes on in those cases where there is wholesale lack of match between cognitive environment and cognitive faculties. In the Gettier cases there is no wholesale lack of match; there is, however, a bit of retail lack of match. Although the cognitive environment is not deeply misleading, it is nonetheless at least mildly misleading. Our design plan leads us to believe what we are told by others; there is what Thomas Reid calls "Credulity", a belief forming process whereby for the most part we believe what our fellows tell us. Of course Credulity is modified by experience; we learn to believe some people under some circumstances and disbelieve others under others. (We learn not to form beliefs about a marital quarrel until we have heard from both parties.) Still, Credulity is part of our design plan. But of course it doesn't work well when our fellows lie to us or deceive us in some other manner, as in the case of Smith who lies about the Ford, or the Wisconsinites who set out to deceive the city slicker tourists, or the wag aiming to hoodwink the Interior Department official.

We might generalize the idea of a design plan: there is a design plan not only for our cognitive faculties, but for the entire cognitive situation. Take the metaphor in this notion of design more seriously for the moment; then the designer of our cognitive powers will have designed those powers to produce mostly true beliefs in the sorts of situations their owners ordinarily encounter. The designer will be aiming at a kind of match between cognitive powers and cognitive environment; there will be, we might say, a sort of design plan not just for cognitive faculties, but for cognitive-faculties-cum-cognitive-environment. In Gettier situations, however, there are relatively minor departures from the design plan for the cognitive situation in question; the cognitive environment then turns out to be misleading for someone with our cognitive powers. And the force of saying that in these cases the beliefs just *happen* to be true, are true *by accident*, is the same as in the case of the counter-examples to reliabilism: the belief's being true is not a result of things working in accordance with the design plan. In the first cases, the problem was with the cognizer's faculties; due to disease or demon they were not functioning in accordance with the design plan. In typical Gettier situations, on the other hand, there is deviation from the design plan for the total cognitive situation, but it is due to the cognitive environment rather than to the cognizer's faculties. But this is a nonessential feature of Gettier situations; no doubt we could think of Gettier situations in which the glitch was internal to the cognizer rather than due to the environment. What is essential to Gettier situations is the production of a true belief despite a relatively minor failure of the cognitive situation to match its design.

D. Theism and Proper Function

But aren't such ideas as that of working properly and related notions such as **cognitive dysfunction, design plan**, and the like, deeply problematic? What is it for a natural organism—a tree, for example, or a horse—to be in good working order, to be functioning properly? Isn't "working properly" relative to our aims and interests? A cow is functioning properly when she gives the appropriate kind and amount of milk; a garden patch is as it ought to be when it displays a luxuriant preponderance of the sorts of vegetation we propose to promote. But here it seems patent that what constitutes proper functioning depends upon our aims and interests. So far as nature herself goes, isn't a fish decomposing in a hill of corn functioning just as properly, just as excellently, as one happily swimming about chasing minnows? But then what could be meant by speaking of "proper functioning" with respect to our cognitive faculties? A chunk of reality—an organism, a part of an organism, an ecosystem, a garden patch—"functions properly", it might be said, only with respect to a sort of grid *we* impose on nature, a grid that incorporates our aims and desires.

Now from a *theistic* point of view—a point of view that I accept—the idea of proper functioning is no more problematic than, say that of a Boeing 747's working properly. Something we have constructed—a heating system, a rope, a linear accelerator—is functioning properly when it is functioning in the way in which it was designed to function. But according to theism, human beings, like ropes and linear accelerators, have been designed; they have been designed and created by God. According to the theistic way of looking at the matter, we human beings have been created by God, and created in his own image; in certain important respect we resemble him. God, furthermore, is an actor, a creator, one who chooses certain ends and takes action to accomplish them. God is therefore a *practical* being. But he is also an *intellectual* or *intellecting* being. He holds beliefs, (even if there are significant differences between his way of holding a belief and ours[30]), has knowledge, apprehends concepts. In setting out to create human beings in his image, then, God set out to create them in such a way that they could reflect his capacity to grasp concepts and hold beliefs. Furthermore, he proposed to create them in such a way that they can reflect his ability to hold *true* beliefs. He therefore created us with cognitive faculties or powers designed to enable us to achieve true beliefs with respect to a wide variety of propositions—propositions about our immediate environment, about the past, about our own interior life, about the thoughts and feelings of other persons, about our universe at large, about right and wrong, about the whole realm of *abstracta* (properties, propositions, states of affairs, numbers, and the like) about modality, and about himself.

From this perspective it is easy enough to say what it is for our faculties to be working properly; they are working properly when they are working in the way they were intended to work by the being who designed them. This, I take it, is the basic root of the idea of proper functioning: an object is functioning properly if and only if it is functioning in the way it was designed to function. Of course from a theistic perspective we must append a qualification to the idea that positive epistemic status is a matter of proper functioning; for clearly enough S's faculties could be working properly, in that root sense, even if S's beliefs have no positive epistemic status for him. S's faculties could have been designed by a mischievous Cartesian demon who finds it diverting to contemplate creatures who are both systematically deceived and proud of their status as the epistemic lords of the universe; or perhaps S's epistemic faculties have been redesigned by an Alpha Centaurian scientist who cares nothing for their relation to truth. So even if we say that S's faculties are working properly, it doesn't follow that S has positive epistemic status for his beliefs. What we must add is what the theistic view does add: that our faculties have been designed by a being who wishes to enable us to achieve a substantial degree of truth in a substantial portion of the range in which we form beliefs.

But can a nontheist also make use of this notion of proper function in understanding positive epistemic status? Well, why not? Can't anyone, theist or not, see that a horse, say, in suffering from a disease, is displaying a pathological condition? Can't anyone see that an injured bird has a wing that isn't working properly? Or that an arthritic hand does not function properly? The question is whether theism is entailed by the claim that we have faculties that function properly or improperly (faculties that have a design plan). The question is whether, on the proposed account of positive epistemic status, the proposition that some belief has positive epistemic status for you entails the truth of theism. Of course it might trivially entail theism, by virtue of the fact (as the theist sees it) that theism is a necessary truth; alternatively, perhaps theism is not a necessary truth, but (as the theist may also think) it is necessary that all contingent beings have been created directly or indirectly by God. But of course if this is true then any account whatever of knowledge (or of anything else) will entail theism. The real question here is something different—something not at all easy to state clearly. Perhaps we can put it like this: the real question is whether the notion of proper function is linked with theism in such a way that the proposition **some organ or system of some organism is functioning properly**, entails theism by way of a series of steps each of which is obvious. Or perhaps the real question is whether there is a satisfactory nontheistic *analysis* or explanation of the notion of proper function. It is certainly not obvious either that there is any such entailment or that there is no such explanation or analysis. More vaguely, the question is whether the notion of proper function can be properly understood from a nontheistic perspective. But even if it can't, that is no real objection to the present account. We all have and constantly use the idea of the proper function of our cognitive faculties; we all have and use the idea of the dysfunction of various systems and organs of human beings and other organisms. If there is no adequate nontheistic way to understand this family of notions, then there lurks here, not an objection to the above account of positive epistemic status, but a powerful theistic argument.

And even if there is no good nontheistic analysis of **proper function**, the nontheist can accept something *like* this notion. Even if he doesn't think we human beings have been designed and created by a powerful and highly competent being who proposed to endow us with the ability to achieve true beliefs, he may nonetheless think of this idea as a convenient and useful fiction. He may join Hans Vaihinger in *Der Philosophie von Als Ob*, and explain proper functioning in terms of this fiction, as he sees it; he may say that our faculties are working properly when they are working the way they would work if the theistic story were true.[31] He may therefore treat this story the way corresponding stories are treated by some who accept ideal observer theories in ethics, or social contract theories in political philosophy, or Piercian theories of truth, or possible worlds theories in metaphysics. I can sensibly explain what it is for an action to be right in terms of what an ideal observer would approve without adding that in fact there exists an ideal observer. A person can see possible worlds theory as a source of insight and understanding, even if he thinks it is not to be taken seriously as sober metaphysics. In the same way a nontheist could help himself to the theistic explanation of positive epistemic status, even if he thinks the notion of proper function has no very good nontheistic explanation.

There is a similar but slightly different tack he may take: He may take towards the idea of design the same attitude Bas van Fraassen takes towards possible worlds, modality, and unobservables in science. These, says van Fraassen, are pictures that guide our inference, but they are not to be taken seriously as part of the sober metaphysical truth of the matter. "Such fictions," he says, "are useful in giving an account of the surface phenomena—and there is in reality, nothing below the surface. In our case the phenomena are the inferential relations among statements, attested in the inferential behavior of those engaged in such discourse."[32] Each of these stances, admittedly, is perhaps vaguely uneasy or a bit awkward; but there is nothing initially incoherent about them. And in the same sort of way a nontheist can accept the present account of positive epistemic status, even if he thinks there is no good way to understand proper function and allied notions from a nontheistic perspective.

By way of conclusion then: the main contemporary accounts of positive epistemic status are all deeply flawed. Each founders on the same rock: each neglects to take into account the ways in which our cognitive faculties can fail to function properly, and each overlooks the crucial connection between positive epistemic status, on the one hand, and our cognitive faculties' functioning properly on the other. Indeed, positive epistemic status, as I see it, just is the proper functioning of our epistemic equipment. In a nutshell, a belief **B** has positive epistemic status for **S** if and only if that belief is produced in **S** by his epistemic faculties' working properly; and **B** has more positive epistemic status than **B*** for **S** iff **B** has positive epistemic status for **S** and either **B*** does not or else **S** is more strongly inclined to believe **B** than **B***. This picture of positive epistemic status, obviously enough, needs articulation, development and qualification; nevertheless, I think, it is a better picture than any of its rivals.

Notes

1. And until Edmund Gettier showed us the error of our ways: see his classic "Is Justified True Belief Knowledge?" *Analysis* 23 (1963) pp. 121-123.
2. See , e.g., *Theory of Knowledge* (New York: Prentice Hall, 2nd Edition), p. 5.
3. See my "Reason and Belief in God" in *Faith and Rationality: Reason and Belief in God*, ed. A. Plantinga and N. Wolterstorff (South Bend: University of Notre Dame Press, 1985), pp. 24 ff.
4. Call the first belief 'A' and the second 'B'; there is the degree of positive epistemic status had by those beliefs that have no more of that quantity (for me) than B, the degree displayed by those that have more than B but less than A, and the degree enjoyed by those that have as much or more than A.
5. For a fuller and more complete version of the ideas of this section, see my "Chisholmian Internalism" in *Philosophical Analysis: a Defense by Example*, ed. David Austin (forthcoming).
6. Although this has perhaps been the dominant internalist tradition in modern (Western) epistemology, it is not the only one. To characterize the other one, we must back up just a bit. According to the second tradition, positive epistemic status is to be understood in terms of rational action. An action I take is rational in case it is appropriately connected with the attainment of my aims or goals—perhaps it is the action (of all those open to me) that is *in fact* most suited to achieving my goals, or perhaps it is the one that I *think* is the one best suited, or perhaps the one such that upon sufficient reflection I *would* think it most suitable. But then epistemic rationality is a special case of rationality generally, and is to be thought of in terms of the aptness of my beliefs or my belief forming policies to fulfill my epistemic goals. See Richard Foley's book *The Theory of Epistemic Rationality* (Cambridge: Harvard University Press, 1987) for an excellent contemporary development of a non-Cartesian variety of internalism.
7. See "Chisholmian Internalism", first section.
8. I ignore, here, the complication provided by the fact that in *Foundations of Knowing* Chisholm recasts his epistemological theory in terms of direct attribution of properties, thus abandoning the earlier formulation in terms of believing or accepting propositions. Everything I say about Chisholm's views can be restated so as to accommodate this shift, though in some cases at the cost of considerable complication.
9. But even if epistemic obligation or requirement is *sui generis*, it shares important elements of structure with moral obligation: there is super-

venience, defeasibility, the application of the *prima facie*/all things considered distinction, the characteristic relations among permission, obligation, and prohibition, and so on.

10. See "Chisholmian Internalism", first section.

11. Much of Chisholm's epistemological work is given over to the project of formulating and defending epistemic principles (see the earlier pages of this section). I do not propose to argue that these principles are mistaken; I mean to argue only that his suggestion as to what positive epistemic status *is*, is mistaken.

12. For example: suppose you were nonculpably convinced that the most likely way to achieve truth was to avoid thinking things over and to believe the first thing that came into your head; would it then be your duty to form beliefs in that way? Suppose you thought, after careful and dutiful reflection, that a given proposition was false: could it nonetheless be your duty to believe it? If you failed to believe it, could you properly be accused of dereliction of duty? See my "Reason and Belief in God", pp.35-37.

13. And it may well be less than that; see "Chisholmian Internalism".

14. For some suggestions as to how coherentism is related to foundationalism, see my "Coherentism and the Evidentialist Objection to Theistic Belief" in *Rationality, Religious Belief and Moral Commitment*, ed. R. Audi and W. Wainwright, (Ithaca: Cornell University Press, 1986).

15. An outstanding exception is Keith Lehrer's book *Knowledge* (Oxford: Oxford University Press, 1974) surely as full and articulate development of coherentist thought as is presently to be found. Although I don't have the space here to give a critical account of Lehrer's conception of coherence (but see my "Coherentism and the Evidentialist Objection to Belief in God") I intend the criticisms that follow to apply to it. Of course there are also probabilistic or Baysian coherentists; I don't here have the space to discuss this position.

16. See, for example, Fred Dretske's *Knowledge and the Flow of Information* (Cambridge: The MIT Press, 1981); Alvin Goldman's "What is Justified Belief" in *Justification and Knowledge: New Studies in Epistemology*, ed. G. Pappas, (Boston, Dordrecht, London: D. Reidel); Robert Nozick's *Philosophical Explanations* (Cambridge: Harvard University Press, 1981; and Marshall Swain's *Reasons and Knowledge* (Ithaca: Cornell University Press, 1981).

17. Nozick, *Philosophical Explanations*, pp.172-178. Nozick points out that conditions (1)-(4), as they stand, are neither necessary nor sufficient for knowledge; he tries to mend matters by adding an epicycle involving "methods" of believing or coming to believe: "This leads us to put forth the following position: S knows that p if there is some method via which S believes that p which satisfies conditions (1)-(4), and that method is not outweighed by any other method(s) via which S actually believes that p that fail to satisfy conditions (3) and (4)". The idea of coming to believe via a "method" isn't very clear; insofar as I see what Nozick means here, I have tried to construct the counterexamples I propose below in such a way that they involve S's coming to believe via just

one method, so that this complication will not be relevant.

18. Hence on Nozick's view, I don't know (4), do know (3), don't know the disjunction of (3) with (4) (if it were false, (4) would be false, so that I would still believe the disjunction) but do know the conjunction of (3) with (4)!

19. Cambridge: MIT Press, 1981.

20. See Richard Foley "Dretske's 'Information Theoretic' Account of Knowledge" forthcoming in *Synthese*.

21. Thus according to Reichenbach, the appropriate reference class is the narrowest class such that we know that Paul is a member of it, and such that we have reliable statistics for the frequency of the attribute in that class. Others have made other suggestions; Wesley Salmon, for example, suggests that the appropriate reference class is the broadest homogenous class containing the instance in question. (See his *Foundations of Scientific Inference*, (Pittsburgh: The University of Pittsburgh Press, 1966) p. 91. All the suggestions made, however, result in the 'probability' for a singular proposition's being relative to some body of knowledge.

22. *The Behavioral and Brain Sciences* (1983) p. 83.

23. Objection: in this example (as in the next) I am conforming to the *letter* of D_5 but not to the spirit of the underlying intuition. That intuition is that in the relevant epistemic situations, there is a source **s** that sends a signal **r** having the property G; K knows that **s** if F in case **r's being G** (1) causes **K** to believe that **s** is F and (2) carries the information that **s** is F (carries that information with respect to **K**). But my last two examples both work by *identifying* **r's being G** with **s's being F**. Reply: In these objections I did indeed collapse **r's being G** into **s's being F**. (My reason for so doing was only to avoid avoidable problems about whether **P(s's being F | r's being G)** really equals 1.) But that is an inessential feature of these examples; we can easily amend them to satisfy the objection. Accordingly, revise the present case as follows: I implant a source of high energy radiation in your dog Spot; it is a lawlike truth that any dog in which a source of high energy radiation has been implanted will lose its hair within seven days; Spot's emitting this high energy radiation causes a brain lesion in you which in turn causes you to form a large number of wildly false beliefs about Spot (that he is in fact a mermaid, that he can speak French but refuses to out of sheer obstinacy, etc.) but also causes you to form the true belief that Spot will lose his hair within the next two weeks. You have no evidence of any sort for your belief and much evidence against it. (You have just had Spot examined by a team of tonsorial experts who assure you that he is entirely normal along these lines.) Here **r's being G** is not collapsed into **s's being F** (**r's being G** is **Spot's emitting high energy radiation** and **s's being F** is **Spot's losing his hair within two weeks**). You satisfy the conditions laid down by D_5 for knowledge; but surely you don't know. The next example (about the doubly rigged lottery) can be similarly amended.

24. "What is Justified Belief?" in *Justification and Knowledge: New Studies in Epistemology*, ed. George Pappas (Dordrecht: D. Reidel, 1979), p. 10.

25. *Monist*, 1986.

26. And perhaps the "such and such lightings and atmospheric conditions" should be deleted; perhaps Goldman's idea is that the types in question must be stateable in psychological terms alone.

27. Robert Shope has called my attention to a passage where Goldman may be proposing a further restriction on the sorts of processes that are relevant: "Justifiedness seems to be a function of how a cognizer deals with his environmental input, i.e., with the goodness or badness of the operations that register and transform the stimulation that reaches him" (12-13). Shope suggests (private communication) that perhaps Goldman intends the processes under discussion to be ones that transform or operate upon external stimuli, a condition that is not met in the brain tumor case. Very well, alter the case accordingly; let the relevant process associated with the tumor be one that takes any visual stimulus, say, as input and yields as output the pathological belief in question.

28. See below, section IV B.

29. See above section III C.

30. See my "Justification and Theism", *Faith and Philosophy*, Oct. 1987, last section.

31. But here he must be careful. If theism were true, then presumably there would be something like Calvin's Sensus Divinitatis, a manysided disposition to accept belief in God or propositions about God in a wide variety of circumstances. (See my "Reason and Belief in God", p. 80-82.) But then our faculties would be functioning properly when we form such beliefs in the basic way—that is, immediately, without believing on the evidential basis of other propositions. And then such belief in God would have positive epistemic status—a conclusion the nontheist may wish to avoid.

32. "Probabilities of Conditionals" in *Foundations of Probability Theory, Statistical Inference, and Statistical Theories of Science, I*, ed. Harper and Hooker, (Dordrecht: D. Reidel Publishing Co., 1976) p. 267.

STRONG AND WEAK JUSTIFICATION*

Alvin I. Goldman
University of Arizona

It is common in recent epistemology to distinguish different senses, or conceptions, of epistemic justification. The proposed oppositions include the objective/subjective, internalist/externalist, regulative/nonregulative, resource-relative/resource-independent, personal/verific, and deontological/evaluative conceptions of justification.[1] In some of these cases, writers regard both members of the contrasting pair as legitimate; in other cases only one member. In this paper I want to propose another contrasting pair of conceptions of justification, and hold that *both* are defensible and legitimate. The contrast will then be used to construct a modified version of reliabilism, one which handles certain problem cases more naturally than my previous versions of reliabilism.

I

I should begin by acknowledging the undesirability of multiplying senses of any term beyond necessity. Lacking good evidence for multivocality of a target analysandum, a unified analysis should be sought. But sometimes there is indeed good evidence for multivocality. Here is a case in point for the term 'justified'.

Consider a scientifically benighted culture, of ancient or medieval vintage. This culture employs certain highly unreliable methods for forming beliefs about the future and the unobserved. Their methods appeal to the doctrine of signatures, to astrology, and to oracles.

Members of the culture have never thought of probability theory or statistics, never dreamt of anything that could be classed as 'experimental method'.[2] Now suppose that on a particular occasion a member of this culture forms a belief about the outcome of an impending battle by using one of the aforementioned methods, say, by consulting zodiacal signs in a culturally approved fashion. Call this method M. Is this person's belief justified, or warranted?

One feels here a definite tension, a tug in opposite directions. There is a strong temptation to say, no, this belief is not justified or warranted. Yet from a different perspective one feels inclined to say, yes, the belief is justified.

The attraction of the negative answer is easily explained. It is natural to regard a belief as justified only if it is generated by proper, or adequate, methods. But method M certainly looks improper and inadequate. This point can be reinforced in the following way. Epistemologists have widely supposed—and I concur—that a necessary condition for having knowledge is having justified belief. But the belief under consideration has no chance to qualify as knowledge, assuming it is wholly based on zodiacal signs. Even if it happens to be true, even if there is nothing 'Gettierized' about the case, the believer cannot be credited with *knowing* (beforehand) the outcome of the battle. The natural explanation is that his belief fails to be justified.

Why, then, is some attraction felt toward a positive answer? This seems to stem from the cultural plight of our believer. He is situated in a certain spatio-historical environment. Everyone else in this environment uses and trusts method M. Moreover, our believer has good reasons to trust his cultural peers on many matters, and lacks decisive reasons for distrusting their confidence in astrology. While it is true that a scientifically trained person, set down in this same culture, could easily find ways to cast doubt on method M, our believer is not so trained, and has no opportunity to acquire such training. It is beyond his intellectual scope to find flaws in M. Thus, we can hardly *fault* him for using M, nor fault him therefore for believing what he does. The belief in question is epistemically *blameless*, and that seems to explain why we are tempted to call it *justified*.[3]

As this case illustrates, there are two distinct ideas or conceptions of epistemic justification. On one conception, a justified belief is (roughly) a *well-formed* belief, a belief formed (or sustained) by proper, suitable, or adequate methods, procedures, or processes. On another conception, a justified belief is a *faultless*, *blameless*, or *non-culpable* belief. As our example suggests, the first of these conceptions is stronger, or more stringent, than the second. It requires the belief to be formed by methods that are *actually* proper or adequate, whereas the second conception makes no such requirement. I therefore call the first conception the *strong* conception and the second the *weak*. Each of these seems to me a legitimate conception. Each captures some chunks of intuition involving the term 'justified' (in its epistemic applications).

Granting the distinction between strong and weak justification, my next task is to delineate more precisely the conditions attached to these respective conceptions. Before turning to this, however, let me mention another distinction relevant to the theory of justified belief.

In *Epistemology and Cognition* (hereinafter *E & C*) I propose a distinction between belief-forming *processes* and belief-forming *methods*.[4] 'Processes' are basic psychological processes, roughly, wired-in features of our native cognitive architecture. 'Methods' are learnable algorithms, heuristics, or procedures for forming beliefs, such as procedures that appeal to instrument readings, or statistical analyses. All beliefs are formed partly by processes. We cannot do anything in the cognitive realm without using basic psychological operations. Learned methods, by contrast, are not universally required, although the vast majority of an adult's beliefs are probably indebted to such methods. Now *fully* justified beliefs, I propose, must be formed by adequate processes *and* adequate methods, if methods are used at all. (At least this is so for strong justification.) But it is possible to form a belief by a combination of adequate process and inadequate method, or by a combination of inadequate process and adequate method. I therefore distinguish two levels of justifiedness: primary justifiedness, corresponding to the level of processes, and secondary justifiedness, corresponding to the level of methods. A complete account of justifiedness must present conditions for both of these levels.

The strong/weak distinction I have introduced enters at each level: the level of processes and the level of methods. So let me try to sketch conditions of strong and weak justification for each level separately. I begin with the level of methods.

II

Strong justification at the level of methods requires the use of *proper* or *adequate* methods. What makes a method proper or adequate? A natural and appealing answer is a reliabilist answer: a method is proper or adequate just in case it is reliable, i.e., leads to truth a sufficiently high percent·of the time. This answer meshes perfectly with our intuitions about the scientifically benighted believer. His belief is not strongly justified precisely because the method of consulting zodiacal signs is not a reliable way of getting truths about the outcomes of battles.

What exactly is meant by calling a method or process 'reliable' needs further discussion. I shall address this issue in due course. Another sort of issue, however, needs comment. High reliability may not suffice for method-level justifiedness because even highly reliable methods may be *less* reliable than other available methods. Some people might argue for a *maximum* reliability condition, not merely a *satisficing* reliability condition. I am going to set this matter aside. There are enough other questions to be dealt with in this paper, and the proposed switch to maximum reliability would not seriously affect the other epistemological topics on which I shall focus.

However, I do not mean to imply that use of a highly reliable method is sufficient for method-level, or secondary, justifiedness. Two other conditions are necessary. First, it is necessary that the method have been *acquired* in a suitable fashion. If a person adopts a method out of the blue, and by chance it happens to be reliable, his use of that method does not confer secondary justifiedness. The method must be acquired by other methods, or ultimately processes, that are either reliable or meta-reliable.[5] A further necessary condition of secondary justifiedness is that the believer's cognitive state, at the time he uses the method, should not *undermine* the correctness, or adequacy, of the method. Very roughly, it should not be the case that the believer *thinks* that the method is unreliable, nor is he justified in regarding the method as unreliable. Of course, the latter condition should be spelled out in non-justificational terms, something I undertake (sketchily) in *E & C* but will not repeat here.[6]

Chisholm expresses the worry that the reliable-method condition is too *easy* to satisfy.[7] He considers the case of a man who comes to believe that there are nine planets by reading the tea-leaves. Now suppose that this reading took place on a Friday afternoon at 2:17, and suppose that nobody on any other occasion consults tea-leaves about the number of planets at 2:17 on a Friday afternoon. Then, says Chisholm, this man followed a method that always leads to truth, a method one could describe by saying, 'To find out anything about the number of planets, consult tea-leaves at 2:17 on a Friday afternoon.'

Notice, however, that *this* is not plausibly the method the man has *used*. For a method to be used, it must be represented in the cognizer's head (though not necessarily consciously). But presumably neither the day of the week nor the time of day was part of the recipe for belief formation that the man represented in his head. Although *we* can introduce those features into a description of his action, it doesn't follow that they were parts of the method *he used*.[8] But the method he *did* use—consulting the tea-leaves—is not reliable.

Admittedly, a cognizer *might* incorporate these temporal factors into a method, and such a method could be reliable (at least in the sense Chisholm specifies). But use of this reliable method would not suffice for secondary (method-level) justifiedness. As indicated, the believer must acquire the method in a suitable fashion. That condition is (apparently) not met in Chisholm's example. If a new example were constructed in which it *is* met, then I think the cognizer's belief *would*, intuitively, be justified.

The plausibility of the reliability approach can be bolstered by considering degrees of justifiedness. Although my main analysandum is the categorical notion of justified belief, a brief digression on the comparative notion may be instructive. Chisholm, of course, has rightly stressed the idea of multiple grades of epistemic status.[9] Can such a notion be captured within reliabilism? Quite naturally, I believe. Ceteris paribus, one belief is better justified than another belief just in case the methods (or processes) that generate (or sustain) the former are more reliable than those that generate the latter.

A simple example will illustrate this idea. Suppose one student does a long addition problem by adding columns from top to bottom, in the canonical fashion. This student arrives at a belief in the answer. A second student goes through the same procedure, yielding the same answer, but then 'checks her work' by doing it all over again. Or perhaps she does the problem the second time by proceeding bottom-up, or by using a calculator. In any event, she uses a *compound* method, M_2, which contains the first method, M_1, as its first component. The compound method involves forming a belief only when both procedures yield the same answer. It is plausible to say that both students have justified beliefs, but that the second has a *more* justified, or *better* justified, belief than her classmate. Why? The natural answer is: method M_2 is more reliable than M_1. Indeed, the difference in degree of justifiedness seems to correspond precisely to the difference in reliability of the methods. If the compound method has only marginally greater reliability, then it yields, intuitively, only marginally greater justifiedness. If the compound method has substantially greater reliability, justifiedness is substantially increased. This supports the idea that reliability is the underlying ingredient in justifiedness.

III

Returning from this digression, but staying at the level of methods, I turn now from strong to weak justification. The weak notion of justification, it will be recalled, is that of blameless, or non-culpable, belief. We must be careful here, however. A well-formed belief, whose method is well-acquired and non-undermined, is also presumably blameless. So the strong notion of justifiedness entails blamelessness. But I want the notions of strong and weak justification to be *opposing* notions. This means that the weak notion of justification that interests me is not precisely that of blamelessness, but the narrower notion of *mere* blamelessness. That is, the weak notion is that of *ill-formed*-but-blameless belief.

With this point clarified, let me propose some conditions for weakly justified belief (at the level of methods). More precisely, I shall try to provide only some *sufficient* conditions for weak justifiedness, not necessary conditions. S's belief in p is weakly justified (at the secondary level) if (1) the method M by which the belief is produced is unreliable (i.e., not sufficiently reliable), but (2) S does not believe that M is unreliable, and (3) S neither possesses, nor has available to him/her, a reliable way of telling that M is unreliable. (By this I mean that S has neither reliable method nor reliable process which, if applied to his/her present cognitive state, would lead S to believe that M is unreliable.) It is plausible that a further condition should also be added, viz., (4) there is no process or method S *believes* to be reliable which, if used, would lead S to believe that M is unreliable.

The proposed conditions seem to capture our case of the scientifically benighted cognizer. That cognizer's belief in the outcome of the impending battle is in fact ill-formed, i.e., formed by an unreliable method. But he does not believe that his method is unreliable. Moreover, there is no reliable method (or process) in his possession, or available to him, that would lead him to believe that his astrology-based method is unreliable. Finally, there is no method or process he *believes* to be reliable that would lead him to this judgment.

Our judgment of the benighted cognizer does depend, admittedly, on exactly what he knows, or has been told, about the accuracy of past astrology-based predictions, especially battle predictions. If he is told that in *all* such cases the predictions were falsified, we would surely deny that his use of the astrology-based method is defensible. After all, he does possess a native process of *induction*, which can be applied to such data! But let the case be one in which he receives relatively few well-substantiated reports of battle outcomes. Some of these corroborate the prior predictions, as chance would dictate. Where outcomes reportedly go against the predictions, the community's astrology experts explain that the predictions had been based on misapplications of the method. The experts have techniques for 'protecting' their theory from easy falsification, and only sophisticated methodologies or astronomical theories would demonstrate the indefensibility of such tactics; but these are not available. (Needless to say, if this particular example of a benighted cognizer does not fully suit the reader, other examples to make the same point might readily be constructed).

Clearly, the truth of the contention that no way of detecting the target method's unreliability is *possessed* or *available* to a cognizer depends on exactly how the terms 'possessed' and 'available' are understood. It might be argued, for instance, that sophisticated scientific methodology is always in fact 'available' to people, even when such a methodology is not in use by members of their culture. The proper response, I suggest, is that the notions of availability and possession are vague and variable. They are open to a number of interpretations, each reasonably plausible and pertinent in at least some contexts.

The vagueness or variability of 'possession' has been stressed in connection with *evidence* possession by Richard Feldman[10]; I also mention it a bit in *E & C*.[11] At one extreme, 'possessing', or 'having', a piece of evidence at a given time could mean consciously thinking of that evidence. At another extreme, it could mean having that evidence stored somewhere in memory, however difficult it may be to retrieve or access the item. An intermediate view would be that a piece of evidence is 'possessed' only if it is either in consciousness or *easily* accessible from memory.

Similar ambiguities arise for the term 'available'. But here there are not only different possible locations *in the head* but different locations and degrees of accessibility in the *social* world. Is a piece of evidence socially 'available' no matter how difficult or costly it would be to find it? There are no clear-cut answers here, neither in the case of *evidence* nor in the case of *methods*, which is what directly concerns me here. Different speakers (and listeners) use varying standards, depending on context and intention. So it is best to leave the notions of possession and availability in their natural, vague state, rather than try to provide artificial precision. It follows, of course, that the notion of weak justification inherits this vagueness. But there is plenty of evidence that epistemic concepts, including justification and knowledge, *have* this kind of vagueness.[12] However, under very natural and commonly used standards, no process or method is possessed or available to our benighted cognizer for telling that his astrology-based battle-predicting method is unreliable. Hence, his battle predictions based on that method are weakly justified. (This probably follows as well from one very moderate constraint I shall later impose on 'availability').

IV

Let me turn now to primary justifiedness: justifiedness at the level of processes. In this treatment I shall adopt the simple format for presenting reliabilism that I used in "What Is Justified Belief?"[13], rather than the preferable but more unwieldy format of process-permitting rule systems found in *E & C*. However, I shall later opt for the preferable rule-system format.

The proposed account of *strong* justification at the primary level closely parallels the account at the secondary level. A belief of person S is strongly justified at the primary level if and only if (1) it is produced (or sustained) by a sufficiently reliable cognitive process, and (2) that the producing process is reliable is not undermined by S's cognitive state.

The proposed conditions for *weak* justification at the primary level also parallel those at the secondary level. S's belief is weakly justified at the primary level if (1) the cognitive process that produces the belief is unreliable, but (2) S does not believe that the producing process is unreliable, and (3) S neither possesses, nor has available to him/her, a reliable way of telling that the process is unreliable. Finally, a further condition may be appropriate: (4) there is no process or method S *believes* to be reliable which, if used, would lead S to believe that the process is unreliable. Once again, interpretation of the terms 'possession' and 'available' is subject to variation. I shall not try to give a unique interpretation to these vague terms. As indicated earlier, though, I shall shortly impose one plausible constraint on availability.

V

I want to turn immediately now to an example of central interest, the case of a cognizer in a Cartesian demon world. Focus on the perceptual beliefs of such a cognizer. These beliefs are regularly or invariably false, but they are caused by the same internal processes that cause our perceptual beliefs. In the Cartesian demon world, however, those processes are unreliable. (I assume that either there is just a lone cognizer using those processes in that world or that the demon fools enough people to render those processes insufficiently reliable.) Then according to the proposed account of *strong* justifiedness, the cognizer's beliefs are not justified.

This sort of case is an ostensible problem for reliabilism, because there is a strong temptation to say that a cognizer in a demon world *does* have justified perceptual beliefs. The course of his experience, after all, may be indistinguishable from the course of your experience or mine, and we are presumably justified in holding our perceptual beliefs. So shouldn't his beliefs be justified as well?[14]

Under the present theory the treatment of the demon case is straightforward. The victim of the demon fails to have *strongly* justified beliefs, but he does have *weakly* justified beliefs. While his beliefs are not *well-formed*, they are *blameless* and *non-culpable*. His cognitive processes are not reliable (in his world), but (A) he does not believe that they are unreliable, (B) he has no reliable way of telling this, and (C) there is no method or process he *believes* to be reliable which would lead him to this conclusion. So on the weak conception of justifiedness, the resulting beliefs are justified.

Is it really true that the demon victim has no reliable way of telling that his perceptual processes are unreliable? What seems fairly clear is that none of his cognitive processes we normally deem reliable would lead him to the conclusion that his perceptual processes are unreliable. Surely if he uses his memories of past perceptual beliefs, memories of subsequent 'validations' of these by further perceptual checks, and then makes a standard inductive generalization, he will conclude that his perceptual processes *are* reliable. However, it might be contended that a reliable method is *available* to him that would yield the conclusion that his processes are unreliable. This is the 'single-output' method that would have him start with his antecedent corpus of beliefs and produce the conclusion, 'My perceptual processes are unreliable'. This single-output method is reliable since the one belief it produces is true!

I make two replies to this proposal. First, to call this is a 'method' is surely to trivialize the notion of a method. I admit, though, that I have no convenient way of restricting methods that would rule this out. (*Perhaps* all single-output formulas should be excluded; but I am unsure of this.) However, even if we persist in calling this a 'method', there is little plausibility in saying that it is *available* to the demon victim. Availability should not be construed as mere in-principle constructibility and usability. It must at least be required that the cognizer could naturally be led to that method by some processes and/or methods he already employs, operating on his actual beliefs and experiences. But that is false in the present case. All his antecedent beliefs, processes, and methods run *against* the acceptance of this single-output 'method'. So there is no relevant sense in saying that this method is possessed by, or available to, this cognizer. Hence, his perceptual beliefs are indeed weakly justified.

VI

It is clear that this version of reliabilism accommodates the intuition that the demon victim has justified beliefs—at least on one conception of justification. What relation does this version bear to other versions of reliabilism? In *E & C* a reliabilist theory is proposed that handles the demon-world case rather differently. That theory is formulated in terms of right systems of process-permitting rules. A belief qualifies as justified (at the process level) just in case it is produced by processes that conform with some right rule system. (A non-undermining proviso is also included.) A rule system is right just in case it is reliable, i.e., compliance with that rule system would produce beliefs with a sufficiently high truth ratio.

These formulations do not resolve all questions of interpretation about the theory. Suppose we ask whether a belief B, in some possible world W, is justified. The answer depends on whether the processes that cause B in W are permitted by a right rule system. But is the rightness of a rule system a function of the system's reliability *in W*? Or is it fixed in some other way?

In *E & C*[15] I suggest that rightness of rule systems is rigid. A given rule system is either right in all possible worlds or wrong in all possible worlds; it does not vary across worlds. Furthermore, rightness is not determined by the system's reliability in the *actual* world, for example, but rather by its reliability in what I call *normal worlds*. A very special sense of 'normal worlds' is delineated. A normal world is understood as a world consistent with our general *beliefs* about the actual world, beliefs about the sorts of objects, events, and changes that occur in the actual world. The upshot of this theory is that the appraisal of a demon victim's beliefs does not depend on whether his perceptual belief-forming processes are reliable in the demon world, but on whether they are reliable in normal worlds. Since they presumably *are* reliable in normal worlds, even this victim's beliefs qualify as justified according to the theory. Moreover, even if it should turn out that the actual world is a demon world, and our own beliefs are systematically illusory, these beliefs would (or could) still be justified. As long as the processes are reliable in normal worlds—which in this scenario does not include the actual world—these beliefs will be justified.

The normal-worlds version of reliabilism has the virtue of saving intuitions about justification in demon world cases. It also has other attractions. It seems to me natural to expect that reliability should be assessed in normal situations (or worlds) rather than all possible situations. When one says of a car that it is very reliable, one doesn't imply that it will start and run smoothly in *all* weather conditions; not at −50 degrees Fahrenheit, for example. One only implies that it will start in *normal* conditions.[16] However, this sense of 'normalcy' probably refers to *typical* situations. It doesn't imply anything like my *doxastic* sense of 'normalcy'. What might rationalize the doxastic sense? In writing *Epistemology and Cognition*, I had planned a chapter on concepts. One thesis I planned to defend is that our concepts are constructed against certain background assumptions, comprised of what we believe about what typically happens in the actual world. I expected this approach to concepts to underpin the doxastic-normalcy conception of reliability. Unfortunately, I did not manage to work out such an approach in detail.

In any case, there are a number of problems facing the account of justification that focuses on normal worlds (construed doxastically). First, *which* general beliefs about the actual world are relevant in fixing normal worlds? There seem to be too many choices. Second, whichever general beliefs are selected, it looks as if dramatically different worlds might conform to these beliefs. Does a rule system count as right only if it has a high truth ratio in *all* those worlds?[17] Third, when the theory says that normal worlds are fixed by the general beliefs *we* have about the actual world, what is the referent of 'we'?[18] Is it *everyone* in the actual world, i.e., the whole human race? Different members of the human race have dramatically divergent general beliefs. How are the pertinent general beliefs to be extracted?[19]

Finally, even if these problems could be resolved, it isn't clear that the normal-worlds approach gets things right. Consider a possible non-normal world W, significantly different from ours. In W people commonly form beliefs by a process that has a very high truth-ratio in W, but would not have a high truth-ratio in normal worlds. Couldn't the beliefs formed by the process in W qualify as justified?[20]

To be concrete, let the process be that of forming beliefs in accord with feelings of clairvoyance. Such a process presumably does not have a high truth ratio in the actual world; nor would it have a high truth ratio in normal worlds. But suppose W contains clairvoyance waves, analogous to sound or light waves. By means of clairvoyance waves people in W accurately detect features of their environment just as we detect features of our environment by light and sound. Surely, the clairvoyance belief-forming processes of people in world W *can* yield justified beliefs.

For all the foregoing reasons, it seems wise to abandon the normal-worlds version of reliabilism. Fortunately, this does not leave reliabilism incapable of meeting the demon-world problem. The present version of reliabilism accommodates the intuition that demon-world believers have justified beliefs by granting that they have *weak-ly* justified beliefs.

If the normal-worlds interpretation of rightness is abandoned, what should be put in its place (in the account of *strong* justification)? As the foregoing example suggests, it is probably unwise to rigidify rightness; better to let it vary from world to world. Perhaps the best interpretation is the most straightforward one: a rule system is right in W just in case it has a high truth-ratio in W.

There are reasons, however, why reliabilism cannot rest content with this interpretation. I shall mention them briefly although I cannot fully address the issues they raise. First, some rule system might be used rather sparsely in a given world, say the actual world. Its performance in that world might therefore be regarded as a poor indication of its true colors: either too favorable or too unfavorable. For this reason, it seems advisable to assess its rightness in W not simply by its performance in W, but by its performance in a set of worlds very close to W. In other words, we should be interested in the probability of a rule-system yielding truths in the propensity, or modal frequency, interpretation of probability.[21]

A similar conclusion is mandated by a related consideration. There are many different possible ways of complying with, or instantiating, a given rule system. Even if we take the outside environment as fixed, some rules might be used frequently in one scenario but infrequently in another. (Remember, the rules are *permission* rules; they do not say what processes *must* be used, or when.) These different scenarios, or compliance profiles, would presumably generate different truth ratios. The multiplicity of compliance profiles is noted in *E & C*,[22] where it is acknowledged that new refinements in the reliability theory are needed. Several plausible developments readily suggest themselves. First, one might require that *all* compliance profiles, even the lowest, should generate a specified, tolerably high, truth ratio. Alternatively, one might propose one or another weaker requirement, e.g., that the mean compliance profile, or the modal profile (in the statistical sense), should have a certain high truth ratio. Although I won't examine these ideas further, all are in the spirit of reliabilism.

Another technical problem is worth mentioning. *E & C* formulates reliabilism in terms of rule *systems* because many single processes would not have determinate truth ratios. Consider an inference process, or a memory process, for example. Whether it yields true or false beliefs depends on the truth values of the prior beliefs which it takes as inputs. Thus, only an entire system of processes, or a system of process-permitting rules, holds the prospect of having associated truth ratios. However, a problem now arises. If you start with a given system, R, that has a very high truth ratio, adding a single unreliable rule might not reduce the truth ratio very much. So R*, obtained from R by adding such a rule, might still pass the reliability test. But if R* contains a poor rule, we don't want to count it as right. Let us call this the epistemic *free rider* problem.

I propose the following solution. It is not enough that a rule system itself have a sufficiently high truth ratio (in whatever fashion this gets spelled out or refined). It must also be required that none of its *subsets* should have an *in*sufficiently high truth ratio. Since the unit set of a member rule is a subset of the rule system, this requirement disbars rule systems with any individually unreliable rules.

VII

Let me leave these detailed points about the strong conception of justifiedness, and consider a worry about its general contours.[23] In particular, let me focus on the 'world-bound' character of reliabilism, as it emerges in the present formulation of strong justifiedness. Since the rightness of a rule system is now allowed to vary from world to world, even from one experientially indistinguishable world to another, it looks as if there is an element of *luck* in whether a belief is strongly justified or not. If we are in the world we *think* we are in, our perceptual beliefs are (in the main) strongly justified. If we are in a demon world, on the other hand, our perceptual beliefs are not strongly justified. But these two worlds are experientially indistinguishable. So it seems to be a matter of luck whether or not our beliefs are strongly justified. But can invidious epistemic judgments properly rest on luck?

Note first that luck is a generally acknowledged component in other epistemic achievements, specifically *knowledge*. Justification does not logically imply truth, so even if one has a justified belief it is still a matter of luck whether one gets truth, and hence a matter of luck whether one attains knowledge. A similar moral follows from Gettier examples. People in experientially indistinguishable worlds might differ in their knowledge attainments because their true justified beliefs are Gettierized in one of the worlds but not the other. Since luck is a component in knowledge, why should it be shocking to find it in justifiedness?

The critic might retort that while it is conscionable to let luck figure in knowledge, it is unconscionable to let it figure in justification, which is an evaluative notion. But, I reply, should luck be excluded from evaluative contexts? Several writers have pointed out that it seems to enter into moral and legal evaluation.[24] Two equally reckless truck drivers, one who unluckily strikes a child and one who does not, may incur different amounts of disapprobation and punishment. A similar point might be made in a slightly different vein about aesthetic evaluation. We can evaluate a painter's artistic feats even while admitting that these feats are partly due to luck: the luck of natural talent and the good fortune of excellent training.

But shouldn't there be *some* style of justificational evaluation that eliminates or minimizes luck? This seems plausible. It is precisely what is captured with the concept of weak justification. So the present theory also makes room for anti-luck cravings.

VIII

Does my duplex theory of justification amount to an acknowledgement that internalism is partly correct? Is it a partial abandonment of externalism? I find this hard to answer because the terms 'internalism' and 'externalism' do not have generally accepted definitions. Internalism might be the view that whether you are justified in believing a proposition is directly accessible to you from the internal perspective, or by immediate reflection. If this is how internalism is defined, though, it is not clear that the weak conception of justification is a brand of internalism. Whether you possess a way of telling, or have available a way of telling, that certain belief-forming processes are reliable or unreliable may not be something directly accessible to you by immediate reflection. I also doubt whether the weak conception of justification would fully appeal to internalists. Most internalists, I suspect, would like a more demanding conception of justification.

So I do not know whether the duplex theory of justification amounts to a marriage of externalism and internalism. I have no objection to this union, if that indeed is what it is. The important point is that it captures many intuitions about justified belief and does so in a broadly reliabilist framework.

Notes

* This paper was read at the 1986 NEH Summer Institute on the Theory of Knowledge and at a conference in honor of Roderick Chisholm at Brown University. It has benefitted from audience comments on both occasions.

1. Objective and subjective senses are distinguished in Pollock (1979) and Goldman (1986), the latter using the terms 'real' and 'apparent' justification. Externalist and internalist conceptions are discussed by Armstrong (1973), Goldman (1980), BonJour (1980, 1985), and Alston (1986). The regulative and non-regulative options are discussed by Kornblith (1983), Goldman (1980, 1986), and Pollock (1986). Resource-relative and resource-independent conceptions are distinguished in Goldman (1986). Lehrer (1981) presents the personal and verific conceptions. Alston (1985) delineates deontological and evaluative conceptions (among many others).
2. Alston (1985) has a similar example of 'cultural isolation'.
3. Justifiedness as freedom from blameworthiness is one of the conceptions discussed by Alston (1985). A related conception of justifiedness as freedom from (epistemic) irresponsibility is presented by Kornblith (1983) and BonJour (1985).
4. See Goldman (1986), pp. 92-95.
5. A process or method is meta-reliable if, roughly, the methods (or processes) it tends to produce or preserve are mostly reliable. There are, however, a variety of alternative ways of spelling out the spirit of this idea. See Goldman (1986), pp. 27, 52-53, 115-116, 374-377.
6. See pp. 62-63, 111-112.
7. Chisholm (1982), p. 29.
8. Similarly, just because a perceptual belief is formed on a Friday, or in an environment with rose-tinted light, this does not mean that the cognizer has used *processes* of 'perceptual belief-formation on a Friday', or 'perceptual belief-formation in rose-tinted light'. In general, external circumstances such as date, time of day, physical objects in the environment, conditions of observation, etc. are not parts of a person's *cognitive processes*. The reason for this is not quite the same, however, as the reason in the case of methods. It isn't because these factors are not represented in the cognizer's head; processes in my sense are not the sorts of things that are represented explicitly in the head. Rather, they are *general operating characteristics* of the cognitive system. This is what restricts them to purely internal features or mechanisms. Many examples of process types given in the critical literature on reliabilism violate the exclusion of external factors, e.g., most cases discussed in Alvin Plantinga (1986), pp. 10-11. Observance of this exclusion does not by itself, of course, solve the 'generality problem' confronting reliabilism. But exclusion of external conditions is essential to understanding the kind of

referent that the term 'cognitive process' is intended to have.

9. See Chisholm (1966, 1977).
10. In Feldman (1986).
11. Goldman (1986), p. 204.
12. For a persuasive discussion of one dimension of contextual vagueness, see Cohen (1986); also Sosa (1974) and Dretske (1980).
13. Goldman (1979).
14. This point has been emphasized by a number of writers, including Pollock (1984), Cohen (1984), Lehrer and Cohen (1983), Ginet (1985), Foley (1985), and Luper-Foy (1985).
15. Page 107.
16. This example is due to Matthias Steup.
17. This point was raised by Alvin Plantinga, in correspondence.
18. This point was raised by Ernest Sosa in a lecture at the NEH Summer Institute on the Theory of Knowledge, Boulder, Colorado, 1986.
19. Sosa also raised other difficulties, in the lecture cited in note 18, but I won't try to review them all.
20. This general point, and the core of the example that follows, is due to Stewart Cohen, in correspondence.
21. See van Fraassen (1980), chap. 6.
22. Chapter 5, note 23, p. 395.
23. A different kind of objection should be addressed as well. I maintain that strong justification, involving generally reliable methods and processes, is necessary for knowledge. But Richard Foley (1985, p. 195) raises the following objection. It is possible for someone to know that a demon has been deceiving most people and himself as well, but no longer is deceiving him. He can then know by means of his perceptual processes, even though these processes are not generally reliable (nor usually reliable *for him*). I grant that a person in such a situation can have knowledge, but I deny that it would be obtained purely perceptually. Rather, it would be obtained *by inference* from the person's knowledge that the demon is *currently* allowing his visual processes to function properly (i.e., reliably). Foley does not specify how knowledge about the demon's new practice might be obtained, but it is compatible with the imagined example that this knowledge be obtained by reliable processes, as reliabilism requires. From such knowledge about the demon's new practice, plus the fact that it now looks to the person as if, say, there is a javelina in the bush (a belief acquired by reliable introspection), the cognizer can reliably infer that there *is* a javelina in the bush. Thus, as Foley says, knowledge acquired with the help of perceptual processes is possible, even if these processes are not generally reliable; but this does not contravene reliabilism.
24. See Williams (1976) and Nagel (1979).

References

Alston, William (1985). "Concepts of Epistemic Justification," *The Monist*, 68: 57-89.

Alston, William (1986). "Internalism and Externalism in Epistemology," *Philosophical Topics*, 14: 179-221.

Armstrong, D.M. (1973). *Belief, Truth and Knowledge* (Cambridge: Cambridge University Press).

BonJour, Laurence (1980). "Externalist Theories of Empirical Knowledge," in P. French, T. Uehling, and H. Wettstein, eds., *Midwest Studies in Philosophy* vol. 5, *Studies in Epistemology* (Minneapolis: University of Minnesota Press).

BonJour, Laurence (1985). *The Structure of Empirical Knowledge* (Cambridge, Mass.: Harvard University Press].

Chisholm, Roderick (1966). *Theory of Knowledge* (Englewood Cliffs, N. J.: Prentice-Hall, 1966).

Chisholm, Roderick (1977). *Theory of Knowledge*, 2nd ed. (Englewood Cliffs, N. J.: Prentice-Hall).

Chisholm, Roderick (1982). *The Foundations of Knowing* (Minneapolis: University of Minnesota Press).

Cohen, Stewart (1984). "Justification and Truth," *Philosophical Studies*, 46: 279-295.

Cohen, Stewart (1986). "Knowledge and Context", *Journal of Philosophy*, 83: 574-583.

Dretske, Fred (1980). "The Pragmatic Dimension of Knowledge", *Philosophical Studies*, 40: 363-378.

Feldman, Richard (1986). "Having Evidence," read at the NEH Summer Institute on the Theory of Knowledge, Boulder, Colorado.

Foley, Richard (1985). "What's Wrong with Reliabilism?" *The Monist*, 68: 188-202.

Ginet, Carl (1985). "*Contra* Reliabilism," *The Monist*, 68: 175-187.

Goldman, Alvin (1979). "What Is Justified Belief?", in George Pappas, ed., *Justification and Knowledge* (Dordrecht: D. Reidel).

Goldman, Alvin (1980). "The Internalist Conception of Justification," in P. French, T. Uehling, and H. Wettstein, eds., *Midwest Studies in Philosophy*, vol. 5, *Studies in Epistemology* (Minneapolis: University of Minnesota Press).

Goldman, Alvin (1986). *Epistemology and Cognition* (Cambridge, Mass.: Harvard University Press).

Kornblith, Hilary (1983). "Justified Belief and Epistemically Responsible Action," *Philosophical Review*, 92: 33-48.

Lehrer, Keith (1981). "A Self Profile," in Radu Bogdan, ed., *Keith Lehrer* (Dordrecht: D. Reidel).

Lehrer, Keith and Stewart Cohen (1983). "Justification, Truth, and Coherence," *Synthese*, 55: 191-207.

Luper-Foy, Steven (1985). "The Reliabilist Theory of Rational Belief," *The Monist* 68: 203-225.

Nagel, Thomas (1979). "Moral Luck," in *Mortal Questions* (Cambridge: Cambridge University Press).

Plantinga, Alvin (1986). "Epistemic Justification," *Nous*, 20: 1-18.

Pollock, John (1979). "A Plethora of Epistemological Theories," in George Pappas, ed., *Justification and Knowledge* (Dordrecht: D. Reidel).

Pollock, John (1984). "Reliability and Justified Belief," *Canadian Journal of Philosophy*, 14: 103-114.

Pollock, John (1986). *Contemporary Theories of Knowledge* (Totowa, N. J.: Rowman & Littlefield).

Sosa, Ernest (1974). "How Do You Know?" *American Philosophical Quarterly*, 11: 113-122.

Van Fraassen, Bas (1980). *The Scientific Image* (Oxford: Oxford University Press).

Williams, Bernard (1976). "Moral Luck," *Proceedings of the Aristotelian Society*, supplementary vol. 1.

Philosophical Perspectives, 2, Epistemology, 1988

THE EVIDENCE OF THE SENSES

Roderick M. Chisholm
Brown University

I return to an ancient philosophical question: What kind of evidence is provided by the senses? Many will feel, I'm sure, that there is nothing new to be said about this question. And perhaps they are right. But, given the present state of philosophy, something, even if it is nothing new, needs to be said about it. For there is still a great deal of confusion about the nature of perceptual evidence. The most unfortunate confusion, I think, gives rise to the belief that there are *no* serious problems about perceptual evidence and that, once one sees that this is so, the other problems of traditional theory of knowledge will disappear.

A typical attitude was that of the members of the Vienna Circle. Carnap, for example, saw the need of referring to one's *total evidence* when speaking of the practical application of inductive logic and the theory of probability.[1] But so far as the concept of evidence itself is concerned, he felt that it was sufficient to say that the *evidence* that a person possesses is "his total knowledge of the results of his observations." One is led to ask, then, what Carnap meant by "the results of one's observations." In his writings on probability, he gives us no answer to this question. And if we look back to his earlier writings on verification, we seem to have traveled in a circle. For he there says, not that the application of probability presupposes the concept of observational knowledge, but that the concept of observational knowledge presupposes the application of probability. He writes, for example: "A predicate 'P' of a language L is called *observable* for an organism (e.g., a person) N, if, for suitable arguments,

e.g., 'b', N is able under suitable circumstances to come to a decision
with the help of a few observations about a full sentence, say 'P(b)',
i.e., to a *confirmation* of either 'P(b)' or '~ P(b)' of such a high degree
that he will either accept or reject 'P(b)'."[2]

The attitude reflects an earlier view developed by Leonard Nelson
in a book on "the so-called epistemological problem." Nelson suggests that the epistemological problems will disappear if we are content to recognize that our knowledge arises out of perception.[3]

My own belief, which I will try to defend here, is that it is only
by investigating the nature of perceptual evidence that we can be
made to see the difficulties of the epistemological problem and how
to deal with them.

The problem of the evidence of the senses involves questions of
three different types: (I) *descriptive* or "phenomenological" questions
about those aspects of our experience that make it a source of
evidence about the external world; (II) *normative* questions about
what it is that those aspects of our experience justify us in believing;
and (III) *epistemic* questions about the nature of these grounding
relations.

This paper, accordingly, is divided into three parts.

Part One: Describing the Objects of Perception

The Objects of Perceptual Verbs

We may approach our subject somewhat indirectly by considering the grammatical objects of perceptual *verbs*—such verbs as "see,"
"hear," and "perceive." These grammatical objects may be of three
different kinds.

(1) Sometimes perceptual verbs take a very simple object, as in
"He sees a cat" and "She hears a dog." This first use has no implications about what the perceiver *believes* and it has no implications
about the *knowledge* or *evidence* that he or she has. For we may
consistently say "He sees a dog but he doesn't think that it is a dog
that he sees"; and similarly for "She hears a cat."

(2) Sometimes the grammatical object of a perception verb is a
"that"-clause, as in "He sees that a cat is on the roof" and "She hears
that the dog is scratching at the door." This use, unlike the first, does
have implications with respect to *belief* and also with respect to

knowledge. If she hears that the dog is at the door, then she knows that the dog is there and thus also believes it.

(3) Sometimes the grammatical object is a "semi-complex" one that seems to fall between the simple grammatical object ("a cat," "a dog") and the propositional object ("that a cat is on the roof," "that the dog is scratching at the door"). Examples of such semi-complex objects are provided by "He sees a cat sitting on the roof" and "She hears the dog scratching at the door." This third use can be misleading, especially in writings on the philosophy of perception.

Such a statement as "He sees a cat on the roof" is relatively simple and straightforward. One philosopher seems to suggest that such statements provide us with no ground for philosophical puzzlement. According to him, they simply refer to the kind of causal process "that standardly takes place when we say that so-and-so sees such-and-such" and the nature of this process is of no special concern to the philosopher: "to a large extent the description of this process must be regarded as a problem for the special sciences, not for philosophy."[4] But a mere description of the causal process has no implications about the perceiver's immediate experience or about what he is justified in believing. And for precisely this reason it does not provide us with what we are looking for.

To get at the nature of perceptual evidence, we must look further at those statements in which the perceptual verb has a complex grammatical object, such statements as "He perceives that a cat is on the roof" and "She hears that the dog is scratching at the door." Ordinarily, when we use our perception words in these ways, our statements commit us to what is affirmed in their subordinate "that"-clauses. "He perceives that a cat is on the roof" implies that there *is* a cat on the roof. And "She hears a dog that is scratching at the door" implies that there *is* a dog that is scratching at the door. *Sometimes*, to be sure we do not take our perception sentences to have such implications. We may say: "Well, *he* perceives that a cat is there, but obviously he is hallucinating once again; he is always seeing some cat or other that isn't really there." But I suggest that, to avoid ambiguity, we renounce this type of use.

If this suggestion is followed, then, "He perceives that a cat is on the roof" will imply, in our use, that there is a cat that is on the roof. And "She hears that the dog is scratching at the door" will imply that there is a dog that is scratching at the door. And when we talk this way, then we may, so to speak, take the subject-term out of the "that"-clause and put it out in front. In other words, we may move from the *de dicto* locution

> He perceives that there is a cat on the roof

to the *de re* locution

> A cat on the roof is perceived by him to be a cat on the roof.

This is a move we cannot make in the case "He believes that there is a cat on the roof" and "He takes there to be a cat on the roof."

How, then, are we to describe the state of the person who is hallucinating—the person of whom one may be tempted to say, "He perceives that a cat is there, but obviously he is hallucinating once again"? The simplest procedure might be to say, "He *thinks* he perceives that a cat is there" or "He *believes* that he perceives that a cat is there." An alternative would be: "He *takes* something to be a cat."

Being Appeared To

The principal source of our philosophical problem lies in the fact that perception is inextricably bound up with *appearing*—with being appeared to in some way. The person who perceives that there is a tree before him *takes* there to be a tree. And when one takes there to be a tree (when one thinks that one perceives a tree), then one is appeared to in a certain way and one believes that *what* it is that is appearing in that way is a tree. In the case of the person who is hallucinating, we may say that, although he is *appeared to* in a certain way, there is nothing that is *appearing* to him in that way.

Let us, then, define "perceives that" in this way:

> S perceives that there is an F =Df (1) There is an F that is appearing in a certain way to S; (2) S takes there to be an F that is appearing to him in that way; and (3) it is evident to S that an F is appearing to him in that way.

"A perceives that there is an F," so defined, will imply "S knows that there is an F."

If you perceive that there is a tree before you, then you believe that your perceptual experience is an experience of a tree—or, in our terminology, you think you are appeared to by a tree. It would be misleading to call the appearance the *"object"* of perception. But it would be accurate to say that, it is *by means of* what you know about the appearance, that you apprehend the object of perception. The philosophical problem of perceptual evidence turns on this question: How is it possible for appearances to provide us with information about the things of which they *are* appearances?

The difficulty, as we know, has to do with what is sometimes called "perceptual relativity." The appearances that we sense are a function, not only of the nature of the things we perceive, but also of the conditions under which we perceive these things. To see that sense-appearances are a function of the conditions of observation, we have only to remind ourselves to this fact: Whenever an external thing appears to us, then, merely by varying the conditions of observation and letting the external thing remain constant, we can vary the appearances that the thing presents.[5]

Sextus Empiricus had cited these examples:

> The same water which feels very hot when poured on inflamed spots seems lukewarm to us. And the same air seems chilly to the old but mild to those in their prime, and similarly the same sound seems to the former faint, but to the latter clearly audible. The same wine which seems sour to those who have previously eaten dates or figs seems sweet to those who have just consumed nuts or chickpeas; and the vestibule of the bathhouse which warms those entering from the outside chills those coming out.[6]

This completes our discussion of the *descriptive* questions involved in explicating the evidence of the senses. We may now turn to the *normative* questions.

Part Two: The Normative Questions

If appearances are so variable, and if we perceive the things around us by means of the appearances that they present to us, then how can such perception provide us with any evidence about the external world?

The third clause in our definition of perceiving ("It is evident to S that he is appeared to in that way") in a *normative* expression, for it contains the epistemic locution "It is evident to S that ...".

The Problem

The normative epistemological problem is analogous to the problem we encounter in ethics or moral philosophy when we attempt to analyze such expressions as "It is right that..." and "It is intrinsically good that..." We want to find a *criterion* stating a non-normative situation that warrants the assertion of a normative statement—a non-normative situation upon which, as it is sometimes said, a normative situation "supervenes."

Our criterion should be of the form:

> So-and-so tends to make it evident to S that he is appeared to by an F.

A criterion might also be formed if we replace "evident" by some epistemic expression, say "probable" or "beyond reasonable doubt." But the expression replacing "So-and-so" should contain no epistemic terms. (We will consider such expressions as "tends to make it evident that" in the final section of the paper.

Three Types of Perceptual Theory

One way to understand the normative questions about perceptual evidence is to consider three theories that we find in ancient Greek philosophy. These are: (1) the *dogmatic* theory; (2) the *inductive* theory; and (3) the *critical* theory.[7] The first was "the theory of the evident perception" set forth by the Stoic, Chrysippus (279-206 B.C.); the second was the so-called "commemorative theory" developed by Sextus Empiricus (c. 150-250); and the third was the theory of the Academic skeptic, Carneades (c. 213-129 B.C.). The first two theories have some initial plausibility, but it is the theory of Carneades, I think, that is closest to the truth.

(1) The Dogmatic Theory

According to "the theory of the evident perception," the appearance presents us with *two* things—the appearance itself and the external thing that appears: there is a way of appearing that presents *itself* to the subject and also presents *another* thing to the subject—a thing that *appears* in a certain way to the subject. It was held that, whenever we have an evident perception, we can tell from the nature of the perceptual experience itself that the perception is veridical. The experience was said to be irresistible. "The perception, being plainly evident and striking, lays hold of us, almost by the very hair, as they say, and drags us off to assent, needing nothing else to help it to be thus impressive."[8] But, more important, it was said that the experience gives us a kind of guarantee.

Just what, then, is supposed to justify what? What is there about the *appearance* that presents the external object to us? And what is it about the *object* that the appearance makes evident to us?

Chrysippus suggested that the nature of the external thing can be "read off" from the nature of the appearances. When I have an evident perception, he said, the external thing "appears so true that it could not appear to me in the same way if it were false."[9]

Hence the "dogmatic" criterion might be put in some way as this:

> Being appeared to in such a way that, if one is appeared to in that way then one cannot resist believing that an F is appearing to one in that way, makes it evident that one is appeared to in that way by an F.

What makes this view "dogmatic" is the fact that the criterion contains the guarantee "makes it evident that" rather than the more tentative "tends to make it evident that".

The criterion seems to imply that the appearance that is yielded by a veridical perception could not be duplicated in an unveridical perception or in an hallucination. And this is contrary to what we know. For what the facts of perceptual relativity tell us is that there is no *logical* connection between the nature of any appearance, or way being appeared to, and the nature of the object that serves to call up that appearance.

The theory is excessively dogmatic. We must go further if we are to have a satisfactory account of the evidence of the senses.

(2) The Inductive Theory

The theory of "the commemorative perception" that was set forth by Sextus was an "inductive" theory.

Sextus agrees with Chrysippus that our perceptual experience provides us with a *sign* of the independently existing external thing. But he rejects the dogmatism of Chrysippus; the nature of the appearance provides no *logical* guarantee of the nature of the object. Sextus points out that normally we do not "read off" the nature of the object from the nature of the appearance—any more than we "read off" the nature of fire from the nature of smoke. Smoke signifies fire for us because we have made an induction that correlates smoke with fire: We have found in the past that smoke is generally accompanied by fire.[10] This much is quite obvious. But now Sextus goes on to take a further step. Many have failed to see just how doubtful this further step is.

He says that the inductive correlation that we have made between smoke and fire give us the clue to the relation between appearances and the external things that the appearances make know to us. He seems to suggest that we have made an inductive correlation between tree-appearances and external trees: We have found that tree-appearances are generally accompanied by an existence of external, physical trees. The nature of an appearance, then, may *make probable* some hypothesis about the nature of the external object. This is what was suggested by our quotation from Carnap above: The content of the observation sentence is *confirmed* by perception. C. I. Lewis, addressing the same problem, says that "the given appearance is a valid *probability-index* of the objective property"; there are, according to him, various "degrees of reliability" that appearances may have with respect to hypotheses about external objects.[11]

We may put one version of the "inductive" criterion this way:

> If, for a certain way in which S is being appeared to, S is such that, more often than not, when he has been appeared to in that way, an F has appeared to him in that way, then it is probable for S that an F is appearing to him in that way.

To see that there is something wrong with this account of perception, we have only to ask: What was the nature of those *earlier* experiences wherein we found that a tree-like appearance was accompanied by the apprehension of an external, physical tree? How was it made known to us *then* that there was a tree there? We are given no clear answers to this question.[12] I would say, therefore, that the "inductive" theory does not provide us with what we are looking for.

An inductive argument need not, of course, be enumerative. That is to say, it need not be of the form: "Most A's are B's and x is an A; therefore it is probable that x is a B." But if any inductive argument tends to make it probable that one is appeared to by something that is F, then, presumably, the premises of the argument should include *some* evidence about external things. But where would S get *that* evidence? Once we try to answer this question, we see that we are left with our original problem. We had wanted to know just how it comes about that we have evidence about the nature of external things. We had assumed that, in the first instance, such evidence must arise out of perception. But the type of inductive theory now being considered tells us only how it is that, once we already have certain *prior evidence* about external things, perception can then go on to supply us with additional evidence about such things. How, then, did we get the prior evidence?

Yet perception *does* tell us something about the external world. Therefore there must be an alternative account of perceptual evidence.

(3) The Critical Theory

Carneades' critical theory was set forth by Sextus Empiricus in his *Outlines of Pyrrhonism* and in his treatise, *Against the Logicians*.[13]

Carneades says, in effect, that if a person has a perception of something being a tree, then, for that person, the proposition that there is a tree is *probable*. What Carneades' here means by "perception," I am convinced, is what we have called "perceptual taking." Carneades begins, then, in the same way that Sextus does. Where, then, does it differ from the view of Sextus?

We have seen that, according to Sextus' inductive theory, the probability of a perceptual taking is derived from an inductive correlation or frequency. But Carneades appeals to no such correlation. When he says that the object of the taking is probable, he does *not* say that this probability derives from any induction. And the reason for not saying this is clear: Carneades knows that we cannot make any inductive inferences about external things until we have some *perceptual data* about such things. And it follows from this that, if we are to have any positive justification for what we believe about the external world, our experience must provide us with a probability that is *not* derived from an induction.

It would miss the point to object: "But probability is, by definition, a matter involving inductive frequencies. You contradict yourself if you say that there is a kind of probable belief that has nothing to do with such frequencies." The sense of "probable" that we have used to express Carneades' view is quite different: It expresses a *nor-*

mative concept. To say that a proposition is probable for a given person, in this normative sense, is to say that the person has a certain positive justification for accepting that proposition. A proposition is *probable*, in this sense, for a given person S, if and only if, S is more justified in accepting that proposition than he is in accepting its negation.

One of the things Carneades was saying seems to have been this:

> Taking something to be F tends to make it probable that there is something one is taking to be F.

Here, then, we have the beginnings of an answer to our question about perceptual evidence: "What aspect of our experience justifies what kind of belief about physical things?" The fact that the perceiver *takes* there to be a tree is a fact that "presents itself" itself to the perceiver: If he takes there to be a tree, then it is probable for him that he takes there to be a tree. And this intentional attitude, this taking, tends to make it probable that the taking has an actual object; it tends to make probable that there *is* in fact an external object upon which the taking is directed.

It should be noted that we have brought the quantifier from the inside to the outside of the intentional object of the "taking"-verb. What is probable to the perceiver is that there *is* something that he takes to be a tree.

We may go beyond this claim in two respects. We may say (1) that, under certain conditions, the perceptual taking yields, not only *probability*, but also *evidence* and (2) that *what* it tends to make evident is its own intentional object. In other words:

> Taking something to be F tends to insure the evidence of there being something that is F.

This view was suggested by Meinong in 1906. He said, using a slightly different terminology from that used here, that perceptual judgments may have *presumptive evidence (Vermutungsevidenz)*: When one takes there to be a tree then the judgment that there *is* a tree that one is perceiving may have presumptive evidence. The qualification "presumptive" was intended to suggest that the judgment may have such evidence without thereby being *true*. Meinong added that there are *degrees* of such justification.[14] This view was subsequently developed further by H. H. Price. He made the following suggestion in his book, *Perception* (1933):

[T]he fact that a material thing is perceptually presented to the mind is *prima facie evidence* of the thing's existence and of its really having that sort of surface which it ostensibly has;...there is *some presumption in favour of* this, not merely in the sense that we do as a matter of fact presume it (which of course we do) but in the sense that we are entitled to do so.[15]

Price adds: "Clearly the principle is *a priori*: It is not the sort of thing we could learn by empirical generalization based upon observation of the material world."[16]

The assumption is that, occasionally at least, the senses provide us with evidence pertaining to the existence of such things as trees, ships and houses. And in answer to the question, "What is the nature of this evidence?", Prices's suggestion is the following. The fact that we *take* there to be a tree is itself sufficient to make it *prima facie* evident for us that there *is* a tree that we perceive. And the fact that we are *appeared to* in certain ways is itself sufficient to make it *prima facie* evident to us that there *is* an external thing that is appearing to us in those ways.

This account of perceptual evidence requires further analysis and explication. We should try to describe more accurately the conditions under which our perceptual takings and the ways in which we are appeared to may inform us about the things around us. But the general view of perception that it represents seems to me to be the only coherent alternative to skepticism.

The view implies that the evidence about external things that is yielded by perception is *indirect* and not direct. What we know about such things is made evident to us by our takings and by the ways in which we are appeared to. It is made evident, therefore, by certain psychological facts that present themselves to us directly.

This use of "indirect" may give pause to some. For one may say: "Ordinarily, we perceive such things as trees, ships and house *directly*. If you were standing here before me, I would perceive you directly. I would perceive you *indirectly* if I were to see your shadow on the floor— in which case I would perceive the floor *directly*." But these facts are consistent with saying that, when I *do* perceive you directly, I do so by becoming aware of *other* things that serve to make it evident for me that you are the object of my perception.

Let us now look more carefully at the epistemic concepts suggested by relational epistemic expressions as "e tends to insure the evidence of h" and "h derives its status as being evident for S from the fact that e is evident for S."

Part Three: The Epistemic Questions

The Epistemic Hierarchy

I make use of these abbreviations: "—A..." for the undefined concept "S is at least as justified in — as in ..."; "—P..." for "S is more justified in — than in ..."; "—S..." for "S's justification for — is equal to his justification for ..."; "Bp" for "Believing p"; "Wp" for "Withholding p"; "~p" for "not-p"; "(p)" for "for every proposition p"; and "(∃p)" for "there is a proposition p such that."

I now set forth a hierarchy of absolute epistemic categories.[17] What I will say presupposes the following definitions:

D1 xPy =Df ~(yAx)
D2 xSy =Df xAy & yAx
D3 Wp =Df ~Bp & ~$B{\sim}p$

It should be noted that withholding a proposition p is identical with withholding the negation of p.

There are 13 epistemic steps or levels each of which is such that, for every conscious subject S, some proposition p occupies that set or level for S. These are the following:

6.	(q)	[(Bp P Wq) & (Bp A Bq)]	Certain
5.	(q)	(Bp P Wq)	Obvious
4.	(q)~	(Wq P Bp)	Evident
3.		(Bp P Wp)	Reasonable
2.		~(Wp P Bp)	In the Clear
1.		(Bp P B~p)	Probable
0.		(B~p A Bp) & (Bp A B~p)	Counterbalanced
-1.		(B~p P Bp)	Probably False
-2.		~(Wp P B~p)	In the Clear to Disbelieve
-3.		(B~p P Wp)	Reasonable to Disbelieve
-4.	(q)~	(Wq P B~p)	Evidently False
-5.	(q)	(B~p P Wq)	Obviously False
-6.	(q)	[(B~p P Wq) & (B~p A Bq)]	Certainly False

Making use of the abbreviations here introduced, we next formulate the axioms for our primitive concept:

(A1) xPy ⊃ ~(yPx)
(A2) [(xPy & yPz] ⊃ (xPz)
(A3) (Bp A Wp) ⊃ (Bp P B~p)
(A4) [(q)(Bp A Wq)] ⊃ (Bp P Wp)
(A5) [(Bp P Wp) & (Bq P Wq)] ⊃ [B(p&q) P (Bp & Wq)]
(A6) [(∃p)(Bp P B~p)] ⊃ [(∃r)(q)(Br P Wq)]

The Relational Epistemic Concepts

Now we may turn to the difficult task of saying what it is for a proposition to *derive* its evidence from another proposition. I have said that the fact that *something appears* to me in a certain way may be evident to me and derive its evidence from the fact that it is evident to me that I am *sensing* in a certain way. And I have said that the fact that I *perceive* there to be a tree may be evident for me and derive its evident from the fact that it is evident to me that I *take* there to be a tree. What is it, then, for certain facts thus to present things *other* than themselves?

Our concern is to explicate what might be expressed by saying this: "h derives its status as being evident for S from the fact that e is evident for S." I believe that it is possible to explicate this concept in terms of those epistemic concepts just set forth.

I begin by considering those properties that may be said to "present themselves" to the person who has them.

Whatever presents itself also presents whatever it entails (whatever it both implies and conceptually involves). Arriving at the belief, say, that some dogs are brown serves to make known not only that one *does* arrive at that belief, but also that one believes that there are dogs, that one believes that there are things that are brown, and more generally, that one has arrived at a belief.

Some things that present themselves *also* present things that they neither imply nor involve. Let us call such things *other-presenting.*[18] Perception provides us with the clearest examples of other-presentation.

Consider once again the experience we have called "taking there to be a tree." From the fact that a person takes there to be a tree we may infer a number of things about what is evident for that person. We may infer that it is evident for the person that he does take there to be a tree. And we may also infer certain further things about the evidence he happens to have. For example, we may affirm this disjunctive proposition: *Either* his *perceiving there for be a tree* is evident to him *or* some further fact about his *taking there to be a tree* is evident for him. No matter how small his body of evidence may be, either it will include the proposition that he perceives there to be a tree (and hence also the proposition that there is a tree) or it will include some proposition about the conditions under which he takes there to be a tree.

Another example of other-presentation is provided by the experience one might express by saying "I seem to remember just having heard a bell ring." (I here use "seeming to remember so-and-so" in such way that, in that use, it does not imply "remember so-and-so.") If we know of a person that he seems to remember just having heard a bell ring, then we can also know that *either* his just *remembering* having heard a bell ring is evident for him *or* something about the *conditions under which he seems to remember* having heard a bell is evident for him. That he seems to remember having heard a bell, therefore, indicates something further about the other things that are evident to him.

It is in virtue of such other-presenting experiences that some of the things that are evident for a given person can be said to *derive their evidence* from other things that are evident for that person.

Let us now try to put these points somewhat more precisely and in the context of the various epistemic concepts we have been using.

We will say that taking there to be a tree *tends to insure the evidence* of perceiving there to be a tree, and that seeming to remember just having heard a bell *tends to insure the evidence* of remembering having just heard a bell. The relation of tending-to-insure-the-evidence-of is a logical relation between propositions; in other words, it is a relation which is such that, if it holds between two propositions, then it holds *necessarily* between those two propositions. And the relation of *deriving its evidence from* is an *application* of this logical relation— the tending-to-insure relation—*to* the evidence of a particular person.

I have referred to one's "*body of evidence.*" saying that, no matter how small a person's body of evidence may be, if it is evident for that person that he takes there to be a tree, then something further—either about the tree or about his taking there to be a tree will also be evident for him. This concept of one's "body of evidence"—one's "total evidence"—will give us the clue to understanding the logical relation, tending-to-insure-the-evidence-of.

Let us say what it is, then, for a proposition to be one's *total evidence*:

> D4 e is the total evidence of S =Df e is evident for S; and every proposition that is evident for S is implied by e.

Your total evidence may thus be thought of as a single proposition—a conjunction of propositions each of which is evident for you.

Suppose now that, under quite ordinary circumstances, you were to look out the train window and take something to be a tree. Then—since taking there to be a tree tends to insure the evidence of perceiving there to be a tree—your total evidence may include *both* "I take there to be a tree" and "I perceive there to be a tree." Let us assume that your total evidence does include both of these propositions. Consider now that proposition w which results from *subtracting* "I perceive there to be a tree" from your total evidence. This proposition could *not* be anyone's total evidence. Anyone for whom *that* much is evident will also have additional evidence not included in w—either evidence to the effect that he perceives a tree and therefore that there is a tree, or evidence about the circumstances under which he takes there to be a tree. Let us, then, define the logical relation expressed by "e *tends to insure* the evidence of h" this way:

> D5 e tends to insure the evidence of h =Df e is necessarily such that, for every x, if e is evident for x, then there is a w such that (i) w is evident for x, (ii) w&e&h is possibly such that it is someone's total evidence, and (iii) w&e is not possibly such that it is anyone's total evidence.

(We could also express the second and third conditions by saying that w&e is *evidentially incomplete* and that it is *evidentially fulfilled* by h.) Our definition allows for the possibility that a proposition e may tend to insure the evidence of a proposition h even though e does not logically imply h. The tending-to-insure relation, therefore, is *inductive*, or *nondemonstrative*.

What if a person S takes there to be a tree but does so under conditions which are such that, under those conditions, he does *not* then perceive there to be a tree? Then his total evidence will include, in addition to w and e, a further proposition d about the conditions under which he takes there to be a tree. An example of such a proposition d would be: "I seem to recall that I have a perceptual disorder which leads me to take there to be trees when no trees are there." This proposition d could be said, in the following sense, to *defeat* the tendency of e to insure the evidence of h:

D6   d defeats e's tendency to insure the evidence of h =Df
     e tends to insure the evidence of h; and d&e does not
     tend to insure the evidence of h.

Now we may consider the application of this logical relation to the evidence of a particular subject S. We will assume that S is a person for whom his perceiving there to be a tree derives its evidence from the fact that he takes there to be a tree. In other words, S's taking there to be a tree *confers* evidence upon—or *lends* evidence to—his perceiving there to be a tree. There are four things to note about this:

(1) It is evident for S that he takes there to be a tree.
(2) Taking there to be a tree tends to insure the evidence of perceiving there to be a tree.
(3) Nothing that is evident for S *defeats* the tendency of taking there to be a tree to insure the evidence of perceiving there to be a tree.
(4) Taking there to be a tree does not logically entail (does not imply and conceptually involve) perceiving there to be a tree.

Why the fourth condition? The first three conditions together imply that it is evident for S that he perceives there to be a tree. But these three propositions do not yield all that is required if we are to define what it is for one proposition that is evident for S to derive its evidence *from* another proposition that is evident for S. For no proposition can derive its evidence *from itself*—any more than a person can lend money to himself.[19] Therefore I add a fourth condition to our definition—a condition which, as we can see, is fulfilled by the relation between "I take there to be a tree" and "I perceive there to be a tree." (Why not use the concept of logical implication instead of the stronger concept of logical entailment? The answer lies in two facts—first, that every *necessary* proposition is logically implied by every proposition and, secondly, that not every necessary proposition that is evident for a person S derives its evidence from *every* proposition that is evident for S.)

Our definition, then, is this:

> D7 h derives its status of being evident for S from e =Df
> (1) e is evident for S; (2) e tends to insure the evidence
> of h; (3) nothing that is evident for S defeats e's
> tendency to insure the evidence of h; and (4) e does not
> logically entail h.

And so we have the desired definition.

Our consideration of perceptual evidence, then, has enabled us to say what it is for one proposition that is evident for a person to derive its evidence from another proposition that is evident for that person. There are other epistemic relations that are similar to this. I suggest that we now have the clue to understanding these concepts.

We may say, for example, that a proposition h which is *probable* for a given subject S *derives* its status of being probable for S from some other proposition e that is evident for S. Here, too, we have the application of a logical relation to the evidence of a particular subject. The logical relation is this:

> D8 e tends to make h probable (e confirms h) =Df e is
> necessarily such that, for every x, if e is evident for x,
> then there is a w such that (i) w is evident for x, (ii) w&e
> could be someone's total evidence, and (iii) h is probable
> for anyone for whom w&e is the total evidence.

This logical probability relation, like that of tending-to-insure-the-evidence-of, admits of *defeat*:

> D9 d defeats e's tendency to make h probable =Df e tends
> to make h probable; and e&d does not tend to make h
> probable.

And the *application* of the logical relation to the evidence of a particular subject S may now be defined this way:

> D10 e makes h probable for S =Df (1) e is evident for S; (2)
> e tends to make h probable; (3) there is no d such that
> d is evident for S and d defeats e's tendency to make h
> probable; and (4) e does not entail h.

Other epistemic relations may be explicated similarly. For example, to get the corresponding explications for "making h such that it is *beyond reasonable doubt* for S," we have only to replace "probable" in the three foregoing formulae by "such as to be beyond reasonable doubt." And analogously for being such as to be *epistemically in the clear*.

Perhaps there are simpler theories which will do justice to the evidence of the senses and which also avoid commitment to skepticism. But I do not know what these theories are.[20]

Notes

1. See Rudolf Carnap, *Logical Foundations of Probability* (Chicago: University of Chicago Press, 1950), p. 211ff.
2. The quotation is from pages 454-455 Carnap's article, "Testability and Meaning," *Philosophy of Science*, Vol. III (1936), pp. 420-471; my emphasis.
3. Compare Leonard Nelson, *Socratic Method and Critical Philosophy* (New Haven: Yale University Press, 1949), pp. 191-2. Nelson felt that, by appeal to such considerations, he could show that all of theory of knowledge rested upon a mistake. See his *Über das sogenannte Erkenntnisproblem* (Göttingen: Verlag Öffentliches Leben, 1930.)
4. Quoted from Alvin Goldman's article, "A Causal Theory of Knowing," reprinted in George S. Pappas and Marshall Swain, eds., *Essays on Knowledge and Justification* (Ithaca: Cornell University Press, 1978), pp. 61-86; the quotation is on p. 69.
5. There had been a tendency in recent Anglo-Saxon philosophy to *deny* that any such variable sense-content is to be found, but this move, of course, is manifestly absurd. Compare J. L. Austin, *Sense and Sensibilia* (Oxford: The Clarendon Press, 1962).
6. *Outlines of Pyrrhonism*, Book I, Chap. 14; abridged from Vol. I of *Sextus Empiricus*, The Loeb Classical Library, pp. 55, 63, 65. Cf. K. Lykos, "Aristotle and Plato on 'Appearing,'" *Mind*, LXXIII (1964), pp. 496-514.
7. I discussed these theories in the second edition of my book *Theory of Knowledge* (Englewood Cliffs, N.J.: Prentice Hall, Inc., 1977), but I was not then fully aware of the importance of the theories or of the fact that they seem to cover almost all the possibilities. I first took note of their significance for contemporary philosophy in "Sextus Empiricus and Modern Empiricism," *Philosophy of Science*, Vol. 8 (1941), pp. 371-384.
8. Quoted by Sextus Empiricus, "Against the Logician," I, 257-8; Vol. II. pp. 137-9.
9. Cicero uses these words in his *De Academica*, II, xi, 34; Cicero, *De Natura Deorum; Academica*, Loeb Classical Library (New York: G. P. Putman's Sons, 1933), p. 511.
10. Thus Sextus distinguished between (1) the "indicative" signs of Chrysippus, where one reads off the nature of the signified from the nature of the sign, and (2) the "commemorative signs" of the "empirical" physicians: a certain symptom signifies a certain disorder in virtue of the fact

that we have experienced symptom and disorder together. See "Outlines of Pyrrhonism," Book II, Ch. X ("Concerning Sign") and Ch. XI ("Does Indicative Sign Exist?"); Loeb Library edition, Vol. I, pp. 213-237.

11. C. I. Lewis, "Professor Chisholm and Empiricism," *Journal of Philosophy*, Vol. XLV (1948), pp. 517-524; the quotations appear on p. 520. This article is reprinted in C. I. Lewis, *Collected Papers of C. I. Lewis* (Stanford: Stanford University Press, 1970), pp. 317-325.

12. Lewis writes: "In my account, objective statements of fact are said to *entail* such probability consequences because it is consequences of this sort which are *contained in what it means*—in one sense of meaning—to assert the objective statements from which they are derivative" (p.524). Unfortunately Lewis seems never to have worked out the details of this suggestion.

13. See the Loeb Classical Library edition of Sextus Empiricus, Vol. I (London: William Heinemann Ltd., 1933), 139-143, and Vol. II (London: William Heinemann Ltd., 1935), 87-103. Compare Charlotte I. Stough, *Greek Skepticism: A Study in Epistemology* (Berkeley: University of California Press, 1969), esp. 50-64.

14. A. Meinong, *Über die Erfahrungsgrundlagen unseres Wissens* (1910); see *Meinong Gesamt Ausgabe*, Vol. V (Graz: Akademische Druck-und Verlagsanstalt, 1973), p. 458-9, 438. Compare his "Toward an Epistemological Assessment of Memory" (1886), reprinted in Roderick M. Chisholm and Robert J. Swartz, eds., *Empirical Knowledge: Readings from Contemporary Sources* (Englewood Cliffs: Prentice-Hall, Inc., 1973), pp. 253-269.

15. H. H. Price, *Perception* (New York: Robert M. McBride and Company, 1933), p. 185.

16. Op. Cit., p. 186.

17. The construction of this hierarchy accords with a suggestion made by Kenneth G. Lucey, in "Scales of Epistemic Appraisal," *Philosophical Studies*, Vol. 29 (1976), pp. 169-179. Lucey there contrasted the "straight steps" hierarchy I had proposed in earlier writings with what he called "a 'mirrored steps' system of epistemic appraisal" (170). The present hierarchy exemplifies the "mirrored steps" approach.

18. A Meinong introduced the expressions "self-presenting" and "other presenting" in 1917. Se Chapter One of his *On Emotional Presentation* (Evanston: Northwestern University Press, 1972). It should be added for the record, however, that Meinong did not use "other-presenting" in the way that I use it here.

19. "For how could anything transmit evidence to itself? The prospect sounds circular at best (like a witness testifying on behalf of his own credibility), impossible at worst (like a man trying to improve his own net worth by borrowing money from himself." James Van Cleve, "Epistemic Supervenience and the Circle of Belief," *The Monist*, Vol. 58 (1984), pp. 90-101; the quotation appears on page 100.

20. I am indebted to Richard Feldman, Richard Foley and Ernest Sosa for criticisms of earlier portions of this manuscript.

References

Austin, J. L., *Sense and Senibilia* (Oxford: The Clarendon Press, 1962).

Carnap, Rudolf, *Logical Foundations of Probability* (Chicago: University of Chicago Press, 1950). Carnap, Rudolf, "Testability and Meaning," *Philosophy of Science*, Vol. III (1936), pp. 420-471.

Chisholm, Roderick M, "Sextus Empiricus and Modern Empiricism," *Philosophy of Science*, Vol. VIII (1941), pp. 371-384.

Chisholm, Roderick M, *Theory of Knowledge*, Second Edition (Englewood Cliffs: Prentice-Hall, Inc. 1977).

Cicero, *De Natura Deorum; Academica*, Loeb Classical Library (New York: G. P. Putnam's Sons, 1933).

Goldman, Alvin, "A Causal Theory of Knowing," in George Pappas and Marshall Swain, eds., *Essays on Knowledge and Justification* (Ithaca: Cornell University Press, 1978).

C. I. Lewis, "Professor Chisholm and Empiricism," *Journal of Philosophy*, Vol. XLV (1948), pp. 517-524.

Lucey, Kenneth, "Scales of Epistemic Appraisal," *Philosophical Studies*, Vol. 29 (1976), pp. 169-179.

Lykos, K., "Aristotle and Plato on 'Appearing,'" *Mind*, Vol. LXXIII (1964), pp. 496-514.

Meinong A., "Toward an Epistemological Assessment of Memory" (1886), reprinted in Roderick M. Chisholm and Robert J. Swartz, eds., *Empirical Knowledge: Readings from Contemporary Sources* (Englewood Cliffs: Prentice-Hall, Inc., 1973).

Meinong A., *Über die Erfahrungsgrundlagen unseres Wissens* (1910), reprinted in *Meinong Gesant Ausgabe*, Vol. V (Graz: Akademische Druck- und Verlagsanstalt, 1973), pp. 369-481.

Meinong A., *On Emotional Presentation* (Evanston: Northwestern University Press, 1972).

Nelson, Leonard, *Über das sogenannte Erkenntnisproblem* (Göttingen: Verlag Öffentliches Leben, 1930).

Socratic Method and Critical Philosophy (New Haven: Yale University Press, 1948).

Price, H. H., *Perception* (New York: Robert M. McBride and Company, 1933).

Sextus Empiricus, *Sextus Empiricus*, Loeb Classical Library, Vol. I (London William Heinemann Ltd., 1933) and Vol. II (London: William Heinemann Ltd., 1935).

Stough, Charlotte, *Greek Skeptics: A Study in Epistemology* (Berkeley: University of California, 1969).

Van Cleve, James, "Epistemological Supervenience and the Circle of Belief," *The Monist*, Vol. 68 (1984).

Philosophical Perspectives, 2, Epistemology, 1988

HOW TO BE A FALLIBILIST

Stewart Cohen
Princeton University

The acceptance of fallibilism in epistemology is virtually universal. Any theory of knowledge that endorses the principle that S knows q on the basis of reason r only if r entails q, is doomed to a skeptical conclusion. Fallibilist theories reject this entailment principle thereby avoiding this immediate skeptical result. The acceptance of fallibilism derives from the widely held view that what we seek in constructing a theory of knowledge is an account that squares with our strong intuition that we know many things. Of course, few believe that skepticism is to be avoided at all costs. But while the entailment principle may look attractive in the abstract, it does not command the kind of assent sufficient to withstand the overwhelming case against it provided by our everyday intuitions concerning what we know. Any residual worry associated with denying the principle is far outweighed by our common sense rejection of its skeptical consequences. Thus, a fallibilist theory allows that S can know q on the basis of r where r only makes q probable.

Unfortunately, skepticism is not so easily dispatched. Other principles that look very difficult to reject threaten to reinstate skepticism—principles that lead to skeptical paradoxes for fallibilist theories. Thus, even fallibilist theories of knowledge are forced to confront skepticism, albeit in the form of a stubborn paradox rather than as a seemingly inescapable result.

The theory of relevant alternatives can be viewed as providing fallibilist theories with a way out of skeptical paradoxes.[1] However, while the theory looks promising in its broad outline, many believe that it faces intractable difficulties on critical matters of detail. Even proponents of the theory disagree over the precise nature of the solution to skeptical paradoxes the theory provides. Because of these problems, there is considerable worry that the theory is unable to provide a satisfactory treatment of the skeptical paradoxes. I propose to show that by restructuring the theory of relevant alternatives, we can obtain a satisfactory solution to these paradoxes. The precise nature of the solution will become clear once we see how the theory can handle other related puzzles that arise for a fallibilist theory. Depending on your perspective, the view I ultimately defend may be considered either a development within the spirit of the relevant alternatives approach or a departure from it.

I. Problems for Fallibilism

We can begin by examining the puzzles and paradoxes that confront fallibilist theories of knowledge. One kind of puzzle results directly from accepting the weaker principle which permits S to know q on the basis of r provided r makes q sufficiently probable.

Suppose S holds a ticket in a fair lottery with n tickets, where the probability $n-1/n$ of S losing is very high. Does S know that his ticket will lose? Although (if n is suitably large) S has good reasons to believe he will lose, it does not seem right to say that S *knows* he will lose.[2] This remains true for arbitrarily large n.

Now, suppose S learns from Jones, the person running the lottery, that Jones intends to fix the lottery so S will lose. Does S, then, know that he will lose? Better still, suppose S reads in the paper that another ticket has won. In both of these cases we are inclined to say that S does know that he loses.

This set of intuitions presents us with a puzzle. In the first case, it seemed, contrary to fallibilist assumptions, that as long as there is a chance that S wins, no matter how small, he does not know that he loses. But the other two cases indicate otherwise. There we said that S can know, on the basis of his reasons, that he will lose. But surely his reasons do not entail that he loses. Generally reliable sources lie, have their intentions thwarted, make mistakes, etc. The probability that S loses conditional on *these* reasons is less than 1.

Why do we attribute knowledge to S in these cases but not in the first case? In each case, his reasons make his conclusion highly probable without entailing the conclusion. And by increasing the number of tickets in the lottery in the first case, we can make it more probable that he loses in the first case than in the latter two.[3] Consider a related puzzle discussed by Gilbert Harman.[4] S does not know that Smith loses the lottery if S's reason is simply that the probability that he loses is $n-1/n$. But if S knows Smith is generally reliable and Smith announces his intention to go to New York tomorrow, S can thereby come to know that Smith will be in New York tomorrow, even though S knows that this entails that Smith loses the lottery (since if he were to win, he would be in New Jersey accepting the prize). So, S knowing that Smith will be in New York would seem to involve S knowing that Smith loses the lottery. But S does not know that Smith loses the lottery (on the basis of the probabilities alone).

Finally, consider skeptical paradoxes. Although fallibilist theories can plausibly reject the entailment principle, other principles with considerable skeptical clout are not so easily rejected. Consider the principle that the set of known (by S) propositions is closed under known (by S) entailment:

(1) If S knows q and S knows that q entails not-h, then S knows not-h.

While this closure principle strikes most people as compelling, it presents difficulties for a fallibilist view.[5] Since fallibilism rejects the entailment principle, S may know q on the basis of r, even though there is a proposition h, compatible with r but incompatible with q. If S fails to know not-h, fallibilism will run afoul of principle (1).

This is how skeptical problems arise for a fallibilist view. Exploiting the appeal of (1), the skeptic points out that, e.g., S knows that he sees a table only if S knows that he is not deceived by a Cartesian Demon, (since the former obviously entails the latter). But since our experience would be just as it is were we to be deceived by a Cartesian Demon, most people are reluctant to say that S knows that he is not so deceived. But then S does not know that he sees a table.

Where q is a proposition we would ordinarily claim to know and h is a skeptical hypothesis whose denial is entailed by q, the skeptic employs (1) in conjunction with

(2) S does not know not-h

to infer the denial of

(3) S knows q

Some philosophers have attempted to resist skepticism by combining (1) with (3) to conclude that (2) is false.[6] Others have argued from (2) and (3) to the rejection of (1). Of course, the problem is precisely that it is difficult to deny any of these propositions. As such, it seems arbitrary and unsatisfying simply to reject one of them on the basis of the other two.

We should view (1), (2), and (3) as constituting a paradox—a set of inconsistent propositions all of which have considerable independent plausibility. The puzzle concerning Smith and the lottery has the same structure (where q is the proposition that Smith will be in New York tomorrow and h is the proposition that Smith wins the lottery).[7]

The burden of the fallibilist is to resolve these puzzles and paradoxes in a way that preserves the truth of our everyday knowledge attributions. But a *satisfying* resolution requires an explanation of why the paradox arises—an explanation of why we have the intuitions that saddle us with the paradox. As I noted, in the case of the skeptical paradox, it is not enough to simply conjoin (3) with a second proposition of the inconsistent triad and then infer the denial of the third. Such a "resolution" would not tell us how the paradox arises in the first place.

II. The Theory of Relevant Alternatives

The resolution of these paradoxes I wish to defend is derived from the theory of relevant alternatives, a theory first developed by Fred Dretske. Before we can see how the resolution works, we need to examine the theory of relevant alternatives in some detail.

Let an alternative to a proposition q, be a proposition incompatible with q. The theory we are to consider says that S knows q relative to a set of *relevant* alternatives. Of course, 'relevance' is used here as a technical term. On Dretske's view, where h is an alternative to q, h is relevant just in case necessarily, S knows q only if S knows not-h.[8] Skeptical alternatives according to Dretske are not relevant.

What makes an alternative relevant? What criteria do skeptical alternatives fail to meet? Notoriously, these questions have been very difficult to answer with any degree of precision or generality. This difficulty has led critics to view the theory as *ad hoc* or obscure. For many, it constitutes the most serious obstacle to accepting the relevant alternatives account.[9] While I agree that there is a problem in specifying precise criteria of relevance, I will later argue that this does not in any way diminish the anti-skeptical force of the theory. For now, we must work with the admittedly problematic characterizations that are available.

The kind of factors that are typically taken to affect relevance can be illustrated through an example discussed by Alvin Goldman.[10] Suppose S sees a barn and believes that he does, on the basis of very good perceptual evidence. When is the alternative that he sees a papier-mache barn replica relevant? If there are many such replicas in the immediate area, then this alternative can be relevant. In these circumstances, S fails to know that he sees a barn unless he knows that it is not the case that he sees a barn replica. Where no such replicas exist, this alternative will not be relevant *(ceterus paribus)*. S can know that he sees a barn without knowing that he does not see a barn replica.

This suggests that a criterion of relevance is something like probability conditional on S's evidence and certain features of the circumstances.[11] Alternatively we could say that an alternative is relevant if S's evidence and certain features of the circumstances constitute a reason to believe h.[12] If the probability referred to in the first formulation is epistemic or inductive probability, then these two formulations come to roughly the same thing.

Of course, there is considerable vagueness here. For example, how many barn replicas must there be? The answer is that there is a continuum of cases with a range of clear cases of relevance at one end, a range of clear case of non-relevance at the other end, and a range of unclear cases in the middle. But there is no reason why relevance cannot be a vague notion provided that skeptical alternatives are sufficiently remote in everyday circumstances to count as clear cases of non-relevant alternatives.

Unfortunately, there is a lack of precision in the suggested formulation of the criterion of relevance that appears more serious. The probability of an alternative conditional on the evidence and certain other features of the circumstances will vary, of course, as the other features vary, and there is no apparent way to specify in general what those other features are. Consider a case where we want the result that the barn replica alternative is clearly relevant, viz., a case where the circumstances are such that there are numerous barn replicas in the area. Does the suggested criterion give us what we want? The probability that S sees a barn replica given his evidence and his location in an area where there are many barn replicas is high. However, that same probability conditional on his evidence and his particular visual orientation toward a real barn is quite low. Thus we want the probability to be conditional on features of the circumstance like the former but not features of the circumstances like the latter. But how do we capture the difference in a general formulation?

At least this much is true. There is some standard according to which, the alternative that S sees a barn replica is relevant in certain circumstances if, e.g., there are many barn replicas in the area, and not relevant if there is just one barn replica thousands of miles away *(ceterus paribus)*. Again I will later argue that this lack of precision should not concern us.

An essential aspect of the version of the theory of relevant alternatives I wish to defend is that the standards that govern relevance are context-sensitive.[13] How probable an alternative must be in order to be relevant will depend on the context in which the knowledge attribution is made. To say simply that skeptical alternatives are not relevant is to fail to do justice to the apparent threat skeptical arguments pose to our knowledge claims. While it is true that we often believe that skeptical alternatives are too remote to threaten our knowledge claims, at other times we find them quite worrisome. By supposing that the standards of relevance are sensitive to the context of attribution we can explain our tendency to vacillate in this way. In normal everyday contexts, the standards are such that skeptical alternatives are not relevant (unless, of course, the circumstances are such that skeptical alternatives are highly probable, e.g., there exist many barn replicas). This explains our confidence in the truth of our everyday attributions of knowledge. However, when we are confronted with skeptical arguments, we may come to consider skeptical alternatives as relevant, thereby lowering our standards (for how probable an alternative must be). Skeptical arguments are forceful precisely because they can have this effect on us. In these contexts, attributions of knowledge which are true in everyday contexts, are false. But we are not thereby constrained to use skeptical standards for our knowledge attributions. Upon further consideration, we may decide that skeptical alternatives are too remote to count as relevant, thereby shifting the standards once more. Again, sometimes we vacillate between considering skeptical alternatives as relevant and dismissing them as irrelevant. By supposing that the truth-value of an attribution of knowledge is context sensitive in just this way, we do justice to both the undeniable force of skeptical arguments and our strong inclination to say that we know things in everyday life.

Thus, the theory I wish to defend construes "knowledge" as an indexical. As such, one speaker may attribute knowledge to a subject while another speaker denies knowledge to that same subject, without contradiction.[14]

III. Closure and Skeptical Paradoxes

If the theory of relevant alternatives provides a resolution of the skeptical paradox, which member of the inconsistent triad does it reject? On Dretskes' view, the theory rejects (1), the closure principle. According to Dretske, (where h is an alternative to q), if S knows q and S knows q entails not-h, then S knows not-h, just in case h is a relevant alternative.[15] Presumably Dretske would argue that the appeal of (1) results from our failure to distinguish it from its qualified version.

Consider a case discussed by Dretske.[16] He observes that when we are at the zoo and encounter the zebra exhibit, we can come to know that the animals we see there are zebras. He then notes that their being zebras entails that they are not cleverly disguised mules. Thus, the proposition that they are cleverly disguised mules is an alternative. Provided that there are no facts concerning, e.g., deceptive practices on the part of the zoo keepers, this alternative is not relevant, and so we know that they are zebras. But, Dretske insists, we do not know that they are not cleverly disguised mules. He claims that we fail to know that they are not cleverly disguised mules because we lack sufficiently good reason to believe that they are not. The evidence for thinking they are zebras does not count against thinking they are cleverly disguised mules. While conceding that we have some statistical reasons for denying this alternative, the normal behavior of zoo keepers, etc., Dretske denies that these reasons are sufficient for us to know that the alternative is false. They fall short of being the sort of knowledge yielding reasons we might obtain by closely inspecting the animals. Dretske points out that the skeptic attempts to exploit this fact in conjunction with (1) to deny that we know that we see a zebra. He proposes that we resist this move by accepting nothing more than the restricted version of (1). Since the alternative that the animals are mules is not relevant in the context, we can know they are zebras even though our evidence does not give us knowledge that they are not disguised mules.

G. C. Stine disputes Dretske's conclusion.[17] While endorsing the theory of relevant alternatives, Stine argues that the theory is most plausibly construed as not entailing the falsity of (1), the closure principle. She accuses Dretske of presupposing that it is always the case that when knowledge of p is attributed to S, the negation of p is a relevant alternative. This allows Dretske to deny (1), since h (the skeptical alternative) fails to be relevant when the issue is whether S knows q, while remaining relevant when the issue is whether S knows not-h. While Stine concedes that this presupposition is normally correct, she denies that it is always correct. In particular, in the special context of making a deductive closure argument, the normal presupposition that the negation of a proposition is relevant is "cancellable". And if this presupposition is cancelled, i.e., if h fails to be relevant, then we should say that S knows not-h. More generally, S knows a proposition in any context where its negation is not relevant. Thus, in a context where we know q, because h is not relevant, we know not-h as well.[18]

Stine's account preserves the closure principle relative to a fixed set of relevant alternatives. If h is relevant, S fails to know not-h, but S fails to know q as well. If h is not relevant, S knows q, but S knows not-h as well. On this interpretation, the relevant alternatives approach to the skeptical paradox amounts to a denial of (2) (relative to the standards that operate in everyday contexts). In those contexts, since h is (normally) not relevant, S knows not-h, as well as q. This is true even though when we consider whether S knows a skeptical alternative like h to be false, we may be led to consider h relevant (thereby shifting our standards) and so fail to know not-h (in *that* context). Stine notes that to object to closure on the basis of examples where the set of relevant alternatives is not held fixed is "to commit some logical sin akin to equivocation".[19]

Stine is certainly correct in characterizing the argument she attributes to Dretske as a form of equivocation. If attributions of knowledge are context-sensitive in the way we have been supposing, i.e., if "knowledge" is an indexical, then the content of knowledge attributions will vary across contexts. What we attribute to S in one context when we assert that S knows, will be different from what we attribute to S in another context when we assert that S knows. As such, if the antecedent and consequent of (1) are evaluated in different contexts, it is problematic to even view (1) as expressing a closure principle. Exactly which set is supposed to be closed?

On the other hand, there would appear to be a problem with Stine's view. For if Dretske is right, we fail to know not-h (in the example he discusses) because we lack sufficient evidence for us to know not-h. The purely perceptual evidence certainly does not count in favor of it not being the case that they are disguised mules and there is considerable plausibility to Dretske's contention that the purely statistical evidence we have regarding the behavior of zoo keepers is insufficient to give us knowledge that they are not cleverly disguised mules.

While Stine agrees that the evidence is insufficient, she contends that Dretske has generalized the evidence requirement when, in fact, some cases of knowledge are such that evidence is not required. She counters that "if the negation of a proposition is not a relevant alternative, then I know it—obviously, without needing to provide evidence..."[20]

Here, I think that Stine's strategy for preserving closure becomes strongly counter-intuitive. Even if it is true that some propositions can be known without evidence, surely this is not true of the proposition that S is not deceived by a cleverly disguised mule.

Moreover, it is not clear that Stine has made much progress in resisting skepticism by defending closure since she (as well as Dretske) claims that we do not have evidence that yields knowledge that not-h while we do have evidence that yields knowledge that q.[21] But then both she and Dretske are committed to the denial of (4):

(4) If S has sufficient evidence to know q and S knows that q entails not-h, then S has sufficient evidence to know not-h.

Surely this principle is as plausible as (1).[22] Moreover, many people think that skeptical doubts about knowledge are, at root, doubts about evidence. So it is peculiar for Stine to defend (1) while implicitly denying (4). Is Stine inadvertently committing the same equivocation in (implicitly) denying (4) as Dretske commits in denying (1)?

It is clear that however we resolve the issue concerning whether knowledge requires evidence, the fundamental skeptical paradox remains if we combine (4) with (5) and (6).

> (5) S does not have sufficient evidence to know not-h.
>
> (6) S does have sufficient evidence to know q.

What should we say about this paradox? If the theory of relevant alternatives is to make any headway against skepticism, the resolution of this paradox must parallel the resolution of the paradox concerning knowledge; S has evidence sufficient for knowledge relative to a set of relevant alternatives determined by the standards that operate in the context. So, our perceptual evidence gives us knowledge of q (the animals are zebras) only given the irrelevance of the alternative h (they are cleverly disguised mules).

But now we must ask which member of this new inconsistent triad is denied by the theory. Again, the theory fails to provide a satisfactory resolution of the skeptical paradox unless it delivers a precise result concerning which proposition we should reject. But now, this issue has merely shifted from the knowledge paradox to the evidence paradox. What are the implications of the theory for (4) and the attendant consequences for (1)?

There is a difficulty in discussing this issue to which we must now turn. As Dretske sketches the theory, an alternative h, to q, is relevant just in case, necessarily, S knows q only if S knows not-h. Thus h is not relevant just in case it is possible that both S knows q and S does not know not-h. With the theory formulated in this way, the failure of closure follows from the claim that skeptical (or for that matter any) alternatives are not relevant. But while all proponents of the theory of relevant alternatives want to claim that skeptical alternatives are not relevant— this is one of the primary motivations for holding the theory—there is a dispute among those proponents over whether closure is preserved by the theory.

We have seen that Stine disputes Dretske's view that the theory involves rejecting closure. But she can claim that closure holds only because she redefines what it is for an alternative to be relevant. Stine presupposes the view that an alternative h, to q, is relevant just in case, necessarily, S knows q only if S knows not-h *on the basis of evidence*.[23] Given her view that knowledge does not require evidence, it does not follow from the fact that h is not relevant that closure fails. All that follows is that it is possible both for S to know q and for S not to know not-h on the basis of evidence. This allows Stine to hold the view that the non-relevant alternatives are known to be false without evidence, thereby preserving closure principle (1). However her way of defining relevance (as well as Dretske's) does have the result that the claim that skeptical alternatives are not relevant entails that closure principle (4) fails (provided that q is known on the basis of evidence). To resolve the closure issue, we need a way of formulating the theory of relevant alternatives that does not prejudge the issue. We need a way of formulating the theory that retains the anti-skeptical force without either denying or affirming closure in the very formulation. We can then *investigate* what implication the theory has for the closure principles.

This is what I propose to do. It is important to remember that the project in which we are engaged, is to rescue fallibilism from the skeptical paradox. On a fallibilist view, S can know q on the basis of (his reason) r, even though r does not entail q. So fallibilism allows that S can know q on the basis of r even though there exist alternatives to q consistent with r. Of course, this is not to say that S knows whenever there are such alternatives. Under certain conditions, S's epistemic position with respect to such alternatives will preclude S from knowing q on the basis of r. Thus, a fallibilist theory, at minimum, is committed to a distinction between conditions in which S's epistemic position with respect to alternatives consistent with r precludes knowledge, and conditions in which S's epistemic position with respect to alternatives consistent with r does not preclude knowledge. We need not decide at this point, whether in these latter conditions, the reason S's epistemic position with respect to the alternatives does not preclude knowledge is that S knows they are false (Stine); or that although S does not know they are false, it is not required that he know they are false in order for him to know q (Dretske).

Let us call an alternative in conditions of this latter kind, a *relevant* alternative:

> an alternative (to q) h is relevant (for S) = df S's epistemic position with respect to h precludes S from knowing q.

Now we can hold that certain alternatives are not relevant, which as fallibilists we must, without thereby being committed either way on the closure issue. We leave it open exactly what S's epistemic situation is with respect to the non-relevant alternatives.

Before we develop the implications for closure of this reformulated theory, we need to say more about the criteria of relevance. Whether

S knows q will depend on whether any alternatives to q are relevant—whether the conditions are such that S's epistemic position with respect to any alternatives precludes knowledge of q. Thus the criteria of relevance should reflect our intuitions concerning under what conditions S does know q. These intuitions are influenced by conditions that are internal to S's evidence and by conditions that are external to S's evidence.[24] The external conditions are reflected in the probabilistic criterion of relevance we discussed earlier.

> (i) an alternative (to q) h is relevant, if the probability of h conditional on reason r and certain features of the circumstances is sufficiently high (where the level of probability that is sufficient is determined by context).

The externality of this criterion is exemplified in its application to Goldman's barn replica case. The mere fact that the replicas exist, whether or not S has any evidence that they exist, is sufficient to render the alternative that S sees a barn replica relevant (in everyday contexts) by this criterion.

If the theory of relevant alternatives is to capture the internal conditions that affect our intuitions, then it must have an internal criterion of relevance, i.e., a criterion that is sensitive to conditions concerning S's evidence alone. Both Stine and Dretske overlook the fact that S's evidence against h plays a role in S coming to know q because they think this evidence is not sufficient for S to know not-h. But even if they turn out to be right in holding that the statistical evidence possessed by S regarding the behavior of zoo keepers is not sufficient for S to know that he does not see a cleverly disguised mule, nonetheless it is surely true that the fact that S possesses this evidence against this alternative is crucial to the alternative not being relevant. If S were to have no evidence at all regarding the behavior of zoo keepers (or even people in general) which would count against this alternative—if as far as S's evidence were concerned, it would be as likely as not that he sees a disguised mule—then surely S would fail to know that he sees a zebra. That is to say, the alternative that he sees a mule would be relevant. The conditions would be such that S's epistemic position with respect to the alternative would preclude S from knowing that he sees a zebra on the basis of his perceptual evidence.

The conditions that make the alternative relevant here are distinct from the conditions governed by the external criterion. It may be that relative to facts beyond S's evidence, it is very improbable that S sees a cleverly disguised mule. But if given S's evidence alone, it is as likely that he sees a disguised mule as that he sees a zebra, S does not know that he sees a zebra.

The point is, perhaps, even more clear when we consider non-perceptual examples.[25] Suppose S believes that there is a zebra at the zoo on the basis of Jones' testimony (alone). Is the alternative that Jones is deceiving him relevant? One factor that will affect relevance here is the actual frequency with which Jones (or people in general) actually provide deceptive testimony. This kind of factor is governed by the external criterion. But clearly, if as far as S's evidence is concerned, it is as likely as not that Jones does deceive him—if S has no evidence concerning the reliability of Jones (or people in general)—then S does not know that there is a zebra at the zoo on the basis of Jones' testimony. Again, factors pertaining exclusively to S's own evidence affect whether alternatives become relevant. This underscores the need for what I have called an internal criterion of relevance. One could deny the need for such a criterion only by denying that, e.g., S's evidence concerning the reliability of Jones' testimony is not relevant to whether S comes to know on the basis of Jones' testimony.[26]

We can augment the theory in the required way by including criterion (ii):

(ii) an alternative (to q) h is relevant, if S lacks sufficient evidence (reason) to deny h, i.e., to believe not-h.

It is a consequence of the internal criterion of relevance that S's evidence against h is, in effect, an essential component of S's total reasons that give him knowledge of q . Thus, we can view the internal criterion as determining a standard that governs how strong S's total reasons to believe q must be in order for S to know q.[27] We noted earlier that in order to explain the appeal of skeptical arguments, we need to suppose that what I am now calling the external criterion of relevance is context-sensitive. The very same considerations apply to the internal criterion. So there will be no general specification of what constitutes sufficient evidence to deny an alternative in order for it not to be relevant, and as such, no general specification of what constitutes sufficient evidence to know q. Rather, this will depend on the context in which the attribution of knowledge occurs.

We can now return to the issue of closure that divided Dretske and Stine. Dretske argues that closure principle (1) is false. S may know q, but fail to know not-h (where h is an alternative to q) where S lacks sufficient evidence to know not-h. On Dretske's view, the fact that S fails to know not-h does not undermine his knowledge of q, provided that h is not a relevant alternative.

Stine defends principle (1) arguing that closure will hold provided we don't equivocate—provided we keep the set of relevant alternatives (and thus the standards of relevance) fixed. When h is relevant, S will fail to know both not-h and q, and when h is not relevant S will know both not-h and q. Stine responds to Dretske's worry that S lacks sufficient evidence to know not-h by claiming that when h is not relevant, S knows not-h without evidence. We noted that the arguments of both Dretske and Stine hinge on the rejection of closure principle (4).

The internal criterion of relevance will enable us to assess more clearly the status of (4). Since this criterion is context-sensitive, we should be alert to the possibility that the rejection of (4) is based on the same sort of equivocation Stine refers to in connection with the external criterion and principle (1). The issue would seem to be this: Suppose S believes q on the basis of his evidence, where h is an alternative to q. If S does not have sufficient evidence to deny h, to prevent h from being relevant in context c, then (given the way I have defined "relevance") S fails to know q on the basis of his evidence, in c. That is to say, S's total evidence is not sufficient evidence for S to know q in c. Thus if S's total evidence is sufficient evidence for S to know q in c, then some subset of that evidence, e, is sufficient evidence to deny h, to prevent h from being a relevant alternative in c. What we need to know is whether e is sufficient evidence, *in that same context* c, for S to know not-h.

(For example, recall Dretske's claim that the statistical evidence concerning the behavior of zookeepers is not sufficient evidence for S to know that he does not see a cleverly disguised mule. I have argued that this evidence certainly plays a role in S knowing that he sees a zebra—it keeps the alternative that he sees a cleverly disguised mule from being relevant. The issue we are confronting is whether this evidence, which enables S to know that he sees a zebra by preventing the alternative that he sees a cleverly disguised mule from being relevant, is sufficient evidence for S to know that he does not see a cleverly disguised mule).

If e is sufficient evidence for S to know not-h in context c, then closure principle (4) holds contrary to both Dretske and Stine. I will argue that e is sufficient evidence for S to know not-h in c.[28] The argument is straightforward: Suppose S has sufficient evidence to know q in c, where h is an alternative to q. I just argued that it follows that some subset of that evidence, e, is sufficient evidence to deny h, to prevent h from being a relevant alternative in c. Thus *in context c*, h is not a relevant alternative to not-h.[29] That is to say (given the way I have defined relevance), in c, e is sufficient evidence to deny h, to prevent knowledge of not-h from being precluded. But the evidence to deny h just is the evidence to believe not-h. Thus, e is sufficient evidence to believe not-h, to prevent knowledge of not-h from being precluded. It follows that e is sufficient evidence to know not-h (since, if e were not sufficient evidence to know not-h, knowledge of not-h would be precluded).

We can now see that closure principle (4) holds, relative to a context. The denial of (4) is based on the same kind of equivocation that Stine alleged in connection with Dretske's denial of (1). The reason we want to say that while S has sufficient evidence to know q, he lacks sufficient evidence to know not-h, is that we inadvertently shift the standards of relevance as we move from the former attribution to the latter.

Moreover, since the status of closure principle (1) depends on the status of (4), (1) remains intact as well, relative to a context. If S knows q and S knows that q entails not-h, then (contrary to Dretske) S does know not-h, but (contrary to Stine) S knows not-h on the basis of his evidence.[30]

Thus, the theory I am proposing handles the skeptical paradox concerning evidence and the skeptical paradox concerning knowledge in precisely the same way. In the evidence paradox, the theory denies (5) (S does not have sufficient evidence to know not-h) in everyday contexts, while denying (6) (S does have sufficient evidence to know q) in skeptical contexts. In the knowledge paradox, the theory denies (2) (S does not know not-h) in everyday contexts, while denying (3) (S knows q) in skeptical contexts. In no context does the theory deny either closure principle (1) concerning knowledge or closure principle (4) concerning evidence sufficient for knowledge.

IV. Contextual Shifts

I have argued that our tendency to say both that S knows q and that S does not know not-h results from our failure to hold the standards of relevance fixed. Since our tendency to shift these standards is what gives rise to the skeptical paradoxes, a satisfactory resolution of the paradoxes requires an account of how this shift occurs. Here is where the fallibilist puzzles I mentioned earlier are germane. Consider the lottery puzzle. Where S's reasons for believing he loses the lottery consist of the testimony of Jones that he will fix the lottery, or the newspaper report that lists another ticket as the winner, S can know that he loses. But S cannot know on the basis of the statistical information concerning the number of tickets, even though the probability that he loses may be greater on the basis of the latter evidence than on the basis of the former. Why should this be?

In the cases where the reasons consist of the testimony or the newspaper report, the reasons do not entail the conclusion that he loses. There are alternatives consistent with the reasons, e.g., the testimony is deceptive, the newspaper report is mistaken. Since ordinarily we attribute knowledge in these cases, these alternatives are not relevant in those contexts.

The situation is different in the case where the reasons consist of the statistical information. Like the other cases, the reasons (the $n-1/n$ probability that the ticket loses) do not entail that S loses. Trivially, there is the alternative that S's ticket wins, which is consistent with the $n-1$ other tickets having an equal chance of winning. Since here we ordinarily deny that S knows that he loses, this alternative is relevant in those contexts.

What makes it relevant? I propose that the explanation lies in the statistical nature of the reasons. Although, as fallibilists, we allow that S can know q, even though there is a chance of error (i.e., there are alternatives compatible with his reasons), when the chance of error is salient, we are reluctant to attribute knowledge. Statistical reasons of the sort that S possesses in the lottery case make the chance of error salient. The specification that S's reason is the $n-1/n$ probability that the ticket loses, calls attention to the $1/n$ probability that the ticket wins. Our attention is focused on the alternative that the ticket wins and this creates a context in which we are reluctant to attribute knowledge, unless S has some independent ground sufficient for denying the alternative. But in this case S has no independent grounds. Since the alternative h is just the contradictory of the believed proposition q, the grounds for denying h just are the grounds for accepting q. Thus the alternative remains relevant and we do not attribute knowledge to S that his ticket loses. The standards of relevance are such that either S lacks sufficient reason to deny h, or the probability of h is too great in the circumstances (or both).[31]

In the cases where we ordinarily attribute knowledge, viz., where S's reasons consist of the testimony or the newspaper report, the chance of error is not salient. Here, there are no relevant alternatives. The standards that operate in these contexts are such that S does have sufficient reason to deny the alternatives, e.g., deceptive testimony, newspaper misprint. But the reasons for denying the alternatives need not be any stronger here than the reasons for denying the alternatives in the statistical case, since we can make the strength of the reasons in the statistical case arbitrarily great by increasing the number of tickets. It follows that the contexts in which we evaluate the two cases are different, i.e., the standards of relevance that operate are different. The explanation for why the standards differ lies in the fact that in the statistical case, unlike the other cases, the nature of the reasons make the chance of error salient.[32]

It might seem as if the alleged difference between the cases does not really exist. Surely facts about testimony or newspaper reports constitute reasons (evidence) only in conjunction with facts about the reliability of testimony or newspaper reports, and surely this reliability will be less than perfect. Thus the reasons are more accurately described as, e.g., Jones says q and Jones is n/m reliable (where $n < m$). But if the reasons are ultimately statistical in this way, why doesn't the chance of error become salient? Why isn't our attention focused on the $m - n/m$ chance that Jones is lying?

The answer is that we do not normally think of the reasons in this way. If we did, we might not say that S knows. How do we think of this case so that the chance of error is not salient?[33] We know that Jones says that he intends to fix the lottery to ensure that S loses. This suggests to us a scenario: Jones announces his intention to fix the lottery because that is, in fact, what he intends, and his intention will lead him to avoid drawing S's ticket and S thereby will lose.

Consider the case where the reasons consist of the newspaper report that a different ticket wins. Newspapers are not perfectly reliable. If the reasons were described in terms of the newspaper's high, but less than perfect reliability, we might begin to wonder whether we really know that what it reports is true. We say that S does know because we do not think of the case in this way. Rather, insofar as we think about it, we imagine a scenario where the information about which ticket loses is transmitted to the paper in one of the usual ways, e.g., the reporter witnesses the drawing and then phones it in to the editor who prints it.

In these scenarios, the chance of error is not salient. Because we think of the cases in terms of these scenarios, we are not led to consider certain alternatives as relevant (and thereby alter the standards). This is unlike the case where the reasons are described in terms of the explicit statistical probabilities. That very description makes salient the chance of error and leads us to consider the alternatives as relevant.

However, there is nothing in the semantics of "know" that requires that we set the standards in this way. Nothing would prevent us from setting the standards in the explicit probability case in such a way that an attribution of knowledge would be correct. If one reflects on the fact that the probability that S loses could be greater based simply on the number of tickets then the probability that he loses conditional on the testimony, one could be led from the tendency to attribute knowledge in the testimony case to attribute knowledge on the basis of the statistical information. One might feel that the chance that S's ticket will be drawn is too remote to count as a relevant alternative.[34]

While a description of the reasons in terms of the statistical probability can be what leads to a lowering of the standards of relevance, imagining *certain* scenarios can have the same effect. When we are told that a lottery is fair, we may imagine a scenario where someone draws blindly from a bin filled with tickets. Viewing the situation in this way underscores the fact that any ticket could be drawn—it makes the alternative that S wins relevant. Indeed the very condition that motivates people to participate in lotteries is the chance that their ticket may win.[35]

We can now gain some insight into how skeptical arguments work. In effect, skeptical arguments make alternatives relevant by forcing us to view the reasons in a way that makes the chance of error salient. Skeptical standards of relevance thereby take effect, creating a context where attributions of knowledge are incorrect.

Consider the case of testimony. As we have noted, in everyday contexts we will attribute knowledge on the basis of testimony. Thus, we ordinarily allow that S knows that his ticket will lose based on the testimony of Jones or the newspaper report. The skeptic poses the question: How does S know that it is not the case that Jones is lying or that the newspaper is mistaken? If he is persistent we can become hesitant to say that S knows that he will lose.

What explains this shift? When the skeptic poses his challenge, he focuses our attention on the chance of error—on the existence of alternatives consistent with S's reasons. When alternatives become salient in this way, we are reluctant to attribute knowledge unless the subject of the attribution has sufficient reason to deny the alternatives. But when we try to meet the skeptical challenge, we are forced to confront the fact that the reasons S has for denying these alternatives are basically statistical, viz., people do not usually lie, newspapers generally do not make mistakes etc.. But reasons of this type serve the cause of the skeptic very well, since they themselves make the chance of error salient. This is why we are reluctant to say that S knows he will lose on the basis of the purely statistical reasons (the number of tickets etc..) To say that people do not *usually* lie or that newspapers do not *generally* make mistakes is to underscore the fact that they sometimes do. In this way, these alternatives become relevant. A skeptical context is created and the reasons for denying the alternatives are not sufficient relative to the standards that apply in this new context. As such, we become reluctant to attribute knowledge to S that he loses on the basis of Jones' testimony (or the newspaper report), because we are reluctant to attribute knowledge to S that Jones is not lying (or that the newspaper report is not mistaken).

The same account applies to Dretske's zebra case. The explanation for why we are hesitant to say that S knows that he does not see a cleverly disguised mule is that S's reasons for denying that he sees one are statistical—people rarely engage in elaborate deceptions. This makes salient the fact that they sometimes do and a skeptical context is created where this alternative becomes relevant. We become reluctant to say that S knows that he sees a zebra because we do not think that he knows that he does not see a cleverly disguised mule.

In everyday contexts, though, the standards of relevance are such that we will attribute knowledge on the basis of testimony and perception.

Skeptical arguments exploit the fact that certain considerations can lead to a shift in the standards of relevance. Failure to recognize the shift can lead us into paradox. We attribute knowledge to S that he loses the lottery on the basis of testimony but we deny that S knows that the report is not mistaken. In Harman's puzzle, we attribute knowledge to S that Smith will be in New York tomorrow on the basis of Smith's announced intention, yet we deny that S knows that it is not the case that Smith will win the lottery and be in New Jersey instead. Both Dretske and Stine attribute knowledge to S that he sees a zebra on the basis of his visual evidence while denying that his evidence gives him knowledge that he does not see a cleverly disguised mule. (Stine contends that he knows without evidence). This pattern of attributions creates the appearance of closure failure which we are hard pressed to accept. Thus we are led to reassess our original judgments often vacillating between skepticism and common sense.

What I am proposing is that we can explain this pattern of attributions in terms of the mechanism of context-sensitivity in a way that endorses our original knowledge attributions, preserves the truth of the closure principles and accounts for the power of skeptical arguments. In all of these cases, S's reason for his belief q gives him knowledge of q, relative to the standards that ordinarily apply. Under skeptical pressure, we are led to view S's reasons for denying alternative h as not sufficient for S to know not-h. However, we have seen that relative to the same standards that ordinarily apply to knowledge of q, S's reason for denying h are sufficient for him to know not-h. If we keep the context fixed, S knows q on the basis of his evidence only if that evidence allows him to know not-h. So, the skeptical pressure results in a shift to a different context where different standards apply. Once we have shifted to the skeptical context, the skeptic will exploit the appeal of closure and insist on the *modus tollens* inference. Thus the skeptic succeeds in getting us to question our original knowledge attribution by getting us to shift the context. When we are confronted with the conclusion of the skeptical argument (e.g., S does not know that he sees a zebra), our ordinary standards often reassert themselves and we resist the skeptical inference, insisting that S does know q. But then we are faced once again with the closure principle. And the *modus ponens* inference to the conclusion that S does know not-h is thwarted by the resurgence of the skeptical standards. Although we find it hard to deny closure, we end up asserting both that S knows q and that S does not know not-h.

Thus we are led into paradox. The theory of relevant alternatives provides a way out of the paradox. According to the theory, attributions of knowledge are context-sensitive. The apparent closure failures are illusions that result from inattention to contextual shifts. In ordinary contexts S does know q, but in those same contexts, S knows not-h. In skeptical contexts S fails to know both q and not-h.

V. Radical Skeptical Hypotheses

If all skeptical hypotheses were like those we have been considering, we could be satisfied that the treatment of these cases generalizes to a complete solution to the skeptical paradoxes. Unfortunately, there are certain skeptical hypotheses that cannot be handled in precisely this way. Let us distinguish between *moderate* and *radical* skeptical hypotheses. A moderate skeptical hypothesis is immune to rejection on the basis of a particular kind of evidence. For example, the hypothesis that the animals are cleverly disguised mules cannot be rejected on the basis of the perceptual evidence available to the observer at the supposed distance. The hypotheses that Smith wins the lottery can not be rejected on the basis of Jones' testimony that he will be in New York. In these cases, the possibility remains that the subject possesses other evidence which counts against these alternatives, e.g., statistical evidence about the likelihood of deception, or the likelihood of a particular ticket winning in a fair lottery.

Radical skeptical hypotheses are immune to rejection on the basis of *any* evidence. There would appear to be no evidence that could count against the hypothesis that we are deceived by a Cartesian demon, or the hypothesis that we are brains-in-a-vat. Radical skeptical hypotheses are designed to neutralize any evidence that could be adduced against them.

If this is correct, then the proposed solution of the paradox is threatened. Where h is a radical skeptical hypotheses, the skeptic can argue that trivially we fail to have evidence sufficient to deny h, *relative to everyday standards* since we fail to have *any* evidence that counts against h. We will not be able to argue, as we did regarding the moderate skeptical hypotheses, that the evidence we do have to deny h really is sufficient relative to everyday standards. Thus h will be a relevant alternative (by the internal criterion) and we will fail to know q.[36]

Where does this leave us? The skeptic would seem to be correct in claiming that we do lack evidence against radical skeptical hypotheses. However, it does not follow that it is not reasonable or rational to deny such hypotheses. I am not, here, referring to non-epistemic senses of rationality (e.g., prudential rationality). Rather I am referring to a way in which it can be rational (or reasonable) to believe a proposition without possessing evidence for the belief. We can call beliefs of this sort intrinsically rational. While we may concede to the skeptic that we lack evidence against radical skeptical hypotheses, I do not think we should be willing to concede that it is not rational to deny these hypotheses (believe they are false). If so we can view the denials of these hypotheses as intrinsically rational. For example I think it is clear that we would think that it is rational to believe that you are not systematically deceived—deceived in a way that cannot in principle be detected.

Is it true that we view matters in this way? Notice that we would characterize someone who believed a radical skeptical hypotheses as crazy, as profoundly irrational. One might claim that we regard acceptance of such hypotheses in this way because we consider suspension of judgment as the only rational attitude to take toward these propositions. On this view it would not be rational to either accept or deny h (the radical skeptical alternative).

However, this is surely an implausible characterization of the way we view the epistemic status of skeptical hypotheses. Typically we think it appropriate to suspend belief about a proposition q, when q and not-q are equally reasonable. In addition, suspension of belief can be the appropriate attitude toward a proposition q even if there is an asymmetry between the degree of reasonability of q and the degree of reasonability of not-q. It may be that while q is more reasonable than not-q, not-q is still sufficiently reasonable to preclude acceptance of q. But this is not our situation with respect to radical skeptical hypotheses. Here there is an extreme asymmetry. We think it would be crazy to believe a radical skeptical hypotheses. This suggests that we think it is rational to deny such a hypotheses.

Perhaps when we are dealing with matters that are paradoxical, it is possible to think that it is crazy to either accept q or deny q. So it would not follow from the fact that we think it is crazy to believe a skeptical hypotheses that we think it is rational to deny skeptical hypotheses. However, this is not our attitude toward accepting skeptical hypotheses. We do not think it is crazy to deny such a hypotheses. Not even the skeptic holds that view. So it must be that we think it is rational to deny skeptical hypotheses even though we recognize that we lack evidence against it.

But doesn't this just beg the question against the skeptic? In a sense it does, but no more than the skeptic begs the question against common sense. While the skeptic may have an argument that we possess no evidence against radical skeptical hypotheses like the demon hypotheses, he has no argument that it is not rational (in the way I have indicated) to deny them. All he can do is insist that rational belief requires evidence, which is just the point at issue.

We need to be very clear about the nature of the enterprise in which we are engaged. What we are confronted with is not an argument that *forces* us to be skeptics. Rather we are faced with a paradox. We are inclined to accept each member of a set of propositions we know to be inconsistent. What we seek is a way out of the paradox—a resolution of our inconsistent inclinations. It is not a constraint on the acceptability of a resolution that it appeal to the skeptic. On the contrary, what we seek is a resolution that rescues common sense from the skeptical worries posed by the paradox. If this is the nature of the problem, then it is perfectly acceptable to appeal to certain aspects of our common sense framework in order to achieve a resolution of the paradox. To resolve the paradox is not to demonstrate to the skeptic that we know. Rather it is to demonstrate to ourselves that we can claim to know without paradox.

However, it does not in itself avoid the paradox to point out that we view the denial of radical skeptical hypotheses as rational. For the problem remains that most of us would deny that the extent to which it is rational is sufficient for us to know that skeptical alternatives are false. If it is not sufficient, then by closure principle (1), we fail to know the common sense propositions we think we know.

What this observation about intrinsic rationality does is provide us with the means for generalizing the resolution that proceeds in terms of context-sensitive closure. Let us say that it is reasonable for a subject S to believe a proposition q just in case S possesses sufficient evidence in support of q, or q is intrinsically rational. We can then amend the internal criterion so that an alternative h is relevant if it is not sufficiently reasonable for S to deny h (to believe not-h). In everyday contexts where S believes an ordinary proposition q, on the basis of reason r, a radical skeptical alternative h will not be relevant. The standard yielded by the internal criterion in those contexts is such that the reasonability (viz., the intrinsic rationality) of denying h is sufficient for S to know q on the basis of r. This explains our intuition that we know q.

Of course, the paradox is generated because, upon reflection, we do not think it is sufficiently reasonable for S to deny h so that S knows not-h. But the reasonability of denying h just is the reasonability of believing not-h. By the argument of the previous section, in contexts where the standards are such that not-h is sufficiently reasonable for S to know q, *according to those same standards*, not-h is sufficiently reasonable for S to know not-h. Thus closure holds, relative to a context, and the paradox is avoided.[37]

Why are we reluctant to say that it is not sufficiently reasonable to believe not-h for S to know not-h? Again, focusing on skeptical alternatives can lead us to consider them relevant. In the case of the moderate skeptical hypotheses we discussed earlier, we saw that the fact that the evidence against those hypotheses is statistical, makes the chance of error salient. Clearly, this explanation does not apply to the radical skeptical hypotheses we are currently considering. As we have noted, we have no evidence against them, statistical or otherwise. Rather we view it as intrinsically rational to deny them. But the very fact that the rationality of denying radical skeptical hypotheses is intrinsic makes the chance of error salient. The fact that the denial of the hypotheses is not supported by any independent considerations, underscores our ultimate fallibility. The skeptic calls our attention to the fact that S has no such independent considerations, thereby focusing our attention on the chance of error. This leads us to consider these alternatives as relevant. By the standards that apply in this skeptical context, it is not sufficiently reasonable for S to deny h and S fails to know q (as well as not-h). But his does not change the fact that relative to the standards that apply in everyday contexts, it is sufficiently reasonable for S to deny h so that S knows q (as well as not-h). Again, we often vacillate between skeptical and non-skeptical contexts. The paradox arises from the illusion of closure failure that results from the shifting contexts.

Let us be more precise about the status of the closure principles. As before, principle (1) concerning knowledge holds relative to a context. Consideration of radical skeptical alternatives has forced us to reject principle (4) concerning evidence sufficient for knowledge, even relative to a context. However, our rejection of (4) is mitigated by our acceptance (relative to a context) of the corresponding closure principle concerning reasonability:

> (4′) If q is sufficiently reasonable for S to know q, and S knows that q entails not-h, then not-h is sufficiently reasonable for S to know not-h.

Thus S's visual evidence is sufficient to give him knowledge, e.g., that he sees a zebra, only if it is sufficiently reasonable for S to deny that he is deceived by a Cartesian demon so that S knows he is not so deceived.

VI. Objections and Replies

This completes my proposal regarding how to be a fallibilist. It remains to defend the theory I propose against two objections.

The first concerns our inability to provide a general account of the criteria of relevance. Recall the earlier discussion of the probabilistic criterion of relevance.[38] The result delivered by the application of the criterion depends on how the reference class is specified. And we noted that we are unable to state in general how the reference class is to be specified. This has led critics to have grave doubts about the relevant alternatives response to skepticism.[39]

Why is it a problem if we lack a general account of the criteria of relevance? Ernest Sosa objects that because of this "... the relevant alternatives defense will remain unacceptably occult."[40] But why is it not enough for the relevant alternatives theorist to define "relevance" and then to point out some of the factors that can sometimes account for relevance? Why must he state in general what factors account for relevance? Why must he provide general criteria of relevance?

For example I have defined "relevance" in this way: an alternative (to q) h is relevant (for S) = df S's epistemic position with respect to h precludes S from knowing q. I have also noted that we can account for some of our intuitions regarding relevance by appealing to "probabilistic" considerations—albeit in an imprecise way. Is it incumbent upon the defender of the relevant alternative theory to do more?

The answer to this question will depend on how we construe the relevant alternatives response to skepticism. One way for the relevant alternative theorist to argue would be to *begin* by appealing to criteria of relevance in the abstract. The claim would have to be that one can see simply by reflecting on the concept of relevance that the proposed criteria capture what it is about alternatives that make them relevant. Having gained assent on the correctness of the proposed criteria, the relevant alternatives theorist would then proceed by arguing that when we apply these criteria to skeptical alternatives, we get the result that skeptical alternatives are not relevant. If we were to proceed in this way, then of course, the failure to provide a precise statement of the criteria would undermine the whole approach. Moreover, to appeal in a vague way to probabilistic considerations and then adjust the reference class as required to yield the desired result for each case would render the whole approach *ad hoc*.[41]

But we should not construe the relevant alternatives theorist as employing this argumentative strategy. Even if we did not worry about the precision problem, surely this strategy would be hopeless. We cannot pull criteria of relevance out of thin air. We formulate such criteria by reflecting on the deliverances of our intuition regarding cases. We try to devise criteria that capture those intuitions. We all have intuitions about relevance (the borderline cases notwithstanding). Since "relevance" is defined in terms of knowledge, our intuitions about relevance are at root, intuitions about knowledge. Even the critics of the relevant alternatives approach demonstrate that they have such intuitions when they criticize various proposed criteria for yielding counterintuitive results.

So we should not construe the relevant alternatives theorist as arguing that skeptical alternatives are not relevant because the criteria show it. The non-relevance of skeptical alternatives is a datum provided by our intuitive judgments concerning what we know. It is illuminating to advert to various factors that account for relevance and it would certainly be desirable to have a general account of the criteria of relevance. But surely it does not follow from our inability to provide a general account, that we cannot legitimately apply the concept. Our inability to provide a general account of the criteria of relevance derives from our inability to provide a general account of the criteria of knowledge. If our inability to formulate a general account made it illegitimate to apply a concept, the skeptic could establish his position simply by appealing to the fact that philosophers have been unable to formulate a general account of knowledge.[42]

Again, one might object that it begs the question against the skeptic to appeal to anti-skeptical intuitions about relevance. And there is a sense in which it does. But of course no more than the skeptic begs the question against the relevant alternatives theorist by appealing to his skeptical intuitions about relevance. In this sense, it is impossible for either side of the dispute not to beg the question against the other side. At the risk of being redundant, I stress that the project is not to demonstrate to the skeptic that we know. What we face is a skeptical paradox. What we seek is a solution that is satisfying to us.

Let me conclude by considering one final objection. One might think that the theory I am proposing really does not provide a reply to skepticism, but instead changes the subject. After all, the skeptic might complain that he denies that we ever know relative to the strictest standards.[43] Thus, to argue that we know relative to looser standards is not to address the skeptic at all.

The problem with this objection is that it gets things backwards. For if the theory of relevant alternatives is correct, it is the skeptic who does not address our everyday knowledge attributions. It is the skeptic who changes the subject.

What is truly startling about skepticism, is the claim that all along, in our day to day lives, when we have claimed to know things, we have been wrong—we have been expressing propositions that are literally false. If the skeptic's position is interesting, it is because he challenges our everyday knowledge attributions. The theory of relevant alternatives addresses the challenge by arguing that our everyday knowledge attributions—properly interpreted—are correct. The propositions we actually express and have been expressing all along are literally true. We do know relative to the standards that ordinarily govern those attributions.

Now it is of considerably less interest (although not devoid of interest) that there is some other proposition involving stricter standards that is false. It is not the case that we know relative to skeptical standards. This a fallibilist readily concedes. What a fallibilist denies is that skeptical standards normally govern our everyday knowledge attributions. If we want to be fallibilists, the challenge is to make that position stick, in the face of the skeptical paradoxes. The theory of relevant alternatives, properly construed, shows us how to do just that.[44]

118 / Stewart Cohen

Notes

1. See Dretske [4], [5], Stine [20], Lewis [13], Goldman [7].
2. Perhaps S does not know that he loses because he does not believe that he loses. But, we would feel the same reluctance to say of someone else who believes that S loses, that he knows that S loses.

   Some philosophers, motivated by the lottery paradox have denied that S even has good reasons to believe that he will lose. See Lehrer [12], Pollock [16]. But the example could be changed so as to avoid the considerations that raise the paradox, e.g., we could suppose that S believes a red ball will be drawn from an urn on the basis of his knowledge that $n-1/n$ of the balls in the urn are red.
3. The probability that S loses conditional on Jones testimony is not well-defined here. For purposes of making the comparison, we can view the probability in both cases as epistemic, and assume that as the statistical probability in the well-defined case increases, so does the epistemic probability.
4. See Harman [8], [10].
5. This closure principle may be subject to certain quibbles. For example, S must believe not-h on the basis of his total evidence. But, surely, something very close to it is very intuitive. See Nozick [14].
6. See Pollock [15], Klein [11].
7. This shows the implausibility of the *modus ponens* strategy (inferring the denial of (2), from (1) and (3)) since I presume no one would argue that S could know that Jones will lose the lottery by inferring it from Jones' announced intention that he will be in New York.
8. This is Dretske's account in [4], although he does not put it in just these words; see pp. 1022-23. In [5] Dretske's characterization of a relevant alternative (p. 371) is very close to Stine's in [20], p. 253. I discuss Stine's characterization later in this paper.
9. See Brueckner [2], Sosa [19], Shuger [18], Yougrau [24]. Yougrau perhaps thinks that there are more serious problems.
10. See Goldman [7].
11. See Dretske [4], Goldman [7], Harman [9], Swain [22].
12. See Stine [20].
13. See Dretske [4], Goldman [7], Lewis [13], Stine [20].
14. Some may think that the claim that attributions of knowledge are context sensitive is an *ad hoc* maneuver against the skeptic. In [3], I argue that context sensitivity can be motivated independently of skeptical issues.

    Since on the view I am defending, "knowledge" is an indexical, many of the issues really should be stated metalinguistically. Thus the issue of whether S knows in a context should really be formulated as the issue of whether the sentence "S knows q" is true in that context.

    The closure principle, as well, should be stated metalinguistically: If the sentence "S knows q" is true in context c, and the sentence "S knows that q entails not-h" is true in c, then the sentence "S knows not-h" is true in c. As such, sentence (1) expresses different closure principles in different contexts, each involving a different knowledge relation (where different knowledge relations involve different standards).

Because the metalinguistic formulations are somewhat cumbersome, I will not always use them. But the reader should not be misled by this.

15. Dretske [4], p. 1023.
16. Dretske [4], p. 1016.
17. Stine [20].
18. The careful reader will have noticed that, given Dretske's definition of "relevance", it appears contradictory to say that the negation of a proposition is not relevant. I discuss this further in the text.
19. Stine [20], p. 256.
20. Stine [20], p. 258.
21. Actually, Stine denies that we know on the basis of evidence in perceptual cases. Obviously, we could change the case to a non-perceptual one where Stine would agree that we do have evidence. Perhaps, Stine's view about perceptual knowledge combined with her focus on perceptual cases accounts for her failure to recognize that her general view entails the denial of principle (4). (See text.)
22. The way that I have stated this principle, it may appear as if Stine's view satisfies the principle vacuously. If no evidence is required to know q, then trivially S has sufficient evidence to know q. (This was pointed out to me by Scott Soames.)

    I intend the principle to be read as follows: If e is sufficient evidence for S to know q (on the basis of e),... then e is sufficient evidence for S to know not-h (on the basis of e). Read this way, Stine's view denies the principle.

    This closure principle, like principle (1), may need to be restricted in certain ways. For example, like principle (1), S must believe not-h on the basis of the evidence in order for the evidence to be sufficient for S to know not-h. This restriction avoids counter-examples to (4), pointed out to me by John Pollock, that exploit the fact that S may know each link of a chain of entailment without knowing that the first member of the chain entails the last. As such, without the restriction, iterated applications of principle (4) would result in counter-examples.
23. Stine [20], p. 253.
24. This "internal/external" terminology is currently popular in epistemology, cf. Bonjour [1], Goldman [6], Pollock [17]. I am doubtful that this distinction can be made very precise. Nonetheless, it is suggestive.
25. Some people find purely externalist analyses of knowledge plausible. Others view such analyses as plausible only for perceptual knowledge. I think that purely externalist analyses are plausible only insofar as we view knowledge as not based on evidence. This is why externalist accounts can seem more plausible for perceptual knowledge. Since I view knowledge (even perceptual knowledge) as based on evidence, I take a dim view of externalist theories. For critical discussion of externalist theories, see Bonjour [1] and Pollock [17].
26. A further example demonstrates the implausibility of any account of

relevance that lacks an internal criterion of relevance: Suppose S believes that the earth was once struck by a large meteorite on the basis of having discovered large amounts of iridium in a certain geological stratum. As it turns out, there is a significant correlation between concentrations of iridium in the stratum and meteor strikes. However as far as S's evidence is concerned there is no significant correlation—S has no evidence that counts against competing explanations for the presence of the iridium. Clearly S does not know that the meteor strikes occurred.

27. Actually this principle is too strong and I will later have to weaken it. But, it will be instructive to work with it and see exactly where it goes wrong.

    Also, I use "reason" and "evidence" interchangeably.

28. Because the argument will depend on the internal criterion, I will later have to take back the defense of (4) as a general principle (see note 27). The argument will remain sound as a defense of (4) against the Dretske/Stine counter-example. For now I will continue to assume the correctness of the internal criterion and so I will present the argument as a defense of (4) as a general principle.

29. One might object that I should not assume that each context selects *one* standard for every proposition-alternative pair, that determines how strong S's evidence must be to deny the alternative, in order for S to know the proposition. Rather, we might assume that the standard will vary within one context depending on the proposition and the alternative at issue. So, in context C, the standard for how strong the evidence for denying h must be in order for S to know q, may differ from the standard for how strong the evidence for denying h must be in order for S to know not-h.

    This view assumes a very complex semantics that would greatly exacerbate the problem of how the context determines the standards. But leaving this problem aside, this view allows for principle (4) to fail even relative to a context, only by allowing (4) to be construed in such a way that it does not express a closure principle. For if the antecedent and consequent of (4) express propositions involving different knowledge relations, i.e., knowledge relative to different standards, then we can not view (4) as expressing a closure principle. Again, exactly which set is supposed to be closed?

    Also, the reader should bear in mind that "relevance" is used here as a technical term. Given my definition of "relevance", there is nothing odd about the negation of a proposition q not being a relevant alternative to q.

30. Stine briefly mentions that one might take this view, but rejects it (without explanation.) See [20], pp. 258-59.

31. I am not sure what determines whether the alternative is relevant by the internal standard or the external standard or both.

32. Jonathan Vogel [24] has arrived, independently, at a similar account. However, he draws a different conclusion.

33. Here I am indebted to Gilbert Harman (in conversation).

34. Some people object to attributing knowledge to S that he will lose the

lottery since it would then be hard to explain why he buys a ticket. However, when S buys a ticket, he is thinking about the possibility of winning and so he will probably not attribute knowledge that he loses to himself. The salience of the alternative that he wins will make that alternative relevant in that context. Since *he* does not believe that he knows he will lose, there is no difficulty in explaining why he buys the ticket.

Moreover, even if he does attribute knowledge to himself that he loses (and the attribution is correct relative to the standards of that context), it might still be rational for him to bet against his losing, provided the odds that he gets are favorable (unlike actual lotteries). Notice that the same is true of the case where S comes to know that he loses on the basis of testimony. Even though he knows that he loses (in that context), it might still be rational to believe that he wins if he is given odds that are favorable relative to the probability of false testimony.

Finally there is no difficulty in reconciling the fact that *we* can know S will lose with the fact that S buys a ticket.

35. I am indebted to David Lewis for this observation (in conversation).

36. Will h be relevant on the external criterion? If, e.g., there is a demon who often deceives us, then this alternative will be relevant. Barring circumstances like this, it will not be relevant. Does this show that we do not know whether we know (in everyday contexts)? No, because these alternatives will fail to be relevant (in those contexts) to whether we know that we know, as well.

These considerations make it clear that skeptical arguments exploit the internal criterion of relevance and thus demonstrate why purely externalist "solutions" to skepticism are so unsatisfying.

37. In effect, I have argued that we know radical skeptical alternatives are false without evidence, in contexts where they are not relevant. Do I, then, agree with Stine after all?

Stine has a *general* view that we know non-relevant alternatives are false without evidence. I have argued that with the exception of radical skeptical alternatives, we know non-relevant alternatives are false on the bases of evidence. It strikes me as highly implausible that we know, e.g., that the zebras are not cleverly disguised mules, yet none of our evidence about the probability of such a deception plays a role in our knowing.

38. Because of the way that relevant alternative theories have been formulated, the discussions in the literature have concerned the external criterion.

39. See Bruckner [2], Shuger [18], Sosa [19], Yourgrau [25].

40. See [19], p. 585.

41. See Sosa [19].

42. It is important to note that if the lack of precision in the criteria of relevance is a problem for the fallibilist, it is a problem for the skeptic as well. For the skeptic must account for the fact that in everyday life, we are strongly inclined to say we know many things. Since these intuitions are *prima facie* evidence against the skeptic, he must explain

them away.

The most promising strategy available to the skeptic (see Stroud [21], Unger [23]) is to claim that in these cases, while it is literally false that we know, nonetheless it is in some way appropriate (serves some social function) for us to say we know. Thus, in Goldman's example, if there are no barn replicas around, although it is literally false that S knows, there can still be many purposes for which it is useful to distinguish such a case from cases where there are lots of replicas around. So according to the skeptic, our everyday pattern of knowledge attributions marks a distinction between cases where it is appropriate to say we know and cases where it is not. But in all cases, the skeptic maintains, it is literally false that we know.

If the skeptic argues in this way, and it is hard to see how he can avoid it, then he needs criteria of relevance as much as the fallibilist does. The only difference is that the alternatives distinguished by the criteria are for the fallibilist relevant to the *truth* of knowledge attributions, whereas for the skeptic, they are relevant to the *appropriateness* of knowledge attributions. Since the skeptic needs criteria of relevance as much as the fallibilist does, our inability to be precise about the criteria should not incline us toward skepticism. If both sides of a dispute share a problem, the existence of the problem cannot favor one side of the dispute against the other.

43. See Yourgrau [21] p. 188.
44. I am indebted to Jamie Dreier, Gilbert Harman, Keith Lehrer, David Lewis, John Pollock, Michael Smith, and Scott Soames for helpful discussion of these issues. I am especially indebted to Jonathan Vogel for insightful comments over the course of many discussions that have helped me to clarify and develop my ideas, and for pressing me to construct a view that preserves closure (although he would not accept my conclusions.)

References

[1]   Bonjour, Laurence: "Externalist Theories of Empirical Knowledge," *Midwest Studies in Philosophy*, Vol. V, 53-73 (Minneapolis, 1980), Peter A. French, Theodore E. Uehling, Jr., Howard K. Wettstein, (editors).

[2]   Brueckner, Anthony L.: "Skepticism and Epistemic Closure," *Philosophical Topics*, (Fall, 1985), 89-117.

[3]   Cohen, Stewart: "Knowledge, Context, and Social Standards," *Synthese* (October, 1987), 3—26.

[4]   Dretske, Fred: "Epistemic Operators", *Journal of Philosophy*, (Dec. 1970), 1007-23.

[5]   Dretske, Fred: "The Pragmatic Dimension of Knowledge", *Philosophical Studies*, 40 (1981), 363-78.

[6]   Goldman, Alvin: "The Internalist Conception of Justification", *Midwest Studies in Philosophy*, Vol. V, 27-51, (Minneapolis, 1980), Peter A. French, Theodore E. Uehling, Jr., Howard K. Wettstein, (editors).

[7] Goldman, Alvin: "Discrimination and Perceptual Knowledge, " *Journal of Philosophy*, 73.20 (1976), 771-91.

[8] Harman, Gilbert: *Thought*, (Princeton, 1974).

[9] Harman, Gilbert: "Reasoning and Evidence One Does Not Possess," *Midwest Studies in Philosophy*, Vol. V, 163-82, Peter A. French, Theodore E. Uehling, Jr., Howard K. Wettstein, (editors).

[10] Harman, Gilbert: *Change in View* (MIT, 1986).

[11] Klein, Peter: *Certainty*, (University of Minnesota, 1981).

[12] Lehrer, Keith: *Knowledge*, (Oxford, 1974).

[13] Lewis, David: "Scorekeeping in a Language Game,"*Journal of Philosophical Logic*, 8 (1979) 339-59.

[14] Nozick, Robert: *Philosophical Explanations*, (Harvard, 1981).

[15] Pollock, John: *Knowledge and Justification*, (Princeton, 1974).

[16] Pollock, John: "Epistemology and Probability", *Synthese*, (May, 1983), 231-52.

[17] Pollock, John: *Contemporary Theories of Knowledge*.

[18] Shuger, Scott: "Knowledge and its Consequences", *American Philosophical Quarterly*, (April, 1983).

[19] Sosa, Ernest: "On Knowledge And Context," *Journal of Philosophy* (October, 1986), 584-85.

[20] Stine, G.C.: "Skepticism, Relevant Alternatives, and Deductive Closure," *Philosophical Studies*, 29 (1976), 249-61.

[21] Stroud, Barry: *The Significance of Philosophical Skepticism* (Oxford, 1974)

[22] Swain, Marshall: "Reasons, Causes, and Knowledge," *Journal of Philosophy* 75 (1978).

[23] Unger, Peter: *Philosophical Relativity* (Minneapolis, 1974)

[24] Vogel, Jonathan: "Are There Counterexamples to the Closure Principle" (forthcoming)

[25] Yourgrau, Palle: "Knowledge and Relevant Alternatives," *Synthese*, (May, 1983), 175-90.

Philosophical Perspectives, 2, Epistemology, 1988

COHERENCE, JUSTIFICATION, AND CHISHOLM*

Keith Lehrer
University of Arizona and University of Graz

I have three objectives in this paper written to celebrate the philosophical career of R. M. Chisholm. The first is to clarify a conception of knowledge that is my explicandum. The second is to present an explication of this conception. The third task is to relate what I shall propose to the work of Chisholm. I shall assume that justification is a condition of knowledge. This justification aims at the attainment of truth and the avoidance of error. Information that is not evaluated as conducive to these goals falls short of knowledge even if the information is correct. The evaluation of information as being conducive to these goals is based on a background system. Coherence with such a system yields positive evaluation, and, therefore, the attainment of the objectives depends on correctness of the background system. Justification must not depend on errors in the background system if it is to yield knowledge.

A Conception of Knowledge. The conception of knowledge that concerns me is one in which a person has information and knows that the information is correct on the basis of some background system used to evaluate the information in question. If a person or my senses inform me that p, but I do not know whether the information that p is correct, then I do not know that p, in the required sense. If, for example, I do not believe that the person or my senses are a trustworthy source of information, then I do not know what they tell me is true, that is, I do not know that p. This conception of knowledge differs from that discussed by Dretske and Goldman in which a person is said to know that p when the person is correctly or reliably informed that p and believes that p as a result.[1] Consider the following argument:

1. S is correctly (reliably) informed that p and believes that p as a result.
2. If S is correctly (reliably) informed that p and believes that p as a result, then S knows that p.
3. S knows that p.

Now consider the following counterargument:

1C. S has been correctly (reliably) informed that p but does not know that the information, that p, is correct.
2C. If S has been correctly (reliably) informed that p but does not know that the information, that p, is correct, then S does not know that p.
3C. S does not know that p.

The conclusions are inconsistent. Obviously, premises (1) and (1C) are consistent with each other. Therefore, either (2) or (2C) must be rejected. I reject (2) on the grounds that a person can be informed, indeed, correctly and reliably informed of something, without having any idea whether they are correctly or reliably informed. It is crucial to notice, moreover, that absence of undermining beliefs is not sufficient. A person can fail to have any idea whether the information that she receives is correct without having any beliefs to the effect that the information is untrustworthy, and she lacks the required sort of knowledge as a result. Those who affirm that some process of receiving information, or some process of reliable belief formation suffices together with true belief to yield knowledge must reject (2C), but I take (2C) as a condition of adequacy for the conception of knowledge I am interested in analyzing. According to this conception, a person must at least believe that the information, that p, is trustworthy, or the person receiving the information does not know that p. A person believes that the information, that p, is trustworthy only if they believe that the origin or source of the information is trustworthy.

Can we say that a person who is correctly informed that p and believes the information, that p, to be trustworthy knows that p? Not in the sense of knowledge in question. For I may be correctly informed of something and believe that the information is correct when the source of the information is untrustworthy. If someone informs me that p who was not in a position to ascertain whether p was true but happens, as luck would have it, to be correct, then I may fail to know that p because my informant does not know that p. What is true of the information I receive from another is also true of the information I receive from my senses. I must believe the information and the source of the information to be trustworthy, and I must be right in this belief, or else I am ignorant. Moreover, it is clear that this is not sufficient. I must believe that I am a trustworthy evaluator of these matters, and I must be correct in this too in order to know.

All this requires more qualification and defense than I can afford. Some brief remarks may be helpful. A person may believe something without reflecting upon it. A person who trusts another without hesitation believes, in the sense that concerns me, that the person they trust is trustworthy, provided, of course, that they understand, as any normal person does, the idea that someone is trustworthy. It is in this sense that a person believes that they are trustworthy as an evaluator of information. They trust themselves and understand that they are trustworthy. A question naturally arises as to whether this conception leads to regress. The regress stops with the conviction that one is a trustworthy evaluator. If one believes one is trustworthy and one is trustworthy, then being right is not a matter of luck but a result, in the normal case, of that very trustworthiness.

Similar remarks apply to the question of whether such justification rests upon a foundation. One could say that it rest on the foundation of the correct conviction of ones own trustworthiness. One may defend the claim that one is trustworthy, of course, but it is difficult not to reason in a circle when doing so, as Reid noted long ago.[2] Following Reid, I should agree that there are beliefs and principles that we are justified in believing without reasoning, though these beliefs and principles hang together like links in a chain. The chain is a system of beliefs and a belief is a link in the chain if it fits or coheres with the system in the appropriate manner. I agree with Reid, and with Chisholm, that there are beliefs that are justified or evident without recourse to reasoning.[3] The justification of such beliefs is not generated by inference. We may, nevertheless, explain why such beliefs are justified in terms of the way they fit into a system of beliefs without assuming that they are inferred from such beliefs.

The sort of knowledge that concerns me is coherence with various systems. The most prominent system is what one accepts in the interests of obtaining truth and avoiding error. But such a system, though aiming at truth, may fall short in many ways. One may think that one is trustworthy in circumstances when one is not. There are many such examples, old ones involving demons, and new ones involving brains in vats, old ones involving wax fruit, new ones involving barn facades. The point is the same. One may assume that ones senses are trustworthy when they are not, or at least not so trustworthy as one believes. Or, as is often noted since Gettier, some error may enter into what one accepts in such a way as to defeat the justification resulting from coherence with what one accepts.[4] There are many ways in which the errors a person makes might be corrected. My proposal, which I shall attempt to articulate in detail below, is an attempt to explicate a simple idea. The idea is that if there is no way that the justification resulting from coherence with the person's system of belief can be defeated by either depriving the person of a false belief, or by substituting the denial of that false belief in his system, then the person has the sort of justification that links conviction with truth and reason so as to yield knowledge.

The Analysis: Undefeated Justification. We are now ready to consider the sort of positive account that combines truth and conviction with reason in such a way as to provide an answer to the socratic question—What must we add to true belief to obtain knowledge? There is a form of justification that is necessary to providing the answer. A belief is justified in the requisite sense only if either it is more reasonable than the competitors of that belief in terms of the system of background beliefs, or the competitors of the belief can be neutralized in terms of that system.

Following Chisholm, I take a comparative notion of reasonableness as an undefined normative notion.[5] Departing from Chisholm somewhat, the notion I assume is conditional on a background system. The background system is a system of things accepted in the interest of obtaining truth and avoiding error. The notion of acceptance replaces the notion of belief in my analysis. I assume, in contrast to some foundationalist theories, that whether it is more reasonable to accept one thing than another depends on a background system used to evaluate incoming information and the source of such information as trustworthy. The positive evaluation or coherence with the background system yields a kind of subjective or personal justification which is a necessary condition of the required sort of knowledge. Such justification is not sufficient, however. The background assumptions yielding a positive evaluation of trustworthiness may be erroneous.

It will be useful to have some definitions to clarify these notions. First let us define the requisite sort of background system which I call the *acceptance* system.

> D1. A system X is an acceptance system of S if and only if X contains only statements of the form—S accepts that p—attributing to S exactly those things that S accepts with the objective of obtaining truth and avoiding error with respect to the specific thing accepted.

Acceptance can have many objectives, only one of which is the obtaining of truth and the avoidance of error. Moreover, that general objective might be furthered by accepting something that one knows to be false, if, for example, accepting that one falsehood was fecund in the acceptance of other truths. Such acceptance is not what is required here, however, and that is why I have added that S must be concerned to forward that general objective with respect to the specific thing accepted. What is meant may be put by saying the person must be furthering those objectives in accepting the specific thing accepted no matter what else the person might accept.

I define without comment a generic notion of justification on the basis of a system and then define the notions used to define that notion taking only a comparative notion of reasonableness as primitive.

> D2. S is justified in accepting p at t on the basis of system X at t if and only if p coheres with X of S at t.
>
> D3. p coheres with X of S at t if and only if all competitors of p are beaten or neutralized for S on X at t.
>
> D4. c competes with p for S on X at t if and only if it is more reasonable for S to accept that p on the assumption that c is false than on the assumption that c is true on the basis of X at t.
>
> D5. p beats c for S on X at t if and only if c competes with p for S on X at t, and it is more reasonable for S to accept p than to accept c on X at t.
>
> D6. n neutralizes c as a competitor of p for S on X at t if and only if c competes with p for S on X at t, the conjunction of c and n does not compete with p for S

> on X at t, and it is as reasonable for S to accept the
> conjunction of c and n as to accept c alone on X at t.

The motivation for the definitions offered is to illustrate the manner in which justification depends on a background system. Let us consider an example. Wendy tells me that Fred Feldman's book is now in print.[6] Am I justified in believing this? My background information includes that I edit a series in which the book appears and that Wendy works for the publisher and is trustworthy about when books appear in the series. Now suppose some skeptic proposes to me that Wendy is lying. The claim that Wendy is lying competes with information that the book is in print, but, on the basis of my background information, it is more reasonable for me to accept that Wendy is telling the truth and that the book has been published than to accept that Wendy is lying.

Imagine the skeptic persists and says, "Well, you know people sometimes lie about when books are in print." Now this skeptical innuendo does compete with the thing I believe in a sort of indirect way. It would be more reasonable for me to accept that Feldman's book is in print on the assumption that people do not ever lie about when books are in print than on the assumption that they do sometimes lie. Moreover, it is quite reasonable for me to accept that people do sometimes lie about these matters. But this skeptical innuendo, though it cannot be beaten, can be neutralized by conjoining the reply that Wendy is not lying. Of course, the reasonableness of accepting the latter depends on my background information about Wendy.

Moreover, appeal to background information shows how one may deal with the skeptic and skeptical alternatives. One may consider all skeptical alternatives as relevant, but such alternatives are beaten or neutralized. It is more reasonable for me to accept that I now see a monitor than to accept that I am asleep and dreaming, or that I am deceived by a powerful demon, or that I am a brain in a vat. To say that it is more reasonable for me to accept what I do on the basis of my acceptance system than to accept the skeptical hypotheses is not to prove those hypotheses to be in error. My background system might itself be challenged. It is, however, still true that I am justified in accepting what I do in terms of my background system. I have here assumed, of course, that my background system is my acceptance system as defined in D1. The sense of justification thus obtained is personal justification which may be simply defined by reference to D2 as follows.

D7. S is personally justified in accepting that p at t if and only if S is justified in accepting that p on the basis of the acceptance system of S at t.

On the basis of the acceptance system of S, S can evaluate incoming information, and when the evaluation is positive, the information will cohere with that system, that is, all competitors will be beaten or neutralized. As the skeptic or the reliablist might note, the acceptance system might be entirely erroneous and, therefore, in no way insures that the information received is trustworthy. Though personal justification is necessary for knowledge, it is not sufficient.

What is sufficient? The answer is contained in the criticism. The justification obtained from the acceptance system must be such that it cannot be defeated by the correction of any error in that system. Note that there are two ways that an error might be corrected. A *weak* correction of an error would result from simply deleting the error from the system as well as any error entailed by it thus obtaining a proper subsystem of the original system. A *strong* correction of an error would result from replacing the error with the acceptance of its denial as well as replacing any error entailed by it in the same way. There is thus a set of systems, a set of sets of statements attributing beliefs to S, that can be constructed from the acceptance system of a person by making one or more weak or strong corrections in the acceptance system of the person. Let us call this the *ultrasystem* of the person and understand it in such a say that it includes the acceptance system as well as any system resulting from making one or more weak or strong corrections in the acceptance system. Undefeated justification is justification on the basis of all the members of the ultrasystem.[7] If a person is justified on the basis of each member of the ultrasystem, then we are assured that the justification does not rest on any error in the acceptance system. It is necessary to consider systems resulting from weak corrections as well as strong corrections in that strong corrections may introduce some new form of justification created by introducing the denial of something erroneously accepted. Similarly, weak corrections may unblock some form of justification not appreciated by the subject. We may now define undefeated justification as follows:

D8. S is justified in accepting that p at t in a way that is undefeated if and only if S is justified in accepting p at t on the basis of every system that is a member of the ultrasystem of S at t.

D9. M defeats the personal justification of S for accepting p at t if and only if S is personally justified in accepting p at t, but S is not justified in accepting p at t on system M at t where M is member of the ultrasystem of S at t.

Definition D8 is crucial for our account, and D9 is not. The latter definition is introduced only to clarify the notion of defeat for whatever intrinsic interest that may have. From D8 it follows that if S is justified in accepting that p at t in a way that is undefeated, then S is personally justified in accepting that p at t. Indeed, the idea behind the definition is that personal justification be undefeated. Moreover, if a person is justified in accepting information that he or she receives in a way that is undefeated because he or she has evaluated the information as trustworthy on the basis of his or her acceptance system, then the information really is trustworthy. Otherwise, the justification would be defeated by some member of the ultrasystem. Assuming, as I do, that people have, as part of their background system, beliefs about when information is trustworthy and when it is not, justification will be undefeated only if those beliefs are correct.

The reply to the skeptic who hypothesizes some invincible deceiver is that if the hypothesis is correct, then our justification is defeated and we lack knowledge. On the other hand, if we are trustworthy at evaluating information, as we assume, then we know that the information we receive from our senses and other faculties is correct, and we possess knowledge. Undefeated justification supplies us with the answer to the socratic question. It does so in an elegant manner, moreover, in that knowledge turns out to be undefeated justification. I propose the following equivalence for knowledge:

E. S knows that p at t if and only if S is justified in accepting p at t in a way that is undefeated.

Undefeated justification entails that S accepts that p at t trivially, and it entails that p is true in that the falsity of p would ensure that one member of the ultrasystem would be a system in which S accepts the denial of p. Thus, the proposed notion of undefeated justification is equivalent to knowledge. I do not claim that this is, however, a definition. The equivalence depends on a psychological assumption, to wit, that we make certain natural assumptions about the trustworthiness of ourselves, our facilities, and the testimony of others which become modified through experience. Those assumptions are, as Reid averred, part of our natural constitution. Given our constitution, however, the conditions of knowledge can be simplified as above. I do not claim that this simple equivalence concerning knowledge holds for all possible worlds. I do claim that it is an adequate account of the knowledge of actual human being in the actual world.

Relation to Chisholm. I should now like to compare the sort of theory that Chisholm has developed over the years and the sort of theory that I am still in the process of articulating. The similarity that is the most marked is that I follow Chisholm in supposing an objective of epistemology is the analysis of knowledge. Another, more distinctive, is that I assume some comparative notion of reasonableness must be taken as a primitive normative term for the explication of a justification condition of knowledge. At one time, when I wrote *Knowledge*, I thought that a comparative notion of probability, an essentially nonnormative notion, would suffice for the analysis of justification.[8] I now think that is a mistake and that naturalized epistemology, however much in vogue, is a mistake. I also assume, though I have not made this at all central, that there are some things that we are justified in accepting without reasoning. That is a good deal to share in common. Moreover, where I differ from Chisholm, I am indebted to things that he has said and written for the fundamental conceptions that I hold. This paper being a contribution to a conference celebrating Chisholm's remarkable career, it might be acceptable for me to explain how I extracted my own views from Chisholm's.

I was most influenced, because I read it at the most formative period of my life, by *Perceiving: A Philosophical Study*.[9] This is a remarkable book. In my opinion, it was the basis for his further thought, and it is the most important book in the English language on perception and epistemology written in this century, perhaps in any century. In this book, we find the analysis of knowledge based on a primitive comparative term, "more worthy of belief". The later comparative notion of reasonableness permitted us to compare different doxastic states, but the primitive comparative epistemic term remained the basis of his definition of epistemic terms. In the same book, we find the articulation of epistemic principles, there said to be synthetic *apriori*. They were principles having a kind of metaphysical necessity as became clearer in the *Theory of Knowledge*. It was also in *Perceiving* that Chisholm articulated his tree of justification where each perceptual claim increasing in content required some *independent information* to justify it in conjunction with the perceptual claim of the next lower level.[10] In the *Theory of Knowledge*, Chisholm explored the question of how we are to select the appropriate epistemic principles. He said that we should select them in such a way as to respect the dual objectives of avoiding believing what is false and, at the same time, attempting to believe as much as we can of what is true.

It is the nature of the student to question his master. When I began to question, the first thing that occurred to me was the matter of the synthetic *apriori*, the metaphysically necessary nature, of the epistemic principles, those principles telling us the conditions under with something is reasonable, evident, and so forth. The principles always looked contingent to me. I saw, of course, that the assumption that such principles were empirical would lead us to reason in a circle if we attempted to justify them by appeal to perceptual beliefs. Nevertheless, it seemed to me to be a contingent fact about us, one grounded in our contingent nature, that beliefs of a specific kind, very simple perceptual beliefs, very simple memory beliefs, for example, were evident. Moreover, these simple beliefs, like that one sees that something is red or that one sees that something is moving, seemed a good candidate for beliefs that are evident in themselves, evident without reasoning, for one clear reason. It is natural to suppose that, given our nature, such beliefs were almost always true.

It may have been the case that my reading of Reid, under the influence of Chisholm and Taylor, made this seem persuasive. Reid held that it was a first principle that such beliefs were true, that, as he put it, those qualities and objects really do exist that we clearly and distinctly perceive. For Reid, the first principles concerned truth, and as I reflected on Chisholm's own explanation for why he selected the principles he did, namely, that they give us the appropriate balance between the objective of avoiding error and that of attaining truth, it seemed to me that Chisholm was assuming, if only implicitly, that his principles of reasonable and evident belief should be cautious enough not to include beliefs that are frequently in error but strong enough to include those beliefs that are almost always true. If, however, that is the motive, it does not seem to me that the evidentness of our cautious perceptual or our cautious memory beliefs is a synthetic *apriori* or metaphysically necessary principle. As Reid noted, our being right about these matters is the result of the way we are fabricated, of our constitution.[11] Of course, Chisholm may reply that epistemic principles are, like principle of ethics, principles that tell us about what it is reasonable to believe and nothing about the truth or falsity of those beliefs. He may then add that it is reasonableness rather than truth that we should seek, unreasonableness rather than error that we should avoid, thus avoiding the objection. Chisholm now seems to have gone in that direction, and that is one consistent way of developing his earlier ideas.

I went the other way. I assumed that principles are based on our conception of those beliefs as ones that are true, or that are almost always true. This rests on a factual assumption about our faculties, consciousness, perception or memory, that they are dependable guides to truth. If we did not assume that, I doubt that we would agree that such beliefs are evident or beyond reasonable doubt without the support of argument. It is a standard philosophical undertaking, much beloved by philosophers who have a taste for logic and order, to see how little they need to assume in order to reconstruct the edifice of common sense. It is worthy enterprise. It has, however, also seemed important to me to reconstruct the edifice on as natural a basis as possible. To say that the basis is natural is to say that we give an account of why we think general principles and particular beliefs are justified that accords with correct beliefs of humanity as to why we think these things are justified. I can give no proof that this should be a philosophical *desideratum*. It has a feeling of naturalism and realism that I value. I am convinced that the reason that people think that beliefs of a general kind are justified is that they think that particular beliefs of that kind are true, or almost always true, and the reason people think that particular beliefs are justified is that they think that beliefs of that kind are trustworthy guides to truth. And that is why coherence yields justification.

There was another pair of strains in Chisholm's work that may have influenced me yet more strongly. Particularly in seminars, which it has been my privilege to participate in over the years, I have been attentive to conflict concerning the influence of subjective factors on what is evident. Suppose I am appeared to in a certain way. Does it automatically follow, as Chisholm suggested early, that it is evident to me that I am appeared to in that way? Chisholm has seen the need to modify his view to insure that the person can understand being appeared to in that way. But suppose a person does understand and yet is under the influence of some charismatic religious figure who convinces him that he is not appeared to in the way in which he, in fact, is. Is it evident to the person that he is appeared to in the way he is, though he disbelieves this, or does his disbelief render it less than evident? Is the person justified in believing that he is appeared to in the way he is, though he disbelieves this, or is he not justified in believing that because he disbelieves it? Suppose I see an apple, but for no reason of any merit, believe it to be made of wax. Am I justified in believing that I see an apple, though I disbelieve it, or am I not justified in believing that I see an apple because I disbelieve that I see one? I think intuition pulls in two directions. The problem is that there is both a subjective and an objective sense of these epistemic terms. That led me to distinguish two notions of justification, first a subjective one and then one based on truth. Moreover, the examples in question need not have involved disbelief to generate the problem. It would suffice that I believe something that sheds doubt on whether I am appeared to in the way I, in fact, am or on whether I see what I, in fact, do.

That leaves us with our fundamental agreement, that there are basic normative conceptions essential to knowledge. Chisholm in his earlier work claimed that there are first principles that do not depend for their justification on any background assumptions. I think that background assumption, like the *independent information* of *Perceiving*, are always actually assumed. In his most recent work in his *Self-Profile*, Chisholm lays great stress on background assumptions as well.[12] He affirms that any uncontradicted belief of a person at a time has some presumption in its favor at this time, and that any undisconfirmed belief of a person at a time is acceptable for the person at that time. Whether a belief is uncontradicted or undisconfirmed depends on the other beliefs a person has at that time, on his system of beliefs. Perceptual taking and self-presenting states continue to yield what is reasonable and evident, but now in conjunction with acceptability, which depends on the background system of beliefs. Moreover, a single reasonable belief combined with acceptability and concurrence among other beliefs, elevates those other beliefs to the level of the reasonable. Similarly, a single evident belief combined with reasonableness and concurrence among other beliefs elevates those other beliefs to the level of the evident. It is clear that various forms of coherence play a central role in Chisholm's epistemology, so much so that I find myself largely in agreement with what Chisholm writes.

My only residual objection is that is seems to me that beliefs about my trustworthiness in matters pertaining to the way I am appeared to and what I see, if acceptable, if a member of a concurrent set, and if correct, would suffice to yield particular justified beliefs concerning how I am appeared to or what I see without appeal to special postulates. If, for example, I believe that I am never wrong about the way I am appeared to, if that belief were acceptable, a member of a concurrent set of beliefs, and moreover, a correct belief, that would seem sufficient to assure that when I believe I am appeared to in some way, I am justified. I think, in fact, that the notion of concurrence may be stronger than necessary to yield justified beliefs of this sort and that coherence would suffice. I do not, however, object to the postulates concerning perceptual takings and the self-presenting. I would only contend that they are contingent truths that can be justified because of the way they cohere with our acceptance system and the various purifications thereof. Technicalities aside, I find myself more in agreement with Chisholm than at any previous point. My work on consensus leads me to think it is probable that we are right.

It is the strains in Chisholm's thought, and sometimes the strain in Chisholm's thought, that has led me to where I am. It is mark of his genius that the most parsimonious prose can contain enough complexity to fuel a theory different from his own. It is a mark of the magnanimity of his generous character that one can turn his work in a direction he did not intend, and perhaps did not welcome, while maintaining a feeling of comraderie in the philosophical enterprise he has created. The truth is hard to find, and some despair, but the nobility of the undertaking, the nobility of Chisholm's undertaking, ennobles our lives.

Notes

*Research for this paper was supported by a grant from the National Science Foundation and a fellowship from the John Simon Guggenheim Memorial Foundation. I am indebted to the members of the Summer Institute in the Theory of Knowledge, Boulder, Colorado, 1986, sponsored by the National Endowment for the Humanities under the auspices of the Council for Philosophical Studies for helpful criticism of the ideas contained in this paper, to Scott Sturgeon and Peter Klein for comments on an earlier version, and to K. Kuys for a positive proposal cited below. The section entitled *The Analysis: Undefeated Justification* overlaps with and is further developed in "Metaknowledge: Undefeated Justification" forthcoming in Synthese. An earlier version of this paper was read at a conference in honor of Roderick Chisholm at Brown University, November, 1986.

1. Dretske, F. I., *Knowledge and the Flow of Information*, Basil Blackwell, Oxford, 1981, and Goldman, A. I., *Epistemology and Cognition,* Harvard University Press, Cambridge, 1986.
2. Cf. *Thomas Reid's Inquiry and Essays*, Beanblossom, R. E., and Lehrer, K., Hackett, Indianapolis, 1983, pp. 87-103.
3. Cf. Chisholm, R. M., *Theory of Knowledge*, second edition, Prentice-Hall, Englewood Cliffs, 1967.
4. Cf. Lehrer, K., "The Gettier Problem and the Analysis of Knowledge," in *Justification and Knowledge*, Pappas, G., ed., Reidel, Dordrecht, 1981.
5. Chisholm, op. cit..
6. Feldman, F., *Doing the Best We Can*, Reidel, Dordrecht, 1986. This example is not fictional. I edit the series in which Feldman's book appeared. Wendy told the truth.
7. This proposal was suggested to me by a similar proposal by Kuys, T., in "Coherentism, Falliblism, and Scepticism" unpublished. See also, Swain, M., *Reasons and Knowledge*, Cornell University Press, Ithaca, 1981, for an account of justification similar to that offered here.
8. Lehrer, K., *Knowledge*, Clarendon Press, Oxford, 1974.
9. Chisholm, R. M., *Perceiving: A Philosophical Study*, Cornell University Press, Ithaca, 1957.
10. Chisholm, ibid..
11. Reid, op. cit..
12. Cf. Bogdan, R., *Roderick M. Chisholm*, Reidel, Dordrecht, 1986, pp. 43-48.

Philosophical Perspectives, 2, Epistemology, 1988

KNOWLEDGE IN CONTEXT, SKEPTICISM IN DOUBT
The Virtue of our Faculties

Ernest Sosa
Brown University

A. Knowledge and Context

Recent epistemology makes knowledge context-relative in many and sundry ways. According to Wittgenstein, ordinary knowledge flows on a riverbed of givens (assumptions, presumptions, background beliefs, things taken for granted), none of which amount to knowledge. Such convictions may be regarded as "beyond being *justified* or *unjustified*; as it were, as something *animal*" (*On Certainty*, par. 359). They provide me with "the *substratum* of all my enquiring and asserting (par. 162)." This substratum is not accepted on the basis of reasoning. "No: it is the inherited background against which I distinguish between true and false (par. 94)."

For J.L. Austin you know when you can rule out knowledgeably all relevant ways in which you might turn out wrong. And what is or is not relevant will vary with context; also, if you happen to consider any of the irrelevant ways in which you might turn out wrong, you must assume that it is not a way in which you do in fact turn out wrong, even if you cannot knowledgeably rule it out at the time.

> Knowing it's a 'real' goldfinch isn't in question in the ordinary case when I say I know it's a goldfinch: reasonable precautions only are taken. But when it *is* called in question, in *special* cases, then I make sure it's a real goldfinch in ways essentially similar to those in which I made sure it was a goldfinch...(J.L.Austin, "Other Minds," in his *Philosophical*

Papers (Oxford:Oxford University Press, 1961), p. 56). These
special cases where doubts arise and require resolving, are
contrasted with the normal cases which hold the field *unless*
there is some special suggestion that deceit, etc., is involved,
and deceit, moreover, of an intelligible kind in the circumstances, that is, of a kind that can be looked into because
motive, etc., is specially suggested. There is no suggestion
that I *never* know what other people's emotions are, nor yet
that in particular cases I might be wrong for no special
reason or in no special way (*Ibid.*, p. 81).

Such forms of contextualism have gained many adherents in recent decades. Irrelevant alternatives (ways in which one might be
wrong) are now widely thought not to require ruling out with the
backing of reasons. Of those who take this approach, some view irrelevant alternatives as things one can rule out *with justification*
despite the lack of any reasoned case against them. Gail Stine, for
example, adopts this view—but provides no explanation of how one
gets to be justified in ruling out such irrelevant alternatives, not all
of which can be denied as *a priori* obviously impossible.[1]

If such "irrelevant" alternatives are contingent possibilities, how
do we know them to be false? According to some, it's the community's approval that enables us legitimately to rule them out. With intellectual as with physical goods we are entitled to what "society let's
us get away with," and there is nothing more to the entitlement than
society's largesse. Thus Richard Rorty:

[We] can think of knowledge as a relation to propositions,
and thus of justification as a relation between the
propositions in question and other propositions from which
the former may be inferred. Or we may think of both
knowledge and justification as privileged relations to the
objects those propositions are about. If we think in the first
way, we will see no need to end the potentially infinite
regress of propositions-brought-forward-in-defense-of-other-
propositions. It would be foolish to keep conversation
going on the subject once everyone, or the majority, or the
wise, are satisfied, but of course we *can*. If we think of
knowledge in the second way, we will want to get behind
reasons to causes, beyond argument to compulsion from the
object known, to a situation in which argument would be

not just silly but impossible . .To reach that point is to reach the foundations of knowledge.[2]
Explaining rationality and epistemic authority by reference to what society lets us say rather than the latter by the former, is the essence of what I shall call "epistemological behaviorism," an attitude common to Dewey and Wittgenstein.[3]

Rorty is not alone. David Annis had indeed already published a defense of such contextualism, including the following passage:

Consider the case either where the objector-group does not require S to have reasons for his belief that h in order to be in a position to have knowledge and where they accept his claim, or the case where they require reasons and accept his claim. In either case there is no regress of reasons.If an appropriate objector-group, the members of which are critical truth seekers, have no real doubts in the specific issue-context, then the person's belief is justified. The belief has withstood the test of verifically motivated objectors.[4]

According to others,it is not the approval of society that enables us to deal legitimately with irrelevant alternatives. Instead, it is rather the objective improbability or impossibility of irrelevant alternatives that renders them negligible or rejectable, if considered at all, even in the absence of any inferential or argumentative backing.[5]

Barry Stroud agrees with the strategy of trying to "...find some way to avoid the requirement [e.g.] that we must know we are not dreaming if we are to know anything about the world around us."[6] For him a way must accordingly be found to deny that "...in order to know something, we must rule out a possibility which is known to be incompatible with our knowing it."[7] Such a strategy is in keeping with the attitude of those who would ignore or dismiss possible ways in which one might be wrong, even absent any knowledge precluding them. In particular, the approaches taken respectively by Wittgenstein, Austin, and Dretske, would permit the neglect or dismissal of various possible ways in which logically one might be wrong, without requiring that one's neglect or dismissal be attended by knowledge or even justification. But the approaches of that ilk taken up by Stroud, either explicitly or by implication (Austin's and, e.g., Dretske's), are all found wanting. For they ill accord with the requirements for simple knowledge commonly imposed in everyday life. Austin's work may suggest the contrary, but that is due to confusion between the requirements for *saying* that one knows, and the requirements for *really* knowing. Reflection on simple and ordinary examples strongly promotes the conclusion that, in everyday life, one's truly attaining knowledge that p requires one not to leave open, not to neglect or dismiss without adequate justification, any possibilities known to one as incompatible with one's attaining such knowledge. Stroud does not resolve this inner tension in his book, and indeed one senses that for him the prospects are dim for any theory of knowledge that would escape skepticism about external surroundings. For such a theory would need to enable the avoidance of a very plausible requirement for the attainment of knowledge: namely, that one rule out appropriately all alternatives known by one as incompatible with one's knowledge.

Knowledge is more confidently placed in context, and skepticism hence in doubt, in recent work by Stewart Cohen, who argues for the relativity of knowledge to epistemic communities.[8] "Being in a position to know" has been my own choice of expression for the requirement of *normal* cognitive equipment combined with the "social requirement" that one not lack or overlook generally known relevant information.[9]*Expert* knowledge would then require not only truth, belief, and justification, but also that one be "in a position to know (from the *expert* point of view)," and similarly *mutatis mutandis* for a layman's knowledge.

Where I have thus favored a *conceptual* relativity of knowledge attributions, however, Cohen favors instead a *contextual* relativity. My proposal has conceived of knowledge attributions as explicitly or implicitly relativized to an epistemic community (actual or possible) or its corresponding standards. For Cohen a knowledge attribution includes no such relativization within its *content* (explicitly *or* implicitly); instead of that, it includes an explicit or implicit indexical (or some kindred resource), such that the *context* of attribution determines the community or standards relative to which the attribution has truth value. I am not sure how significant this difference may turn out to be, especially in view of the emphasis placed by Cohen on the standards *intended* by the attributor. But it does seem a distinction abstractly worth making for the alternative form of relativization which it provides.[10]

Cohen compares two moves in recent epistemology: first, the

relativization of knowledge attributions to an epistemic community or its correlative standards, by way of the requirement that the subject satisfy the (conceptually *or* contextually) specified standards; and, second, the appeal to relevance of alternatives in response to the skeptic. An important similarity is then found in the two moves. Just as the knowledge attributor can slide his cutoff point up or down the scale of required standards, depending on his intentions (or, perhaps, depending on other features of the context of attribution), so the relevance of an alternative can also vary depending on the context: on *how probable* that alternative is in the context.

These intriguing ideas are worth closer consideration. Knowledge is said to be twice contextual. It is said to be contextual first of all in respect of how sensitive one must be to the weight of evidence in one's possession for or against a belief that p. One's evidence may often provide premises for long and complex arguments that only a genius could see after long concentration. But it can be seen by examples that one's missing such an argument does not necessarily invalidate one's claim to know that p, a claim that of course could not survive a *blatant* inconsistency between one's evidence and the proposition believed (that p). Knowledge is thus said to be contextual in respect of how sensitive one must be to such evidence if it is to be effective in determining whether one knows that p. It is said to be contextual in what, for short, we shall call *the first way*. In addition, knowledge is said to be contextual in a second respect, in respect of which "alternatives" to the proposition that p count as *relevant*. Knowledge is thus said to be contextual in *the second way*.

Even given a fixed subject S, proposition that p, and time of utterance t, the attribution of knowledge that p to S at t will vary in truth value from context of attribution to context of attribution. So it is argued; but what in particular is it about the context that determines the truth value of such an utterance? Presumably it is believed that something in the context determines standards that entail whether or not one is appropriately sensitive to the weight of one's evidence. And presumably it is believed further that something in the context determines how probable an alternative must be (and relative to what factors) in order to be a relevant alternative to P: "relevant" in that it must be ruled out (independently of P) in order that one may know.

Finally, appealing to the irrelevance of skeptical alternatives is now said to be more than just an *ad hoc* response to the skeptic, since there are independent reasons why the truth of an attribution of knowledge is context-dependent. Context *also* determines, with regard to one's evidence, just how sensitive one must be to the bearing of what it contains for or against belief that p, in order to qualify for knowledge that p. (Only the most gifted could be perfectly sensitive, but knowledge is fortunately to be found as well in those less favorably endowed, depending on the context.)

Suppose now that knowledge is indeed contextual in *the first way*. This does reduce the ad hoc character of the claim that skeptical alternatives (evil demon, brain in a vat, etc.) are irrelevant in *ordinary* contexts and need not there be ruled out; that they need not there be ruled out for one to know about one's surroundings, neighbors, past, etc.; though in a *philosophical* context those alternatives may yet remain relevant alternatives that do need to be ruled out. Such a claim is now less *ad hoc*, for in responding to the skeptic that knowledge is contextual in this *second* way, one is not now introducing relativity to context on the sole basis that it permits such a response to the skeptic. Relativity to context now has a further basis, one said to supplement the response to the skeptic: namely, the basis provided by the fact that knowledge is contextual in the *first* way.

That much seems quite plausible.Nevertheless, it bears mention that responding to the skeptic with the charge that skeptical alternatives are *irrelevant* may be *ad hoc* in more ways than one. For example, it may be thought *ad hoc* to introduce contextuality of knowledge attributions in that response, and it may also be thought *ad hoc* to introduce an unexplained notion of relevance, *whether its application is contextual or not*. In order to ward off this second objection one would seek some explanatory account of relevance, no matter how partial and tentative, as is sometimes done with the suggestion that relevance of alternatives is a matter of their probability. But the explanatory account may yet in its turn leave a residue of the *ad hoc*. And that is I fear what happens with the account of relevance in terms of probability. For we are not told how to pick a reference class for the pertinent probability assignments. Suppose the skeptic presents a possibility A as a skeptical alternative to some proposition P that we believe, urging that for all we have to go on A might be the case rather than P. Now it is replied by the relevant alternatives response that A is *irrelevant* and needn't be ruled out, because it is too little probable relative to some factors. But too little probable relative to which factors? Or, at least, relative to factors of what sort, along what dimension?

An alternative may be said to be "relevant" relative to S, P, and t, in a certain context, *by definition*, iff it needs to be ruled out in that context for S to know P at t. Then the *concept* of relevance is relatively clear (though not transparent), but what we still need is some minimal understanding of what accounts for the relevance or irrelevance of hypotheses. If on the other hand we are told that a certain alternative is negligible (and need not be ruled out) *because* it is irrelevant, then we need some more substantial account of relevance. And if we appeal to probability at this point, then we need some minimal explication of the *sort* of reference class relative to which the relevant probabilities are to be determined.

The reference-class problem might be viewed as adequately defused by remarks like the following: "that at least there is some standard according to which the alternative that S sees a barn replica is relevant if, e.g., there are many barn replicas in the immediate area, and not relevant if there is just one barn replica in Antarctica." But that is open to doubt. For one thing, let d = the information that a reliable source reports the existence of numerous barn replicas in the area. It seems plausible that S's possessing d makes it relevant (relative to the normal standards) that S sees a barn replica. But S's possessing d is compatible with there being just one barn replica in Antarctica. So it looks like the alternative that S sees a barn replica might after all be relevant even when there is just one barn replica in Antarctica. So we are back to square one with the reference-class problem. Even leaving aside the sort of problem of misinformation posed by d, moreover, it is clear *neither* that the barn-replica alternative is relevant (and must be ruled out specifically) when there are many barn replicas in the vicinity, *nor* that it is *not* relevant when there is only one barn replica in Antarctica. Suppose there are many barn replicas in the vicinity but it is part of your background knowledge that you are on the one working farm in the area. Is it then incumbent on you to come up with some specific way of ruling out the replicas alternative? Is that any more incumbent on you here than it would be when out for an ordinary drive in an ordinary countryside? As for the Antarctica case, suppose your access to the barn-like items is via TV and the transmission is alternating between the facsimile at the South Pole and a real barn. Then the existence of that facsimile would seem relevant, as it would if one knew oneself to be *either* before the facsimile at the Pole *or* before a real barn in some other wintry setting, the decision having been made by the toss of a coin. Here again the existence of that South Pole facsimile becomes relevant after all.

Suppose it is replied that these unusual contexts are not to be allowed. Take again the standard that rules the facsimile alternative irrelevant when there is only the lone South Pole facsimile. That standard, we may be told, is supposed to operate in ordinary circumstances. In that case the "standard" in question would seem not to go very deep. It would seem to depend on some deeper principle which together with the contingencies of our ordinary circumstances determines which alternatives are "relevant" and require specific ruling out. And concerning such deeper principles of "relevance" we would still be about as much in the dark as before.

So far we have considered two ways in which knowledge is said to be contextual, and a defense of the relevant alternatives response to the skeptic, a defense based on that dual contextuality of knowledge.[11]

B. Intellectual Virtue

For further varieties of epistemic relativity, we turn next to our intellectual virtues, which might be viewed as ways of coping that are cognitively effective, a view however that would invite the question of just what might make a way of coping "cognitively effective." According to my dictionary, 'cognition' means "the act or process of knowing ...: *also*: a product of this act." As for 'effective', it is said to mean "producing or capable of producing a result," with an emphasis on "...the actual production of or the power to produce an effect <effective thinking>." Putting all this together, it would appear that what makes a way of coping "cognitively effective" is its power to produce effects relating to or involving knowledge. But now look where that leaves us:

> What is "knowledge"? True belief that is at least justified.
> And what makes a true belief "justified"? That it have its source in intellectual virtue.
> And what is "intellectual virtue"? A skill or ability that enables one to cope in a cognitively effective way.
> And what makes a way of coping "cognitively effective"?

That it have the power to produce effects relating to or involving knowledge.

Thus we start with knowledge and return to it in a narrow circle.

For a more illuminating account we need to escape the circle. One way to do so understands intellectual virtue not as a "cognitively effective" skill or ability, but rather as one that is truth conducive (or as the ground of such a disposition). This might elicit objections as follows.

"*First*, accepting such an account of intellectual virtue drives us back upon the question about the nature of justified belief—back, in short, to the foundationalist-coherentist dispute. For if we understand "intellectual virtues" as truth-conducive dispositions or the like, then we will want to ask how we know which dispositions are virtues, how we know which are truth-conducive. But since, by wide agreement, our best access to truth is justified belief, this strategy leaves us with the primary notion of justification as that of justified beliefs; justified dispositions would remain secondary.

"*Second*, it is doubtful that the ordinary notion of justification can be captured by the idea of a reliable generating mechanism for beliefs. Just as there is presumably some way in which one has a say in the matter whether or not one is morally virtuous, so there should be also a way in which one has some say in the matter whether or not one is intellectually virtuous. But it is nonsense to attribute such "say" to someone regarding his reliable belief-generating mechanisms or their exercise."

Taking the two objections in reverse order, I admit first a narrow Aristotelian conception of virtue according to which a virtue is a certain disposition to make appropriate deliberate choices. And this is of course much narrower than any simple notion of a truth-conducive belief-generating mechanism. For whether or not belief is *ever* a product of deliberate choice, it surely is not *always* a product of such choice. Thus perceptual and introspective beliefs are often acquired willy-nilly. And yet even where deliberate choice is thus absent, some mechanism may yet generate one's belief. For example, it may be one's faculty of sight operating in good light that generates one's belief in the whiteness and roundness of a facing snowball. Is possession of such a faculty a "virtue"? Not in the narrow Aristotelian sense, of course, since it is no disposition to make deliberate choices. But there is a broader sense of "virtue," still Greek, in which anything with a function—natural or artificial—does have virtues. The eye does, after all, have its virtues, and so does a knife.[12] And if we include grasping the truth about one's environment among the proper ends of a human being, then the faculty of sight would seem in a broad sense a virtue in human beings; and if grasping the truth is an intellectual matter then that virtue is also in a straightforward sense an intellectual virtue.

As for the first objection, it charged truth-conduciveness accounts of intellectual virtues with driving us "... back upon the question about the nature of justified belief ...[and leaving] us with the primary notion of justification as that of justified beliefs." But when and how are we supposed to be thus driven back? When we try to determine the credentials of a candidate intellectual virtue, and when we ask more generally "... how we know which dispositions are virtues, how we know which are truth-conducive." The problem is supposed to be that to determine whether a disposition is truth-conducive we must determine whether the beliefs that manifest that disposition are mostly true. And, since "... our best access to truth is justified belief," in order to determine whether a belief is true we must determine whether it is a justified belief.

If that is the problem, it is apparently captured by the following argument.

A1. To determine that a disposition of one's own is truth-conducive one must determine that beliefs manifesting it are mostly true. (Assumption)

A2. To determine that a belief of one's own is true one must determine that it is a justified belief. (Assumption)

A3. To determine that a disposition of one's own is truth-conducive one must determine that beliefs manifesting it are mostly justified. (From 1, 2)

Even if conclusion A3 is true, that does not immediately refute the account of justified belief as belief that manifests a truth-conducive intellectual virtue—not even if we take such an "account" to be a philosophical analysis. For how we must determine something is an epistemological question, whereas our philosophical analysis of justified belief would be something semantical or ontological, and there is no immediately obvious connection between the two. In particular, there is no manifest absurdity in the notion that X be analyzable (semantically or ontologically) as Y despite the fact that to determine whether Y applies in a certain situation you need to determine (first) whether X applies. Thus to be a cube may be analyzable as being a six-sided closed solid with sides all square but in a certain situation it may be easier to see that there is a cube before you than to determine that there is a closed solid that both: has six sides, and has sides all square. You may be able to *see* right away that it's a cube you are holding as you turn it in your hands, though you lack the time and patience to count the sides keeping track of which you have already counted; and hence you may *conclude* that it has six sides from your analysis of cubicity and from your perceptual knowledge that it is a cube.

For *some* sort of philosophical or semantical analysis, however, it may perhaps turn out that if X has Y as its analysis of that sort, then it cannot in consistency turn out that to determine whether Y applies you must determine whether X applies. That there is such a connection between meaning and justification is of course a familiar theme of recent decades.

But the argument before us still does not rule out the account of justified belief as belief issuing from an intellectual virtue, even if this account is understood as a meaning analysis requiring the mentioned connection between meaning and justification. My objection now pertains not to what the conclusion would show even if we accepted it, but pertains rather to the truth of the second premise. Consider the following argument.

B1. It rains.
B2. I (occurrently) believe that it rains.
B3. It rains and I believe that it rains. (From B1, B2)
B4. If it rains and I believe that it rains, then my belief that it rains is true. (Obvious)
B5. My belief that it rains it true. (From B3, B4)

It seems plain I can determine [B5]—that my belief that it rains is true—by means of this argument (where square brackets will function as nominalizers, so that [It rains] = that it rains).Since [B4] is obvious, since [B5] is deduced by modus ponens from [B3] and [B4], and since [B3] is deduced by conjunction from [B1]and [B2], it all goes back to the premises [B1] and [B2]. But I may just start from the following two bits of knowledge: (a) my knowledge of the fact [B1], which I have as a result (in part) of being outside and looking up and putting out my bare arms; and (b) my knowledge of the fact [B2], which

I have by simple introspection. So it appears I can after all determine that a belief of my own is true without considering whether it is justified, and without considering in the course of that determination whether any particular belief of mine is or is not justified.

Accordingly, if it is true that "our best access to truth is justified belief," that is so only in a certain sense. For our best access to truth may be justified belief simply in the sense that in our search for truth we are better served by harboring beliefs that *are* justified rather than those that are unjustified. But it is not entailed that in order to determine that a belief of one's own is true, one must first *determine* it to *be* justified. Hence the sense in which indeed "our best access to truth is justified belief" is not after all one that dooms as viciously circular our account of what it is for a belief to be justified: namely, our account that for a belief to be justified is for it to manifest a truth-conducive faculty or intellectual virtue.

But what, again, is such a faculty or intellectual virtue? The primary meaning attributed to 'faculty' by my dictionary is "ability, power." Faculties are abilities to do certain sorts of things in certain sorts of circumstances, but how more specifically should we conceive of them? One possibility is to *define* each faculty as the ability to attain certain accomplishments. But of course an accomplishment attainable in given circumstances may be unattainable in other circumstances. Abilities correlate with accomplishments only relative to circumstances. There is for example our ability to tell (directly) the color and shape of a surface, so long as it is facing, "middle-sized," not too far, unscreened, and in enough light, and so long as one looks at it while sober, and so on. And similarly for other perceptual faculties. Compare also our ability to tell simple enough necessary truths, at least once having attained an age of reason and discernment; and our ability to retain simple enough beliefs in which we have sufficient interest. In each case our remarkably extensive species-wide accomplishments of a certain sort are explained by appeal to a corresponding ability, to a cognitive faculty; or at least we are thus provided the beginning of an explanation, an explanation sketch. But in none of these cases is there really any pretense to infallibility. All we're in a position to require is a good success ratio. Common sense is simply in no position to specify substantive circumstances in which the exercise of sight is bound to be infallible. Of course that is not to rule out underlying abilities which are in fact infallible in specifiable circumstances; it is only to imply that if there are such abilities common sense is at this point unable to formulate them.

What powers or abilities do then enable a subject to achieve knowledge or at least epistemic justification? They are presumably powers or abilities to distinguish the true from the false in a certain subject field, to attain truth and avoid error in the field. One's power or ability must presumably make one such that, normally at least, in one's ordinary habitat, or at least in one's ordinary circumstances when making such judgments, one *would* believe what is true and *not* believe what is false, concerning matters in that field.

A faculty is, again, an ability. An ability to do *what*? To *know*? That would be circular. To believe with justification? Still circular. To believe correctly propositions of a certain sort: perceptual ones, say, or mathematical ones? That can't be enough since *every* correct belief of a proposition of the sort involved will manifest *that* ability, i.e., that *mere* ability. To tell the true from the false with a good success ratio? A similar problem arises here, since one might just through a fantastic coincidence *actually* get mostly true beliefs in a certain field, and this would manifest *that* ability, i.e., that *mere* ability.

Indeed it is probably better to think of a faculty *not* as an ability but rather as a virtue or a *competence*. One has a faculty only if there is a field F and there is a set of circumstances C such that one *would* distinguish the true from the false in F in C. But of course whenever one *happens* to have a true belief B, that belief will manifest *many* such competences, for many field/circumstance pairs F/C will apply. How then can one rule out its turning out that just *any* true belief of one's own is automatically justified? To my mind the key is the requirement that the field F and the circumstances C must be accessible within one's epistemic perspective.[13] (Note that this requires considering servomechanic and animal so-called "knowledge" a lesser grade of knowledge, or perhaps viewing the attribution of "knowledge" to such beings as metaphorical, unless we are willing to admit them as beings endowed with their own epistemic perspectives.)

C. A Social Component of Knowledge

In earlier discussion above we took note of a certain contextual relativity in our attributions of knowledge. It seems that linguistic and/or epistemic communities conceive of knowledge and, more specifically, justification, by reference to community correlated standards. Why is that so? We can now suggest an answer as follows.

All kinds of justification are a matter of the cognitive or intellectual virtue of the subject. We care about justification because it indicates a state of the subject that is important and of interest to his community. And that holds good for all sorts of epistemic justification, from mere "animal" justification to its more sophisticated, reflective counterpart. In all cases we have a state of interest and importance to an information-sharing social species. What sort of state? Presumably, the state of being a dependable source of information over a certain field in certain circumstances. In order for this information to be obtainable and to be of later use, however, the sort of field F and the sort of circumstances C must be projectible, and must have some minimal objective likelihood of being repeated in the careers of normal members of the epistemic community. For it is through our cognizance of such relevant F and C that we grasp the relevant faculties whose possession by us and others makes us dependable informants and cognizers.

Recall now that we are in no position to require *infallibility* for possession of a cognitive faculty or virtue. All we are in a position to require is a good success ratio. But how good a success ratio might we agree on in order to have a commonly shared standard for knowledge? A concept of knowledge requiring a perfect success ratio would not be very discriminating, and would not help us to keep track of the facts regarding epistemic dependability, our own and others'. Nor would that concept of perfect knowledge aid intercommunication of such facts amongst members of the group. It seems a reasonable conjecture that a concept of knowledge tied to virtues of approximately normal attainment would be most useful to the group. But of course what is normal in one group may be far from it in another.

The foregoing has displayed a contextual relativity of knowledge attributions to an epistemic community; and we have sketched a sort of explanation for the implied social component of knowledge. Our explanation sketch may be summed up most briefly as follows: We are social animals. One's linguistic and conceptual repertoire is heavily influenced by one's society. The society will tend to adopt concepts useful to it. A concept of epistemic justification that measures the pertinent virtues or faculties of the subject relative to the normal for the community will be useful to the community. The community will hence tend to adopt such a concept.[14]

D. Summary

Concerning the relevant alternatives response to the skeptic, I have emphasized the large element of adhocness that remains even if we grant that knowledge is contextual in ways other than the way required by that response. This problem bears emphasis, I believe, because the elements of adhocness that remain beyond the question of contextuality seem to me much more serious problems of adhocness for the relevant alternatives view. Speaking for myself, at least, the main problem has been not the contextuality of relevant alternatives, but rather the obscurity of the concept (except when *defined* as alternatives that need to be ruled out), and the implausibility or adhocness or incompleteness of any explication so far offered (except possibly for Nozick's, which of course we cannot stop for at this point). The foregoing has also discussed whether knowledge *is* indeed contextual in the way proposed or whether the reasons adduced for considering it to be contextual cannot be taken into account with comparable overall success by the view that knowledge can vary in *content* from context to context. We next turned to intellectual virtue: the concept, its realization in humans, and its relation thereby to cognitive justification and human knowledge. Finally we considered the relativity of knowledge to epistemic communities, and offered a tentative sketch of an explanation for such relativity, whether viewed as contextual or contentual, in terms of a certain conception of intellectual virtue.[15]

Notes

1. "Skepticism, Relevant Alternatives, and Deductive Closure," *Philosophical Studies* 29 (1976) 249-61.
2. *Philosophy and the Mirror of Nature* (Princeton, NJ: Princeton University Press, 1979), p. 159.
3. *Ibid.*, p.174
4. "A Contextualist Theory of Epistemic Justification," *American Philosophical Quarterly* 15 (1978) 213-19. Also in Paul Moser (ed.), *Empirical Knowledge* (Totowa, NJ: Rowman & Littlefield, 1986).
5. Compare here Marshall Swain's "Revisions of "Knowledge, Causality, and Justification"," in M. Swain and G. Pappas (eds.), *Essays on*

Knowledge and Justification (Ithaca, NY: Cornell University Press, 1978). Also Fred Dretske's "The Pragmatic Dimension of Knowledge," *Philosophical Studies* 40 (1981) 363-78. For a review of the appeal to relevant alternatives, see also Palle Yourgrau's "Knowledge and Relevant Alternatives," *Synthese* 55 (1983) 175-190. We shall return to this appeal below.

6. *The Significance of Philosophical Scepticism* (Oxford: Oxford University Press, 1984).

7. *Ibid.*

8. "Knowledge and Context," *The Journal of Philosophy* 83 (1986) 574-584.

9. "How Do You Know?" *American Philosophical Quarterly*, XI, 2(April 1974): 113-122; also in G. Pappas and M. Swain, eds. *Essays on Knowledge and Justification* (Ithaca, N.Y.: Cornell, 1978), esp. sec. II. According to that paper, the relativity of knowledge to an epistemic community" is brought out most prominently by the requirement that inquirers have at least *normal* cognitive equipment (e.g., normal perceptual apparatus, where that is relevant)" (117). The reference to perception is explicitly *illustrative*, since the same sorts of consideration apply to other cognitive equipment—e.g., reason and memory—as Cohen has well made explicit.

10. Attributions of knowledge are said to vary in truth value depending on standards picked out in the context, even once we fix the subject, proposition, and time. And what is it in the context that picks out the pertinent standards? This is left wide open, but it is mostly the intentions of the speaker that are cited and discussed. Suppose accordingly that it is really the intentions of the speaker, explicit or implicit, that determine at least sometimes the standards relative to which we must assess an attribution of knowledge. In that case, it is less than obvious that such attributions remain uniform in *content* from context to context, while nevertheless shifting in truth value. For it seems at least equally plausible to suppose that the content itself expressed by the speaker shifts from context to context, though it may do so in a regular and explicable way. Cohen's only reason against this is that it would make the *concept* of knowledge too shifty. But surely the contextual view for its part owes us the resources for disagreeing, arguing, and perhaps eventually agreeing about knowledge, and especially for doing so across significantly different contexts. What Cohen provides here involves the possibility of fusing one's own context with that of one's interlocutor by intending the other's standards. That being so, at present it is hard to see any very weighty reason for opting between the following two possibilities:

(1) Statements of the form "At t, S knows that p" vary in truth value from context to context, *without varying in content*, though it is always possible to fuse one's own context with that of another (whose own context is otherwise as different as could be), by simply intending the other's intended standards.

(2) Statements of the form "At t, S knows that p" vary in truth value from context to context *because they vary in content*, though it is always possible to adopt the content of another (whose situation may be quite different from one's own) by adopting a content correlated with the other's intended standards.

With option 2 we do have ambiguity of knowledge attributions. But that is quite compatible with a shared and uniformly univocal term 'knowledge', one standing for a generic sort of knowledge that spans a variety of species keyed to a corresponding variety of standards. Option 1 imposes no such ambiguity but still yields just as serious an obstacle to the meeting or clashing of minds by use of a common language. What is needed for minds to meet or clash according to the *context-intention* view is for one of the interlocutors to accommodate the other by adopting the other's standards, at least for the sake of communication, discussion, or argument. But such explicit or implicit intending of standards can of course be equally well accommodated by the *content* view of the matter. For the *content* view, the intention of certain standards by the speaker would of course have a different bearing. Instead of determining a factor in the *context* of knowledge attributions, it would determine their *content*, or it would do so at least in part.

At present I see no sufficient reason for favoring either over the other of the two possible options before us.

11. Skepticism is discussed further in my "The Skeptic's Appeal," forthcoming in *Theory of Knowledge: the State of the Art*, ed. by Marjorie Clay and Keith Lehrer.

12. See Plato's *Republic*, Bk I, 352.

13. The theme of this paragraph is developed in section B4 of my "Beyond Skepticism, to the Best of Our Knowledge," *Mind* (1988).

14. For more on the concept of epistemic justification and doubt that it can serve all the purposes which epistemology has given it, see my "Methodology and Apt Belief," forthcoming in *Synthese* (1988), a special issue on epistemology, edited by Steven Luper-Foy.

15. This paper has benefited from the work and comments of John Greco, Stewart Cohen, and Stuart Rosenbaum, to all of whom go my appreciative thanks.

Philosophical Perspectives, 2, Epistemology, 1988

KNOWLEDGE AND CONDITIONALS[1]

Risto Hilpinen
University of Turku and University of Miami

I

Everyone agrees that knowledge is either a superior form of belief, or not a variety of belief at all.[2] In this paper I shall disregard the latter view, and take it for granted that knowledge is a cognitively superior form of belief. Let '$B_a p$' mean that p belongs to a's belief system (a system of propositions accepted by a), and let '$K_a p$' mean that a knows that p. In its simplest form, the view under consideration may be expressed as follows:

(CK) $K_a p \rightarrow B_a p \;\&\; C_a p,$

where 'Ca' expresses a condition which the cognitively superior beliefs should satisfy. I shall call such a condition here a *K-condition*. A K-condition may be either necessary for knowledge or a necessary part of some set of conditions which are jointly sufficient for knowledge, or it may be a condition which is positively relevant to knowledge ascriptions without being either necessary or sufficient for knowledge.[3] Below I shall use 'B_a' both as a belief operator, as in (CK), and as an expression which refers to a's belief system (the system of propositions accepted by a). A belief system is relative to a person and a time (or situation); and can thus be identified by an expression of the form '$B_{a,t}$', where the second index refers to time. In the sequel one (or both) of the two indices will often be omitted. Points of time or situations will usually be indicated by integers (1, 2,..).

True beliefs are cognitively superior to false ones, but it has generally been felt that truth alone is not a sufficient K-condition, because it does not distinguish knowledge from "lucky guesses" or irrational beliefs which happen to be true. It has been thought that something else is required as well.

What *kind* of a condition can a K-condition be? Philosophers have put forward two main kinds of K-conditions:

(i) In addition to being true, the superior beliefs should be appropriately related to the other beliefs accepted by the person, that is, to other propositions in B_a.

(ii) The superior beliefs should be appropriately related to the facts (that is, to the world).

It is clear that these alternatives do not exclude each other: perhaps knowledge should satisfy both kinds of conditions.

If we picture a person's belief system as a system or a construct which "covers" part of the world, relations of type (i) might be called *horizontal* relations among beliefs, and relations of the second kind *vertical* relations; conditions concerning these two kinds of relations may be termed *horizontal* and *vertical* conditions or requirements, respectively. The distinction between horizontal and vertical conditions is related to the well-known distinction between "internal" and "external" conditions of knowledge and justification.[4] Horizontal relations are internal to a person's belief system, whereas vertical relations connect a person's beliefs to external circumstances.

Requirements of the first kind, horizontal requirements, are based on the assumption that in order to know something, a person must have reasons or evidence for his belief, and these reasons must be propositions which are believed or accepted by the person.[5] The theories of knowledge based on this approach may be called *evidence theories* of knowledge.

The second approach, the attempt to distinguish knowledge from true belief in terms of additional vertical requirements, is based on the intuitive idea that a person can know something only if it is not *accidental* that he is right (that the belief is true).[6] Thus there should be an appropriate relationship of *dependence* between a's belief that p and the fact p; it is not enough that the belief "correspond" to the facts (or reality). In Charles Peirce's terminology, we might say that a person's beliefs are knowledge only if they are indexical and not merely iconic signs of the facts to which they refer.[7] It has often been thought that in the case of empirical beliefs, the relationship of dependence should be some form of *causal* dependence.[8]

II

It seems fairly obvious that no matter how a person's beliefs are related to each other, some of them may nevertheless be only accidentally correct. This suggests that no horizontal condition or set of horizontal conditions is sufficient to distinguish knowledge from "lucky guesses". Even a well-justified belief may be true by accident. This has been shown by numerous examples of the following kind, due to Edmund Gettier and therefore called "Gettier examples":[9]

(i) a has good evidence for p, say e; both e and p belong to B_a, and a infers $p \lor q$ from p.

(ii) Assuming that the following principle of evidence is valid,

(CC) If a has good (conclusive) evidence for p, and infers r correctly from p, then a has good (conclusive) evidence for r,

a's evidence for p counts as evidence for any proposition correctly inferred (by a) from p. Thus we may assume that in the situation described in (i), a is justified in believing the disjunction $p \lor q$.

(iii) Let us suppose now that despite a's evidence, p is actually false, but the disjunction is true because q is true. If a's evidence for p is not at all relevant to q, a cannot be said to know that $p \lor q$, even though this belief is well-justified and true.

Examples of this kind show that even well-justified beliefs may be only accidentally correct. Thus, if we accept the condition[10]

(CA) a knows that p only if it is not accidental that a's belief that p is correct,

horizontal conditions do not seem sufficient for knowledge: such conditions cannot distinguish knowledge from merely true beliefs, and some vertical requirements seem therefore necessary.

III

In its simplest form, the dependence of belief on fact may be expressed as follows:

(CB) If p were not the case, a would not believe that p,

or briefly,

(CB1) $\sim p >> \sim B_a p$,

where '$>>$' is an expression for a counterfactual (or subjunctive) conditional. The negation of (CB1) may be read: "If p were not the case, a might (still) believe that p", and expressed briefly as

(1) $\sim p <> B_a p$.

It is easy to see that (CB) does not hold in the example given above (or in examples which have the form specified in (i)-(iii)): the conditional

(2) $\sim (p \lor q) >> \sim B_a (p \lor q)$,

that is,

(3) $\sim p \, \& \sim q >> \sim Ba(p \lor q)$

does not hold, because a's belief in the disjunction is not at all dependent on the truth of q, and a would believe $p \lor q$ even if q were false (which in this case is the same as the assumption that $p \lor q$ is false, since p is actually false).

Robert Nozick has regarded (CB1) as a necessary K-condition.[11] Nozick has suggested that in addition to (CB1), the concept of knowledge should satisfy the condition

(CB2) $p >> B_a p$,

that is, "If p were the case, a would believe that p". (CB1) and (CB2) together say that a's believing that p is counter-factually dependent on the truth of p (whether a believes that p depends on whether p is true).[12] According to the standard semantics of subjunctive (or counterfactual) conditionals, (CB2) follows from the truth of p and $B_a p$,[13] and consequently (CB2) holds for all true beliefs:

(4) $p \, \& \, B_a p \rightarrow (p >> B_a p)$.

Nozick interprets conditionals in a way which does not make (4) valid,[14] and takes both (CB1) and (CB2) as necessary and nonredundant K-conditions. The question of the possible redundancy of (CB2) will be left here open.[15] I shall argue below that the kind of dependence of belief on fact expressed by (CB1) and (CB2) (jointly) is not necessary for knowledge; in particular, I shall argue that (CB1) is not a necessary K-condition.

IV

Let us consider the following example. Suppose that a person a is interested in the temperature of a certain object o, and a has a thermometer M which is reasonably accurate within the range of (say) 0 to 100 degrees Celsius. Let '$T(o) = x$' be the statement that the temperature of o is x degrees Celsius, and let '$M(o) = x$' be the proposition that M indicates that the temperature of o is x degrees C.

If a's beliefs about the temperature of o are determined on the basis of M, he can know on the basis of the reading '$M(o) = 30$' (for example) that $T(o) > 25$. If the thermometer is very accurate, condition (CB1) may in this case be satisfied: if the temperature of o were not more than 25 degrees, a would not believe that it is more than 25 degrees C:

(5) $\sim(T(o) > 25) >> \sim B_a(T(o) > 25)$.

In this situation a apparently also knows that $T(o)$ is more than -40 degrees C. However, since the thermometer is not at all accurate for subzero temperatures, the following condition need not be satisfied:

(6) $\sim(T(o) > -40) >> \sim B_a(T(o) > -40)$.

Under the conditions specified in the antecedent of (6), the thermometer would not work properly, and a would not be able to determine the temperature of o. If $T(o)$ were actually -40 degrees, a might well believe that it is (say) -35 degrees, but this does not prevent him from knowing that $T(o) > -40$ when it is actually 28 degrees, and M indicates a temperature of 30 degrees C. Thus the truth of (CB1) is not necessary for knowledge; (CB1) is not a necessary K-condition.

Apparently vertical K-conditions cannot do justice to *inferential* knowledge: in the example given above, a's belief that $T(o) > -40$ is inferred from (or based on) the belief that $T(o) > 25$, and is therefore an instance of inferential knowledge.

Many philosophers, for example, Brian Skyrms and Fred Dretske, have assumed that inferential knowledge depends on relations of counterfactual dependence between facts. Such relationships may be termed *external* horizontal relationships. According to Dretske, an evidential relation between e and h can give knowledge about the truth of h—that is, e can be *conclusive* evidence for h—only if the following counterfactual holds:[16]

(CC) $\sim p >> \sim e$;

if p were not the case, e would not be the case. However, the example just given can also be regarded as a counterexample to (CC). According to (CC), a can know that $T(o) > -40$ on the basis of the evidence provided by the thermometer (i.e., on the basis of $M(o) = 30$) only if

(7) $\sim (T(o) > -40) >> \sim (M(o) = 30)$.

But in the present example this conditional need not be true: if $T(o)$ were less than -40 degrees C, the thermometer would break, and it might indicate 30 degrees C even under those circumstances. This does not prevent the thermometer from being a reliable indicator of temperature under the actual circumstances, when $T(o)$ is about 30 degrees Celsius.

The case against the necessity of (CC) (as a K-condition) is not quite as convincing as that against (CB1), because it might be argued that in the example discussed above the thermometer reading *alone* cannot be sufficient or "conclusive" evidence that $T(o) > -40$. One problem with this defense of (CC) is that it seems to be applicable to almost all non-monotonic (non-demonstrative) reasoning because such reasoning is always context-sensitive and depends on tacit *ceteris paribus*-clauses.[17] Condition (CB1) cannot be defended in a similar way, because neither (CB1) nor the argument against it involves any assumptions about the evidential basis of a person's beliefs.

V

The counter-example to (CB1) discussed above is an example of inferential knowledge, and seems to depend on the principle that knowledge is transmissible by valid deductive reasoning. Fred Dretske, Robert Nozick and other authors have challenged this principle, and argued that the concept of knowledge is not closed under known logical implication: a person may fail to know the truth of a proposition which he has correctly inferred from what he knows.[18] The most plausible examples of this possibility are cases in which the proposition inferred is the negation of some "skeptical" hypothesis (for example, "there is no evil demon deceiving me into believing that ..."),[19] but the example given above does not seem to be of this kind, but a perfectly normal and common instance of knowledge: if someone knows that $T(o)$ is more than 25 degrees C, he obviously also knows that $T(o)$ is above the freezing point (above zero). Here is a slightly different counter-example to (CB1): A mother suspects that her child has temperature, and when she measures the temperature and looks at the thermometer, she takes it to read 40.0 degrees Celsius. Let us call the child 'c' and the thermometer again 'M'. If the thermometer is fairly accurate and the mother has reasonably good eyesight, we can say under these circumstances that she knows that the child has temperature, i.e., that $T(c) > 37.0$. (To say that the child has temperature is just another way of saying that the temperature of the child is more than 37 degrees Celsius.) But the mother need not have perfect eyesight and the thermometer need not be completely accurate (few ordinary thermometers are): the actual thermometer reading might be $M(c) = 39.8$, and the actual temperature of the child might be 39.2 degrees Celsius. If the child did not have temperature, that is, if it were the case that $T(c) \leq 37.0$, the thermometer might read (say) 37.3 degrees Celsius, and the mother might believe that the child has temperature, but this does not prevent her from knowing in the *actual* circumstances that $T(c) > 37.0$. Thus (CB1) is not a necessary K-condition.

In this example the mother's "reasoning" can be represented as an inference from

(8) $M(c) = 40.0$

to

(9) $T(c) = 40.0$

and from (9) to

(10) $T(c) > 37.0.$

If the mother knows that the child has temperature, she knows that (10) is true, in spite of the fact that both (8) and (9) are false. This example suggests that a person can know things not only on the basis of (valid) inference from what he or she knows, but in some cases even on the basis of inference from what is *not* known (or even true), provided that the latter (evidential) propositions are sufficiently close to the truth. Thus the example can also be regarded as a counter-example to the foundationalist view that knowledge can be justified only by propositions which are true and known to be true: perhaps relatively vague knowledge-claims can sometimes be justified by "sharp" (or informative) but false beliefs which are reasonably close to the truth. This seems to be common in experimental science, where (correct) theoretical claims are often justified by fallible and inaccurate experimental results. In his paper 'Experiment, Theory Choice, and the Duhem-Quine Problem' (forthcoming) Allan Franklin has pointed out that incorrect experimental outcomes need not result in incorrect (or unjustified) theory choices. For example, Franklin notes that "the fact that Millikan's value of e, the charge of the electron ... disagrees with the currently accepted value ... has not changed the support for charge quantization".[20]

The thrust of the present argument is, in a sense, the very opposite of those presented by Dretske and Nozick: according to Dretske and Nozick, a proposition correctly inferred from known truths may *fail* to be knowledge, whereas I have argued that a proposition inferred from other propositions which are *not* known to be true *may* be knowledge.

Many philosophers have recently argued that (CB1) and (CB2) are not *sufficient* to distinguish knowledge from true belief, because intuitively unjustified beliefs may satisfy (CB1) and (CB2),[21] but I have tried to argue above that (CB1) is not a *necessary* K-condition.[22] (CB1) and (CB2) are reliability conditions, and Nozick's analysis of knowledge is a form of reliability analysis. The argument given here is not directed against all reliability theories, but only against theories in which knowledge is analyzed in terms of direct vertical connections between beliefs and the world (or facts).[23]

It should not be surprising that knowledge cannot be distinguished from true belief by direct vertical connections alone, and that such connections are not even necessary for knowledge. Beliefs derive their meaning and identity from their inferential relationships to other beliefs, and (in my view) it is not even *prima facie* plausible to assume that they should be correlated with facts one by one in the way required by (CB1).

VI

The preceding arguments seem to show that neither horizontal relationships among a person's beliefs nor vertical connections between beliefs and facts can distinguish knowledge from (merely) true belief. Many philosophers have suggested that this distinction also depends on horizontal relations between a person's beliefs and the propositions *outside* his belief system, that is, propositions which are merely *potential* beliefs. Below I shall consider horizontal conditions of this more general kind.

To formulate such conditions, I shall use the concept *justification within a belief system*,

'p is justified within $B_{a,t}$'.

This concept of justification should be understood as nondemonstrative or "non-monotonic" justification which can in principle be undermined or "defeated" by new evidence. If certain propositions $e_1,..., e_n$ justify a conclusion p, but there is an evidential proposition i such that p is not justified by $e_1,...,e_n, i$, we say that i *defeats* (or undermines) the justification of p by $e_1,...,e_n$.[24] The concept of justification within a belief system is subject to the following condition:

(CD1) If p is justified within Ba on the basis of evidence $e_1,..., e_n$, then there is no proposition i in B_a such that i defeats the justification of p by $e_1,..., e_n$.

Both p and the evidential propositions e_i are here assumed to belong to B_a. According to the classical "justificationist" interpretation of the concept of knowledge, a person a can know that p only if p is justified within his belief system.

(CD1) is a version of the well-known *principle total evidence*, according to which the credibility (or acceptability) of a hypothesis should be determined on the basis of the total evidence available in a given situation. This principle can be interpreted in two different ways. According to the first interpretation, the principle refers to all the evidence which is already in a person's possession, that is, belongs to his belief system. But "the total evidence available" can also be understood as all the relevant evidence which a person *could* (or perhaps *should*) find by inquiry and take into account.[25] (CD1) reflects the former interpretation of the principle of total evidence. According to the second interpretation, the following two conditions are not necessarily equivalent:

(CD2) a knows that p only if p is justified within B_a.
(CD3) a knows that p only if p is justified by all the relevant evidence.

According to the second interpretation of the principle of total evidence, the justification conditions for knowledge should include both (CD2) and (CD3), and thus imply the following "condition of indefeasibility":

(CD4) a knows that p only if p is justified within B_a and there is no relevant evidence i such that i defeats the justification of p.

Condition (CD4) reflects the classical view that a person knows that p only if he is able to defend his opinion successfully against objections and counter-arguments. Siger of Brabant expressed this view as follows:[26]

> Finding truth presupposes the ability to solve any objection or dubitation against the proposition accepted as true. For if you do not know how to solve the objections that may arise, you are not in possession of the truth, since in that case you have not assimilated *the procedure of finding* truth and thus will not know whether or when you have arrived at truth.

Jaakko Hintikka has formulated a similar view about knowledge in a slightly different way. Hintikka notes that a person is in a position to say that he knows that p (in the "full" or "strong" sense of knowledge) only if his grounds for p are in some sense "conclusive" or "adequate". This does not mean logical but *factual* (or empirical) conclusiveness: if a knows that p, further inquiry concerning p would be pointless (for a), in other words:[27]

If somebody says "I know that *p*" in this strong sense of knowledge, he implicitly denies that any further information would have led him to alter his view.

In Charles Peirce's words, we might say that a person who knows something has reached the "final opinion" concerning the matter in question.[28] Condition (CD4), and other horizontal conditions similar to it, have sometimes been called "indefeasibility conditions" (or "defeasibility conditions").[29] These conditions express several inter-related intuitions about the "strong" concept of knowledge, for example, that genuine knowledge should be *extendable*, and that knowledge-claims should be justified by evidence which is in some sense conclusive or complete—not logically, but empirically conclusive.[30] Thus conditions similar to (CD4) may also be termed "conclusiveness conditions" or "extendability conditions".[31]

What evidence is (potentially) relevant to a person's knowledge claim, that is, what propositions can be used in the attempts to refute *a*'s claim that he knows that p? (The expression "evidence" does not mean here *actual* evidence, but potential evidence or evidence which may be *available* to a person in a broad sense of the word "available".) It is clear that *a*'s own beliefs, regardless of whether they are true or false, may provide grounds for admissible counterarguments: principle (CD1) is based on this assumption. But admissible counter-evidence is obviously not restricted to a person's own beliefs: condition (CD2) is not enough. It is not implausible to suggest that any *true* proposition may be potential counter-evidence, regardless of whether it is believed by *a* (or any other person):

> (CD5) Any true proposition may constitute potential counter-evidence against *a*'s claim to know that *p*.

(CD5) is a strong requirement. In the second interpretation of the principle of total evidence, the total evidence available in a given situation is interpreted as the evidence which a person could and (given enough time and resources) perhaps should find and take into account. In the light of this interpretation, it seems reasonable to restrict (CD5) to truths which are in some sense *cognitively accessible* to *a*:[32]

> (CD5*) Any true proposition accessible to *a* may constitute potential counter-evidence to a's claim to know that *p*.

On the other hand, it might also be suggested that the beliefs accepted by all or most members of the "cognitive community" to which *a* belongs may provide potential counter-arguments against *a*'s knowledge-claims in the same way as *a*'s own beliefs, even if these beliefs are false. (Such beliefs are always readily accessible to *a*.) According to this view, knowledge is an essentially social notion, dependent on the standards of argument of a whole community and not just a single person. This suggests the following condition:[33]

> (CD6) If *q* is believed by many persons, it may constitute possible counter-evidence against *a*'s knowledge-claim even if it is false.[34]

Below I shall not try to give a sharp characterization of the semantic and pragmatic requirements for what may be regarded as potentially relevant evidence; I shall call such propositions simply 'evidential propositions', and assume that they satisfy one of the conditions (CD5), (CD5*) or (CD6), or some other condition of the same type.

VII

The general form of conclusiveness conditions can be expressed in an convenient and perspicuous way by using the concept of a *revision* of a belief system. If B_a is a belief system, let B_a/d be a system which results from B_a by *a*'s coming to believe that *d*. I assume that B_a/d is a *minimal* revision of B_a in the sense that all the differences between the two systems depend on or are associated with *a*'s acceptance of *d* (or *a*'s coming to believe that *d*). I shall call such a revision of B_a a *minimal d-revision* of *Ba*. Intuitively speaking, a minimal *d*-revision of a belief system tells us what a person *might* believe if he were to learn that *d* (accept *d*). I assume that a given belief system may have several minimal *d*-revisions: a person may come to believe that *d* in several, equally "minimal" ways. The concept of "minimality" can be interpreted in different contexts in different (more or less relaxed) ways; in this way it is possible to represent part of the context-dependence of knowledge ascriptions. Many authors have recently formulated the conditions of acceptability of various types of conditionals in terms of the minimal revisions of belief systems; thus the formulation of conclusiveness conditions in terms of the minimal revisions of belief systems is closely related to the formulations in terms of subjunctive conditionals.[35]

Let us now assume that d is a proposition outside a's belief system. Many philosophers have suggested that d may defeat a's knowledge-claim p if a would no longer be justified in believing that p if he were to learn (or come to believe) that d (provided that d is an appropriately qualified evidential proposition).[36] This defeasibility condition may be expressed in the following form:

> (CD7) An evidential proposition d defeats the justification of p within B_a if and only if every B_a/d fails to justify p (if p is not justified in any B_a/d).

This condition implies the following K-condition:

> (CDK1) a knows that p only if there is no evidential proposition d such that every B_a/d fails to justify p,

which is equivalent to

> (CDK1*) If a knows that p, then, for every evidential proposition d, p is justified within some B_a/d.

Intuitively, (CDK1) says that a knows that p only if he *might* be justified in believing that p even if he were to learn that d, where d is any evidential proposition or "potential defeater" of p. If this requirement seems too weak, we might consider the following condition:

> (CDK2) a knows that p only if, for every evidential proposition d, p is justified within every B_a/d.

This condition expresses the requirement that a knows that p only if he *would* be justified in believing that p even if he were to learn that d (for any evidential proposition d).[37] (CDK.2) follows from the following defeasibility condition:

> (CD8) d defeats the justification of p within B_a if and only if some B_a/d fails to justify p.

Again, we have to assume here that d is an appropriately qualified evidential proposition.

(CDK2) may be criticized on the ground that it is too strong a requirement, and is apt to lead to skepticism. According to (CDK2), a knows that p only if all possible ways of expanding the evidential basis of p keep it justified. It has been suggested that there may be peculiar, "misleading" ways of adding new evidence to B_a which may make p unjustified without falsifying the original knowledge-claim. According to this view, we should make a distinction between (new) evidence which is apt to undermine (or which might undermine) a person's justification for p (in the sense expressed by (CD8)), and new or potential evidence which also makes it impossible for a to know that p on the basis of his original evidence.[38] The philosophers who hold this view may be willing to accept (CDK1), which requires only that given any (appropriately qualified) evidential proposition d, *some* ways of including d in B_a will keep p well-justified. This requirement may be termed the *weak* interpretation of the principle of extendability of knowledge. Condition (CDK2), or the assumption that a person knows that p only if all possible ways of coming to know the truth of any evidential proposition will keep p justified, may be termed the *strong* principle of extendability.[39] If the different "ways of coming to know" something do not have to satisfy any minimality condition, the weak principle of extendability is (almost) obviously valid, and if the requirement of minimality is relaxed for (CDK1), it is equally unproblematic.[40] But (CDK1) is only a necessary K-condition: it is not an exhaustive account of the circumstances under which an evidential proposition may defeat a knowledge-claim. The critics of defeasibility conditions have usually not distinguished (CDK1) and (CDK2) (or (CD7) and (CD8)) from each other, but have apparently assumed that there is just one "preferred" (or "minimal") way of coming to know the truth of any evidential proposition d. This assumption makes (CD7) equivalent to (CD8), and (CD1) equivalent to (CD2) (provided, of course, that there is some way of coming to believe d, i.e., that d is potential evidence). One is unwittingly committed to this assumption if one (mistakenly) takes the negation the subjunctive conditional 'If r were the case, then s would be the case' to be 'If r were the case, then s would not be the case'.

VIII

Some philosophers have suggested that an evidential proposition d which makes p unjustified may not prevent a person from knowing that p if d is a "misleading" proposition (that is, misleading with respect to p).[41] This possibility has often been illustrated by examples in which the evidential relevance of the proposition which seems to make p unjustified depends on some tacit, incorrect presumption; if this presumption is corrected, the original justification of p is restored. The recent literature on the analysis of knowledge contains several attempts to define the concept of misleading evidence by means of defeasibility conditions, and many of these definitions are based on the assumption that the relevance of the incorrect presumption can been seen from the propositions justified or supported by B_a/d. For example, according to Peter Klein, d is a misleading evidential proposition (with respect to B_a and p) if and only if it would make p unjustified only by justifying some false proposition f.[42] In accordance with this proposal, we might give the following account of the circumstances under which a proposition is "misleading". Let us say that a belief system B_a *supports* a proposition q which does not belong to B_a if the system gives good grounds for accepting q; thus the relation of support is analogous to the relation of justification, with the distinction that the latter expression is used about propositions which belong to the system, and the former also about propositions outside the system. Now we might define the concept of misleading evidence as follows:

(CD9) d is misleading with respect to p and B_a if and only if there is a false proposition f such that (i) for any B_a/d, p is not justified within B_a/d if and only if B_a/d supports f, and (ii) for any evidential proposition e, if $B_a/d/e$ does not support f, it justifies p.

We are assuming here that p is justified within B_a, and d is a proposition which undermines the justification of p in the sense expressed by (CD8) or (CD7), in other words, some or all d-revisions of B_a fail to justify p. Thus, if d is misleading with respect to p, some or all d-revisions of B_a support f. Condition (ii) expresses part of the meaning of the assumption that the failure of B_a/d to justify p depends on the support for f: as soon as this support is withdrawn, p is again justified. (CD9) is just one of several definitions of misleading counter-evidence which might be considered here; alternative definitions can be obtained from (CD9) by changing the scopes of the various quantifiers in it. However, the conclusions reached below about (CD9) hold for the alternative definitions as well, and I shall therefore consider only (CD9).

According to the view under consideration here, a proposition d which satisfies the right-hand side of (CD9) does not prevent a from knowing that p (on the basis of his belief system B_a). But philosophers disagree on this point: some philosophers have suggested that a false and misleading (but apparently reliable) testimony may prevent a person from knowing that a certain proposition p is true, even though the person is not aware of the existence of the testimony (and is therefore justified in believing that p is true).[43] Such cases usually have the following form: Let t be a (false) report which asserts that q, where q is either inconsistent with p or otherwise strongly negatively relevant to p. Let $t(q)$ be the proposition

(11) According to t, q.

If t is apparently reliable, $t(q)$ is a true proposition which supports q and consequently undermines a's justification for p. But if there is no other evidence against p, we may assume that the justification of p can be restored by new evidence which suggests that t is unreliable; thus we may assume that p is justified within every $B_a/t(q)/e$, where 'e' is (for example) the statement that t is an unreliable report. $t(q)$, q and e therefore satisfy the right-hand side of condition (CD9) (with $t(q) = d$ and $q = f$; e may be the statement 'Report t is unreliable', or any evidential proposition which implies that t is unreliable). Once a has learned that t cannot be relied on, the evidential significance of $t(q)$ has been discredited, and p is again justified on the strength of a's original evidence. Nevertheless many philosophers have interpreted examples of this kind as cases in which a does *not* know that p on the basis of his original evidence (included in B_a). According to this view, (CD9) cannot distinguish the cases in which an evidential proposition d which would undermine a's justification for p does not prevent a from knowing that p, from cases in which d also falsifies a's original knowledge-claim.[44]

According to Carl Ginet, such a distinction exists: in some cases a person's ignorance of new evidence against p "protects" only his justification for p, but not his knowledge; in other cases it protects his knowledge that p as well. In cases of the latter sort it is possible to (come to) "know less by knowing more".[45] Ginet has argued that the distinction between these two cases cannot be made in the way indicated by (CD9), i.e., in terms of "misleading evidence"; he notes that "to say that evidence against a truth is misleading is just to say that it is evidence against a *truth*".[46] According to Ginet, the difference between the two cases is a matter of degree:[47]

> Given a particular justification for a knowledge claim,
> contrary evidence that would render that claim false always
> differs from contrary evidence that would not do so because
> the subject's justification for believing the proposition in
> question would be weakened much more by her learning
> the first sort of contrary evidence than it would by her
> learning of the second sort.

The fact that people disagree on the interpretation of many examples involving "misleading" new evidence lends some support to Ginet's conclusion. A comparison of conditions (CDK1) and (CDK2) suggests a somewhat similar conclusion. Condition (CDK2) requires that every (minimal) d-revision of a person's belief system should sustain the justification for p, and this requirement seems too strong. On the other hand, according to (CDK1), a person knows that p only if, for any (appropriately qualified) evidential proposition d, some minimal d-revisions of the person's belief system would sustain his justification for p. This is a relatively weak requirement, and may be accepted as a necessary K-condition. Unlike (CDK2), (CDK1) does not justify the possibility of defeating a knowledge claim by "gerrymandering" (potential) evidence, that is, by selecting bits and pieces of evidence in a misleading way,[48] because (CDK1) implies that a does not know that p only if all possible ways of coming to know the "bits and pieces" undermine a's justification for p. (In this context we should adopt a somewhat relaxed conception of the "minimal revisions" of belief systems.) It should be observed here that condition (CDK1) and the requirement that a knows that p only if no evidential proposition d defeats a's justification for p do not entail the defeasibility condition (CD7), but only the condition

> (CD10) An evidential proposition d defeats the justification of p
> within B_a if every B_a/d fails to justify p (if p is not justified
> in any B_a/d).

If the right-hand side of (CD10) holds for some evidential proposition d, a does not know that p. But we may wish to deny that a knows that p also if many but not all d-revisions of B_a fail to justify p. Whether a knows that p depends on how *easily* a's justification for p may be shaken by new evidence. But the boundary between the cases in which the existence of (potential) *prima facie* counter-evidence makes it impossible for a person to know that p and those in which it is only capable of undermining his justification for p may well depend on considerations other than extendability (or defeasibility). If this is the case, defeasibility conditions of the sort considered above express an important *aspect* of knowledge,[49] even though knowledge cannot always be distinguished from (*prima facie*) justified true belief by means of such conditions alone.[50]

The concept of knowledge is a quasi-normative notion; it is used for the purpose of evaluating the epistemic credentials of a person's beliefs. "Knowledge" refers to ideal (or perfect) cognition,[51] and our beliefs may fall short of this ideal in different respects; but if the shortcomings are unimportant and a person's belief comes close to the ideal, we are willing to grant him knowledge.[52] The cogency of the potential counter-evidence to a knowledge claim may be evaluated in the same way as the claim itself; and if the epistemic credentials of an evidence proposition are unsatisfactory in some important respect, a person may have a "right" to disregard the (apparent) counter-evidence (or perhaps he *ought to* disregard the evidence): the existence of such evidence does not stand in the way of the ascription of knowledge to the person. If we accept the view that the epistemic credentials of propositions depend on several criteria which are not necessarily concurrent, it is possible that the epistemic shortcomings of putative evidential propositions cannot be expressed exhaustively in terms of defeasibility conditions, but depend also on requirements of a different sort, for example, on some "objective" reliability criteria.[53]

If the concept of knowledge is characterized in terms of features which are either positively or negatively relevant to the application of the concept to various situations, rather than by means of a fixed set of necessary conditions, it is easy to see why hardly any K-condition (except truth, perhaps) seems to be necessary for all knowledge ascriptions. In a certain situation we might wish to ascribe a person knowledge that p since the situation exemplifies an important aspect of knowledge (or what I have called above a K-condition), without necessarily satisfying other relevant conditions; but in another situation we might refuse knowledge ascription on the ground that the situation *fails* to exhibit a feature which is for some reason considered important in that situation.[54]

IX

In his book *The Analysis of Knowing* Robert K. Shope has criticized the defeasibility conditions of knowledge on the ground that they involve what he calls the "conditional fallacy".[55] The conditional fallacy is, roughly speaking, the mistaken assumption that a statement q can be analyzed in terms of a subjunctive conditional 'If r (were the case), then s (would be the case)', when the truth of q depends on r in such a way that (i) q is actually false although the conditional (the proposed analysans) is true, but if the antecedent r were the case, q would also be the case, or (ii) q is true although the conditional is false, but if the r were the case, q would be false. Shope calls (i) the "first version" of the conditional fallacy, and case (ii) "the second version" of the fallacy.[56] In both cases the truth of the analysandum depends on the truth or falsity of the antecedent of the conditional in question.

Let us consider a very simple extendability condition, for example:[57]

(12)a knows that p only if there is no true proposition d such that if a were justified in believing that d, a would not be justified in believing that p.

This condition resembles condition (CD7) given above. Let p be the proposition 'a is not justified in believing that r', where r is some true proposition. It is clearly possible for a to know that he is not justified in believing a certain proposition r (which happens to be true). But if a were justified in believing that r, and also justified in believing that he is justified in believing that r, a would no longer be justified in believing that p. According to Shope, this example shows that condition (12) involves the second version of the conditional fallacy. (In this case a knows that r is not justified, but if a were justified in believing that r, he might not be justified in believing that r is not justified; thus the conditional is false.)[58]

It is easy to see that the defeasibility conditions (CDK1), (CDK2), (CD7) and (CD8) avoid this difficulty. In these conditions, the concept of justification is expressed in the form 'p is justified within $B_{a,i}$', where $B_{a,i}$ refers to a certain belief system. The index 'a' refers to a person, 'i' to time; here the first index may be omitted. In the example given above, the statement that a is not justified in believing that r may be formulated as

(13) r is not justified within B_1,

where '$B1$' refers to a's current belief system. If a knows that (13) is true, then, according to (CD7) and (CDK1), the following condition should be satisfied:

(14) There is no evidential proposition d such that 'r is not justified within B_1' is not justified within any $B1/d$,

which is equivalent to

(14*) For any evidential proposition d, 'r is not justified within B_1' is justified within some B_1/d.

The acceptance of (CD8) (instead of (CD7)) yields the following K-condition:

(15) For any evidential proposition d, 'r is not justified within B_1' is justified within every B_1/d.

If we assume here, for the sake of simplicity, that any truth may serve as an evidential proposition, (14) holds only if

(16) 'r is not justified within B_1' is justified within some B_1/r,

and (15) entails

(17) 'r is not justified within B_1' is justified within every $B1/r$.

(It was assumed above that r is a truth.) But (16) and (17) can obviously be true: nothing prevents the proposition that r is not justified within B_1 from being justified in an r-revision of B_1. (B_1 and each B_1/r are distinct belief systems.) This point can also be expressed by saying that even if a were justified in believing that r (and even if a were to believe that r), he might (or would) still be justified in believing that he was not justified in believing that r. Thus conditions (13) and (14) do not make it impossible for a to know that he is not justified in believing that r. The present formulation of the extendability (or indefeasibility) conditions does not involve any fallacy or paradox. According to the present analysis, Shope's criticism of the defeasibility analyses of knowledge depends on his failure to distinguish the propositions 'p is justified within B_1' and 'p is justified within B_1/r' from each other.

Notes

1. This paper is based on research supported by a Finnish State Council of the Humanities grant No. 09/053. Part of the work was done during the spring term 1986 while I enjoyed a research fellowship at the Center for Philosophy of Science, University of Pittsburgh. Earlier versions of the paper have been presented in a seminar on epistemology and philosophy of science at the University of Miami during the autumn semester 1985, and at Philosophy Colloquia at Cornell University, Ohio State University, Wayne State University, and the University of Uppsala during the spring and autumn semesters of 1986. I wish to thank the participants of these seminars and colloquia and in particular Professors Carl Ginet, Alan Goldman, Michael McKinsey, Lawrence Powers, and Nicholas Rescher for their comments and criticisms, and Miss Rita Heino for her assistance in the preparation of the paper.

2. The second disjunct here is occasioned by Colin Radford's claim that a person can know something he does not believe, and by Zeno Vendler's argument that belief and knowledge have different objects, and knowledge cannot therefore be regarded as a variety of belief at all; see Colin Radford, 'Knowledge-By Examples', *Analysis* 27 (1966), 1-11, and Zeno Vendler, *Res Cogitans*, Cornell University Press, Ithaca 1972, ch. V.

3. Condition (CK) represents the simplest case, in which a K-condition is a necessary condition of knowledge. The recent work on the analysis of knowledge has been mainly concerned with K-conditions of this kind.

4. For a discussion of this issue, see Alvin Goldman, 'The Internalist Conception of Justification', *Midwest Studies in Philosophy, Vol. V: Studies in Epistemology*, ed. by Peter A. French et al., University of Minnesota Press, Minneapolis 1980, pp. 27-51, and Laurence Bonjour, 'Externalist Theories of Empirical Knowledge', *Midwest Studies in Philosophy, Vol. V: Studies in Epistemology*, pp. 53-73.

5. Cf. Donald Davidson, 'Empirical Content', *Grazer Philosophische Studien* 16-17 (1982), 471-489 (pp. 476-77), and 'A Coherence Theory of Truth and Knowledge', in *Kant oder Hegel? Über Formen der Begründung in der Philosophie* (Stuttgarter Hegel-Kongress 1981), ed. by Dieter Henrich, Klett-Cotta, Stuttgart 1981, pp. 423-438 (see p. 426).

6. See Peter Unger, 'An Analysis of Factual Knowledge', *Journal of Philosophy* 65 (1968), 157-170.

7. For the distinction between iconic and indexical signs, see *The Collected Papers of Charles Sanders Peirce*, Vol. 2, ed. by Charles Hartshorne and Paul Weiss, Harvard University Press, Cambridge, Mass., 1932, paragraphs 2.247-2.248 and 2.275-2.291. Causal accounts of knowledge are often formulated by using expressions similar to "the fact to which the belief that *p* refers" ("the state of affairs which makes the belief true", "the state of affairs designated by a belief", etc.); cf. David Armstrong, *Belief, Truth, and Knowledge*, Cambridge University Press, London 1973, ch. 12 (p. 166); Marshall Swain, 'Knowledge, Causality, and Justification', *Journal of Philosophy* 69 (1972), 291-300, and *Reasons and Knowledge*,

Cornell University Press, Ithaca 1981, pp. 196-202. These expressions are highly problematic, and their careless use gives rise to the old problem of false belief, but I shall not try to clarify their meaning here.

8. For causal theories of knowledge, see Robert K. Shope, *The Analysis of Knowing: A Decade of Research*, Princeton University Press, Princeton, N.J. 1983, pp. 119-121, and Fred Dretske and Berent Enc, 'Causal Theories of Knowledge', *Midwest Studies in Philosophy, Vol. 9, 1984: Causation and Causal Theories*, ed. by P. French et al., University of Minnesota Press, Minneapolis 1984, pp. 517-527.

9. Edmund Gettier, 'Is Justified True Belief Knowledge?', *Analysis* 23 (1963), 121-123. Other philosophers have been presented similar examples before Gettier, for example, Bertrand Russell in *The Problems of Philosophy*, Oxford University Press, London 1912, ch. 13, and in *Human Knowledge: Its Scope and Limits*, Allen and Unwin, London 1948, but Gettier's predecessors did not present such examples as counter-examples to the justified true belief analysis.

10. See Peter Unger, 'An Analysis of Factual Knowledge', p. 158.

11. Robert Nozick, *Philosophical Explanations*, Clarendon Press, Oxford 1981, pp. 172-196. Nozick's analysis of knowledge resembles in many respects that presented by Fred Dretske in 'Epistemic Operators', *Journal of Philosophy* 67 (1967), 1007-1023, and in 'Conclusive Reasons', *Australasian Journal of Philosophy* 49 (1971), 1-22, as well as David Armstrong's "thermometer model" of non-inferential knowledge; cf. David Armstrong, *Belief, Truth, and Knowledge*, Cambridge University Press, London 1973, ch. 12. Unlike Armstrong, Nozick regards (CB1) as a general K-condition, not as one restricted to non-inferential knowledge.

12. For the concept of counterfactual dependence, see David Lewis, 'Causation', *Journal of Philosophy* 70 (1973), 556-567; reprinted (with Postscripts) in David Lewis, *Philosophical Papers, Vol. II*, Oxford University Press, Oxford 1986, pp. 159-213 (see pp. 167-169).

13. See David Lewis, *Counterfactuals*, Basil Blackwell, Oxford 1973, pp. 27-28.

14. Robert Nozick, *Philosophical Explanations*, p. 176.

15. If the truth-conditions of conditionals are defined in such a way that (CB2) is not redundant, it is far from obvious that it is necessary for knowledge, since one may learn (and hence know) something as a result of an accident or a coincidence; see Graeme Forbes, 'Nozick on Scepticism', *The Philosophical Quarterly* 34 (1984), 43-52; p. 47.

16. Fred Dretske has defined the concept of conclusive evidence or conclusive reason in this way in 'Conclusive Reasons', *Australasian Journal of Philosophy* 49 (1971), 1-22. Brian Skyrms presented a somewhat similar account (in terms of the sufficiency of e to p) in 'The Explication of 'X knows that p'', *Journal of Philosophy* 64 (1967), 373-389. I have discussed some implications and problems of this analysis in my paper 'Knowledge, Causation, and Counterfactuals', *Kausalitet (Foredrag og*

diskusjonsinnlegg ved et Nordisk seminar om kausalitet i Oslo, 11-12 april 1975), Institutt for filosofi, Universitetet i Oslo, Oslo 1976, pp. 71-82.

17. See David Lewis, *Counterfactuals*, ch. 3.

18. See Fred Dretske, 'Epistemic Operators', p. 1010, Robert Nozick, *Philosophical Explanations*, pp. 204-211, and Colin McGinn, 'The Concept of Knowledge', *Midwest Studies in Philosophy, Vol. IX, 1984: Causation and Causal Theories*, ed. by Peter A. French et al., University of Minnesota Press, Minneapolis 1984, pp. 529-554 (cf. section 4).

19. Cf. Nozick, *op. cit*, p. 198.

20. Forthcoming in *Theory and Experiment: Proceedings of the 6th Joint International Conference of History and Philosophy of Science* (Ghent, Belgium, 25.-30. August, 1986), ed. by D. Batens and J. van Bendegem, D. Reidel, Dordrecht 1988.

21. See Alvin Goldman, *Epistemology and Cognition*, Harvard University Press, Cambridge, Mass. 1986, pp. 45-46, and Laurence Bonjour, 'Externalist Theories of Empirical Knowledge', in *Midwest Studies in Philosophy, Vol. 5: Studies in Epistemology*, ed. by P. French et al., University of Minnesota Press, Minneapolis 1980, pp. 53-73. Bonjour's objection is not directed specifically against Dretske's and Nozick's conditional analyses, but against reliability conditions in general.

22. Alan Goldman has also argued that (CB1) is not necessary for knowledge; see his paper 'An Explanatory Analysis of Knowledge', *American Philosophical Quarterly* 21 (1984), pp. 106-107.

23. It seems clear that vertical requirements similar to (CB1) should be restricted to noninferential knowledge, as suggested by David Armstrong in *Belief, Truth, and Knowledge*, ch. 12.

24. The concept of defeasibility seems to have been introduced into contemporary philosophical discussion by H. L. A. Hart, who pointed out that may legal concepts are *defeasible* in the sense that their use depends (i) on conditions which are necessary but not (logically) sufficient for their application to a given situation, and (ii) on conditions which determine when the concept is not applicable even when conditions of the first kind are satisfied. (Thus conditions of first kind are *prima facie* reasons for the application of the concept, whereas conditions of the second kind are reasons against its application.) Hart adopted the concept of defeasibility from the characterization of the legal interest in property as subject to possible "termination" or "defeat" under various circumstances; see H. L. A. Hart, 'The Ascription of Responsibility and Rights', *Proceedings of the Aristotelian Society* 49 (1948-1949); reprinted in *Logic and Language, First Series*, ed. by Anthony Flew, Basil Blackwell, Oxford 1952, pp. 147-149.

25. These two interpretations of the principle of total evidence are discussed in Risto Hilpinen, 'On the Information Provided by Observations', in *Information and Inference*, ed by J. Hintikka and P. Suppes, D. Reidel, Dordrecht 1970, p. 100, and in Teddy Seidenfeld, *Philosophical Problems of Statistical Inference: Learning from R. A. Fisher*, D. Reidel, Dordrecht 1979, ch. 8.

26. Quoted from Anthony Kenny and Jan Pinborg, 'Medieval Philosophical Literature', *The Cambridge History of Later Medieval Philosophy*, ed by N. Kretzmann et al., Cambridge University Press, Cambridge 1982, p. 82. The reference is to Siger of Brabant, *Quaestiones super librum de Causis*, ed. by A. Marlasca, Publications Universitaires de Louvain, 1972, p. 35.

27. Jaakko Hintikka, *Knowledge and Belief*, Cornell University Press, Ithaca 1962, p. 20. Keith Lehrer expresses the justification condition in form "*a* is completely justified in believing that *p*". The qualification "completely" presumably refers to some kind of empirical conclusiveness, even though it is not analyzed by Lehrer and his analysis contains a separate condition of indefeasibility; cf. Keith Lehrer, *Knowledge*, Clarendon Press, Oxford 1974, pp. 18-23, and 'The Coherence Theory of Knowledge', *Philosophical Topics* 14:1 (1986): *Papers in Epistemology*, p. 6.

28. See *The Collected Papers of Charles Sanders Peirce*, Vol. V, ed. by Charles Hartshorne and Paul Weiss, Harvard University Press, Cambridge, Mass., 1934, paragraph No. 5.408.

29. See Robert K. Shope, *The Analysis of Knowing: A Decade of Research*, Princeton University Press, Princeton, N.J. 1983, ch. 2.

30. Jeffrey Tlumak and Scott Shuger have called this feature of knowledge the "hardiness" of knowledge; see their paper 'The Hardiness of Knowledge', *American Philosophical Quarterly* 18 (1981), 23-31.

31. In my paper 'Knowledge and Justification', *Ajatus* 33 (1971), pp. 1-39, I called the assumption that knowledge cannot be 'lost' simply as a result of learning something new "the extendability thesis" (p. 25).

32. The concept of accessibility has been used in this way by William G. Lycan, 'Evidence One Does Not Possess', *Australasian Journal of Philosophy* 55 (1977), 114-126.

33. Gilbert Harman's example about the public denials of a true report of a political assassination illustrates this possibility; see *Thought*, Princeton University Press, Princeton, N.J. 1972, pp. 143-145. I have discussed the "social" aspect of knowledge in my paper 'Remarks on Personal and Impersonal Knowledge', *Canadian Journal of Philosophy* 7 (1977), 1-9.

34. We might also take the relevant evidential proposition to have here the form,'It is generally believed that *r*'; examples of this kind could then be interpreted in the way suggested in section VIII.

35. Cf. Risto Hilpinen, 'Conditionals and Possible Worlds', *Contemporary Philosophy: A New Survey*, Vol. 1: *Philosophy of Language and Philosophical Logic*, ed. by G. Fløistad, Martinus Nijhoff, The Hague 1981, pp. 302-303; Peter Gardenfors, 'Conditionals and Changes in Belief', *The Logic and Epistemology of Scientific Change: Acta Philosophica Fennica 30, Nos. 3-4*, ed. by I. Niiniluoto and R. Tuomela, North-Holland, Amsterdam 1979, pp. 381-401, 'An Epistemic Approach to Conditionals', *American Philosophical Quarterly* 18 (1981), 203-211, and 'Epistemic Importance and Minimal Changes of Belief', *Australasian Journal of Philosophy* 62 (1984), 136-157.

36. Definitions of this kind have been put forward by Peter Klein, 'A Proposed Definition of Propositional Knowledge' *Journal of Philosophy* 68 (1971), p. 475, and by Carl Ginet, *Knowledge, Perception, and Memory*, D. Reidel, Dordrecht 1975, p. 80.
37. The analysis of knowledge proposed in my paper 'Knowledge and Justification', pp. 30-31, resembles (CDK2) rather than (CDK1).
38. See Carl Ginet, 'Knowing Less By Knowing More', *Midwest Studies in Philosophy, Vol. V, 1980: Studies in Epistemology*, ed. by P. French et al., University of Minnesota Press, Minneapolis 1980, pp. 151-161.
39. John A. Barker has made this distinction between two versions of the extendability thesis in his paper 'What You Don't Know Won't Hurt You?', *American Philosophical Quarterly* 13 (1976), p. 303.
40. By relaxing the minimality condition in appropriate ways it is possible to avoid various apparent (and often somewhat extravagant) counterexamples to (CDK1) and other similar conclusiveness conditions. Some far-fetched counterexamples are also blocked by the requirement that d should be "accessible to a" or an "appropriately qualified" evidential proposition.
41. See Keith Lehrer and Thomas Paxson, Jr., 'Knowledge: Undefeated Justified True Belief', *Journal of Philosophy* 66 (1969), p. 228; Keith Lehrer, 'The Gettier Problem and the Analysis of Knowledge', in *Justification and Knowledge*, ed. by George S. Pappas, D. Reidel, Dordrecht 1979, pp. 70-72; Steven R. Levy, 'Misleading Defeaters', *Journal of Philosophy* 75 (1978), 739-742.
42. See Peter Klein, 'Knowledge, Causality, and Defeasibility', *Journal of Philosophy* 73 (1976), p. 809, and 'Misleading "Misleading Defeaters"', *Journal of Philosophy* 76 (1979), p. 383; Steven R. Levy, 'Misleading Defeaters', p. 740.
43. For example, the case of Tom's theft of a book from a library and his mother's misleading testimony (in which the mother is not known to be demented or a pathological liar), and the case of the misleading letters about Donald's trip, as described by Gilbert Harman in *Thought*, Princeton University Press, Princeton, N.J. 1973, pp. 142-143, are examples in which the existence of misleading evidence can, according to Harman, prevent a person from knowing something.
44. This has also been pointed out by Jeffrey Tlumak and Scott Shuger in 'The Hardiness of Knowledge', p. 30. In his paper 'Knowledge, Causality, and Defeasibility' (cf. note 42) Peter Klein has presented an analysis of "misleading evidence" which resembles (CD9), and Tlumak and Shuger show that according to Klein's definition, many cases in which the existence of new evidence prevents a person from knowing something should be regarded as instances of "misleading evidence".
45. Carl Ginet, 'Knowing Less By Knowing More', *Midwest Studies in Philosophy, Vol. V: Studies in Epistemology*, ed. by P. French et al., University of Minnesota Press, Minneapolis, pp. 151-161.
46. Carl Ginet, 'Knowing Less By Knowing More', p. 153.
47. Carl Ginet, 'Knowing Less By Knowing More', p. 159.

48. Gilbert Harman is worried about this possibility in 'Knowledge, Inference, and Explanation', *American Philosophical Quarterly* 5 (1968), p. 173.

49. I am using the expression "aspect of knowledge" here roughly in the way Peter Unger has used this expression in his paper 'The Cone Model of Knowledge', *Philosophical Topics* 14:1 (1986): *Papers on Epistemology*, pp. 128-138.

50. The analysis presented here leaves room for the influence of several different factors on knowledge ascriptions. For example, the "minimality" of a belief revision and the epistemic qualifications of (potential) evidence propositions can be interpreted in different contexts in different ways, but the choice of an interpretation need not be arbitrary.

51. The word "perfect" is used here in the same way as in the expression "deontically perfect world" in the semantics of deontic logic.

52. Cf. Peter Unger, *Ignorance*, Clarendon Press, Oxford 1975, ch. 2, and 'The Cone Model of Knowledge', pp. 128-129; John Tienson, 'On Analyzing Knowledge', *Philosophical Studies* 25 (1974), pp. 292-293; Marshall Swain, *Reasons and Knowledge*, Cornell University Press, Ithaca 1981, pp. 160-162.

53. As was pointed out earlier, the argument presented in sections III-IV against condition (CB1) is not an argument against reliability conditions (or reliability theories of knowledge) in general; it is only an argument against the view that (CB1) is necessary for knowledge in the "classical" sense of philosophical analysis, according to which the objective of an analysis is to find a set of conditions which are individually necessary and jointly sufficient for the correct application of the *analysandum*.

54. Peter Unger has expressed this feature of the concept of knowledge by speaking about the "profile of context" which determines how the knowledge ascriptions depend in a given situation or context on various aspects of knowledge; see Peter Unger, 'The Cone Model of Knowledge', p. 139.

55. Robert K. Shope, *The Analysis of Knowing*, pp. 48-52.

56. See Robert K. Shope, 'The Conditional Fallacy in Contemporary Philosophy', *The Journal of Philosophy* 75 (1978), 397-413.

57. This condition resembles those put forward by Risto Hilpinen, 'Knowledge and Justification' Ajatus 33 (1971), pp. 29-30, Peter Klein, 'A Proposed Definition of Propositional Knowledge', *Journal of Philosophy* 68 (1971), p. 475, and Carl Ginet, *Knowledge, Perception, and Memory*, D. Reidel, Dordrecht 1975, p. 80.

58. This example is from Robert K. Shope, *The Analysis of Knowing*, p. 52.

Philosophical Perspectives, 2, Epistemology, 1988

ON KNOWING ONE'S OWN MIND

Sydney Shoemaker
Cornell University

I

One of the views associated with Descartes is that it is of the essence of mind that each mind has a special, privileged access to its own contents. Recently, I think, this view has been very much out of favor. Those who have rejected it have not, in general, denied that there is something that might be called a "special access" to one's own mental states. Usually they have not denied that normally a person knows of his own beliefs, desires, sensations, thoughts, etc. in a way that is utterly different from that in which one person knows of such mental states in another person. And in the case of at least some mental phenomena, in particular sensations and occurrent thoughts, it would generally be allowed that a person's access to those phenomena in himself is both more comprehensive and less subject to error than his access to the same sorts of phenomena in other persons. What is denied, when this Cartesian doctrine is rejected, is, first, that the special access a person has to his own mental states is necessarily infallible or "incorrigible," or at least yields knowledge having a kind of certainty which empirical knowledge about other matters cannot attain, and second, that it is in any way constitutive or definitive of mental states, or of minds, or of the concepts of these, that these states intimate their existence to their possessors in a special and direct way.

In the present paper I shall assume, at least for the sake of discussion, that the first of these denials is correct—that it is logically possible for a person to be mistaken about his own mental states, of whatever kind, and that the certainty we can attain about our own mental states is not of a different order than that we can attain about other matters of fact. The anti-Cartesian view that concerns me here is the second denial—the denial that having a special access to its mental states, what I will sometimes call "self-acquaintance," is of the essence of mind, or that being accessible in this special way is any way definitive of mental states. The anti-Cartesian sees self-acquaintance as analogous to sense-perception in one important respect; just as the existence of a tree or mountain is logically independent of its being perceived, and even of there being creatures who could perceive it, so, on the anti-Cartesian view, the existence of a belief or desire or sensation is logically independent of its being actually, or even potentially, the object of self-acquaintance. Typically the anti-Cartesian will see self-acquaintance as analogous to sense-perception in another respect as well. He will see it as involving a mechanism whereby, under certain circumstances, the existence of a certain states of affairs causes in a person a belief in the existence of that state of affairs, the cause and the effect being logically independent. And the important thing, for him, is that the existence of this belief-producing mechanism is something over and above the existence of the mental states about which it yields belief and knowledge, in the same sense in which the existence of our perceptual mechanisms is something over and above the external facts about which they yield belief and knowledge.

It is approximately true that it is only the mental states of a person that directly produce in that person beliefs in their occurrence. To be sure, excess acidity in my stomach may produce in me the belief that there is excess acidity in my stomach; but it is natural to suppose that here the belief production is mediated by the production of a sensation, something mental, and requires the background belief that sensations of that sort indicate excess acidity in the stomach. Now it seems perfectly conceivable that there should be creatures, otherwise like ourselves, who have a "special access" to physical states of themselves which is not in this way mediated by sensations and background beliefs. We can imagine, for example, that the blood pressure of these creatures varies from one moment to the next, but that if you ask one of them what his blood pressure is he is always able (after some preliminary training) to answer correctly, and is unable to give any account of how he is able to do this, except by saying that once the question is put to him he "just knows" that his blood pressure is such and such. The anti-Cartesian, as I am conceiving him, sees no important difference between the special access we in fact have to our own mental states and the access these creatures would have to their blood pressure, or which analogous creature might have to their pulse rates, their body temperatures, their blood sugar levels, and so on. And it is on his view just a contingent fact that we have the one sort of access and not the other; logically speaking, it could just as well have been the other way around.

As is probably apparent by now, I have set up this anti-Cartesian position so as to oppose it. In opposing it I will be embracing a moderate Cartesianism—a version of the view that it is of the essence of mind that each mind has a special access to its own contents, or more soberly expressed, that each person has a special access to his own mental states. Embracing this Cartesian thesis does not, of course, commit me to holding the other thesis about the mental which is most commonly associated with Descartes, namely mind-body dualism. The Cartesianism I accept is perfectly compatible with materialism.

II

As a preliminary to arguing for the essentiality of this special access, i.e., of self-acquaintance, I want to say something about its utility—about the role it plays in our lives.

The self-knowledge I will focus on in the present paper is knowledge of our own beliefs, desires and intentions. There are at least two areas in which this is important. One is in our dealings with other persons. When one is engaged in a cooperative endeavor with another, it is essential to the efficient pursuit of the shared goal that one be able to communicate to the other information about one's beliefs, desires and intentions; and in order to communicate this information one must possess it. Often an action of one's own will contribute to the shared goal only if it is followed up by an appropriate action by the other—and for the other to know what action is appropriate it may be necessary for him to know with what intention one does what one does, what one expects its consequences to be, and what one intends to do next. When in such circumstances one conveys one's beliefs to another, this is not merely for the purpose of conveying what one takes to be information about the world, namely the contents of the beliefs; it is also for the purpose of giving him information about oneself which will assist him in predicting one's behavior and so in coordinating his own behavior with it, and also to enable him to correct those of one's beliefs he knows to be mistaken. To be sure, one needn't say "I believe that P" in order to convey to another that one believes that P—usually just saying "P" will serve as well. But if one doesn't believe that one believes that P, one cannot say either of these things with the intention of conveying to the other person that one believes this. And unless that second-order belief is true, one cannot succeed in fulfilling this intention. In the absence of self-knowledge, information about a person's mental states could not be conveyed to others as the result of speech acts aimed at facilitating cooperative endeavors by conveying such information. In such circumstances, cooperative endeavor would be considerably more difficult, to say the least. And here the utility of self-knowledge depends crucially on its being acquired by self-acquaintance; if I had to figure out from my behavior what my beliefs, goals, intentions, etc. are, then in most cases it would be more efficient for others to figure this out for themselves than to wait for me to figure it out and then tell them about it.

The other useful role of self-knowledge I am going to comment on is its role in deliberation, both about what to do and what to believe. It may seem tempting to view deliberation about what to do as a battle in which one's various desires are pitted against one another, the strongest prevailing and determining one's course of action. Similarly, one might try to view deliberation about what to believe as a battle between contending beliefs or inclinations to believe. If this were right, it would seem unnecessary that the deliberator should have knowledge of the contending beliefs and desires; he would merely be the subject of them, and the battleground on which the struggle between them takes place. But this model seems hopelessly unrealistic, in part because it leaves out entirely the role of the person as an *agent* in deliberation; it represents deliberation as something that happens in a person, rather than as an intentional activity on the part of the person. That this is wrong seems obvious; what is perhaps not quite so obvious is that the agency involved in deliberation essentially involves self-knowledge.

Deliberation is a self-critical enterprise. One's beliefs, desires and intentions are up for review, and for this to occur one must not only have them but be aware of having them. Suppose that one's standing beliefs include the belief that P and the belief that if P then Q, and that one now comes up against evidence that Q is false. To see that there is a problem here that calls for resolution, it is not enough to be aware that the propositions "P," "If P, then Q," and "Not-Q" form an inconsistent triad; one must also be aware that these are all propositions one believes or is disposed to believe or has *prima facie* reason to believe. It is this awareness, plus one's desire to avoid error, that motivates the various intentional activities involved in putting one's beliefs in rational order—the review of one's reasons for believing the various propositions, and perhaps the conducting of tests and the collection of new evidence. Someone who had no idea what he believed could not entertain the possibility that any specific one of his beliefs was wrong, and could not be led by doing so to initiate activities aimed at testing that possibility. If such a person's beliefs were inconsistent, and he were aware of the inconsistency between the propositions believed, he would have to think, incoherently, that the *facts* were inconsistent! As long as he remained ignorant of the fact that these propositions were believed by him, the objective of changing his beliefs so that they are no longer inconsistent would be one that he would have no way of forming or pursuing.

Similar remarks apply to deliberation about what to do. This often stems from competing desires. But the mere fact that certain of one's desires are in conflict will not by itself motivate activity directed at resolving the conflict. The activity I have in mind involves a critical assessment of one's desires, aimed either at deferring satisfaction of certain of them, or at denying satisfaction to some of them and if possible extinguishing them. This obviously involves the operation of what Harry Frankfurt has called "second-order desires"—desires to the effect that certain first-order desires, and not others, be operative in the determination of one's behavior.[1] But to the extent that the influence of desires is rational, desires will influence behavior, including mental behavior, only in conjunction with appropriate beliefs; and where the operative desires are second-order desires, the beliefs would have to include beliefs about what one desires. Suppose that I have a desire for something the pursuit of which would conflict with other aims I have, or with fundamental values I have, and that as a result of deliberation I suppress the desire or at least deny it satisfaction. This can scarcely be a direct effect of the operation of my first-order desires together with relevant beliefs. It cannot be that the offending desire simply lost out in a tug of war between first-order desires. What we may suppose to have happened is that I noticed the conflict between this desire and others that I had, and that I then drew upon my knowledge of the world to calculate the consequences of pursuing these various competing goals (this would involve both calling up memories of relevant facts, and reasoning on the basis of what one takes to be the facts), and that I called to mind my more basic values, second-order desires, and the like, and, viewing the results of my empirical reasoning in the light of these desires, "identified" (as Frankfurt would put it) with certain of my first-order desires and resolved to restrain or suppress others of them. Like any other rational activity, this activity must have been motivated by a set of desires and beliefs which "rationalized" it. The desires will have included a higher order desire aimed at maximizing my utility or desire satisfaction in the long run, or something of the sort. The only sort of belief which could combine with this desire in such a way as to rationalize the activities involved in deliberation is a belief about one's system of desires, namely that it involves conflicts that are bound to give rise to imprudent action unless one engages in effective deliberation. And some of what goes on in the deliberative process requires for its explanation more specific beliefs about one's desires, namely beliefs to the effect that one has desires with such and such objects; only so could one be motivated to find out how the pursuit of certain objects would affect one's ability to pursue certain other objects.

III

Nothing I have said about the utility of self-knowledge and self-acquaintance entails the Cartesian thesis that it is of the essence of mental states, or of any central kind of mental states, that they be accessible to their possessor by self-acquaintance. It seems offhand that it is open to the anti-Cartesian to hold that while the higher-order intentions involved in at least some communication are no doubt useful, and while they do require a capacity for self-acquaintance, they are not essential to mentality. Likewise, even if deliberation, as it exists is in us, requires self-acquaintance, it may be, for all I have argued so far, that one could have the benefits of deliberation without such self-acquaintance.

Now on one understanding of the claim that self-acquaintance is not essential to mentality I am prepared to concede it. I am prepared to ascribe beliefs, desires, and intentions to such lower animals as chimpanzees and dogs. And offhand it seems outrageous to ascribe to such creatures beliefs about their mental states. Such animals do not engage in the sorts of communicative and cooperative endeavors that would warrant such ascriptions. Nor is there any reason to think that they go in much for deliberation. This requires me to refine the Cartesian thesis I wish to defend.

What I wish to maintain is the impossibility of something I shall call "self-blindness." A self-blind creature would be one which has the conception of the various mental states, and can entertain the thought that it has this or that belief, desire, intention, etc., but which is unable to become aware of the truth of such a thought except in a third-person way. In other words, a self-blind creature could frame and understand ascriptions to itself of various mental states, but would be incapable of knowing by self-acquaintance whether such self-ascriptions were true. Only if self-blindness were a conceptual possibility would it be appropriate to think of the capacity for self-acquaintance as a quasi-perceptual capacity which is something over and above the capacity to have and conceive of the mental states in question. And it is the appropriateness of so thinking of it that I am anxious to deny. Now, whatever else may be the case with dogs and chimpanzees, there is no reason to think that they are self-blind in this sense. If it is true that dogs lack knowledge of their beliefs, this is not because a dog can wonder whether it has a certain belief but has no way (except by observing its behavior) of establishing whether what it wonders is true!

To deny the possibility of self-blindness is to hold that it is implicit in the nature of certain mental states that any subject of such states that has the capacity to conceive of itself as having them will be aware of having them when it does, or at least will become aware of this under certain conditions (e.g., if it reflects on the matter). And this seems to me to qualify as a Cartesian thesis. In the remainder of this paper I shall be arguing in its support.

IV

Suppose a man confronts evidence which contradicts things he believes, and he makes suitable modifications in his beliefs—he modifies them in the way rationality dictates, or at any rate in one of the ways rationality allows, instead of sticking with an inconsistent or incoherent set of beliefs. Does this show self-knowledge? Specifically, does it show awareness that there was inconsistency in his beliefs and that modification was called for? I think it plainly does if the modification of belief is the effect of deliberation or reflection—we have already seen the central role self-knowledge plays here. But I wish to argue that even if no explicit rationalization or deliberation went on such a readjustment of one's beliefs requires self-knowledge, or at least something very much like it. The man, or something in him, must be sensitive to the fact that there is the inconsistency, and must know what changes in his body of belief would remove it—and this requires knowledge (or something like it) of what beliefs he has.

Someone might object that self-knowledge is no more involved here than in any other case in which a man acts on his beliefs and desires. Suppose that my beliefs and desires call for (i.e., they "rationalize," to use Donald Davidson's term) a certain course of action, and I undertake that course of action, from those beliefs and desires. Does this show that I am aware that my beliefs and desires call for that course of action? It might be thought that the fact that I so act shows that I, or something in me, is sensitive to the fact that these beliefs and desires call for that course of action. But this is true only in the sense in which a bomb, in going off, shows that it, or something in it, is sensitive to the fact that the combustion in the fuse has reached the explosive. In the case of the bomb, the "sensitivity" is nothing over and above the various properties of the bomb having their natural effects. And in the case of the person acting on his beliefs and desires, the sensitivity is nothing over and above the particular beliefs and desires having their natural effects. Roughly speaking, it is the *existence* of the beliefs and desires, not *knowledge* of their existence, that gives rise to the behavior they rationalize. This needs to be qualified, since someone who was irrational could have had those beliefs and desires and not so acted. Perhaps, then, we should add the rationality to the causal factors. The fact that the person is rational might be compared to the fact that the powder in the bomb was dry. In order that the dryness of the powder should play its enabling role, it is not necessary that the bomb, or anything in it, should *know* that the combustion in the fuse has reached the powder. And no more is it necessary that I or something in me should *know* that my beliefs and desires are such and such in order for my rationality to play its enabling role. Indeed, you might say that for me to be rational just *is* for me to be such that my desires and beliefs tend to give rise to behavior they rationalize. Perhaps what is comparable in the bomb to the rationality of the person is its "explodability"—a property which is realized in, among other things, the dryness of its powder.

Applying this to the readjustment of my beliefs in the face of new evidence, someone might say that just as we need no self-awareness in order to explain my acting on my beliefs and desires, we need none in order to explain my modifying my beliefs and desires in the light of new experience. What produces the modifications is just the existence of the beliefs and desires and experiences, plus the fact that I am rational.

But the cases seem to me importantly different. I agree that we don't need any self-awareness in order to explain why beliefs and desires jointly produce effects which they rationalize—i.e., actions which it is rational for the subject of such a set of beliefs and desires to perform. Given that the agent is rational, the mere existence of such beliefs and desires is sufficient to explain their having the appropriate effects. But if the beliefs and desires are all first-order beliefs and desires, i.e., beliefs and desires that are not themselves *about* the agent's beliefs and desires, then one thing they do not rationalize is changes in themselves. For such changes to be rationalized the beliefs and desires would have to include second-order beliefs and desires—desires to promote consistency and coherence in the system of beliefs and desires, and beliefs about what changes in the beliefs and desires would be needed in order to satisfy the second-order desires, which in turn would require beliefs about what the current beliefs and desires are.

In a rational being, there are two sorts of causal efficacy exerted by the first-order beliefs and desires. They jointly produce such effects as their contents make it rational for them to produce. And they jointly produce such effects as are needed in order to preserve or promote consistency and coherence in the belief-desire system. The latter may require the initiation of investigations aimed at discovering which of two inconsistent propositions is true, and of reasoning aimed at discovering which of two such propositions coheres best with certain other propositions, which are the contents of beliefs that are part of the system. Now it seems to me that the least we can say of this case is that it is *as if* the system contained a desire to be a rational and coherent belief-desire system, and beliefs (true beliefs) about what beliefs and desires it contains. If it is viewed as containing such second-order desires and beliefs, then the second sort of effect of beliefs and desires (the changes in the belief-desire system) can in a sense be assimilated to the first (the production of effects "rationalized" by the belief-desire system). The first-order desires and beliefs will be seen as producing knowledge of themselves, this knowledge of course consisting of true second-order beliefs. And this knowledge, given the rationality of the system and the desire to be rational (a second order desire), will produce the behavior (perhaps only "mental behavior," like reasoning) which it, together with the second-order desire, rationalizes, and which eventually results in changes in the system of beliefs and desires. But perhaps we needn't suppose that each belief or desire produces a separate state which is the knowledge or belief in its own existence. Perhaps instead it is the case that insofar as a person is rational, each belief and desire tends to double as knowledge or belief in its own existence. For perhaps in making its contribution to the preservation or restoration of consistency and coherence in the system, each desire and belief plays the causal role appropriate to a second-order belief to the effect that one has the first-order belief or desire in question. Either way, rationality would be seen as requiring self-knowledge.

I am tempted to say that if everything is *as if* a creature has knowledge of its beliefs and desires, then it *does* have knowledge of them. There is no phenomenology of self-knowledge of such states that is in danger of being ignored if we say this—there is nothing it is like to believe something, and there need not be anything it is like to know or believe that one believes something. What I am inclined to say is that second-order belief, and the knowledge it typically embodies, is supervenient on first order beliefs and desires—or rather, it is supervenient on these plus a certain degree of rationality, intelligence, and conceptual capacity. By this I mean that one has the former *in* having the latter—that having the former is nothing over and above having the latter.[2]

If this is right, then of course the "self-blind man" is an impossibility. But I realize that some will be skeptical about what I have just been saying. Why couldn't there be a creature which is simply "hard-wired" to make, in the light of new experience, the adjustments in its belief-desire system that are required to preserve rationality, without there being any second-order beliefs and desires that rationalize these adjustments? Any why couldn't this show itself in the creature's behavior, in particular in its unwillingness to avow the relevant second-order beliefs and desires? To meet this challenge, I want to present an argument aimed more directly at showing the impossibility of self-blindness. I will call it the argument from Moore's Paradox.

V

To say "It is raining, but I don't believe that it is raining" is not to assert an explicit contradiction, for both conjuncts may be true—it can be raining even though the speaker believes that it is not. But some sort of logical impropriety has been committed if this sentence is assertively uttered. This sort of impropriety—that manifested in utterances of the form "P, but I don't believe that P"—was first noticed by G. E. Moore, and has come to be discussed under the heading "Moore's Paradox."

Now there are, it seems offhand, conceivable circumstances in which such an utterance might be expected from someone who was self-blind. Assuming that self-blindness is possible, it would not of course prevent its victim from having beliefs about his environment, such as that it is raining. And offhand it would seem that it should not prevent him from expressing such beliefs by making assertions. But since he would have plenty of information about his behavior, and can be presumed not to be cognitively or conceptually deficient in any way (his deficiency is supposed to be quasi-perceptual), it ought also to be possible for him to have, and give verbal expression to, behaviorally based beliefs about his own beliefs—first-person beliefs he acquires in a "third-person way." Now it seems entirely possible that the total evidence available to a man at a given time should support the proposition that it is raining, while the total "third-person" evidence available to him should support the proposition that he does not believe that it is raining. This could happen even if the third-person evidence included the fact that he had just said "It is raining"; for the rest of the third-person evidence might support the proposition that in circumstances like these he is likely to lie! So if a self-blind man were in such circumstances, it seems that he might be led, on perfectly reasonable grounds, to assert the Moore-paradoxical sentence "It is raining, but I do not believe that it is raining."

Let us call our self-blind man George. As I have said, George's deficiency is supposed to be perceptual, or quasi-perceptual, rather than cognitive or conceptual. And this provides a reason for thinking that, contrary to what I just said, he would *not* make Moore-paradoxical utterances in such circumstances. Being as conceptually sophisticated as any of us, George ought to be as capable as anyone of recognizing the paradoxical character of Moore-paradoxical sentences. Unfortunately, there appears to be no generally agreed upon account of what exactly the logical impropriety involved in asserting such sentences is. But I suppose it would be generally agreed that the assertive utterance of such a sentence would be self-defeating. Since in asserting the first conjunct one would, if sincere, be expressing the belief which the second conjunct denies one has, one could not hope to get one's audience to accept both conjuncts on one's say so, and could have little hope of getting them to accept either. In any case, whatever the details of the right account, it ought to be possible to get George to recognize that the assertive utterance of Moore—paradoxical sentences involves some sort of logical impropriety, and defeats the normal purposes of assertion. Since we can assume him to be a rational man, we can assume that this recognition would lead him to avoid Moore-paradoxical utterances.

But let us suppose that it does so. What leads him to avoid such utterances is, presumably, his grasp of the nature of assertion and its relation to belief. But it would seem offhand that if George's conceptual grasp could have the effect of leading him to avoid Moore-paradoxical utterances, it should also have certain related effects. If asked "Do you believe that P?" he ought to answer "yes" just in case he would answer "yes" to the question "Is it true that P?" (and this should be so whether his intention is to tell the truth or to lie). Moreover, he will recognize that the meaning of "believe" makes it appropriate for the words "I believe" to function as a kind of assertion sign, but will be capable of appreciating the Gricean considerations that lead to its omission except when there are special reasons for including it (e.g., when the assertion is guarded or hesitant); so it is to expected that he will preface his assertions with "I believe" in just the circumstances in which this is pragmatically appropriate. But now George is beginning to look just like a normal person. It would appear that there would be nothing in his behavior, verbal or otherwise, that would give away the fact that he lacks self-acquaintance. This seems to conflict with what I said earlier about the benefits of self-acquaintance; for on the supposition we are now making, those same benefits would be available to a self-blind man whose cognitive and conceptual resources were comparable with ours. And how can we be sure, if this is so, that self-blindness is not the normal condition of mankind? But rather than conclude that self-acquaintance provides no benefits that would not be available without it, and that it is questionable whether we have it, it seems better to take the considerations just mentioned as a *reductio ad absurdum* of the view that self-blindness is a possibility.

What I just said was all on the supposition that George's awareness of the logical impropriety of Moore-paradoxical utterances, and in general his grasp of the concepts involved, would lead him to avoid such utterances. And it may be objected that this is unwarranted. George's conceptual grasp does lead him to see the following as a sensible rule: "If you have the intentions (Gricean or whatever) that make appropriate an assertive utterance of a sentence 'P,' don't conjoin this utterance with an assertive utterance of the sentence 'I don't believe that P.'" The trouble, it may be said, is that because of his self-blindness George is incapable of recognizing (except on third-person evidence) that the antecedent of this rule is true, and so is incapable of being guided by the rule in his linguistic activity.

But there is something peculiar about this view of the matter, if it is legitimate to suppose that George is capable of making assertive uses of language. If he has this capability he has to be capable of acting in accordance with, and in some sense following, rules of the form "If you have such and such intentions, utter 'P' assertively," even though he would, if self-blind, be incapable of detecting (except on third-person evidence, which would usually be unavailable) whether the antecedents of such rules were true. Suppose, now, that we accept the general claim that if a creature is capable of following a rule of the form "If you are in circumstances C, do X," it is in some sense capable of recognizing that it is in circumstances C. It follows right away that a self-blind creature could not possess the assertive use of language.

Here a natural rejoinder is that this general claim about rule following is false. A well constructed Celsius thermometer "acts in accordance with" the rule "When your temperature is X degrees Celsius,
register X degrees Celsius," but it does not literally recognize anything
at all. Why shouldn't the following of linguistic rules sometimes be
like this? Someone's being taught the assertive use of language is
just a matter of certain causal connections being set up between person's mental states and certain behavior, namely the making of certain sorts of utterances. And it might be said that for a person to
be such that certain mental states cause him to make certain utterances, so that he acts in accordance with rules of the form "When
in mental state M, do X," it is not necessary that he be able to *establish*
that he has those mental states— any more than a thermometer must
be able to *establish* that it has a certain temperature in order for it
to be such that its having that temperature causes it to register that
temperature.

This rejoinder sounds *prima facie* plausible. But if it applies to rules
of the form "If you have such and such intentions, utter 'P' assertively," why shouldn't it apply to the only slightly more complicated rules
which enjoin the avoidance of Moore-paradoxical utterances, require
one to assent to "I believe that P" if one assents to "P." and so on?
It is conceivable, I suppose, that a creature might be capable of being taught to act in accordance with rules of the first sort while being incapable of being taught to act in accordance with rules of the
second sort. The additional complexity of the latter might be the
straw that breaks the camel's back. But this additional complexity
should not tax the abilities of our man George, whom we are supposing to have cognitive and conceptual capacities comparable to
our own. It therefore seems to me that if despite his self-blindness
George could acquire the assertive use of language, then in doing
so he would also learn to use "believe" in such a way as to avoid
pragmatic paradox, and what goes with this, to give appropriate
answers to questions of the form "Do you believe that P?", to preface
certain kinds of assertions with the words "I believe," and in general,
to be indistinguishable from someone having the faculty of self-
acquaintance. But the truth of this conditional seems to me a *reductio ad absurdum* of its antecedent. So the immediate conclusion of
the argument from Moore's paradox is that for creatures having
cognitive and conceptual capacities comparable with our own, the
ability to acquire the assertive use of language excludes self-

blindness—more specifically, this ability necessarily goes with a capacity for self-acquaintance with respect to beliefs.

Anyone persuaded of the view that self-blindness is possible will of course reply that the most this argument shows is not that there could not be a self-blind man but only that such a man could not have the assertive use of language—or, more guardedly, that he could use language assertively only in cases in which he had third-person knowledge (i.e., a behaviorally grounded knowledge) of his own beliefs. This goes with the view that assertion is an expression of second-order beliefs (beliefs about one's beliefs) rather than first-order beliefs. This is, indeed, in line with one version of H.P. Grice's account of meaning—that according to which (leaving out some complications) meaning that P is doing something with the intention to bring about in one's audience the belief that one believes that P, through their recognition that one has this intention. Assuming that asserting involves meaning what one says, this account would suggest that sincerely asserting that P involves believing that one believes that P while insincerely asserting that P involves believing that one does not believe that P. And assuming that assertion must be sincere or insincere, this would imply that assertion involves a second-order belief as to whether one believes the thing asserted.

Now *in a way* this is what I hold myself. Since I think that anyone with the relevant conceptual and cognitive abilities will have the second-order beliefs if he has the corresponding first-order beliefs, I think that the person who makes sincere assertions expressive of his first-order beliefs will believe that he has those beliefs. But the opponent I have in mind thinks of assertion as directly the expression of second-order beliefs; and given that he thinks this, he thinks that there is a possibility which my argument cannot rule out without begging the question—namely that the self-blind man would not have the assertive use of language, except insofar as he gets second-order beliefs by third-persons means, and that he would be distinguishable from normal persons by just that fact.

What I need to support my case is a reason for thinking that someone with first-order beliefs plus human conceptual capacity and normal rationality would thereby have the use of language, where this reason does not beg the question by assuming from the start that such a person would have to have second order beliefs as well. I will now try to present such a reason. As before, George will be a supposedly self-blind man who has human intelligence and conceptual capacity. My aim will be to reduce to absurdity the supposition that he is self-blind.

Given his intelligence and conceptual capacity, George should have no difficulty coming to *understand* language—i.e, learning rules that enable him to know what the truth conditions are for utterances of indicative sentences, what intentions, desires, feelings, etc. are expressed by utterances in the various moods, and what the standard effects of such utterances are. The question is whether he could employ this knowledge in the making of assertions. Well, it would seem that he could see that certain ends he has would be furthered by his saying certain things, and that this could motivate him to say those things, in just the way in which in other cases he is motivated to do what tends, according to his beliefs, to bring about the satisfaction of his ends. More specifically, he could know that the standard effect of hearing a sentence uttered in certain circumstances is to come to believe a certain proposition, and this could lead him in certain circumstances to utter a sentence with the object of making his audience believe the proposition expressed by it. (It may be objected that he can use language to further his aims only if he knows what his aims are. But if it is true in general that purposive action requires knowledge of what one's aims are, then I need argue no further, since this implies the impossibility of self-blindness. I have been assuming, however, that at least sometimes it is one's *having* an end, not one's knowing that one has it, that combines with one's beliefs to produce action, and that this can be true when the action is one of uttering a sentence assertively.)

Earlier I mentioned a version of Grice's theory of meaning according to which the intended effect, when one means that P by uttering something, is that one's audience believe that one believes that P. But in Grice's first formulation of the theory the intended effect was said to be that the audience believe that P.[3] Obviously both sorts of intentions are possible. If someone intends by doing something to bring it about that his audience believes that it is raining, and intends that this effect come about through his audience's coming to believe that he has this intention, let us say that he has a Grice-1 intention. If the intention is that the audience should believe, through recognizing the intention, that the speaker believes that it is raining, let us say that the speaker has a Grice-2 intention. I do not wish to deny that our intentions in speaking are often Grice-2 intentions. But what I have argued is that given a general ability to engage in practical reasoning, Grice-1 intentions are enough to account for a good deal of what looks like assertion. If the self-blind man is a possibility at all, he will be capable of such intentions, and will have (or appear to have) an assertive use of language.

Does it follow that George would be indistinguishable from a normal person—and thus that we get a *reductio ad absurdum* of the supposition that he is self-blind? Well, not immediately. For what about cases in which there would be a point in his speaking with Grice-2 intentions (if only he had them), but no point in his speaking with Grice-1 intentions? Consider, for example, a case in which he knows that his hearer already believes that P (so there would be no point in his saying "P" with the object of getting his hearer to believe this), but in which there would be a point in his conveying to his hearer that he believes that P—perhaps he knows that his hearer is looking for a fellow P-believer with whom to start a partnership, so that it would be to his advantage that his hearer believe that he is a P-believer if, but only if, he actually is one. It might seem that this is the case that would provide a behavioral difference between George and the normal man. The normal man, who has self-acquaintance, would straightforwardly express his belief (either by saying "I believe that P," or by saying "P"), while George, being self-blind, would just stand there—knowing that the other already believes that P he has no motive to assert P in order to get him to believe this, and not knowing his own belief he lacks a motive for trying to get his hearer to believe that he believes that P.

But it seems to me that George would have a motive for saying "P," or "I believe that P," in this case. He could reason as follows. "P is true. [This expresses his belief, but it of course doesn't say that he has it.] It is therefore to anyone's advantage, by and large, to act on the assumption that P is true, for, ceteris paribus, one is most likely to achieve one's ends if one acts on assumptions that are true. Since this applies to anyone, it applies to me—ceteris paribus it is to my advantage to act on this assumption. But that means acting as if I believed that it is true. In this instance so acting would mean saying 'I believe that P,' or just 'P.' And plainly this would have good consequences for me. For it would lead this man to choose me as his partner, and given that what this man believes is true, a team consisting of him and someone else who will likewise act on the assumption that P is likely to be successful (since they will be acting on the assumption of a truth)."[4] Having given himself a good reason for saying "P" or "I believe that P," he then says one of these. It seems to me that he would always have such an argument available to him, in any case in which it would be rational for a self-aware believer to avow his belief. So again it looks as if he would speak, as well as act, just as a rational self-aware man would. And this calls into question the supposition that he lacks something the self-aware man has.

I should mention in passing that one thing this reasoning assumes is that having concluded that it is to his advantage to act on the assumption that P is true, George has reason to think that he will so act. Only so does he have reason to think that if he teams up with the other, the two together will act as if P were true. But if he can't do this, i.e., if his beliefs about what is the case and how he ought to behave in the future (given what he takes to be the case) give him no indication of how he will in fact behave in the future, then it seems to me that we don't have the rational sort of creature we are supposed to have. We don't have the sort of creature who can plan, or who can undertake projects that take time to execute—i.e., ones such that the initial stages make sense only on the supposition that they will be followed up in certain ways. Perhaps what we have uncovered here is a connection between knowledge of one's own mental states and intentional knowledge of one's own future behavior—knowledge that one will do something because one has excellent reasons for doing it and for that reason intends to do it. What I am inclined to think is that one cannot have the latter without the former, and that the capacity to have the latter is indispensable for any creature to which anything like human rationality can be ascribed.

One might think that George's self-blindness could show itself in his response to a request like "Tell me some things you believe." But there is no reason why this should leave him speechless. He could be sure of making an appropriate and correct response to this request by treating it as equivalent to the request "Tell me some things that are true." Interestingly enough, *trying* to satisfy the latter request, whether successful or not, guarantees *successfully* satisfying the earlier one. And there is no reason why George should not realize this.

VI

Before going on to consider how the argument from Moore's Paradox applies to states other than belief, I want to consider a pair of objections to the argument as stated so far. One of these will require me to qualify the conclusion I have drawn from it.

I began by saying that it seems offhand that there are conceivable circumstances in which the total evidence available to a man supports the proposition that it is raining while the total third-person evidence supports the proposition that he does not believe that it is raining, and that if the man were self-blind he might well come up, in such circumstances, with the Moore-Paradoxical utterance "It is raining but I don't believe that it is raining." I then went on to argue that it follows from the stipulation that the self-blind man is not in any way conceptually deficient that he would avoid such utterances, would assent to "I believe that it is raining" just in case he would assent to "It is raining," and in general would use "believe" in first-person utterances in pragmatically appropriate ways. And I wrote as if this showed that even in the sort of case envisioned his behavior would be indistinguishable from that of a normal person. The first objection is that it does not show this. As before, let George be the putatively self-blind man. If George is self-blind, then in the envisaged circumstance he is going to be very puzzled. He knows that Moore-Paradoxical utterances are to be avoided. Yet it will seem to him that such an utterance is warranted by the evidence. His grasp of the concepts of belief, assertion, etc. may prevent him from making such an utterance. But it doesn't appear that there is anything that would prevent him from giving expression to his puzzlement. And now there will be something—namely his expression of puzzlement—that distinguishes him from the normal person. This may seem to ruin my attempt to reduce to absurdity the supposition that he is self-blind.[5]

The answer to this is that the case envisioned is not really conceivable. There is a contradiction involved in the idea that the total evidence available to someone might unambiguously support the proposition that it is raining and that the total third-person evidence might unambiguously support the proposition that the person does not believe that it is raining. For the total third-person evidence concerning what someone believes about the weather should include what evidence he has about the weather—and if it includes the fact that his total evidence concerning the weather points unambiguously towards the conclusion that it is raining, then it cannot point unambiguously towards the conclusion that he doesn't believe that it is raining. So the situation I said seems "offhand" to be conceivable is not really conceivable. Since the objection now under consideration depends on the conceivability of that situation, and none of my own claims depend on it, the objection would seem to be answered.

But a related objection is not so easily answered. Consider George's knowledge of his *past* beliefs. To a large extent it can be just like the knowledge a normal person has of his past beliefs. Often one knows of one's past beliefs on the basis of "third-person evidence." One remembers what one did and said, and draws conclusions from that about what one believed. Or one knows things about what evidence was then available to one (perhaps because it was the evidence available to everyone), and concludes from that that one must have believed that such and such. Such ways of knowing about past beliefs will be available to George. But there is an additional way normal people can know about past beliefs. Sometimes a belief does not manifest itself in any behavior, verbal or otherwise. And in some such cases information about what evidence was available concerning a certain matter may be insufficient to indicate what the person believed about it. This might be because the belief was due to wishful thinking, or it might be because it arose from complex inferences which the person's behavior gave no indication that he was performing or capable of performing. Now in some such cases a normal person will nevertheless know later on what he believed— he will have known this by "self-acquaintance" at the time, and will have retained this knowledge in memory. This is the sort of memory one expresses by saying "I remember thinking at that time that," or "I remember that despite the evidence to the contrary, I was convinced that...". But if George is self-blind, and lacks the faculty of self-acquaintance, then he won't have this sort of knowledge of his past beliefs. And this is a difference between him and other people that should be detectable; if a person never has beliefs about his past beliefs that are not grounded on third-person evidence, this fact should reveal itself. Of course, George might make himself indistinguishable from other people by *pretending* to have such beliefs. But the claim that he might be indistinguishable from normal people for *this* reason can hardly be used as part of a reductio ad absurdum argument against the supposition that he is self-blind.

I think that this objection does require me to qualify my claims. If someone's access to his own past beliefs is completely a third-person access, let us say that he suffers from DAPB (for direct access to past beliefs) deficiency. It does seem that self-blindness would bring DAPB deficiency with it, and that DAPB deficiency would be detectable. It doesn't follow, however, that there is self-blindness wherever there is DAPB deficiency. For why couldn't there be someone whose faculty of self-acquaintance is unimpaired, but who has a memory impairment that results in DAPB deficiency but does not interfere with the memory of facts known otherwise than on the basis of self-acquaintance? If there could be, then I can modify my claim as follows: while the self-blind man would not be indistinguishable from a normal person, he would be indistinguishable from someone who has self-acquaintance but suffers from DAPB deficiency.

Let's come at this from another direction. Our earlier discussion suggests that when George has the belief that P, his behavior will be that of someone who believes that he believes that P. This implies that George has a state that plays at least a good part of the causal role of the second-order belief expressed by "I believe that P." That is, he has a state that combines with his desires and other beliefs to produce the sorts of behavior that that second-order belief, together with those other beliefs and desires, would rationalize. All of this he would have simply in virtue of being rational, having normal conceptual capacities, and having the relevant first-order beliefs. Let's call this a "quasi" second-order belief, where this leaves it open whether it is a genuine second-order belief or an "ersatz" one. The supposition that George is self-blind is the supposition that it is ersatz. What the objection just raised comes to is that on this supposition this quasi second-order belief would lack one part of the causal role of the genuine second-order belief that one believes that P. Part of the causal role of such a second-order belief is to have, to borrow a term of David Kaplan's, a certain sort of "cognitive dynamics"—such a state produces, or turns into, a past tense second-order belief to the effect that one did at the time in question have the first-order belief in question. And this state will be causally independent of the corresponding past tense first-order belief. For example, if at t I believe that it is raining, and believe that I believe this, then the latter belief will turn into a belief that I believed at t that it was raining, and this is a belief I may continue to have even if I cease to believe that it was raining at t. But now let us imagine someone, call him

George*, who is just like George except that when he believes that P, his quasi-belief that he believes that P not only plays the causal role that George's plays but also has the cognitive dynamics of a genuine second order belief—it produces, or turns into, a state that plays the causal role of a past tense belief on his part that he previously believed such and such. Anyone who thinks George*'s present tense quasi second-order beliefs are ersatz will probably think that his past tense ones are ersatz too. And anyone who thinks that George's present tense quasi second-order beliefs are ersatz will probably think that George*'s are ersatz too. For it hardly seems plausible that adding this additional bit to the causal role of a state turns it from an ersatz belief to a real one, and bestows on its possessor a faculty of self-acquaintance—especially if, as I suggested earlier, someone possessing such a faculty could suffer from DAPB deficiency. But George* will not be distinguishable from a normal person even in the way George was. It does not seem at all plausible to me to deny that George* has a faculty of self-acquaintance. And I think that if we allow that he has one, we should allow that George has one as well, and that self-blindness with respect to belief is an impossibility.

VII

At best, the argument I have given so far shows that George, the putatively self-blind man, would give every indication of having knowledge of his own *beliefs*—it says nothing about his situation *vis a vis* his other propositional attitudes, such as desire, hope, intention, etc.. Now there are counterparts to Moore's paradox in the case of these other propositional attitudes. In the case of desire, the Moore-paradoxical utterances would be ones like "Please close the window, but I don't want you to" and "How old are you?—but I don't want you to tell me." In the case of hope there is "Would that he would come, but I hope that he doesn't." For the case of intention there is "I'll be there, but I intend not to be." Will my argument from Moore's paradox, and the related points I have made, show that George will give indications of having knowledge of his own desires, hopes and intentions?

Up to a point it will. Given his intellectual abilities, George will see the advisability of avoiding the Moore-paradoxical utterances relating to desire, etc., just as he saw the advisability of avoiding those relating to belief. So, for example, even when the behavioral evidence indicates that he doesn't want something, and he does in fact want it and so is disposed to ask for it, he will not come up with the likes of "Please close the window, but I don't want you to." But as in the case of belief, if he is capable of avoiding Moore-paradoxical utterances, he should in other ways be capable of using the verbs of propositional attitude in pragmatically appropriate ways. He should answer affirmatively to "Do you want X" if he answers affirmatively to "Shall I give you X?" If he is capable of using language at all, he should be capable of giving linguistic expression to his desires, e.g., by making requests and other speech acts aimed at the attainment of things he wants. And if he is capable of doing this, he should be capable of learning to do it by saying things of the form "I want X" or "I would like X." Similar considerations suggest that words like "hope" and "intend" will turn up in his first-person utterances, used in pragmatically appropriate ways.

But there are two parts of my argument about belief for which there are no counterpart arguments about desire and other propositional attitudes (from now on, I will talk only about desire). I could claim without begging any questions that simply in having the belief that P George has a premise, namely P, from which he can reason that it is to his advantage to act in ways expressive of belief that P, including saying that he believes it. But belief is unique among propositional attitudes in being such that having the attitude entails having available as a premise the proposition that is the "object" of the attitude. Obviously this is not true of desire. Also, and what goes with this, there seems to be no formula for satisfying the request "Tell me some of your desires" that is comparable with the one I suggested for satisfying the request "Tell me some of your beliefs," namely treating this as equivalent to "Tell me some things that are true."

Perhaps, however, these differences between belief and desire are made up for by another one. As practical reasoning is usually represented, in the basic case statements about the agents's beliefs will not figure among the premises—the premises will of course be expressions of the agent's beliefs, but what they will be about is the nature of the world and the agent's situation in it. With desire, however, it seems different; it is natural to include among the premises statements about the agent's desires or goals. So, in a simple case, the premises might be "I want X" and "The most efficient way of getting X is to do A," and the conclusion "I should do A."

Earlier I said that it seems that it is the *having* of beliefs and desires, not believing that one has them, that leads to action. But when the action is the result of practical reasoning, this seems at best half true—the premises need not express a belief about the agent's beliefs, but they must, it may seem, express a belief about his desires. If we further claim that rationality plus human conceptual and intellectual capacity requires engaging, or appropriate occasions, in practical reasoning which results in actions rationalized by the agent's desires, we get the conclusion that it requires self-knowledge with respect to desire, and hence that self-blindness is impossible. This is of course a much quicker argument than the one I gave about belief, and bypasses the argument from Moore's paradox.

It can be objected, however, that the premises in practical reasoning need not be explicitly about the agent's desires. The work done by premises about the agent's desires or goals can be done instead by premises about what is good or desirable. Instead of "I want X" we might have "It is desirable that I should have X." This brings us to a tangled issue: the connection between regarding something as desirable and actually desiring it. If the former entailed the latter, we could have our man George reasoning as follows: "X is desirable. Therefore [by my earlier argument] I should act as if I believed that X is desirable, and so, among other things, should include the claim that I believe this among the premises I employ in my reasoning. From this premise it follows that I desire X. So if I am asked what I desire I should say that I desire X, in the absence of reasons for doing otherwise." In that case George's behavior would presumably be that of a normal person. And assuming that regarding something as desirable and desiring it generally go together, it would seem that such reasoning would for the most part lead to George's acting as if he has self-acquaintance with respect to his desires. Indeed, if we could suppose that George is a perfectly rational being, we would have no problem—for in a perfectly rational being, presumably, desiring and regarding as desirable would always go together. But all I have been supposing is that George is rational to the extent that normal human beings are—it is on that degree of rationality, plus first-order beliefs and desires and normal human intelligence, that I want to claim that self-acquaintance supervenes. And in normal human beings desiring and regarding-as-desirable do sometimes come apart. So I need an argument to show that in the exceptional cases in which this happens George will still behave as if he had knowledge of his desires—or as much such knowledge as the rest of us do.

I have no argument for this that satisfies me. Still, the claim seems to me plausible. We have already seen that George can be expected to say things of the form "I want X" as the expression of his desires, and it is to be expected that he will sometimes say this even when he would admit that the thing wanted is not objectively desirable. Similarly, it is to be expected that he will sometimes say "I don't want X" as the expression of a desire not to have something, say a painful medical treatment, even when he would admit that the thing is objectively desirable. The difficulty of producing a decisive argument here is due in part to the fact that, issues about self-knowledge aside, it is difficult to know what to say about cases in which there seems to be a discrepancy between what a person wants and what he thinks is objectively desirable, valuable, or worthwhile. It is natural to say that if the person really does regard something as objectively desirable then in some sense he wants the thing, although in another sense he doesn't. Given what I have said about George, it does not appear to me that the conflicting indications about what he wants, and about what he thinks about what he wants, would be different from what we find in normal people.

Although I do not claim to have a decisive argument, I think that my consideration of Moore's paradox gives support to the claim that normal human rationality and intelligence plus first-order beliefs and desires gives you everything, in the way of explanation of behavior, that second-order beliefs can give you—from which we should conclude either that second-order beliefs are superfluous or, what I think is the correct conclusion, that second-order beliefs, and the self-knowledge they constitute, are supervenient on first-order beliefs and desires plus human rationality and intelligence. To accept the latter conclusion is to reject the possibility of self-blindness, and with it the perceptual model of self-awareness.

VIII

Let me end by trying to forestall one possible objection to what I have been saying. It may be thought that in denying the possibility of self-blind man I am denying the possibility of unconscious beliefs, desires and intentions. And it may be objected that we know, from the work of Freud and others, that any such denial has to be wrong.

Fortunately, the question of whether self-blindness is a possibility is not the same as that of whether there can be unconscious beliefs, desires, etc.. Clearly, a man with the unconscious belief that he is a failure is not someone who is prepared to assert "I am a failure" but not "I believe that I am a failure." Presumably he will be no more disposed to assert the first than the second, and in fact can be expected to deny both. Nor, presumably, will he be someone whose nonverbal behavior is always, or normally, what rationality would dictate for someone having the beliefs and desires he has, including the belief that he is a failure. That belief may manifest itself in his behavior in devious ways, but it is not to be expected that he will act on it, in the sense of performing actions which it, in conjunction with his other beliefs and desires, "rationalizes." Here, admittedly, things begin to get messy, for it is arguable that there is a *kind* of rationality, albeit very limited rationality, involved in self-deception about such matters—in failing to face up to what deep down he knows, the man is protecting himself against situations that would be very painful. Still, I take it that overall such a man's actions, in relation to his beliefs, values, etc., exhibit a failure of rationality. What I have asserted, in denying the possibility of self-blindness, is a connection between self-knowledge and rationality; that given certain conceptual capacities, rationality necessarily goes with self-knowledge. It is entirely compatible with this that there are failures of rationality that manifest themselves in failures of self-knowledge. And such I assume we have in cases of unconscious belief. All of this, I realize, puts a rather heavy burden on the concept of rationality. Fortunately, that is a matter for another paper, which I haven't the slightest idea of how to write.[6]

Notes

1. See Frankfurt's "Freedom of the Will and the Concept of a Person," *Journal of Philosophy*, 68 (1971), 5-20.
2. A very similar view is expressed by Colin McGinn, in *The Character of Mind* (Oxford, 1982), pp. 20-21.
3. For Grice's earlier formulation, see his "Meaning," *The Philosophical Review*, 66, (1957), 377-88. For his later formulation, see his "Utterer's Meaning and Intentions," *The Philosophical Review*, 78 (1969), 147-77.
4. Our (putatively) self-blind man would of course have to contend with the point that acting as if one believed a true proposition may not conduce to the attainment of one's goals if at the same time one is acting

on other beliefs that are false. But here he is no worse off than someone who is not self-blind. Many philosophers (e.g., Davidson) have offered more or less a priori arguments in favor of the presumption that beliefs are generally true; and our man is as entitled as anyone to avail himself of such arguments. And even if this presumption cannot be supported on a priori grounds, there would seem to be good empirical evidence in its favor, which likewise would be available to our man, even if (*ex hypothesis*) he doesn't know what in particular his own beliefs are. And of course, the argument I imagine him giving about P is one he can give about any proposition which in fact he believes—so if someone points out that acting on P will advance his aims only if Q is true and he acts on it, then if in fact he believes that Q he will be able, arguing as above, to give himself reason for acting as if he believed that both P and Q are true.

5. This objection was raised by a member of the audience when I read an earlier version of this paper at Berkeley. At the time I had no answer to it.

6. I am grateful to Carl Ginet, Richard Moran and Robert Stalnaker, to members of my 1985 NEH Summer Seminar on "Self-Consciousness and Self-Reference," and to audiences at Berkeley, Duke, Harvard, Trinity College, Dublin and the University of South Carolina, for comments and criticisms of earlier versions of this paper.

References

Frankfurt, Harry: 1971, "Freedom of the Will and the Concept of a Person," *Journal of Philosophy*, 68, 5-20.

Grice, H.P.: 1957, "Meaning," *The Philosophical Review*, 66, 377-88.

Grice, H.P.: 1969, "Utterer's Meaning and Intentions," *The Philosophical Review*, 78, 147-77.

McGinn, Colin: 1982, *The Character of Mind*, Oxford University Press.

Philosophical Perspectives, 2, Epistemology, 1988

KNOWLEDGE AND EPISTEMIC OBLIGATION

Hector-Neri Castañeda
Indiana University

> But our first assumptions must be
> examined more carefully.
> PLATO

Introduction

Basic epistemology is the general study of the uses and meanings of sentences, whatever the language they belong to, that can be paraphrased as or translated into instances of the schema '*x* knows that *p*'. After Edmund Gettier the problem has been customarily put in terms of the formula:

(BF) *x* knows that *p* = *x* has a justified true belief that *p* that satisfies some condition C.

The disputes pertain mainly to condition C. There are, however, several difficulties with the pursuit of that mysterious condition C within the framework of (BF). But here we shall discuss only one crucial component of (BF), namely: the notion of *justifiedness* that enters in the definientia of (BF). This notion is considered by most specialists to be normative. Hence, basic epistemology turns out to be a normative discipline, aiming at determining in general terms what we ought, or what it is permissible for us, to believe, sometimes knowledge being equated with the state of truly believing what one ought to believe. Yet it is a scandal, yes, a *scandal*, that the many efforts at analysis have included no sustained attempt at developing the requisite deontic logic for epistemology. Thus, it seems, a good deal of work in basic epistemology has ensued in floating theories crying out for an anchor.

Here I first develop an epistemic counterpart of the deontic paradox that has been called The Good Samaritan. This development sheds some light on the nature of knowledge, and shows that in epistemology we need some distinctions analogous to similar distinctions that have proven to be so fruitful in actional deontic logic. This suggests that we may have a unified theory of epistemic and actional deontology. This theory is outlined in the final section of the paper. It happens to be the most comprehensive actional deontic logic available.

We leave for further studies to develop a *two-tier multiple-pronged epistemology* suggested by the structure of morality and moral conflicts. That theory would be a multiple-pronged doxastic deontology, pertaining to what one is justified in believing, subordinated to a conflict-solving epistemic deontology.[1]

I. Epistemic Justification: General Deontology

1. The Scandalous Lack of an Epistemic Deontology

The concept of belief justification is generally claimed to be normative. Yet, curiously, no sustained effort has been made to clarify its normative, or deontic, structure. One deontic principle that has received some discussion is so-called Kant's axiom:

(K.1) Ought implies Can.

The context of discussion has been the general fact that we are caused to have most of the beliefs we have with apparently little control over them. Yet this principle has been discussed in a deontic vacuum. As a consequence, most proposed theories of epistemic justification are floating balloons lacking anchor. In particular it is seldom remarked that beyond logical consistency, it is not clear what sense of *Can* is at issue. Much less has it been observed that in strong senses of *Can* on which the axiom holds some obligatory actions are bound to be ones the agent cannot do, e.g., in the case of conflicts of duties. We will here have much more to say about conflicts of duties, hence we will simply assume that Kant's axiom holds for logical and other *Can*'s without bothering to demarcate their limits.

More significant is a prevailing ambivalence about the normative character of epistemic justification. Most epistemologists, concerned with person's actual beliefs, tend to understand the schematic sentence 'S is justified in believing that p' as:

(EN.1) S believes that *p* and S has a right to believe that *p* (or, S believes that *p* and it is permissible for S to do so).

Sometimes, however, the schema is understood as meaning:

(EN.2) *S should (is obligated to) believe that p.*

Obviously, this semantic decision is not without importance.

Alvin Goldman has, with his characteristic sophistication, proposed to employ both normative interpretations[2]. With most epistemologists, he has adopted as primary the permissibility interpretation (EN.1) for the justification of "*an actual* belief," and he calls it *ex post justifiedness*. But he broadens his discussion to include cases of propositions "one would (could) be justified in believing, ... *ex ante* justifiedness [requiring] obligation rules" (*op. cit.*, p. 112), thus adopting (EN.2) as well. Undoubtedly, this combination of (EN.1) and (EN.2) places a heavier demand on the needed logics of obligation and permission. Goldman does not, however, stoop to raise the question of the requisite epistemic deontic logic.

The combination of (EN.1) and (EN.2) is intrinsically serious. Since (EN.1) is a conjunction of a psychological statement and a normative one, the question arises as to how the normative conjunct of (EN.1) relates to (EN.2). The answer to this question is of both theoretical and practical importance. For one thing, a standard principle of most deontic logics for action is this:

(O ~ P ~) *It is Mly obligatory for X to do A* is equivalent to *It is not Mly permissible for X to fail to do A.*

Here the adverb 'Mly' does duty for any expression that indicates a type of deontic structure, e.g., adverbs like 'morally', 'legally', 'in accordance with Peter's promise 157', 'by virtue of article 117 (clause i) of the Alabama Income Tax Law'[3].

If principle (O ~ P ~) holds for epistemic deontology, we can have a unified theory of justification. We can then ask questions about the justification of belief in one and the *same* sense, regardless of whether the beliefs are actual or not. Indeed, furthermore, independently of $(O \sim P \sim)$ we should be able to ask the question of justifiedness about present or merely possible beliefs in the same sense. It is of the essence of normativity that deontic status and actuality are mutually independent, that is:

(NF*) *It is Mly obligatory (permissible, wrong, optional) for X to do A (be in state S) neither implies nor is implied by X does [has done, will do] A (X is [will be, has been] in state S).*

Consequently, *no* obligatory action loses its obligatoriness by being performed: "She was obligated to do it, and she did it," or "She did it because she was obligated to do it"—we say consistently.

It seems, then, that we should aim at a general theory of epistemic justification that treats S's believing that p as possessing a deontic status, determined by a set of epistemic rules and facts, regardless of whether S's believing that p obtains or not. It is clearly perplexing to suppose that S's believing that p can give rise only to the question whether S is permitted to believe that p, but not to the question whether it is obligatory for him to do so. If this perplexity is a fact, it should be resolved in a fuller theory of epistemic justification erected on the proper epistemic and doxastic deontic logic. Now, if obligation and permission to believe are not related as indicated by $(O \sim P \sim)$, then this principle is false for the values *epistemically* and *doxastically* of the variable 'Mly', and we urgently need a theory of epistemic and doxastic deontology—one without $(O \sim P \sim)$.

Thus, from every side there is a cry for an epistemic and doxastic deontic logic.

2. Ideal Epistemic Deontic Logic

The standard approach that interprets doxastic justification primarily in terms of permissibility vents an important insight. In general deontic logic there are good reasons for considering obligatoriness to be closed under logical implication. This has to do with the objectivity of obligatoriness, which in its turn arises from the ultimate orientation of obligatory action, namely: the guidance of conduct and the production of behavior of certain kinds. In contrast, psychological attitudes are very much subjective in being finite in content and, hence, not closed under logical implication. E.g., we cannot even think of, let alone believe, some of the consequences of what we believe. Thus, it seems excessive to demand that we ought to believe everything whatever that our beliefs imply. Yet it does not seem out of order to claim that it is permissible to believe any consequence of what one believes. Nothing untowards seems to ensue even from being permitted to believe *all* the consequences of the totality of our beliefs, if this totality is logically consistent—even though we may be unable to satisfy that permission.

Some epistemologists argue that one may be justified in believing contradictions, although not obligated to believe contradictions. Here we would be abandoning the weak version of Kant's axiom, namely:

(K.2) What is permitted is possible.

Now, (K.2) and $(O \sim P \sim)$ are incompatible with the principle:

(OT) Tautological acts (or states) are obligatory.

The finitude of psychological acts and states makes it excessive to make a person actually responsible for believing all tautological propositions just because they are tautological. More specifically, it is morally and epistemologically outrageous to hold a person liable to criticism—not to mention other forms of epistemic or social punishment-for not believing tautologies that she or he cannot even think. It seems, then, that the best policy is to deal exclusively with *doxastic permissibility*—even for the case of Goldman's *ex ante* justifiedness.

On the other hand, it seems somewhat too licentious merely to allow a person to believe tautologies that she is clearly able to think and even needs to think for certain inferences. We must certainly regard it as epistemically wrong to believe obvious available contradictions. Thus, here are some decisions for epistemological deontology[4].

We need a minimally objective sense of epistemic obligation. Believing truly is a state we desire to gain in the pursuit of truth. This imposes an obvious constraint. Epistemological deontology cannot sanction believing everything whatever. But epistemological deontology cannot sanction with equanimity our believing falsehoods just because we believe falsehoods that imply them. *Objectively*, epistemology in its concern with truth frowns upon our expanding the domain of believed falsehoods. Yet it should be tolerant of, without condoning, our major doxastic faults—let alone our doxastic foibles. Thus, *subjectively* epistemology can succeed by not demanding blame for our inferring falsehoods from falsehoods.

It seems, then, that we need a two-storied epistemology: a lower level where believers are blamed and held responsible for certain false beliefs, and a higher level, where objectivity reigns, a realm of *ideal* doxastic fittingness, or requiredness. Even Goldman's *ex post* justifiedness can, by being closed under logical implication, fruitfully guide our acquisition of beliefs: being ideal, that fittingness would *not* be intimately tied to blame for violating it; blame would be adjudicated only to those agents who in some special ways, e.g., deliberately, resist conforming with some special manifestations of it when they confront it.

We already have a model of objective normative idealization of practical (practitional, we will call them) attitudes in the key principle of hypothetical imperatives. This is *one* bridging principle of implication between an agent's motivation and her recognition of obligations or commitments in order to comply with them. It projects from logically not closed wants and desires into logically closed ideal wants or hypothetical *oughts*. This is a principle of rationality that guides deliberation[5]. Here lie exciting issues we cannot go into.

In brief, in the case of doing, we must distinguish blame and responsibility from primary obligation. An agent ought Rly (= by a certain rule R) to do an action A; he fails to A; yet it is in general an open matter whether the agent is (i.e., ought Rly or otherwise) to be blamed for not doing A. Likewise, in the case of believing, we must distinguish between the wrongness possessed by a certain state of believing and the epistemic or doxastic blame that may, or may not, accrue to the believer for exemplifying that belief state.

It still remains the case that to believe is not a typical action, but a state, indeed a dispositional state that need not be manifested in anything occurrent at a given time. Furthermore, it is a crucial fact that many, perhaps most, of our beliefs lie beyond our control. Moreover, it is still true that in epistemology we need a much stronger separation than in morality between what a person ought to do and what a person is to be blamed for. For these reasons it may be better to speak neither of believers as agents nor of believing as an action, our epistemic normative judgments being, not so much of the Ought-to-Do type, but rather of the Ought-to-Be type. Then we can distinguish the fundamental epistemic and doxastic Ought-to-Be-Believed's from the derived Ought-to-Be-Blamed-For's[6].

3. A Deontic Logic Suitable for Epistemology

We urgently need a carefully formulated ideal deontic logic of belief. Fortunately, at this juncture we can resort to the work of deontic logicians. Naturally, we must resort to the richest and most comprehensive deontic logics in the market. There is, as luck has it, at least one simplest and richest and most comprehensive deontic logic. This is a two-sorted logic that distinguishes between circumstances or *grounds* of obligation and *foci* of obligatoriness, and caters to quantification and identity. One notable feature of that deontic logic is its faithfulness to ordinary deontic English; another is its being paradox-free, indeed fruitfully so by having *pre*-solved the so-called deontic paradoxes—discovered for other systems. Moreover, that theory of deontic logic has pre-solved all the paradoxes—except for the Powers paradox, which delves into the defeasibility of obligations—in a unified single fell swoop[7]. In the next section we discuss a deontic epistemic paradox in order to see the importance of the deontic ground/focus distinction in epistemology.

Consequently, we adopt the above mentioned system of deontic logic, called D^{**} as the basic structure of ideal epistemic deontology. It is outlined in Part II below. Since the system takes the strong modality of the *ought* type as central, a reader who prefers epistemic permissibility as his or her primitive deontic operator may, in accordance with $(O \sim P \sim)$ above, rephrase our strong deontic modalities in terms of the weaker modality *is permissible*.

D^{**} must be enriched with principles peculiar to epistemic deontic logic. We must, however, appreciate the fundamental distinction between grounds and foci of obligatoriness, which is the simplifying trademark of system D^{**}. The distinction between deontic grounds and deontic foci is itself a manifold of distinctions, which together with other distinctions are subsumed in the theory of practical reasoning embodied in D^{**} under the heading *the proposition/practition distinction*. It is of the utmost importance in epistemology to see that some epistemic distinctions can, and with a great economy of theory, be subsumed under the proposition/practition distinction. We show this in the ensuing sections.

4. Circumstances or Grounds vs. Foci of Obligatoriness

Here is no room for an illuminating exploration in detail of all the manifestations in epistemic justification of the known paradoxes of deontic logic and of intentional action. But at least one illustration is *de rigueur*. We will consider the Good Samaritan paradox.

Counterparts of The Good Samaritan, a celebrated paradox affecting many actional deontic calculi, can be formulated for doxastic and epistemic deontology. The lessons to be derived are the same, mainly, that we must distinguish between the *circumstances* that originate, or surround, obligations and the *foci* of such obligations. To illustrate consider:

(e.1) John ought Rly to do the following:
(a) *if the Library finds a copy of Plato's Theaetetus for him*, READ the *Theaetetus*, and
(b) only if *he reads the Theaetetus*, WRITE an essay proposing a new definition of knowledge, and
(c) if and only if *he proposes a new definition of knowledge*, LEAD an oral discussion of his definition.

In (e.1) the whole conjunction (a)&(b)&(c) is within the scope of, and is the argument of, the deontic operator *ought Rly to do the following*. The argument is a conjunction of three mixed conditionals: the conditions-sufficient in the case of (a), necessary in the case of (b), and both necessary and sufficient in the case of (c)—are just *that*: conditions or grounds for the other components of the conditionals. These other components are the *foci* of obligatoriness. This semantico-pragmatic contrast between deontic conditions and foci is neatly signaled in English by the grammatical contrast between the indicative mood of the expressions of conditions and the infinitive mood of the deontic foci. The grammar is, however, just a signal of a fundamental difference. More importantly, the two components are logically asymmetric. In the case of (a) there is a valid internal *modus ponens*, but a fallacious internal *modus tollens*: the first inference schema (s.1) below is valid, whereas (s.2) is invalid:

(s.1) (e.1)
The Library finds (will find) a copy Plato's *Theaetetus* for John;
therefore, John ought to read the *Theaetetus*.

(s.2)   (e.1)
> John won't read the *Theaetetus*;
> therefore, the Library ought not to find a copy of Plato's
> *Theaetetus* for John.

In the case of (b) the situation is reverse: It allows an internal *modus tollens*, but not an internal *modus ponens*. In the case of (c) there are both a valid internal *modus ponens* and a valid internal *modus tollens* just in case the minor premise is the condition *John proposes a new definition of knowledge* or its denial, the deontic focus *(John to) LEAD an oral discussion of his definition* remaining within the scope of the deontic operator. These special roles of allowing internal inferences are of the essence of deontic foci: They allow the foci to be the whole argument of a deontic operator as in the conclusion of (s.1) above, and they also allow deontic grounds or conditions to function as independent premises, as shown also by (s.1).

Deontic foci have other logical and syntactic properties. But this should suffice to establish the distinction between deontic conditions (or grounds) and deontic foci. The former I have called *propositions* because they are true or false, and are believed to obtain or not; the latter I have called *practitions*, which are neither true nor false, but are the basic characteristic irreducible contents of practical thinking, the core contents of commands, of intentions, of deontic judgments, of the practical mental states of desiring, wanting, purposing, planning, etc. They are the proprietary accusatives of intending oneself or wanting others to do something, but cannot function as accusatives of believing, or supposing that; nor are they the accusatives of knowing that, yet they are the accusatives of knowing *what to do*. (This expression 'what to do' is here a practitional variable.) Thus, the propositional and practical powers and acts of the mind differ both in their content and in their causal psychological reality, and the two differences are intimately connected[8].

Here we are concerned with only one surface, but significant aspect of the cartography of mind and of the syntax and semantics of the natural language through which that aspect is realized. Specifically, here we aim at establishing three things:

(i) The Doxastic Good Samaritan reveals an important duality of thought content within claims about what is permitted or obligatory to believe;

(ii) that duality has to be taken into account by *any* theory of doxastic justification minimally rich enough to deserve our attention, and

(iii) the theoretical *posit* to identify that duality with the proposition/practition duality, which has proven so fruitful in action theory, is a simplifying, perhaps the simplest, stroke of theorization about doxastic and epistemic deontology: It merely embeds the solution within an already comprehensive and tested theory.

5. The Doxastic (Epistemic) Paradox of the Good Samaritan

The Good Samaritan was a problem for certain actional deontic calculi because it involved a person's duty or right to do something in order to palliate a wrong done before. But it soon became clear that the Good Samaritan need not be different from the wrongdoer. Furthermore, it soon became obvious to some of us that the problem arises even in the case of duties to make amends for future wrongdoing. As discussed above, in the doxastic situation we must consider not so much the wrong*doing* of a state of believing and the actions of *making* amends, but the fittingness, or the rational Ought-to-Beness of a state of believing.

Alvin Goldman has developed examples in which a person, Millicent, believes what she remembers (or perceives), correctly in fact, in spite of warnings by persons (parents, neurosurgeons) in a position to know, that those memories (or perceptions) are false. He claims that such a person believes without epistemic permission, or right, to do so (see citations above). Other philosophers disagree on this. But that is not the issue here. The point is that sometimes a person can believe without justification. Let us, for once, forgo the tradition in basic epistemology of setting examples within literary gems, and allow ourselves a prosaic schematic example. Imagine a situation illustrating the following:

(1) It is not epistemically permitted that X believe that *p*.

(2) Yet X believes that *p*.

(3) Clearly, it ought epistemically to be that X makes a sort of amends: has and believes an explanation of why he believes that *p*.

(3′)Alternatively put, it is not epistemically permissible that X not have and believe an explanation of why he believes that *p*.

An important principle of deontic logic is expressed in colloquial English as follows:

> (DL*) If doing A implies doing B, then:
> (a) the obligation to A implies the obligation to B;
> (b) not being permitted not to A implies not being permitted not to B;
> (c) not being permitted to B implies not being permitted to A.

There are crucial problems concerning the proper interpretation of (DL*). In fact, we are anxious both to show this and to promote the sound interpretation of (DL*).

To prepare the ground for an application of (DL*) note that:

> (4) *Having and believing an explanation of why one believes that p* $= = >$ *believing that p.*

NOTE: Hereafter we may use the symbol '$= = >$' to denote logical (or conceptual or analytic) implication. Hence, from (3) and (DL*):

> (5) (a) it ought epistemically to be that X believe that p;
> (b) it is not epistemically permissible that X not believe that p.

Now, another standard deontic principle is this:

> (DL.1) It is Mly obligatory that A $= = >$ It is Mly permissible that A.

Hence, (5), in either form, implies:

> (6) It is epistemically permissible that X believe that p.

Clearly, (6) contradicts (1). This reasoning (1)-(6) is an epistemic (doxastic) counterpart of The Good Samaritan.

Some comments on the preceding argument may not be amiss.

First, the argument depends crucially on the present tense and on the duty to explain implying the duty to believe what is explained. The paradox does not arise, as Harald Pilot showed to me, in cases in which a person has *changed* his mind from believing that p to believing that $\sim p$. In this case the duty to explain why one believed that p does not yield that one believes that p. Pilot's example: At time T Hobbes believed that the circle is squarable, and that at time T', later than T, he believed that the circle is not squarable.

The paradox can be reached in an interesting circuitous way, which brings out the role of the present tense. Consider:

(11) At T Hobbes believed that CS (= the circle is squarable).

(12) At T' Hobbes believed that ~CS.

(13) Hobbes ought epistemically to explain at T' (and later) why at T he* beiieved that CS.

NOTE: Here 'he*' is the quasi-indicator 'he himself' representing Hobbes's first-person references[9].

(14) Explanation E satisfyies (13) = = > (11).

From (14) by (DL*):

(15) At T' Hobbes ought epistemically to believe that E = = > At T' Hobbes ought epistemically to believe that at T he* believed that CS.

From (13) and (15) we merely deduce:

(16) At T' Hobbes ought epistemically to believe then* that at T he* believed that CS.

NOTE: the quasi-indicator 'then*' depicts Hobbes's uses of the indicator 'now' at the time in question. There is no problem here. But suppose that times T and T' are the same. Then (16) has a special instance:

(16*) At T' Hobbes ought epistemically to believe then* that he* believed then* that CS.

Now, many philosophers subscribe to a principle of incorrigibility of beliefs about certain *current* states of belief. A relevant principle is this:

(BB*) At T x believes that he* then* believes that p = = > At T x believes that p.

This may be too strong. But perhaps a person who is rehearsing his believing that p, e.g., by asserting reflectively: *I believe now that p*, gains the belief that p. In any event, in the case of Hobbes rehearsing his current belief that he* then* believes that CS does imply his believing that CS. Hence, the epistemic obligation to believe explanation E rehearsing it why he* then* believes that CS does seem to require by (DL*) his obligation to believe that CS[10].

Second, recall that we are dealing with the ideal epistemological deontology, not with the lower epistemology where epistemic blame and epistemic punitive measures are taken. Thus, the question of *epistemic amends* introduced in premise (3) does not have a temporal factor: at one time the wrong doing and later the amends. The objectivity of knowledge, which must be captured by epistemic deontology, requires this basic principle:

(EB.D*) At T x believes that p and $\sim p$ = = > It ought epistemically to be the case that x has an explanation of why he* believes that p.

In fact, the coherence of knowledge, which demands belief grounded on reasons, seems to require an even stronger ideal guiding principle:

(EB.Dg) At T x believes that p = = > At T x OUGHT epistemically to BE able to explain why then* he* believes that p.

Principle (EB.Dg) seems to be at the heart of the justification of belief capable of constituting knowledge. Its importance lies both in its being stronger than Goldman's *ex post* justifiedness and in its applying a unified deontology to believing, whether actual or potential[11].

6. Ordinary Deontic Language and Logic Converging at the Proposition/Practition Distinction

Paradoxes can be solved only by both rejecting some premises and substituting for them premises that capture the grains of truth the rejected premises were supposed to bring in.

What are we to give up in the preceding Epistemic Good Samaritan? Patently, there are several choices, and each one *must* be explored for our greater understanding of epistemic justification. Equally patently, a good theory of this problem must be the simplest subsumption of this paradox under a comprehensive simple theory. Thus, without more ado, I propose to solve this paradox by cutting it with the same fell swoop that has solved all the deontic paradoxes (except the Lawrence Powers's Suzy-Mae paradox), to wit: by means of the proposition/practition distinction.

As remarked above, the very grammar of ordinary English provides a clue. The contents or arguments of the deontic operators appear formulated in infinitive clauses. For instance: *X is permitted (ought) Mly to A* has as argument of the deontic operator *is Mly permitted (ought Mly)* what the infinitive clause expresses: *X to A*. This is not a circumstance that gives rise to an obligation, but the obligation itself. We have already pointed out how crucial logical asymmetries distinguish practitions from practitions. The examples above illustrate these fundamental principles:

(D*.F1) Deontic operators take practitions as arguments and propositions as values.
(D*.F2) Mixed connective compounds of propositions and practitions are practitions.

7. The Actional Good-Samaritan Paradoxes Solved in One Fell Swoop

Let us return to (DL*). In the above application of (DL*) the Good Samaritan paradox issues from two connected assumptions: i) the proposition/practition distinction is not acknowledged, and ii) the gerundial phrases in the above statement of (DL*) are taken to represent propositions. Obviously, ii) is a proper consequence of i), which is in its turn supported by the view that propositions (or declarative true-or-false sentences) alone have implications. This assumption makes it difficult to understand the nature and function of practical thinking. And we can see that it creates problems in action theory as much as in epistemology.

The proper interpretation of (DL*) is to take the gerunds as denoting practitions, to wit:

(*D.L) If the practition *X to A* logically implies the practition *Y to B*, then:
(a) *X ought Mly to A* implies *Y ought Mly to B*;
(b) *X is not Mly permitted not to A* implies *X is not Mly permitted not to B*;
(c) *X is not Mly permitted to B* implies *X is not Mly permitted to A*.

To illustrate the simplest solution to the Good Samaritan consider:

(17) It is Mly obligatory for X to do the following: help Jones, to whom he has done A, which is Mly wrong.

Here within the scope of the deontic operator lies the practition:

(18) X to help Jones, to whom he has done A, which is
Mly wrong.

This practition logically implies each of the following:

(18.a) [The practition] X to help Jones;
(18.b) [The proposition] X has done A to Jones;
(18.c) [The proposition] X's having done A to Jones is Mly wrong.

By (D*.F1) these propositions (18.b)-(18.c) do not allow the derivation of the corresponding deontic judgments. We need practitions
as arguments of deontic operators. But practition (18) does NOT imply the practition *X to do A to Jones*, NOR does it imply the practition *X to do something wrong*. Hence, (17) implies neither *X ought
to do A* nor *X ought to do something wrong*.

In brief, circumstances—which may very well be the performances
of forbidden actions—can be within the scope of a deontic operator
of the *ought*, or the *is permissible*, type, as in (17), and be implied
by the resulting deontic judgment without any contradiction.

8. Subsumption of The Doxastic (Epistemic) Good Samaritan

The doxastic paradox (1)-(6) above is automatically resolved once
we adopt a counterpart of (*DL), the right interpretation of (Dl). In
the doxastic situation we are not dealing with agents, actions, or the
Ought-to-Do, but with subjects, subjective states, and the Ought-to-
Be. Thus, we need a generalization of the notion of *practition*. We
hereby extend this notion to include *all* deontic foci, whether of the
Ought-to-Do or of the Ought-to-Be type. If the word 'practition' is
too reminiscent of action, the reader may substitute 'deontic focus'
for it, or may read it as an abbreviation of 'ideal practition'.

Recall premise (3):

(3) Clearly, it ought epistemically to be that X makes a sort
of amends: that he has and believes an explanation of why
he believes that *p*.

In this premise the clause 'he believes that *p*' at the end does *not*
express a deontic focus, but merely expresses a circumstance involved in the obligation, a ground of obligation. Using the above
capitalization mechanism we can highlight the generalized proposi-
tion/practition contrast present in (3), as follows:

(3a) It ought epistemically to be the case that: X HAS and BELIEVES an explanation of why he believes that p.

To be sure, in the global infinitive clause 'to be the case that X has and believes an explanation of why he believes that p' we blur syntactically the distinction between the deontic foci and deontic circumstances. But the syntactically unaided semantics remains the same. For this reason we might resort to the strict practition formulation, signaling that we are dealing with subjective states and subjects and the Ought-to-Be by introducing the adverb 'ideally'. With this notation we can paraphrase (3a) thus:

(3b) X ought-ideally epistemically to HAVE and BELIEVE an explanation of why he *believes* that p.

Here again the contrast between the infinitive clauses 'to have and believe an explanation of why he believes that p' and the indicative clause 'he believes that p' signals the distinction between a generalized practition and a proposition.

At any rate, proposition (3), however canonical notation for it may be adopted, has the following implicates, using notation of (3b):

(3b.1) X ought-ideally epistemically to have an explanation of why he believes that p;
(3b.2) X ought-ideally epistemically to BELIEVE an explanation of why he believes that p;
(3b.3) X believes that p.

Palpably, X need not fall into contradiction when she has an explanation, and even expounds it, of why she is in the state of believing that p. For instance, Alvin Goldman's Millicent can, having been brainwashed by Goldman, concede that she ought to believe that her perceptions are in error, and explain that she is so overwhelmed by the force of her visual appearances that she cannot help, against the Goldmanian better reasons, but believe that "a chair is before her, that the neurosurgeon is wearing a yellow smock, and so on" (*op. cit.*, pp. 53f)—yet remaining not only in full grasp of the facts but also logically consistent.

9. The General Deontic Foundation of Epistemology

The preceding discussion provides powerful data (not of course a deductive proof[12]) of the adequacy of our theory of deontic logic embodied in system D** as a general deontology. We have thus a solid framework on which to erect a theory of doxastic and epistemic deontology. We proceed to formulate system D**.

II. A Comprehensive Second-Order System of Basic Deontic Logic

We proceed now to formulate a system of deontic logic which aims at capturing the criteria of adequacy distilled from many investigations on the nature of practical reasoning (e.g. in *Thinking and Doing*), the interpretation of legal texts[13], and the discussion of epistemic paradoxes. My proposal is that the formal system here sketched out represents the fundamental logical structure of deontic concepts in general, whether they be applied to prospective agents, in external systems of rules as in laws and institutions, whether they be applied to real agent's internal motivational hierarchies, or whether they belong to ideal norms pertaining to an Ought-to-Be. Thus, when below we speak of practitive expressions we refer to expressions of generalized practitions, or deontic foci, whatever the deontic modalities in whose scopes they belong to. Understandably, because of the intimate connection between the motivational *ought* and action, there are some principles that govern exclusively the motivational deontic structure, and some principles that govern ideal epistemic obligations. Hence, the theory about the general form of deontology here proposed is only the foundation for the specific investigations pertaining to the particular types of deontic modalities. In particular, we must develop the full theory of epistemic deontology.

1. *Formal deontic languages* D_i*. We start by constructing a large number of such syntactical structures, one for each type of obligatoriness. These languages will be called D_i*, for $i = 1, 2, 3, .$

Because of Russell's paradox of self-predication, we adopt here for expedience a modest type theory. We allow action types and properties of individuals to function both as predicates and as subjects of predication; but we require their predicated properties to belong to a higher type of entity.

A. *Primitive signs*: We assume the following types of symbols.

1. Individual constants: denumerably many signs denoting individuals, whether physical objects, persons, institutions, or other legal entities.

2. Individual variables: denumerably many symbol variables whose semantic ranges are individuals as understood above.

3. Predicate constants of the lower type, which denote properties of individuals or actions that individuals can perform.

4. Predicate variables, which range over lower properties.

5. Predicate constants of the higher type, which denote second-order properties that are predicated of properties of the lower order.

6. The connectives '~' and '&' expressing negation ('it is not the case') and logical conjunction ('and', 'but', 'although'), respectively.

7. The round parentheses '(' and ')', which paired denote propositional (circumstantial) predication, as we shall see, but are also used to demarcate well-formed formulas; the square brackets '[' and ']' which paired constitute the sign of practical or practitional predication.

8. The operator '$' which maps practitives (i.e., formulas expressing practitions) into indicatives (i.e., formulas expressing propositions); the sign 'O_i' of oughtness$_i$ or obligatoriness$_i$; the identity sign '='.

B. *Rules of Formation*: We use Quine's corners implicitly throughout. Let the small letters 'p', 'q', 'r', range over *indicatives* (i.e., expressions of propositions or propositional functions); let the capital letters 'A' and 'B' without subscripts or superscripts range over *practitives* (i.e., expressions of practitions or practitional functions); let '$p*$' and '$q*$' range over both indicatives and practitives. We use indexed capital letters of the form 'Z_n^j,' for $j = 1, 2$, and $n = 1, 2, 3, ...$, to represent predicate variables or constants of type j, 1 for the lower type, and 2 for the higher type, and of rank n. Small letters toward the end of the alphabet, 'x,' 'y,' 'z,' with or without subscripts will be used here to denote individual variables; letters at the beginning of the alphabet, 'a', 'b', with subscripts or not, will denote individual constants, and 'd' and 'e,' with subscripts if necessary, to represent individual signs, whether constants or variables. The letters 'f' and 'g', with or without subscripts, will denote predicate variables (of the lower type), as is opportunely indicated.

(a) The INDICATIVES of D_i* are the sequences of signs of D_i* having one of the following forms:

1. $Z_n^1(d_1, ...,d_n)$, where Z_n^1 is an n-adic lower predicate constant or variable and each d_i is an individual constant or variable;

2. $Z_n^2(Z_1^1, ..., Z_n^1)$, where Z_n^2 is a predicate constant of the higher type and each Z_1^1, $i = 1, ..., n$ is a predicate constant or variable of the lower type;

3. $(\sim p)$;   4. $(p \, \& \, q)$;

5. $((\forall x)p)$;   6. $(O_i A)$;

7. $(\$ A)$;   8. $(d = e)$.

(b) *Practitives* or *imperative-resolutives* of D_i^* are the sequences of signs of D_i^* having one of the following forms:

1. $C[x_1, ..., x_n]$, where C is an n-adic predicate, each x_i is an individual variable or constant;

2. $(\sim B)$;   3. $(p \, \& \, B)$;

4. $(B \, \& \, p)$;   5. $(B \, \& \, A)$;

6. $((\forall x)B)$;

(c) The Indicatives and the practitives of D_i^* are all the wffs of D^{i*}.

C. *Definitions.* We adopt the usual definitions of 'bound variable' and the definitions of the other connectives and the existential quantifier but we generalize them so as to cover practitives. For brevity we use 'h' with subscripts if necessary to represent either an individual or a predicate variable. We say that the occurrence of an individual, or predicate, variable h in a wff p^* is *bound* in p^*, if and only if it is an occurrence in a wff which is a part of p^* and is of the form $(\forall h)q^*$. An occurrence of an individual, or predicate, variable h in wff p^* is *free* in p^*, if and only if it is not bound in p^*. The *bound* [free] *variables* of a wff p^* are the variables which have bound [free] occurrences in p^*.

Def. 1 $(p^* \vee q^*)$ for $(\sim(\sim p^*) \, \& \, (\sim q^*)))$.

Def. 2 $(p^* \supset q^*)$ for $(\sim(p^* \, \& \, (\sim q^*)))$.

Def. 3 $(p^* \equiv q^*)$ for $((p^* \, \& \, q^*) \vee ((\sim p^*) \, \& \, (\sim q^*)))$.

Def. 4 $((\exists h)p^*)$ for $(\sim((\forall h)(\sim p^*)))$

We introduce the following deontic definitions:

Def. 11 $(P_i A)$ for $(\sim(O_i(\sim A)))$.

Read: It is permitted$_i$ that A, if and only if it is not obligatory$_i$ that not-A.

Def. 12 $(F_i A)$ for $(O_i(\sim A))$.

Read: It is forbidden$_i$ that A, if and only if it is obligatory$_i$ that not-A.

Def. 13 (L_iA) for $((\sim(O_iA)) \& (\sim(O_i(\sim A))))$.

Read: It is optional$_i$ (or there is a liberty$_i$ that A) if and only if neither is it obligatory$_i$ that A nor is it obligatory$_i$ that not-A.

Def. 14 ($A) represents the indicative wff resulting from the substitution of each practitional copula in A with a propositional copula, i.e., by the substitution of each pair of square brackets '[' and ']' in a each wff of the form 2.(a).1 which is a sub-formula of A for a pair of round parentheses: '(' and ')'.

We adopt the standard conventions on parentheses: (1) we drop the pair of outermost parentheses of each wff; (2) we associate chains of conjunctions, or disjunctions, to the left; (3) we rank the connectives in the following order of increasing scope or bindingness: $=$; \$; deontic operators and quantifiers; $\sim$; &; $\vee$; $\supset$; and $\equiv$.

2. The *desired primary interpretation* for each language D_i^* is this: (1) indicatives should express propositions; (2) practitives should express practitions; (3) predicates should express properties or conditions, and in this system we simply take actions to be first-order properties. Patently, each language D_i^* satisfies some crucial data: (i) the difference between atomic propositions and corresponding atomic practitions is represented by the difference between the two expressions of copulation: '(...)' and '[...]'; (ii) deontic judgments are represented as propositions; (iii) mixed indicative-practitive compounds are practitive; (iv) the deontic operators expressed by 'O_i', 'P_i', 'F_i' and 'L_i' apply to practitions, not to propositions; (v) there are no iterations of deontic operators. NB: The practitional copula [ ] may be considered the value of an operation t on atomic wffs: $t(C(X_1,...,X_n)) = C[X_1,..., X_n]$. In English t corresponds to the transformation of an indicative clause into an infinitive one, and it can be taken as an abbreviation of 'to'.

The part of each language D_i^* that includes neither quantifiers nor identity will be called D_i^{c*}.

3. *The axiomatic systems D_i^{**}*

We build on each deontic language D_i^* an axiomatic system D_i^{**}, which is constituted by the axioms and rules of derivation enunciated below. We shall take advantage of the above definitions and conventions on parentheses. We shall also use the following convention. Let X be a wff, and let v and w be individual variables or constants of the same type, and if variables of the same rank; that v be the same as w is not excluded. Then an expression of the form 'X(v/w)' stands for any wff resulting from X by replacing some, perhaps all, occurrences of v in X with occurrences of w, where all occurrences in question of v or w (or both) are free if v or w (or both) are variables. X($v//w$) is the wff X(v/w) that results when *all* occurrences of (free) v in X are replaced with (free) occurrences of w.

Axioms. The axioms of D_i** are all and only the wffs of D_i* that have at least one of the following forms:

A0. $O_iA \supset C_i$, where C_i is the conjunction of the necessary or "cancellation" conditions of *ought$_i$-ness*.

Propositional-practitional logic:

A1. $p^* \supset (p^* \& p^*)$
A2. $(p^* \& q^*) \supset p^*$
A3. $(p^* \supset q^*) \supset (\sim(r^* \& q^*) \supset \sim(r^* \& p^*))$

Deontic non-quantificational logic:

A11. $O_iA \supset \sim O_i \sim A$

General quantificational logic:

A111. $(\forall h)p^* \supset p^*(h//v_1)$, where v is a constant of the same type as h or a variable of the same type and rank as h.

Identity (definable in second-order logic):

A1111. $d = e \equiv (\forall f)(f(d) \equiv (f(e)))$
A1112. $(\exists f(\forall x1, ..., \forall x_n)(f(x_1, ..., x_n) \equiv p)$, where p is any indicative well-formed formula of D_i**.

We adopt the standard definitions of 'proof' and 'theorem.'

1. A *proof* of D_i** is a sequence of wffs of D_i* such that each member of it is either (i) an axiom of D_i** or (ii) a wff derivable from previous members of the sequence by one application of the derivation rules R1, R11, or R111 of D_i**, formulated below.

2. A *theorem of D_i*** is the last member of a proof of D_i**. We write $\vdash_i$ X to abbreviate 'X is a theorem of D_i**'.

3. $p_1^*, p_2^*, ..., p_n^* \vdash_i q^*$, if and only if $\vdash_i p_1^* \& p_2^* \& ... \& p_n^* \supset q^*$.

4. *Rules of Derivation.* The rules of derivation of D_i^{**} are:

R1. *Modus ponens:* From p^* and $p^* \supset q^*$, derive q^*.
R11. OG: If $\vdash_i (p \ \& \ A_1 \ \& \ ... \ \& \ A_n \supset B)$, then $\vdash_i (\forall h)(p \ \& \ O_i A_1 \ \& \ ... \ \& \ O_i A_n) \supset Oi(\forall h)B \ \& \ (\forall h)O_i B$, where $n > 0$.
R111. UG: If $\vdash_i p^* \supset q^*$, then $\vdash_i p^* \supset (\forall h)q^*$, provided that p^* has no free occurrences of h.

Notes

1. Part of this essay is a revised version of a paper presented at the Brown University Symposium in honor of Roderick Chisholm during November 20-23, 1986. An earlier version was presented at a colloquium at the University of Heidelberg in June 1987. It benefited from the discussion by the Heidelbergian philosophers, both in general terms and in the specific suggestions acknowledged in the footnotes.
2. Alvin Goldman, *Epistemology and Cognition* (Cambridge, Massachusetts: 1986).
3. For a fuller discussion of the adverbial, institutional modality *Mly* and for the fundamental actional deontic logic, see Hector-Neri Castañeda, *Thinking and Doing: The Philosophical Foundations of Institutions* (Dordrecht: Reidel, 1975). Ch. 7.
4. This paragraph and the preceding one have been written at the urging of Ulrich Brandt's.
5. For the major principle of the logic of hypothetical imperatives, i.e., of ends-means relationship, see Hector-Neri Castañeda, "Reply to Michael Bratman: Deontic Truth, Intentions, and Weakeness of the Will," in James E. Tomberlin, ed., *Agent, Language, and the Structure of the World* (Indianapolis: Hackett Publishing Company, 1983), to be cited as "Tomberlin 1983."
6. The original essay was revised to accommodate the Ought-to-Be at Hans Friedrich Fulda's suggestion. He has made other important suggestions, which require special treatment, e.g., to compare the esthetic normativity with epistemic and actional normativity, and to apply my thesis of the multiple species of knowledge in a comparative hermeneutics of philosophical views. I hope to be able to act on Fulda's suggestions in the near future. The history of skepticism can be illuminated by that thesis.
7. For a unified solution of the actional deontic paradoxes see *Thinking and Doing*, Ch. 7, and Hector-Neri Castañeda, "The Paradoxes of Deontic Logic: The Simplest Solution to All of Them in a Fell Swoop," in Risto Hilpinen, ed., *Deontic Logic and the Foundations of Ethics* (Dordrecht: Reidel, 1980). For a complementary discussion, including consideration of some main deontic alternatives, see the exchange between James E. Tomberlin and Hector-Neri Castañeda in J. E. Tomberlin, ed., *Hector-Neri Castañeda* (Dordrecht: D. Reidel, 1986). Additionally, see the ex-

change between Tomberlin and Castañeda in Tomberlin 1983.

8. For the differences between practical and propositional attitudes see Myles Brand's "Intending and Believing" and Hector-Neri Castañeda's "Reply to Myles Brand: Intentions, Properties, and Propositions," both in Tomberlin 1983.

9. For the major syntactic, semantic and pragmatic properties see Hector-Neri Castañeda, "The Semiotic Profile of Indexical (Experiential) Reference," *Synthese* 49 (1981): 275-316, and "Indicators and Quasi-indicators," *American Philosophical Quarterly* 4 (1967): 85-100.

10. This *First* Comment has been prompted by Harald Pilot's excellent observations about time and obligation to explain.

11. This *Second* Comment was motivated by valuable observations from Christel Fricke.

12. For this and related methodological matters see Hector-Neri Castañeda *On Philosophical Method* (Bloomington, Indiana: Nous Publications, 1980).

13. See Hector-Neri Castañeda, "The Basic Logic for the Interpretation of Legal Texts," in Charles Walter, ed., *Computer Power and Legal Language* (Westport, CT: Greenwood Press, Quorum Books, 1988).

Philosophical Perspectives, 2, Epistemology, 1988

EPISTEMIC OBLGATIONS

Richard Feldman
University of Rochester

I

Suppose an unfortunate student, Jones, is about to take an oral exam with an unusually difficult teacher. In fact, the failure rate on oral exams with this teacher is grim indeed: only 10% of the students who take the exam pass it. One slightly encouraging fact is that people who are optimistic about their chances for passing the exam tend to do a little better: 20% of them pass it. Apparently, the teacher's evaluations are improved by sincere manifestations of confidence. Let us also suppose that Jones, the student, has no particularly good information about his own abilities on the material to be covered on the tests. Assume next that Jones is a relatively normal person and that he has a strong desire to pass the test. Assume finally that Jones is aware of all of this and is considering the proposition that he will pass the exam.

We may ask what, given this information, Jones ought to believe. Should he believe that he will pass the oral exam?[1] When Jones considers the proposition that he will pass the exam, he must take exactly one of three attitudes toward it: he must either believe it, disbelieve it, or suspend judgment with respect to it. One of these attitudes will be the one that he ought to have.[2]

One may find oneself with conflicting intuitions about what Jones should do. On the one hand, it surely is in Jones's interest to believe that he'll pass; one could hardly blame him for doing whatever he could to improve his chances. Since he wants to pass and knows that the best way to increase his chances is to believe that he'll pass, he should believe that he'll pass. At the very least, this way of thinking about the case makes it seem clear that it is permissible for him to believe that he'll pass. In other words, it is not the case that he ought to believe that he won't pass.

On the other hand, his evidence makes passing look unlikely, and this inclines us to say that believing that he'll pass "flies in the face of the facts." After he finds out that he's failed and we're dealing with his disappointment, we might say that he should have realized that he wouldn't pass. That is, given his information, he should not have believed that he would pass. So, it seems that there is some basis for saying that he shouldn't believe that he'll pass, as well as some basis for saying that he should believe that he'll pass.

The apparent conflict between these inclinations can be resolved easily. The inclination to say that Jones ought to believe that he'll pass concerns a *practical* or *prudential* sense of obligation. Sometimes it makes sense to treat beliefs like other actions and to evaluate their practical or prudential merit. Jones's optimistic belief scores well in this evaluation, and this accounts for our judgment that it is a belief he ought to have. The contrary intuition concerns *epistemic* obligation. The peculiarly epistemic judgment concerns not these practical merits but rather the propriety of a disinterested believer in Jones's situation having that belief. Since Jones's optimistic belief does not come out so well on these grounds, it is epistemically improper. Epistemic obligation, then, concerns obligations to believe to which the practical benefits of beliefs are not relevant. They are obligations that arise from a purely impartial and disinterested perspective.[3]

Epistemic obligation also differs from *moral* obligation. There may be cases in which having a belief is morally significant. If there are such cases, then it may be that the moral factors lead one to a different belief than the epistemic factors. Thus, for example, one might have a moral duty to trust one's friends and family, thereby making it morally obligatory that one believe their claims. At the same time, one's purely epistemic obligation may well lead the other way. In allowing for this possibility, I may be disagreeing with the well-known claim of William K. Clifford (1886), who said that "It is wrong, always, everywhere, and for every one, to believe anything upon insufficient evidence." (p. 346). If 'wrong' here expresses moral wrongness, as the context suggests it does, then Clifford is claiming that one never is morally permitted to believe what is not supported by one's evidence.[4] And, given what I will argue later, this is equivalent to saying that one is never morally permitted to believe what one is not epistemically permitted to believe. Equivalently, if one epistemically ought to believe something, then, on Clifford's view, one also morally ought to believe it. That, as I said, seems wrong to me, since the moral consequences of an epistemically obligatory belief might be very bad. Thus, I think epistemic and moral obligation are distinct.

This discussion of the ethics of belief, of the moral status of beliefs, suggests an obvious and important issue. It is generally held that something can be obligatory only if it is a free action, only if it is something over which the agent has control. But it is doubtful that beliefs are, for the most part, free, voluntary, or controllable actions. Hence, it seems that there can't be any epistemic obligations to have believes. I respond to this claim in the next section. In subsequent sections I will develop an account of what our epistemic obligations are.

II

The objection to there being any epistemic obligations concerns doxastic voluntarism, the view that having a belief is something a person does voluntarily and can control. Alvin Plantinga (1986) has recently defended a version of this objection, arguing that if accepting a "proposition is not up to me, then accepting ...[that]...proposition cannot be a way in which I can fulfill my obligation to the truth, or, indeed *any* obligation." (p. 12). Plantinga thinks that it is as absurd to hold that one has epistemic obligations if doxastic voluntarism is false as it is to hold that one has obligations regarding which way to fall-up or down-after one has gone off a cliff.

Plantings's point can be formulated as a simple argument, which I will call 'The Voluntarism Argument':

1. Doxastic voluntarism is false.
2. If doxastic voluntarism is false, then no one has epistemic obligations.
3. Therefore, no one has epistemic obligations.

The Voluntarism Argument has considerable plausibility. There is a long tradition that makes only voluntary or controllable actions the subject of obligations, so (2) seems true. And it does seem that we can't control our beliefs. In the ordinary course of events, one finds oneself with some beliefs and rather little one can do about them. If revelations about your favorite politician cause you to believe that he is dishonest, then you might wish that you didn't have this belief. Although you may be able to put the matter out of mind, you can't, at will, change your belief about the topic. Similarly, all the perceptual beliefs that you have seem just to come over you. When I go outside on a typical winter day in Rochester, the belief that it is cold and gray outside just comes over me. In general, there is rather little we can do about our beliefs. They seem not to be matters under our control. So, (1) seems to be correct as well.

Despite the apparent truth of (1) and (2), philosophers have denied each premise. Although some philosophers, perhaps Descartes, have thought that beliefs are voluntarily adopted and maintained, few have rejected (1) on this basis. A more plausible reason for rejecting (1) has been advanced by John Heil (1983). His idea is that although we can't "directly" control our beliefs (in some sense of 'direct'), we can indirectly control them. There are things we can do to alter the ways in which we form beliefs and the kind of information which we receive. I can, for example, study logic and probability theory with the aim of reducing the number of mistaken inferences I draw. I might read the publications of some political or religious groups with the aim of eventually coming to accept the general set of beliefs they support. These and any number of other voluntary actions will affect my beliefs, and I may perform the actions for that very purpose. Hence, I do have some sort of indirect control over my beliefs. And this indirect control over beliefs makes some sort of doxastic voluntarism true, so (1) is false.

Heil is surely right about there being some sense in which we can indirectly control our beliefs. Perhaps, this shows that not every version of doxastic voluntarism is true. However, defenders of The Voluntarism Argument are likely to contend that (1) and (2) are true when 'doxastic voluntarism' is taken to refer the view that people have the relevant sort of "direct" control over their beliefs. They would argue that indirect control of the sort Heil discusses is not sufficient for there to be epistemic obligations. At most, they would grant that Heil has shown that there can be obligations to perform the sort of belief inducing actions Heil mentions. He has not shown that there can be epistemic obligations to believe or disbelieve anything. I'm inclined to agree with Heil's critics here, although the meanings of 'direct' and 'indirect' are sufficiently obscure to make these issues extremely difficult to sort out.

In any case, we are willing to say of people that they should or should not believe things even in cases in which they do not have the ability to undertake courses of action that might affect their beliefs in the relevant way. So, our intuitive judgments do not limit epistemic obligations to cases in which we have the sort of indirect control Heil describes. Thus, an equally damaging version of The Voluntarism Argument, restricted to cases of this sort, can be constructed.

Examples of the sorts of cases I have in mind are ones in which seemingly unchangeable psychological factors determine one's beliefs. For example, I just can't help believing that I see some tables and chairs now. Moreover, it is unlikely that I could embark upon any course of action, even the study of skepticism, which would lead me to believe otherwise in similar situations. Despite my inability to avoid this belief, this is exactly what I should believe in my current situation. Similarly, as a result of some psychological factors one may be unable to do anything about some of one's beliefs about oneself or one's family. For example, some people never believe that they are successful or talented, no matter what their accomplishments. Such people often should have better opinions of themselves, but there may be nothing they can do to change their negative attitude. Thus, there seem to be epistemic obligations even in cases in which we don't have the limited sort of control Heil describes. But the modified Voluntarism Argument has the conclusion that we don't have epistemic obligations in these cases. Thus defenders of epistemic obligations need a response to that argument that goes beyond Heil's. They need a way to reconcile the apparent truth of doxastic involuntarism with their inclination to ascribe epistemic obligations even in these cases.

Another way to respond to the Voluntarism Argument is to deny (2), the claim that if voluntarism is false, then there are no epistemic obligations. One might reject (2) on the basis of the idea that epistemic obligations pertain not to doxastic states but rather to actions that lead to doxastic states. Thus, my epistemic obligations may be to gather lots of evidence, to listen carefully of evidence, to listen carefully to critics, and the like. While I grant that there may be obligations to perform actions such as these, I think that this response simply evades the point at issue here. My concern is with obligations to believe and the question is whether there can be any such obligations if doxastic voluntarism is false. The existence of these other obligations, whether they are called 'epistemic obligations' or not, is thus beside the point.

A more promising variant on this objection to (2) has been proposed by Keith Lehrer (1981). Lehrer suggests that the notion of belief should be replaced in some epistemological analyses with that of acceptance. The difference between the two "concerns the element of optionality. Sometimes a person cannot decide what to believe at a moment, but he can decide what to accept....Believing is not an action. Accepting is." (pp. 79-80). Since accepting is an action over which one has control, one can have obligations to accept or not accept certain propositions. Accounts of these obligations could be constructed that are perfectly analogous to the accounts of obligations to believe that will be considered later. This sort of view preserves the traditional connection between obligation and voluntariness, is consistent with the apparent fact that beliefs are voluntarily formed or retained, yet makes sense of something like epistemic obligation. I will argue shortly that it is possible to have obligations with respect to involuntary behavior, but those who reject that conclusion may translate all subsequent discussion of obligations regarding beliefs into talk of obligations to accept propositions.[5]

I think that the best response to The Voluntarism Argument is to deny (2) on the grounds that there can be obligations concerning involuntary behavior. It may be true that with respect to *some* sorts of obligation, one has obligations of those sorts only if one has control over the relevant actions, only if one can act (and can avoid acting) in the obligatory way. This seems most clearly true with respect to moral obligation. Perhaps there are also notions of prudential obligation and "all things considered" obligation that obtain only when the person has control over the obligatory behavior. It is never the case that one is obligated, in these senses, to do things one can't avoid doing (or must do).

However, it is equally clear that there are obligations and requirements that obtain in the absence of our ability to fulfill them. Here are some examples. In the beginning of a semester teachers typically tell their students what they are obligated to do as students in the class. We might say that students have an academic obligation to do that work. We also say, more naturally, that they are required to do the work. It often happens that later in the semester students report that they are unable to complete the work. Teachers respond to such claims in any number of ways, but I doubt that any say, "Well, if you can't do it, it follows that you are not required to do it." We are more apt to tell them what we do to students who don't complete their requirements.

To make the case more concrete, and like some Plantinga (1986) considers in his defense of The Voluntarism Argument, suppose a student comes to me and says that he cannot write a term paper because he has a brain lesion that makes him fall asleep whenever he thinks about the paper topic. In this case, it may be best for me to change his requirements or to advise him to switch to another course in which he can fulfill his requirements. His inability plainly does not make it the case that he does not have these academic obligations or course requirements. (His inability makes him not morally required to do the work.) Thus, the student's course requirements include doing work he is unable to do. Similarly, course requirements may include doing something that a student can't refrain from doing. If, somehow, a brain lesion or a malicious demon makes a student unable to avoid doing logic problems identical to those assigned by the logic teacher, it does not follow that he was not required to do those problems. These kinds of obligations or requirements do not imply freedom or control.

Similar considerations apply to some other obligations. When I took out a mortgage on my house I incurred a legal obligation to pay the bank each month a certain sum of money. The amount is roughly equal to my entire monthly salary. If my salary goes down, or I lose my job and I can't pay, I'm sure that officials in the bank's foreclosure department would properly be unimpressed by the argument: "I can't pay you the money you say I owe you; therefore, I have no financial obligation to pay you that money." I still am legally (or financially) obligated to pay, even though I can't do it. On the other hand, if I arrange things so that the money is automatically taken out of my bank account and it is impossible for me to change that, I may be unable to avoid paying the mortgage. I retain my obligation to pay.

I conclude from these examples that there can be non-moral and non-prudential obligations that one can't fulfill and ones that one can't avoid fulfilling. Thus, I think that it is plausible to hold that there can be epistemic obligations that one can't fulfill and ones that one can't avoid fulfilling. Sometimes, one can't believe what one ought to believe and sometimes one can't help believing what one ought to believe. There can be epistemic obligations even if doxastic voluntarism is false.

Some examples, mentioned above, seem to me to give this view support. Normally, while observing the world one forms a lot of perceptual beliefs that are in the relevant sense unavoidable. Yet, many of those beliefs are ones that one should have. For example, when one is looking at a table in clear light one should believe that one sees a table, rather than deny or suspend judgment about the proposition. Fortunately, then, in these cases most of us can't help doing what we epistemically ought to do. But people who are driven to beliefs by hopes, fears, or other emotions may be unable to believe what they epistemically ought to believe.

I can think of two objections to my claim that epistemic obligations don't require doxastic voluntarism. The first grants that some sorts of obligations don't carry implications of freedom and control, but adds that some do and that epistemic obligations are of the latter sort. I've admitted that moral and prudential obligations may obtain only where there is control, but claimed that legal and financial obligations can obtain in the absence of freedom and control. My suggestion is that epistemic obligations are of the latter sort and the response is that they are of the former sort.

I believe that this objection is mistaken. Two remarks are in order. First, I think that the examples support my side. That is, it is natural to say things like "He should (or shouldn't) believe that" even in cases in which there is no freedom or control. The examples already described indicate that. Second, as I hope to show later in this paper, a plausible account of epistemic obligations can be developed which makes it clear that epistemic obligations don't have much to do with freedom and control. Of course, the force of this point turns on the merits of the account to be developed later.

I turn now to the second response to my claim that (2) is false. Recall that my defense relies on the claim that there are some obligations, such as academic and legal ones, that do not require voluntarism. The response is that academic and legal obligations are not, strictly speaking, cases of simple obligation at all. They are, rather, cases of conditional obligation. What's true of the student might be put this way: given that he wants to pass this course, he ought to write the paper. What's true of me is: given that I want to keep my house, I ought to pay my mortgage. Couple these accounts of the obligations present in these cases with the denial of a rule of detachment for obligation statements and one then has the basis for denying that I have presented any cases of obligations that cannot be fulfilled. That is, from these conditional obligations and the facts that the student does want to pass the course and I do want to keep my house, it does not follow that the student ought to do the work or that I ought to pay the mortgage. Hence, we do not yet have cases of unfulfillable unconditional obligations.

If financial and academic obligations are best understood as conditional obligations, and one can have conditional obligations that one cannot fulfill (or cannot avoid fulfilling), then, I think, epistemic obligations can also be understood as conditional obligations that one might be unable to fulfill. If epistemic obligations are best interpreted as conditional obligations, then perhaps they are conditional upon the desire to be epistemically excellent: to say that you epistemically ought to believe *p* is to say that given that you want to achieve epistemic excellence, you ought to believe *p*.

I don't particularly want to defend this analysis. However, I will concede to anyone who insists that the examples I have given of unfulfillable obligations are really only examples of unfulfillable conditional obligations. My claim about epistemic obligations could then be recast as the claim that epistemic obligations are also conditional obligations and they may also be unfulfillable. And if this is the case, then my main claim is this section remains unrefuted: ordinary talk about epistemic obligations, talk about what one ought to believe, carries no implications about doxastic voluntarism. We can, then, look into the nature of epistemic obligations without worrying further about whether doxastic voluntarism is true.

III

I turn next to discussion of the most widely accepted account of what our epistemic obligations are. This view traces back at least to William James (1911). James says,

> There are two ways of looking at our duty in the matter of opinion,—ways entirely different, and yet ways about whose difference the theory of knowledge seems hitherto to have shown little concern. We *must know the truth*: and *we must avoid error*,—these are our first and great commandments as

would-be knowers; but they are not two ways of stating an identical commandment, they are two separable laws....By choosing between them we may end by coloring differently our whole intellectual life....For my part, I can believe that worse things than being duped may happen to a man. (pp. 17-19.)[6]

James states his view in terms of two related "commandments" or imperatives: know the truth and avoid error. In telling us to avoid error, James is telling us that we should not believe falsehoods. And his directive that we know the truth implies that we should believe truths. So, James's idea seems to be that we should believe truths and should not believe falsehoods. His claim that these are two separable and independent commandments can be easily demonstrated. We can succeed in believing lots of truths by believing everything. If one does this (assuming that one can believe both a proposition and its negation), then one will surely have managed to believe all the truths, or at least all the truths among the propositions one considers. But that hardly achieves any sort of epistemic excellence. On the other hand, by believing very little we surely manage to avoid error. But this excessive conservativism does not achieve epistemic excellence either. It is by attaining a suitable mix of the two goals that we will achieve epistemic excellence. That, according to the Jamesian view, is what we ought to do.

An account of epistemic obligation along Jamesian lines has become a philosophical commonplace. In setting out his own account of epistemic requirements, Roderick Chisholm (1977) cites the passage from James just quoted as his source. Keith Lehrer (1981) uses a notion of reasonableness as the fundamental notion in his account of knowledge, and he says the following about his concept: "When we use the notion of reasonableness in our definition, we mean reasonable for the purpose of pursuing truth. The pursuit of truth involves an interest in obtaining a story free of error, or as much so as we can, and obtaining the whole story, or as much as we can. These combined interests may pull in opposite directions, but they both bear the stamp of legitimacy in the quest for truth." (p. 87). Roderick Firth (1978) discusses, but does not ultimately defend, an analysis of epistemic warrant in terms of "a duty to believe propositions if and only if they are true." (p. 224.) The Jamesian flavor in these passages is obvious.

Other writers describe a view very much like James's as 'standard' or 'familiar'. Paul Moser (1985) writes, "A familiar characterization of epistemic obligation states that it is the *(prima facie)* obligation one has, *qua* truth-seeker, to maximize true belief and to minimize, if not to avoid, false belief." (p. 214). Peter Markie (1986) describes the end (or goal) of believing all and only what is true about the matter under investigation as "the standard epistemic imperative". (p. 37). Richard Foley (1987) says that "... a distinctly epistemic goal ...[is]... what epistemologists often have said it to be, now to believe those propositions that are true and now not to believe those propositions that are false." Each of the three writers just mentioned eventually defends an account of epistemic obligation along Jamesian lines and describes such accounts as familiar or standard.

While James's view may seem straightforward enough, there actually is some difficulty in figuring out exactly what his claims amount to. James speaks of "commandments", Chisholm speaks of "requirements", Moser speaks of "obligations", Markie and Foley both speak of "ends" and Markie frames the idea in terms of an imperative. While all of these ideas may be fairly similar, there are differences worthy of our attention, and it is not entirely obvious just how the Jamesian line can be put into plausible account of epistemic obligations.

As a first attempt at a Jamesian view about epistemic obligation, we might try the following:

(1) S is epistemically obligated to believe p if p is true and S is epistemically obligated to disbelieve p if p is false.

(1) is subject to several obvious and decisive objections.

First of all, it is clear that sometimes one epistemically ought to suspend judgement about some propositions. However, (1) implies that everyone should believe every truth and disbelieve every falsehood, thereby leaving no room for suspension of judgment. Suppose a coin I know to be fair has been tossed, I have not seen how it landed, and do not have any other information about how it landed. Surely, I ought to suspend judgment about the proposition that it came up heads. But (1) says that I ought to believe it came up heads if it did come up heads and disbelieve that if it didn't. That's clearly wrong. I ought to suspend judgment in this and many other cases in which I have no good information about the truth value of the proposition in question.

It is equally clear that sometimes people should believe propositions that are in fact false. Suppose that some proposition, p, is false but all the evidence anyone has indicated that p is true, and some person carefully collects and weighs all the evidence, and then believes p on the basis of that evidence. Then surely that person is believing what he epistemically ought to believe. It may be that the evidence is in some sense misleading, but if the person has no way to know that, then the mere falsity of his belief does not demonstrate that he failed to do what he epistemically should have done. To say, for example, that ancient school children should have believed that the Earth was (roughly) round, since it is roughly round, is to miss the point of epistemic obligation altogether. By believing that the Earth is flat such children were believing exactly what they should have believed, given the situation they were in.

But if (1) is false, and so seriously off the mark, what could James have had in mind in asserting it? And what have others had in mind in endorsing his view? I believe that we can arrive at an answer to these questions by considering an analogy. Investors are often urged to "buy low and sell high". That is, they should buy stocks that are at a low point and will go up and they should sell stocks that are at a high point and will go down. Thus, we might say

(2) S ought to buy stock x if the price of x will go up and S ought to sell x if the price of x will go down.

While (2) may seem to express some truth, there is at least one straightforward interpretation under which it is plainly false. Suppose that, as a matter of fact, some stock is about to go up, but all available indications are that it is about to go down. Perhaps it has just been discovered that the company's sole product is defective, e.g., house paint that is water-soluble after it dries. There seems to be a clear sense in which, assuming one knows this, one ought not buy the stock. (Ignore the possibility that one might do well by being a "contrarian".) If all the information one has suggests that a stock will go down, then it is a bad idea to buy it. In some sense of 'ought', one ought not buy such stocks. One ought to follow the best indicators of future price that one has. So, (2), at least with "ought' understood this way, is false.

There is, however, some truth in the vicinity of (2). It is:

    (3) One's goals as an investor are to buy stocks that will go
        up and to sell stocks that will go down.

(3) specifies some *goals* of investing. Although (3) may seem trivial, it is not. You might explain to children who know nothing about the stock market that these are the goals of investing. One could, in fact, disagree about whether (3) is entirely accurate or complete. Some would claim that one's goals are, or should be, different, or at least broader. Profits may not be the only goal. Perhaps investing in companies that meet some political or social values one has is important as well. So (3) is a plausible and non-trivial claim about investment objectives.

More specific investment advice can be seen as advice about how best to satisfy the goal specified in (3). So, when one is told that one ought to buy stocks in companies in expanding rather than declining industries, one is being told about a means to an end. Our obligations, perhaps, are to do what is best (in some sense) to accomplish some end. There is much that remains to be said about all of this. There are, in particular, questions about what exactly counts as the "best" means for achieving these investment ends. But I will ignore these issues for now and return to the epistemic case, which I think is quite similar.

I think that James's remarks are best seen as comments about epistemic ends, not about epistemic obligations. This makes James's view most similar to the one expressed by Foley in the passage quoted above. He has told us what we are to strive for as epistemic agents. He has told us nothing about what means we ought to follow in order to achieve those ends. Thus, I think that a truth about epistemic ends can be formulated as follows:

    (4) One's goals as a rational believer are to believe things
        that are true and to avoid believing things that are false.

Again, this may seem trivial, but it isn't. (4) calls our attention to what the proper epistemic ends are. According to this view, it is not to believe things that are edifying or expansive. It is not to believe what makes us feel good. It is not to have opinions that differ from those of our parents. It is to get at the truth. Telling this to children, or to college freshman, could be useful and enlightening. But (4) leaves open entirely what the proper means to this end are. The passage from James simply has nothing to say about how we ought to go about achieving this end.

Thus, I think that what's true and Jamesian is (4). But (4) isn't a statement about epistemic obligations. One simple statement about obligations somehow connected to (4) is (1). But (1) is false. We have, then, no adequate account of epistemic obligations.

IV

Chisholm (1977) has defended an account of epistemic obligations that is clearly derived from James's account, but which seems to avoid the objections to (1) raised in the previous section. Chisholm writes,

> We may assume that every person is subject to a purely intellectual requirement—that of trying his best to bring it about that, for every proposition h that he considers, he accepts h if and only if h is true. (p. 14).

This statement may be formulated as the following account of epistemic obligation:

> (5) For any proposition p and person S, if S considers p then S is epistemically obligated to try his best to bring it about that S believes p if and only if p is true.

This could, of course, be broken up into two principles, one saying that a person is obligated to try to believe p if p is true and the other saying that the person is obligated to try to avoid believing p if p is false. Thus Chisholm's view connects with James's in an obvious way. James has said, in principle (4), that the two epistemic ends are to believe truths and to avoid believing falsehoods. Chisholm has said that our epistemic obligation is to try our best to achieve these ends with respect to the propositions we consider.

One obstacle to determining exactly what implications (5) has is the fact that (5) gives no directive about the relative weights given to the obligation to try to believe truths and the obligation to try to avoid believing falsehoods. One might be cautious, and weigh the obligation to try to avoid error more heavily. On the other hand, one might advocate a more adventurous attitude, and emphasize the obligation to try for the truth more strongly. James himself seems to support the latter view, in his remark that he "can believe that worse things than being duped may happen to a man." (1911), p.

19). I think that this is a suggestion to the effect that it is better to be bold, and form beliefs in an effort to get at the truth, than it is to be cautious and avoid belief in an effort to avoid error. I will not pursue this issue, however, because I think that there are more fundamental questions to be raised about (5), and I want to turn to them instead.

I will consider two objections to Chisholm's view. The first objection is that it construes our epistemic obligations far too narrowly, mentioning only obligations to try for the truth and to try to avoid error, omitting many other important epistemic goals. Plantinga (1986) raises this sort of objection in his discussion of Chisholm. He writes, "Obviously, something must be said about *other* epistemic values: the importance of considering *important* propositions, of having beliefs on certain topics, of avoiding unnecessary clutter and trivial dilettantism, etc." (p. 6). Thus, Plantinga thinks Chisholm construes our epistemic obligations too narrowly, considering only our obligation to the truth and ignoring our obligation to be what we might call "good epistemic agents".

I do not wish to deny that there is plausibility in the view that we ought, in some sense, to be good epistemic agents. However, I think that being a good epistemic agent in this sense is irrelevant to the central notion of epistemic obligation, and irrelevant to the sort of obligation with which Chisholm is concerned. Thus I deny that Chisholm has given too narrow an account of our epistemic obligations. I grant, however, that there may be another sort of obligation, distinct from the one with which he is concerned, to which Plantinga is calling attention. Thus, I think that Plantings's objections to (5) fails.

To see what Chisholm has in mind, it is useful to focus on these questions: given that I am in the situation that I am in, and given that I am considering proposition p, what should I do—believe it, disbelieve it, or suspend judgment about it? Which of these three options is epistemically best? In thinking about these questions, one is to consider only these three options and only the end of getting at the truth about p. The particularly epistemic aspect of this is supposed to exclude from consideration other factors, such as which attitude would feel good or be comforting or be morally valuable. Also irrelevant to this judgment are the long-term epistemic consequences of adopting the belief. It is the truth about p now that matters. Thus, if believing something now would somehow lead me to believe lots of truths later, that long-term epistemic benefit is also irrelevant to this judgment. Foley, in the passage quoted previously, brings out the relevant point by emphasizing the key question related to epistemic obligation is "what should I believe *now*?"

In thinking about this question, being a good epistemic agent in the broader ways that Plantinga mentions is just irrelevant. Whether I have been, am, or will be a good agent—whether I consider important propositions, etc.—has no bearing on what attitude I epistemically ought to take toward *p* now. A person can fulfill the narrower obligations without being a good epistemic agent in the broader sense. He might have the attitude he ought to have toward each proposition he considers even though he spends most of his time considering a sequence of "unimportant" propositions of the form "$n+1 > n$" and even if he seeks his intellectual stimulation by going bowling. All that he must do in order to fulfill his narrower epistemic obligations is to have the appropriate attitude toward the propositions he does consider.

Other things that have broader epistemic relevance are also irrelevant to this core notion of epistemic obligation. Consider the suggestion that one ought to seek and consider all relevant evidence. That may be a good idea, but when my question is what I should believe *now*, seeking more evidence just isn't one of my options. Suppose I haven't thought very carefully about some proposition, but the little evidence I have seen suggests that the proposition is true. I ask, "Should I believe that proposition now?" If you tell me that I should seek more evidence, than my original question remains unanswered. Perhaps I should seek more evidence or think about the matter further, but until I have a chance to do that, what should I believe? What should I believe *now*? It is this latter question, I think, that is the central epistemic question, and these issues about epistemic agency are quite clearly irrelevant to it.

It is clear, I think, that there are at least two different questions associated with epistemic obligation. One is the question about what to believe, or what attitude to take toward a particular proposition. This is the question I have been trying to focus on in the preceding paragraphs. There is also a legitimate set of questions about what actions ought to be pursued in an effort to obtain evidence, what issues ought to be the focus of attention and the like. My main point here is that these latter questions are distinct from and independent of the former one. The reason for this, again, is that even if it is true that I should seek more evidence or perform some other action in connection with some proposition, there always remains the question of what attitude I should take toward that proposition now, before (or while) I perform that action.

Sometimes it seems true that a person should seek more evidence concerning some proposition. It is important to realize that this does not imply that the person should suspend judgment about the proposition until that additional evidence is in. Whether I should seek additional evidence typically depends upon how important it is that I get a well-founded belief about the topic in question. An example, described by Heil (1986) makes the point well. Suppose that you are in charge of an agency responsible for testing drugs and deciding whether they are to be sold to the public. You might have considerable evidence indicating that a particular drug is safe, sufficient evidence to make it reasonable for you to believe that it is safe. Of your three doxastic options, believing that it is safe is the one you ought to have. At the same time, it may also be true that because of the importance of being right, and the potential risks of allowing an unsafe drug on the market, you ought to seek further evidence about its safety.

This example shows the independence of questions about what actions regarding evidence gathering ought to be performed from questions about what ought to be believed. Since it is this latter sort of obligation with which Chisholm is concerned, the example helps us to see the error in Plantings's contention that Chisholm has construed epistemic obligations too narrowly.

The example just considered, as well some others to be described below, suggest that the sorts of considerations Plantinga mentions are really relevant to some sort of practical obligations, not to any purely epistemic concerns. Whether the drug tester should seek more evidence seems to be a clear case of a decision problem in which the expected value of the possible actions is to be weighted. If the potential side effects of the drug are severe, more testing may be appropriate. If the drug offers a cure for a serious illness not yet treatable, perhaps foregoing additional testing would be prudent. There seems to be no purely epistemic considerations that decide this matter.

Other cases also suggest that epistemic considerations do not determine what evidence gathering activities are appropriate. To someone who tells me that I should seek additional evidence about some proposition, I might appropriately respond that there are better things for me to do with my time. Maybe it would be better for me to play with my daughter or take my dog for a walk. But these considerations are practical, not epistemological. There's never any purely epistemological considerations that decide these practical questions. Whether I should be a better epistemic agent is always a practical question. The narrower question about what I should believe now, the question I want to focus on, is the central epistemological question.

Thus, I conclude that this first objection to (5) is mistaken. In thinking that these broader sorts of vaguely epistemological obligations that we may have are relevant to the central notion of epistemic obligation, Plantinga has conflated the epistemic aspects of a broader notion of practical obligation with the central notion of epistemic obligation.

A second objection to Chisholm's view, is, I think, more successful. Chisholm says very little about what counts as "trying one's best", but on at least one plausible interpretation, his view is clearly unsatisfactory. Other, more satisfactory interpretations, are possible, but then the view is in serious need of additional detail.

On Chisholm's view, one's goal is to believe all and only the truths one considers, and one's obligation is to try one's best to achieve that goal. But what counts as trying one's best? Suppose p is a truth I consider. In one straightforward sense of 'try my best to believe truths,' if p is true, then I've tried my best with respect to p if I bring it about that I do believe p. And if p is false, then I've tried my best to avoid error if I've tried in a way that brings it about that I don't believe p. More generally, on one reading of 'try my best to believe truths and avoid falsehood', I've fulfilled my obligation to do this if I've tried in the way that in fact makes me believe all and only truths. What could possibly be a better way to try to achieve a goal than to do what in fact makes one achieve that goal? There's at least one reading of 'try my best' that makes the answer "Nothing". In this sense, one has tried one's best when one has tried in the way that has the best results.

But this reading of 'try my best' saddles (5) with implausible implications that Chisholm surely did not intend. On this reading, when I've done whatever I can to bring it about that I believe truths, then I've done my best. Thus, if there is any way I can try that will make me believe p, and p is true, then I am obligated to try in that way. This is the case even if what I must do is make myself believe what my evidence clearly suggests to be false. Plainly, this is not what Chisholm intended. He surely agrees that there are times when doing one's epistemic best, doing what one epistemically should, will lead to avoidable false beliefs.

I suspect that what Chisholm has in mind is that some general ways or methods to try to believe the truth are better than others and that we epistemically ought to follow the best method. Thus, we might pose the following:

(6) For any proposition p and person S and time t, if S considers p at t, then S is epistemically obligated to believe p at t if and only if, if S were to follow the best available method for trying to believe truths and avoid believing falsehoods at t, then S would believe p at t.

The methods in (6) are limited to methods to be followed at the moment. They are not to include longer term strategies such as looking for lots of evidence. But if this sort of account is to work, some possibly successful ways must be eliminated from the running. For example, one might concoct a way to try for the truth by listing all the truths a person considers and describing the way to try for the truth as trying to believe all the propositions on that list at the appropriate times. Perhaps trying in this way would in fact lead him to believe all the truths. Or, perhaps there is some other way in which the person could try that would have this result. This would saddle (6) with the same absurd consequences as (5). It would have the plainly mistaken result that one is epistemically obligated to believe each of the truths one considers, or at least those one can believe, regardless of the evidence one has and the situation one is in. As we have seen, that is plainly mistaken. The problem, in short, is that there are unnatural and gerrymandered "methods" for trying to believe truths that one could follow. Some of these cooked up methods can be very successful. But their mere success does not make them the ones one ought to follow.

In the next section I will discuss a different account of epistemic obligations. It is possible that the account to be discussed differs from (6) only in that it makes explicit what would have been said in a generous interpretation of (6). It may also be that it is what Chisholm had in mind originally. That is, it may be that the account to be suggested simply specifies what Chisholm was thinking of when he said that one should try one's best to believe truths and avoid believing falsehoods. It has the advantage, however, of avoiding the problems found in formulations (5) and (6).

V

In objecting to (6) I assumed that the best method for trying to believe truths and disbelieve falsehoods is the one that is in fact most effective. There is another way to try to believe truths and perhaps Chisholm would regard this as the best way to do so. In any case, I believe that this other way to try for the truth leads to a more satisfactory account of epistemic obligations.

This other method to try to believe truths and avoid believing falsehoods is to believe what is supported or justified by one's evidence and to avoid believing what is not supported by one's evidence. One who follows this method does not believe things because it feels good to believe them or because of some long-term benefits that result from doing so. One who follows this method just believes at any time exactly what the evidence he then has supports.[7] Thus, I propose:

(7) For any person S and proposition p and time t, S epistemically ought to believe p at t if and only if p is supported by the evidence S has at t.

Since psychological or other factors may force or preclude one from believing what is supported by one's evidence, (7) does not imply that one always can believe, or can avoid believing, what one should believe. It is therefore an account of epistemic obligation that does not require the truth of doxastic voluntarism. Moreover, (7) obviously avoids the successful objections to the other accounts of epistemic obligation previously considered.

In his most recent published discussion of this topic, Chisholm (1986) proposes something along the lines of (7). He writes: "I have previously written, incautiously, that one's primary intellectual duties are to acquire truth and to avoid error. What I should have said is that one's primary intellectual duties are to believe *reasonably* and to avoid believing *unreasonably*." (pp. 90-91). Since what it is reasonable for a person to believe at any time is what is supported by the person's evidence, what Chisholm says here turns out to be quite similar to (7). To accept (7) as an account of epistemic obligations is not to reject a Jamesian view entirely. (4), the claim that one's epistemic goal is to get at the truth, is consistent with (7) and I believe that it is also true. But one's epistemic duties or obligations concern the way to get to this goal and the epistemically dutiful way to get there is to believe in accordance with one's evidence. That's what one is epistemically obligated to do.[8]

Notes

1. I will use the phrases 'ought to believe', 'should believe', and 'is obligated to believe' interchangeably. It is possible that there are contexts in which it is useful to distinguish among their meanings, but I don't think the present context is one of those.
2. It is consistent with the view expressed here that there are also other attitudes one can take toward a proposition. For example, one can hope that it is true or be despondent over its truth. One can also choose to act as if it is true, or take it to be true for the sake of argument or further inquiry. Still, one is always either believing it, disbelieving it, or suspending judgment about it.
3. It is also possible that there is only one sense of 'ought' at issue here, and that there are conflicting considerations about whether it applies. That is, there are practical considerations supporting the conclusion that Jones ought to believe that he'll pass and epistemic considerations opposing that same conclusion. I believe that the "two senses" resolution is clearly preferable in this case. The reason is just that, upon reflection, it seems clear that the two intended conclusions— that Jones ought to believe that he'll pass and that he ought not believe that—are compatible.
4. It is possible that Clifford is making the more modest claim that the fact that a belief is based on insufficient evidence is a factor that counts against its moral permissibility. Other considerations, however, might outweigh this one.
5. This is not to say that I find Lehrer's notion of acceptance entirely clear. I don't know if a accepting is identified with any overt behavior, such as saying that a proposition is true, or any familiar mental activity, such as mentally assenting to it.
6. This passage, except for the last part, is cited by Chisholm (1977, p. 22).
7. One who follows this method will also have only epistemically justified beliefs. For an account of epistemic justification that has this implication, see Feldman and Conee (1985).
8. Earlier versions of this paper were read at Brown University and at the University of Miami. I would like to thank the participants in discussions at those places, as well as Earl Conee, for helpful comments.

References

Chisholm, R.: 1977, *Theory of Knowledge, 2nd edition*, Prentice-Hall, Englewood Cliffs, NJ.
Chisholm, R.: 1986, 'The Place of Epistemic Justification', *Philosophical Topics* 14, pp. 85-92.
Clifford, W.L.: 1866, *Lectures and Essays, 2nd Edition*, Macmillan, London.
Feldman, R. and Conee, E.: 1985, 'Evidentialism', *Philosophical Studies* 48, pp. 15-34.
Firth, R.: 1978, 'Are Epistemic Concepts Reducible to Ethical Concepts?' in A.I. Goldman and J. Kim, (eds.) *Values and Morals*, D. Reidel, Dordrecht, pp. 215-225.
Foley, R.: 1987, *The Theory of Epistemic Rationality*, Harvard University Press, Cambridge.
Heil, J.: 1983, 'Doxastic Agency', *Philosophical Studies* 43, pp. 355-364. Heil, J.: 1986, 'Believing Reasonably,', presented at The University of Rochester, October, 1986.
James, W.: 1911, *The Will To Believe and Other Essays in Popular Philosophy*, David McKay, New York, 1911.
Lehrer, K.: 1981, 'A Self Profile', in Bogdan, R. (ed) *Keith Lehrer*, D. Reidel, Dordrecht, pp. 3-104.
Markie, P.: 1986, *Descartes's Gambit*, Cornell University Press, Ithaca.
Moser, P.: 1985, *Empirical Justification*, D. Reidel, Dordrecht.
Plantinga, A: 1986, 'Chisholmian Internalism', presented at Brown University, November, 1986.

Philosophical Perspectives, 2, Epistemology, 1988

THE DEONTOLOGICAL CONCEPTION OF EPISTEMIC JUSTIFICATION

William P. Alston
Syracuse University

I. The Deontological Conception

The terms, 'justified', 'justification', and their cognates are most naturally understood in what we may term a "deontological" way, as having to do with obligation, permission, requirement, blame, and the like. We may think of *requirement*, *prohibition*, and *permission* as the basic deontological terms, with *obligation*, and *duty* as species of requirement, and with *responsibility*, *blameworthiness*, *reproach*, *praiseworthiness*, *merit*, *being in the clear*, etc. as normative conse- quences of an agent's situation with respect to what is required, pro- hibited, or permitted. More specifically, when we consider the justification of *actions*, something on which we have a firmer grip than the justification of beliefs, it is clear that to be justified in hav- ing *done* something is for that action not to be in violation of any relevant rules, regulations, laws, obligations, duties, or counsels, the ones that govern actions of that sort. It is a matter of the action's being *permitted* by the relevant system of principles.[1] To say that the action was justified does not imply that it was required or obligatory, only that its negation was not required or obligatory. This holds true whether we are thinking of moral, legal, institutional, or prudential justification of actions. To say that Herman was (morally) justified in refusing to take time out from writing his book to join in a peace march, is to say that the relevant moral principles do not require him to march; it is not to say that he is morally obliged to stick to writing his book, though that may be true also. Likewise to say that Joan was legally justified in leaving the state is to say that her doing so contravened no law; it is not to say that any law required her to do so. Finally consider my being justified in giving my epistemology class a take home final rather than one to be taken in the classroom. Here we might be thinking of institutional justification, in which case the point would be that no regulations of my department, college, or university require a classroom final exam; but my being so justified does not imply that any regulations require a take home exam. Or we might be thinking of pedagogical justification, in which case the point would be that sound pedagogical principles allow for a take home exam for this kind of course, not that they require it; though, again, the latter might be true also.

The most natural way of construing the justification of beliefs is in parallel fashion. To say that S is justified in believing that p at time t is to say that the relevant rules or principles do not forbid S's believing that p at t. In believing that p at t, S is not in contravention of any relevant requirements. Again, it is not to say that S is required or obligated to believe that p at t, though that might also be true. With respect to beliefs we can again distinguish various modes of justification: moral, prudential, and epistemic. These may diverge. I may, e.g., be morally justified in trusting my friend (believing that he is well intentioned toward me), and I may even be morally required to do so, though all my evidence tends strongly against it, so that the belief is not epistemically justified. In this paper our concern is with epistemic justification. How is that distinguished from the other modes? The justification of anything, X, consists in X's being permitted by the relevant principles: epistemic, moral, or whatever. Thus the crucial question is: What distinguishes epistemic principles from moral principles? Well, the "epistemic point of view" is characterized by a concern with the twin goals of believing the true and not believing the false. To set this out properly we would have to go into the question of just how these goals are to be weighted relative to each other, and into a number of other thorny issues; but suffice it for now to say that epistemic principles for the assessment of belief will grade them in the light of these goals. Just how this is done depends on the conception of justification with which one is working. On a deontological conception of justification, the principles will *forbid* beliefs formed in such a way as to be likely to be false and either *permit* or *require* beliefs formed in such a way as to be likely to be true.[2] Thus on the deontological conception of the epistemic justification of belief that is as close as possible to the standard conception of the justification of action, to be justified in believing that p at t is for one's belief that p at t not to be in violation of any epistemic principles, principles that permit only those beliefs that are sufficiently likely to be true.[3] Let's say, for example, that beliefs in generalizations are permitted only if based on adequate inductive evidence, otherwise forbidden; and that a perceptual belief that p is permitted only if (a) it is formed on the basis of its perceptually seeming to one that p and (b) one does not have sufficient overriding reasons; otherwise it is forbidden. One will be justified in a belief of the specified sort if the relevant necessary conditions of permissibility are satisfied; otherwise the belief will be unjustified.

Since this is the natural way to use 'justification', it is not surprising that it is the one most often formulated by those who seek to be explicit about their epistemic concepts. Perhaps the most eminent contemporary deontologist is Roderick Chisholm.[4] However because of the complexities of Chisholm's view, I shall take as my model deontologist Carl Ginet. He sets out the conception with admirable directness.

> One is *justified* in being confident that p if and only if it is not the case that one ought not to be confident that p; one could not be justly reproached for being confident that p.[5]

Now this conception of epistemic justification is viable only if beliefs are sufficiently under voluntary control to render such concepts as *requirement, permission, obligation, reproach,* and *blame* applicable to them. By the time honored principle that "Ought implies can", one can be obliged to do A only if one has an effective choice as to whether to do A.[6] It is equally obvious that it makes no sense to speak of S's being permitted or forbidden to do A if S lacks an effective choice as to whether to do A. And it seems even more obvious, if possible, that S cannot be rightly blamed for doing (not doing) A if S is incapable of effectively deciding whether or not to do A.[7] Therefore the most fundamental issue raised by a formulation like Ginet's is as to whether belief is under voluntary control. Only if it is can the question arise as to whether the epistemic justification of beliefs can be construed deontologically. As we shall see, there are various modes of voluntary control that have usually not been fully distinguished in the literature and that require separate treatment.

I will be arguing in this paper that (a) we lack what I will call direct voluntary control over beliefs, (b) that we have only a rather weak degree of "long range" voluntary control over (only) some of our beliefs, and (c) that although our voluntary actions can influence our beliefs the deontological notion of justification based on this indirect influence is not the sort of notion we need for the usual epistemological purposes to which the term 'justification' is put.

II. The Problem of Voluntary Control of Belief

There are many locutions that encourage us to think of believing as subject to requirement, prohibition, and permission. We say "You shouldn't have supposed so readily that he wouldn't come through", "You have no right to assume that", "I had every right to think that she was honest", "I ought to have given him the benefit of the doubt", and "You shouldn't jump to conclusions". We also often seem to suggest the voluntary control of belief: "I finally decided that he was the man for the job", "Make up your mind; is it coreopsis or isn't it?", "I had to accept his testimony; I had no choice" (the suggestion being that in other cases one does have a choice). And philosophers frequently fall in with this, speaking of a subject's being in a situation in which he has to decide whether to accept reject, or "withhold" a proposition.[8] All these turns of phrase, and many more, seem to imply that we frequently have the capacity to effectively decide or choose what we are to believe, and hence that we can be held responsible for the outcome of those decisions. It is natural to think of this capacity on the model of the maximally direct control we have over the motions of our limbs and other parts of our body, the voluntary movements of which constitute "basic actions", actions we perform "at will", just by an intention, volition, choice, or decision to do so, things we "just do", not "by" doing something else voluntarily. Let's call the kind of control we have over states of affairs we typically[9] bring about by basic actions, "basic voluntary[10] control." If we do have voluntary control of beliefs, we have the same sort of reason for supposing it to be basic control that we have for supposing ourselves to have basic control over the (typical) movements of our limbs, viz., that we are hard pressed to specify any voluntary action by doing which we get the limbs moved or the beliefs engendered. Hence it is not surprising that the basic voluntary control thesis has had distinguished proponents throughout the history of philosophy, e.g., Augustine, Aquinas, Descartes, Kierkegaard, and Newman.[11] Though distinctly out of favor today, it still has its defenders.[12]

Before critically examining the thesis we must make some distinctions that are important for our entire discussion. First, note that although the above discussion is solely in terms of belief, we need to range also over propositional attitudes that are contrary to belief. Chisholm speaks in terms of a trichotomy of "believe", "reject", and "withhold" that p.[13] Since rejecting p is identified with believing some contrary of p, it brings in no new kind of propositional attitude; but withholding p, believing neither it nor any contrary, does. The basic point to be noted here is that one has control over a given type of state only if one also has control over some field of incompatible alternatives. To have control over believing that p is to have control over whether one believes that p or not, i.e., over whether one believes that p or engenders instead some incompatible alternative.[14] One cannot effectively choose to believe that p without refraining from choosing an incompatible alternative; nor can one choose such an alternative without refraining from believing that p. Voluntary control necessarily extends to contraries; the power to choose A at will *is* the power to determine at will whether it shall be A or (some form of) not-A. Therefore, to be strictly accurate we should say that our problem concerns voluntary control over propositional attitudes. Although in the sequel the formulation will often be in terms of belief, it should be understood as having this more general bearing.

Second, something needs to be said about the relation between the control of *actions* and of *states of affairs*. Thus far we have been oscillating freely between the two. Now a belief, in the psychological sense that is being used here (as contrasted with the abstract sense of that which is believed), is a more or less long-lived *state* of the psyche, a modification of the wiring that can influence various actions and reactions of the subject so long as it persists. And the same holds for other propositional attitudes. Thus in speaking of voluntary control of beliefs, we have been speaking of the control of states.

But couldn't we just as well speak of the voluntary control of, and responsibility for, the action of bringing about such states: accepting, rejecting, or witholding a proposition, forming a belief, or refraining from believing?[15] The two loci of responsibility and control may seem strictly correlative, so that we can equally well focus on either.

For one exercises voluntary control over a type of state, C, by voluntarily doing something to bring it about or inhibit it. And from the other side, every action can be thought of as the bringing about of a state of affairs. Whenever we are responsible or blameworthy for a state of affairs by virtue of having brought it about, we may just as well speak of being responsible for the action of bringing it about. However there are the following reasons for proceeding in terms of states.

First, in holding that beliefs are subject to deontological evaluation since under voluntary control, one need not restrict oneself to beliefs that were formed intentionally by a voluntary act. I can be blamed for believing that p in the absence of adequate evidence, even though the belief was formed quite automatically, not by voluntarily carrying out an intention to do so. Provided believing in general is under voluntary control, any belief can be assessed deontologically. It is enough that I could have adopted or withheld the proposition by a voluntary act, had I chosen to do so. This definitely favors a focus on responsibility for states of belief, since we want to evaluate beliefs deontologically where there is no *action* of forming them.

Another consideration that decisively favors the focus on states is that, as we shall see latter, there is a way in which one can be responsible and blameworthy for a state of belief, or other state, even if one lacks the capacity to bring about such states intentionally.

The final preliminary note is this. Our issue does not concern free will or freedom of action, at least not in any sense in which that goes beyond one's action's being under the control of the will. On a "libertarian" conception of free will this is not sufficient; it is required in addition that both A and not-A be causally possible, given all the causal influences on the agent. And other requirements may be imposed concerning agency. A libertarian will, no doubt, maintain that if deontological concepts are to apply to believings in the same way as to overt actions, then all of his conditions for freedom will have to apply to believings as well. However in this paper I shall only be concerned with the issue of whether believings are under voluntary control. If, as I shall argue, this condition is not satisfied for believings, that will be sufficient to show that they are not free in the libertarian sense as well.

III. Basic Voluntary Control

Let's turn now to a critical examination of the basic control thesis, the thesis that one can take up at will whatever propositional attitude one chooses. Those who have attacked this view are divided between those who hold that believing at will is logically impossible and those who hold that it is only psychologically impossible, a capacity that we in fact lack though one we conceivably could have had.[16] I cannot see any sufficient reasons for the stronger claim, and so I shall merely contend that we are not so constituted as to be able to take up propositional attitudes at will. My argument for this, if it can be called that, simply consists in asking you to consider whether you have any such powers. Can you, at this moment, start to believe that the U. S. is still a colony of Great Britain, just by deciding to do so. If you find it too incredible that you should be sufficiently motivated to try to believe this, suppose that someone offers you $500,000,000 to believe it, and you are much more interested in the money than in believing the truth. Could you do what it takes to get that reward? Remember that we are speaking about believing at will. No doubt, there are things you could do that would increase the probability of your coming to believe this, but that will be discussed later. Can you switch propositional attitudes toward that proposition just by deciding to do so? It seems clear to me that I have no such power. Volitions, decisions, or choosings don't hook up with anything in the way of propositional attitude inauguration, just as they don't hook up with the secretion of gastric juices or cell metabolism. There could conceivably be individual differences in this regard. Some people can move their ears at will, while most of us cannot. However, I very much doubt that any human beings are endowed with the power of taking on propositional atittudes at will. The temptation to suppose otherwise may stem from conflating that power with others we undoubtedly do have but are clearly distinct.[17] If I were to set out to bring myself into a state of belief that p, just by an act of will, I might assert that p with an expression of conviction, or dwell favorably on the idea that p, or imagine a sentence expressing p emblazoned in the heavens with an angelic chorus in the background intoning the Kyrie of Mozart's Coronation Mass. All this I can do at will, but none of this amounts to taking on a belief that p. It is all show, an elaborate pretense of believing. Having gone through all this, my doxastic attitudes will remain just as they were before; or if there is some change it will be as a *result* of these gyrations.

We should not suppose that our inability to believe at will is restricted to propositions that are obviously false. The inability also extends, at least, to those that are obviously true. A few pages back we made the point that voluntary control attaches to contrary pairs, or to more complex arrays of alternatives. If the sphere of my effective voluntary control does not extend both to A and to not-A, then it attaches to neither. If I don't have the power to choose between A and not-A, then we are without sufficient reason to say that I did A *at will*, rather than just doing A, accompanied by a volition. It is even more obvious, if possible, that responsibility, obligation, and their kindred attach to doing A only if the agent has an effective choice between doing and not doing A. If I would still have done A whatever I willed, chose, or preferred, I can hardly be blamed for doing it.

Thus, even if I willingly, or not unwillingly, form, e.g., perceptual beliefs in the way I do, it by no means follows that I form those beliefs at will, or that I have voluntary control over such belief formation, or that I can be held responsible or blameworthy for doing so. It would have to be true that I have effective voluntary control over whether I do or do not believe that the tree has leaves on it when I see a tree with leaves on it just before me in broad daylight with my eyesight working perfectly. And it is perfectly clear that in this situation I have no power at all to refrain from that belief. And so with everything else that seems perfectly obvious to us. We have just as little voluntary control over ordinary beliefs formed by introspection, memory, and simple uncontroversial inferences.

The discussion to this point will suggest to the voluntarist that he can still make a stand on propositions that do not seem clearly true or false, and hold that there one (often) has the capacity to adopt whatever propositional attitude one chooses. In religion, philosophy, and high level scientific matters it is often the case that, so far as one can see, the relevant arguments do not definitively settle the matter one way or the other. I engage in prolonged study of the mind-body problem or of the existence of God. I carefully examine arguments for and against various positions. It seems to me that none of the positions have decisively proved their case, even though there are weighty considerations that can be urged in support of each. There are serious difficulties with all the competing positions, even though, so far as I can see, they leave standing more than one contender in each case. So what am I do in this situation? I could just abandon the quest. But alternatively I could, so it seems, simply decide to adopt one of the positions and/or decide to reject one or more of the contenders. Is that not what I must do if I am to make any judgment on the matter? And isn't that what typically happens? I decide to embrace theism or epiphenomenalism, and forthwith it is embraced.

There are also practical situations in which we are confronted with incompatible answers to a certain question, none of which we see to be clearly true or false. Here we often do not have the luxury of leaving the field; since we must act in one way rather than another, we are forced to form, and act on, some belief about the matter. It would be a good idea for me to plant these flowers today if and only if it will rain tomorrow. But it is not at all clear to me whether tomorrow will be rainy. I must either plant the flowers today or not, and it would surely be unwise to simply ignore the matter, thereby in effect acting uncritically on the assumption that it will not rain tomorrow. Hence the better part of wisdom would be to make some judgment on the matter, the best that I can. On a larger scale, a field commander in wartime is often faced with questions about the current disposition of enemy forces. But often the information at his disposal does not tell him just what that disposition is. In such a situation is it not clear that, weighing available indications as best he can, he simply decides to make a certain judgment on the matter and act on that? What else can he do?

Before responding to these claims I should point out that even if they were correct, it would still not follow that a deontological conception of justification is adequate for epistemology. For the voluntarist has already abandoned vast stretches of the territory. He has given up all propositions that seem clearly true or false, and these constitute the bulk of our beliefs. Controversial and difficult issues force themselves on our attention, especially if we are intellectuals, just because we spend so much of our time trying to resolve them. But if we survey the whole range of our cognitive operations, they will appear as a few straws floating on a vast sea of items about none of which we entertain the slightest doubt. Consider the vast number of perceptual beliefs we form about our environment as we move about in it throughout our waking hours, most of them short-lived and many of them unconscious. By comparison just with these the controversial beliefs we have in religion, politics, philosophy, and the conduct of our affairs are negligible in number, however significant they may be individually. Hence if only the uncertain beliefs are under voluntary control, that will not enable us to form a generally applicable deontological concept of epistemic justification.[18]

To return to our philosopher, gardener, and military commander, I would suggest that in each case the situation is better construed in some way other than as initiating a belief at will.[19] The most obvious suggestion is that although in these cases the supporting considerations are seen as less conclusive, here too the belief follows automatically, without intervention by the will, from the way things seem at the moment to the subject. In the cases of (subjective) certainty belief is determined by that sense of certainty, or, alternatively, by what leads to it, the sensory experience or whatever; in the cases of (subjective) uncertainty belief is still determined by what plays an analogous role, the sense that one alternative is more likely than the others, or by what leads to that. Thus when our philosopher or religious seeker "decides" to embrace theism or the identity theory, what has happened is that at that moment this position seems more likely to be true, seems to have weighter considerations in its favor, than any envisaged alternative. Hence S is, *at that moment*, no more able to accept atheism or epiphenomenalism instead, than he would be if theism or the identity theory seemed obviously and indubitably true. This can be verified by considering our capacities in a situation in which the above conditions are not satisfied; theism and atheism, or the various contenders on the mind-body issue, really seem equally likely to be true, equally well or ill supported. If that were strictly the case (and perhaps it seldom is), then could S adopt, e.g., theism, just by choosing to do so? When I contemplate that possibility, it seems to me that I would be as little able to adopt theism at will as I would be if it seemed obviously true or obviously false. Here, like Buridan's ass, I am confronted with (subjectively) perfectly equivalent alternatives. If it were a choice between actions, such as that confronting the ass, I need not perish through indecision. I could arbitrarily make a choice, as we often do in a cafeteria line when two alternative salads look equally tempting. (Some people negotiate this more quickly than others.) But doxastic choice is another matter. How *could* I simply choose to believe one rather than the other when they seem exactly on a par with respect to the likelihood of truth, especially when that subjective probability is rather low? To do so would be to choose a belief in the face of the lack of any significant inclination to suppose it to be true. It seems clear to me that this is not within our power.[20]

The above account in terms of comparative subjective probability might be correct for all our cases, theoretical and practical. Thus the military commander might adopt the supposition about the disposition of enemy forces that seems to him at the moment best supported by the reports at his disposal. But I believe that there are cases, both theoretical and practical, in which the upshot is not triggered by some differential subjective probability of the alternatives. I have already argued that in those cases the upshot cannot be the formation of a belief, whether at will or otherwise. But then what? Here is one possibility. What S is doing is to resolve to act as if p is true, adopt it as a basis for action. This is often a correct description of situations like the military commander's. He may well have said to himself: "I don't know what the disposition of enemy forces is; I don't even have enough information to make an educated guess. But I have to proceed on some basis or other, so I'll just assume that it is X and make my plans accordingly." This is not to form the belief that the disposition is X; it is not to *accept* the proposition that the disposition is X, except as a basis for action. It would simply be incorrect to describe the commander as *believing* that the disposition of enemy forces is X, or having any other belief about the matter. He is simply proceeding on a certain assumption, concerning the truth of which he has no belief at all. One may also make an assumption for theoretical purposes, in order to see how it "pans out", in the hope that one will thereby obtain some additional reasons for supposing it to be true or false. Thus a scientist can adopt "as a working hypothesis" the proposition that the atomic nucleus is positively charged, draw various consequences from it, and seek to test those consequences. The scientist need not *form* the belief that the atomic nucleus is positively charged in order to carry out this operation; typically he would be doing this because he didn't know what to believe about the matter. Likewise a philosopher might take materialism as a working hypothesis to see how it works out in application to various problems. There may also be blends of the theoretical and the practical. One may adopt belief in God, or some more robust set of religious doctrines, as a guide to life, setting out to try to live in accordance with them, seeking to act and feel one's way into the religious community, in order to determine how the doctrines work out in the living of them, both in terms of how satisfatory and fulfilling a life they enable one to live and in terms of what evidence for or against them one acquires.

Where the "acceptance" of a proposition in the absence of a significant subjective probability is not the adoption of a working hypothesis, there are other alternatives. (1) S may be seeking, for whatever reason, to bring himself into a position of believing p; and S or others may confuse this activity, which can be undertaken voluntarily, with believing or judging the proposition to be true. (2) As noted earlier, S may assert that p, overtly or covertly, perhaps repeatedly and in a firm tone, and this, which can be done voluntarily, may be confused with a "judgment" that p, of the sort that inaugurates a state of belief. (3) S may align herself, objectively and/or subjectively, with some group that is committed to certain doctrines-a church, a political party, a movement, a group of thinkers-and this, which can be done voluntarily, may be confused with coming to believe those doctrines. I am convinced that the analysis of a wide variety of supposed cases of believing at will in the absence of significant subjective probability, would reveal that in each case forming a belief that p has been confused with something else. Thus I think that there is a strong case for the proposition that no one ever acquires a belief at will. But even if I am wrong about that, the above considerations do at least show that it is of relatively rare occurrence, and that it certainly cannot be used as the basis for a generally applicable deontological concept of epistemic justification.

IV. Non-Basic Immediate Voluntary Control

However the demise of basic control is by no means the end of "voluntarism", as we may term the thesis that one has voluntary control of propositional attitudes. Many deontologists, after disavowing any commitment to what they usually call "direct voluntary control of belief" and what we we have called "basic voluntary control", proceed to insist that beliefs are subject to what they term "indirect voluntary control".[21] All of them use the term 'indirect control' in an undiscriminating fashion to cover any sort of control that is not "direct", i.e., basic. As a result they fail to distinguish between the three sorts of non-basic control I shall be distinguishing.[22] Some of their examples fit one of my three categories, some another. The ensuing discussion will show important differences between these three modes of control.

To get into this, let's first note that we take many familiar non-basic overt actions to be voluntary (and their upshots to be under voluntary control) in a way that is sufficient for their being required, permitted, and prohibited. Consider opening a door, informing someone that p, and turning on a light. To succeed in any of these requires more than a volition on the part of the agent; in each case I must perform one or more bodily movements and these movements must have certain consequences, causal or conventional, in order that I can be said to have performed the non-basic action in question. In order for it to be true that I opened a certain door I must pull it, push it, kick it, or put some other part of my body into suitable contact with it (assuming that I lack powers of telekinesis), and this must result in the door's coming to be open. In order to inform H that p, I must produce various sounds, marks, or other perceptible products, and either these products must fall under linguistic rules in such a way as to constitute a vehicle for asserting that p (if we are thinking of informing as an illocutionary act), or H, upon perceiving these products, must be led to form the belief that p (if we are thinking of informing as a perlocutionary act). Hence actions like these are not immediately consequent on a volition and so are not strictly done "at will". Nevertheless I might be blamed for my failure to turn on the light when it was my obligation to do so. The point is that in many cases we take the extra conditions of success for granted. We suppose that if the agent will just voluntarily exert herself the act will be done. Here we might say that the action, and its upshot, is under the "immediate voluntary control" of the agent (more strictly, *non-basic* immediate voluntary control), even though more than an act of will is required of the agent. I call this "immediate"[23] control since the agent is able to carry out the intention "right away", in one uninterrupted intentional act, without having to return to the attempt a number of times after having been occupied with other matters.[24] I will use the term "direct control" for both basic and immediate control. It is clear that if beliefs were under one's immediate control that would suffice to render them susceptible to deontological evaluation.

But are beliefs always, or ever, within our immediate voluntary control? Our discussion of this will be largely a rerun of the discussion of basic control, with some added twists. As in the earlier discussion we can first exempt most of our doxastic situations from serious consideration. With respect to almost all normal perceptual, introspective, and memory propositions, it is absurd to think that one has any such control over whether one accepts, rejects, or witholds the proposition. When I look out my window and see rain falling, water dripping off the leaves of trees, and cars passing by, I no more have immediate control over whether I accept those propositions than I have basic control. I form the beliefs that rain is falling, etc. willy-nilly. There is no way I can inhibit these beliefs. At least there is no way I can do so *on the spot*, in carrying out an uninterrupted intention to do so. How would I do so? What button would I push? I could try asserting the contrary in a confident tone of voice. I could rehearse some sceptical arguments. I could invoke the Vedantic doctrine of *maya*. I could grit my teeth and command myself to withold the proposition. But unless I am a very unusual person, none of these will have the least effect. It seems clear that nothing any normal human being can do during the uninterrupted operation of an intention to, e.g., reject the proposition that it is raining (in the above situation) will have any chance at all to succeed. And the same can be said for inferential beliefs in which it is quite clear to one that the conclusion is correct. Since cases in which it seems perfectly clear to the subject what is the case constitute an enormously large proportion (I would say almost all) of propositions that are either the object of a definite attitude or considered as a candidate for such, the considerations of this paragraph show that immediate voluntary control cannot be a basis for the application of deontological concepts to most of our propositional attitudes.

But what about situations in which it is not clear whether a proposition is true or false? This is where voluntarists tend to take their stand. After all, they say, that is what inquiry is for, to resolve matters when it is not clear what the correct answer is. One certainly has voluntary control over whether to keep looking for evidence or reasons, and voluntary control over where to look, what steps to take, and so on. Since one has control over those matters that amounts to what I have called immediate voluntary control over one's propositional attitudes.

> If self-control is what is essential to activity, some of our
> beliefs, our believings, would seem to be acts. When a man
> deliberates and comes finally to a conclusion, his decision is
> as much within his control as is any other deed we attribute

to him. If his conclusion was unreasonable, a conclusion he should not have accepted, we may plead with him: "But you needn't have supposed that so-and-so was true. Why didn't you take account of these other facts?" We assume that his decision is one he could have avoided and that, had he only chosen to do so, he could have made a more reasonable inference. Or, if his conclusion is not the result of a deliberate inference, we may say, "But if you had only stopped to think", implying that, had he chosen, he could have stopped to think. We suppose, as we do whenever we apply our ethical or moral predicates, that there was something else the agent could have done instead.[25]

To be sure, the mere fact that one often looks for evidence to decide an unresolved issue does not show that one has immediate control, or any other sort of control, over one's propositional atittudes. That also depends on the incidence of success in these enterprises. And sometimes one finds decisive evidence and sometimes one doesn't. But let's ignore this complexity and just consider whether there is a case for immediate control of propositional attitudes in the successful cases.

No, there is not, and primarily for the following reason. These claims ignore the difference between doing A in order to bring about E, for some definite E, and doing A so that some effect within a certain range will ensue. In order that the "looking for more evidence" phenomenon would show that we have immediate voluntary control over propositional attitudes in basically the way we do over the positions of doors and light switches, it would have to be the case that the search for evidence was undertaken with the intention of taking up a certain particular attitude toward a particular proposition. For only in that case would the outcome show that we have exercised voluntary control over *what* propositional attitude we take up. Suppose that I can't remember Al Kaline's lifetime batting average and I look it up in the Baseball Almanac. I read there the figure .320, and I thereby accept it. Does that demonstrate my voluntary control over my belief that Kaline's lifetime batting average was .320? Not at all. At most it shows that I have immediate voluntary control over whether I take up *some* propositional attitude toward *some* proposition ascribing a lifetime batting average to Kaline. This is not at all analogous to my exercising my capacity to get the door open whenever I choose to do so. Its nearest analogue in that area would be something like this. I am a servant and I am motivated to bring the door into whatever position my employer chooses. He has an elaborate electronic system that involves automatic control of many aspects of the household, including doors. Each morning he leaves detailed instructions on household operations in a computer. Doors can only be operated through the computer in accordance with his instructions. There is no way in which I can carry out an intention of my own to open or to close a door. All I can do is to actuate the relevant program and let things take their course. Since the employer's instructions will be carried out only if I actuate the program, I am responsible for the doors' assuming whatever position he specified, just as I was responsible for taking up some attitude or other toward some proposition within a given range. But I most emphatically am not responsible for the front door's being open rather than closed, nor can I be said to have voluntary control over its specific position. Hence it would be idle to apply deontological concepts to me vis-a-vis the specific position of the door: to forbid me or require me to open it, or to blame or reproach me for its being open. I had no control over that; it was not subject to my will. And that's the way it is where the only voluntary control I have over my propositional attitudes is to enter onto an investigation that will eventuate in some propositional attitude or other, depending on what is uncovered. That would be no basis for holding me responsible for believing that p rather than rejecting or witholding it, no basis for requiring me or forbidding me to believe that p, or for reproaching me for doing so.

If Chisholm's claim is only that one can voluntarily put oneself in a position from which some doxastic attitude to p will be forthcoming (or perhaps that one can put oneself in a position such that a desirable doxastic attitude to p will be forthcoming), *this* capacity extends to all sorts of propositions, including those over which we obviously have no voluntary control. Consider propositions concerning what is visible. I have the power to open my eyes and look about me, thereby putting myself in a position, when conditions are favorable, to reliably form propositions about the visible environment. Again, with respect to past experiences I can "search my memory" for the details of my experiences of the middle of yesterday, thereby, usually, putting myself in an excellent position to reliably form beliefs about my experiences at that time. No one, I suppose, would take this to show that I have immediate voluntary control over what I believe about the visible environment or about my remembered experiences. And yet this is essentially the same sort of thing as the search for additional evidence, differing only in the type of belief forming mechanism involved.

I suspect that deontologists like Chisholm secretly suppose that the additional evidence, rather than "automatically" determining the doxastic attitude, simply puts the subject in a position to make an informed choice of an attitude. That is, despite their official position, they really locate the voluntary control in the moment of attitude formation rather than in the preliminary investigation, thus in effect taking the direct voluntary control position. But then, faced with the crashing implausibility of that position, they think to save the application of deontological concepts by pushing the voluntary control back to the preliminary search for decisive considerations. It is, then, their secret, unacknowledged clinging to the basic control thesis that prevents them from seeing that voluntary control of the investigative phase has no tendency to ground the deontological treatment of propositional attitudes. I must confess that I have no real textual evidence for this speculation, and that I am attracted to it by the fact that it explains an otherwise puzzling failure of acute philosophers to see the irrelevance (to this issue) of our voluntary control over the conduct of inquiry.

Thus far I have been considering one way in which deontologists seek to defend a claim of immediate voluntary control over beliefs. We have seen that way to fail by irrelevance, since it has to do with voluntarily putting oneself in a position to form the most rational attitude, whatever that may be, rather than voluntarily taking up some specific attitude. However, there is no doubt but that people do sometimes set out to get themselves to believe that p, for some specific p. People try to convince themselves that X loves them, that Y will turn out all right, that the boss doesn't really have a negative attitude toward them, that the Red Sox will win the World Series, that materialism is true, or that God exists. Epistemologists don't like to cite such disreputable proceedings as a ground for the application of deontological concepts. To try to get oneself to believe that p, prior to being in a good position to tell whether p is true or not, is not a procedure to be commended from the epistemic standpoint. Nevertheless, these undertakings have to be considered in a comprehensive survey of possible modes of voluntary control. Proceeding in that spirit, the point to note here is that such goings on provide no support for a supposition of *immediate* voluntary control over belief. For such enterprises can be successfully carried out only as long-term projects. If I, not currently believing that X loves me, were to set out to bring about that belief in one fell swoop, i.e., during a period of activity uninterruptedly guided by the intention to produce that belief, then, unless I am markedly abnormal psychologically, I am doomed to failure. We just don't work that way. Again, I wouldn't know what button to push. My only hope of success would lie in bringing various influences to bear upon myself and shielding myself from others, in the hope of thereby eventually moving myself from disbelief to belief. This might include dwelling on those encounters in which X had acted lovingly toward me, shutting out evidences of indifference or dislike, encouraging romantic fantasies, etc. Thus this sort of enterprise belongs, rather, to the category of *long range voluntary control*, a topic to which we now turn.

V. Long Range Voluntary Control

We have seen that we cannot plausibly be credited with either sort of direct control over our propositional attitudes. Taking up such an attitude can be neither a basic action like raising one's arm nor a non-basic action like flipping a switch. Hence the deontological treatment of belief can borrow no support from the applicability of deontological terms to actions like these. But the possibility still remains that we have more long-range voluntary control over belief. The considerations of the last paragraph encourage this supposition, at least for some cases. Before examining this possibility I will firm up the distinction between this type of control and the previous one.

In introducing the notion of "immediate control" I said that when one has this species of control over a type of state, C, one is able to bring about a C "right away, in one uninterrupted intentional act". When conditions are propitious, one can get a door open, get a light on, get one's shoes on, or tell Susie the mail has come, by doing various things under the direction of a single uninterrupted intention to bring about that state of affairs. One does not have to return to the attempt a number of times after having been occupied with other matters, when the intention to bring about C was not performing a monitoring and directing function.[26] And since one is not ordinarily capable of keeping an intention in an active state for more than a relatively short period of time, the sorts of actions over which one has immediate control must be capable of execution within a short time after their inception.

Long range control is simply the foil of immediate control. It is the capacity to bring about a state of affairs, C, by doing something (usually a number of different things) repeatedly over a considerable period of time, interrupted by activity directed to other goals. One has this sort of control, to a greater or lesser degree, over many things: one's weight, cholesterol concentration, blood pressure, and disposition; the actions of one's spouse or one's department. One can, with some hope of success, set out on a long-range project to reduce one's weight, improve one's disposition, or get one's spouse to be more friendly to the neighbors. The degree of control varies markedly among these examples. I have, within limits, complete control over my weight; only sufficient motivation is required to achieve and maintain a certain weight. My ability to change my disposition or to change behavior patterns in my spouse is much less. But all these cases, and many more, illustrate the point that one can have long range control over many things over which one lacks direct control. I cannot markedly reduce my weight right away, by the uninterrupted carrying out of an intention to do so, e.g., by taking a pill, running around the block, or saying "Abracadabra". But that doesn't nullify the fact that I have long range control.

It does seem that we have some degree of long range voluntary control over at least some of our beliefs. As just noted, people do set out on long range projects to get themselves to believe a certain proposition, and sometimes they succeed in this. Devices employed include selective exposure to evidence, selective attention to supporting considerations, seeking the company of believers and avoiding non-believers, self-suggestion, and (possibly) more bizarre methods like hypnotism. By such methods people sometimes induce themselves to believe in God, in materialism, in Communism, in the proposition that they are loved by X, and so on. Why doesn't this constitute a kind of voluntary control that grounds deontological treatment?

Well, it would if, indeed, we do have sufficient control of this sort. Note that people could properly be held responsible for their attitudes toward propositions in a certain range only if those who set out to intentionally produce a certain attitude toward such a proposition, and made sufficient efforts, were frequently successful.[27] For only if we are generally successful in bringing about a goal, G, when we try hard enough to do so, do we have effective control over whether G obtains. And if I don't have effective control over G, I can hardly be held to blame for its non-occurrence. Even if I had done everything I could to produce it, I would have had little chance of success; so how could I rightly be blamed for its absence? (I might be blamed for not *trying* to produce it or for not trying hard enough, but that is another matter.) This is a generally applicable principle, by no means restricted to the doxastic sphere. If I am so constituted that the most I can do with respect to my irritability is to make it somewhat less likely that it will exceed a certain (rather high) average threshold, I can hardly be blamed for being irritable.

It is very dubious that we have reliable long range control over any of our beliefs, even in the most favorable cases, such as beliefs about religious and philosophical matters and about personal relationships. *Sometimes* people succeed in getting themselves to believe (disbelieve) something. But I doubt that the success rate is substantial. To my knowledge there are no statistics on this, but I would be very much surprised if attempts of this sort bore fruit in more than a small proportion of the cases. In thinking about this, let's first set aside cases in which the attempt succeeds because the subject happens onto conclusive evidence that would have produced belief anyway without deliberate effort on his part to produce belief. These are irrelevant because the intention to believe that p played no effective role. Thus we are considering cases in which the subject is swimming against either a preponderance of contrary evidence or a lack of evidence either way. S is fighting very strong tendencies to believe when and only when something seems true to one. Some of these tendencies are probably innate and some engendered or reinforced by socialization; in any event they are deeply rooted and of great strength. To combat or circumvent them one must exercise considerable ingenuity in monitoring the input of information and in exposing oneself to non-rational influences. This is a tricky operation, requiring constant vigilance as well as considerable skill, and it would be very surprising if it were successful in a significant proportion of the cases. I am not suggesting that it is unusual for people to form and retain beliefs without adequate grounds, reasons, or justification. This is all too common. But in most such cases the proposition in question seems clearly true, however ill supported. The typical case of prejudice is not one in which S manages to believe something contrary to what seems to him to be the case or something concerning which he has no definite impression of truth or falsity. It is a case in which his socialization has led it to seem clearly true to him that, e.g., blacks are innately inferior.

Thus a long-range control thesis does not provide much grounding for deontologism, even for the sorts of propositions people do sometimes try to get themselves to believe or disbelieve. Much less is there any such grounding for those propositions with respect to which people don't normally even try to manipulate their attitudes. We have already noted that most of our beliefs, e.g. perceptual beliefs, spring from doxastic tendencies that are too deeply rooted to permit of modification by deliberate effort. Most of the matters on which we form beliefs are such that the project of deliberately producing belief or disbelief is one that is never seriously envisaged, just because it is too obvious that there is no chance of success. Thus even if we were usually successful when we set out to produce a propositional attitude, the voluntary control thus manifested would not ground the application of deontological concepts to beliefs generally. So, once again, the most we could conceivably have (and I have argued that we do not in fact have even that) would fall short of a generally applicable deontological concept of justification.

VI. Indirect Voluntary Influence: A Different Deontological Conception of Epistemic Justification

Up to this point I have been examining the support for a deontological conception of epistemic justification provided by the treatment of propositional atttitude formation on the model of intentional action. We have considered whether, or to what extent, it is in our power to carry out an intention to take up a certain propositional attitude, either at will (basic control), or while uninterruptedly guided by the intention to do so (immediate control), or as a complex long term project (long-range control). We have seen that for most of our beliefs we have control of none of these sorts, and that for the others we have, at most, some spotty and unreliable control of the long-range sort. I conclude that we do *not* generally have the power to carry out an intention to take up a certain propositional attitude. Insofar as the conception of epistemic justification as *believ-*

ing as one is permitted to depends on that assumption, it must be rejected. The inauguration of propositional attitudes simply does not work like intentional action.

However this is not necessarily the end of the line for the deontologist. As I point out in Alston (1985), he has another move. We can be held responsible for a state of affairs that results from our actions even if we did not produce that state of affairs intentionally, provided it is the case that something we did (didn't do) and should have not done (done) was a necessary condition (in the circumstances) of the realisation of that state of affairs, i.e., provided that state of affairs would not have obtained had we not done (done) something we should not have done (done). Suppose that, although I did not do anything with the intention of bringing about my cholesterol build up, still I could have prevented it if I had done certain things I could and should have done, e.g., reduce fat intake. In that case I could still be held responsible for the condition; it could be my fault. This is a way in which deontological concepts can be applied to me, with respect to a certain state of affairs, even though that state of affairs did not result from my carrying out an intention to produce it.

This suggests that even if propositional attitudes are not under our effective voluntary control, we might still be held responsible for them, provided we could and should have prevented them; provided there is something we could and should have done such that if we had done it we would not have had the attitude in question. If this is the case it could provide a basis for the application of deontological concepts to propositional attitudes, and, perhaps, for a deontological concept of epistemic justification, one that bypasses the above critique. Let's use the term "indirect voluntary influence" for this kind of voluntary control, or better, "voluntary impact" we may have on our beliefs.

It may be helpful to display in outline form the various modes of voluntary control we have distinguished.

    I. Direct control.
      A. Basic control.
      B. Non-basic immediate control.
    II. Long-range control.
    III.Indirect influence.

Now it does seem that we have voluntary control over many things that influence belief. These can be divided into (1) activities that bring influences to bear, or withold influences from, a particular situation involving a particular candidate, or a particular field of candidates, for belief, and (2) activities that affect our general belief forming habits or tendencies.[28] There are many examples of (1). With respect to a particular issue, I have voluntary control over whether, and how long, I consider the matter, look for relevant evidence or reasons, reflect on a particular argument, seek input from other people, search my memory for analogous cases, and so on. Here we come back to the activities that people like Chisholm wrongly classify as the intentional inauguration of a propositional attitude. Although the fact that it is within my power to either look for further evidence or not to do so, does not show that I have voluntary control over what attitude I take toward p, it does show that I have voluntary control over influences on that attitude. The second category includes such activities as training myself to be more critical of gossip, instilling in myself a stronger disposition to reflect carefully before making a judgment on highly controversial matters, talking myself into being less (more) subservient to authority, and practicng greater sensitivity to the condition of other people. It is within my power to do things like this or not, and when I do them with sufficient assiduity I make some difference to my propositional attitude tendencies, and thus indirectly to the formation of such attitudes.[29]

Actually, there would be no harm in including in the first category attempts to bring about a certain specific attitude, and the successful carrying out of such an attempt when and if that occurs. For these too would be things over which we have voluntary control that influence our propositional attitudes. The point of stressing other things is that, since our earlier discussions have provided reason for thinking that such attempts are rarely successful, I want to emphasize the point that even if we are never successful in carrying out an intention to believe (reject, withhold) p, still there are many things over which we have voluntary control that do have a bearing on what propositional attitudes are engendered.

It hardly needs argument that voluntary activities of the sorts mentioned do influence our propositional attitudes, so that it will sometimes be the case that had we performed (not performed) some voluntary actions A, B, . . ., we would have (not have) taken up some attitude we did not (did) take up. The only remaining question is as to whether deontological concepts apply to the sorts of activities we have been discussing. Is it ever the case that we ought or ought not to engage in some activity of searching for new evidence or refraining from doing so? Is it ever the case that we ought (ought not) to strive to make ourselves more (less) critical of gossip or more (less) sensitive to contrary evidence? Deontologists typically aver that we have *intellectual* obligations in such matters, obligations rooted in our basic intellectual obligation to seek the true and avoid the false, or, alternatively, rooted in our basic aim, need, or commitment to believe the true and avoid believing the false. Let's go along with our opponents on this point. I can do so with a clear conscience, since I am seeking to show that even if we admit this, and make the other concessions I have been making, a deontological conception of epistemic justification is not viable.

Thus it will sometimes be the case, when I believe that p, that I would not have done so had I done various things in the past that I could and should have done but failed to do. Suppose that I accept some idle gossip to the effect that Jim is trying to undermine Susie's position as chair of the department. It may be that had I been doing my duty by way of making myself more critical of gossip, and by way of checking into this particular matter, I would not have formed that belief, or would not have retained it for so long. In that case I could be held responsible for believing this in the same way as that in which I can be held responsible for my cholesterol build up. I can be properly blamed for it, even though I did not intentionally bring it about.

Note that this application of deontological concepts to beliefs is a derivative one. What is primarily required, permitted, and forbidden are the voluntary activities we ranged in two categories, various sorts of activities that influence belief. Deontological concepts are applied to beliefs only because of some relation these attitudes have to those primary targets of permission, etc. This asymmetrical relation of dependence attaches to all those cases in which one is responsible for a state of affairs without being responsible for an action of intentionally bringing it about.

Now let's consider just what deontological terms can be applied to beliefs in this derivative way and how this application is to be understood. Remember that we are taking requirement, prohibition, and permission to be the basic deontological concepts. When dealing with intentional actions it is best to think first of general principles that lay down conditions under which an action of a certain sort is required, forbidden, or permitted; and then consider a particular action to have one of these statuses because it exemplifies some general principle. Thus if we take the forming of a belief to be an intentional action, we will envisage general principles that hold, e.g., that it is forbidden to believe that p in the absence of sufficient evidence. Then if I form a particular belief without sufficient grounds that belief is forbidden, or, if you prefer, I have violated a prohibition in forming that belief. We can then apply other deontological terms like 'responsible', 'blame', and 'praise' on this basis. If one intentionally does something that falls under a principle of one of the above sorts, one is responsible for what one has done. If in doing it one has violated a requirement or a prohibition, one can rightly be blamed for it. If one has not violated any requirement or prohibition, one is justified in doing it.

But on the present way of looking at the matter, we can have no principles laying down conditions under which a belief is required, forbidden, or permitted, just because we lack sufficient voluntary control over belief formation. What the relevant principles will require, etc., are activities that are designed to influence factors that, in turn, will influence belief formation.[30] Hence there is no basis for taking a particular belief to be required, prohibited, or forbidden. And so if we are to say, on the rationale given above, that one can be responsible and blameworthy for a belief, that will be the case even though the belief is not prohibited. If one is puzzled by this, the cure comes from realizing that responsibility and blame supervene on requirement, prohibition, and permission in two quite different ways. First, and most simply, one is to blame for doing something forbidden or for failing to do something required. But second, one is also to blame for the obtaining of some fact if that fact would not have obtained if one had not behaved in some manner for which one is to blame in the first sense, i.e. for doing something forbidden or failing to do something required.

So far, in discussing indirect influence, we have seen that one can be to blame for a certain propositional attitude provided one wouldn't have that attitude had one not failed to conform to some intellectual requirement or prohibition. But this formulation must be refined. On reflection it turns out to be too broad. There are certain ways in which dereliction of duty can contribute to belief formation without rendering the subject blameworthy for forming that belief. Suppose that I fail to carry out my obligation to spend a certain period in training myself to look for counter-evidence. I use the time thus freed up to take a walk around the neighborhood. In the course of this stroll I see two dogs fighting, thereby acquiring the belief that they are fighting. There was a relevant intellectual obligation I didn't fulfill, which is such that if I had fulfilled it I wouldn't have acquired that belief. But if that is a perfectly normal perceptual belief, I am surely not to blame for having formed it.[31]

Here the dereliction of duty contributed to belief-formation simply by facilitating access to the data. That is not the kind of contribution we had in mind. The sorts of cases we were thinking of were those most directly suggested by the two sorts of intellectual obligations we distinguished: (a) cases in which we acquire or retain the belief only because we are sheltered from adverse considerations in a way we wouldn't have been had we done what we should have done; (b) cases in which the belief was acquired by the activation of a habit we would not have possessed had we fulfilled our intellectual obligations. Thus we can avoid counter-examples like the above by the following reformulation:

> (1) S is (intellectually) to blame for believing that p *iff* if S had fulfilled all her intellectual obligations, then S's belief forming habits would have changed, or S's access to relevant adverse considerations would have changed, in such a way that S would not have believed that p.

Another issue has to do with the "absoluteness" of the counterfactual involved in this formulation. (1) involves the flat requirement that S *would not have believed that p* under these conditions. But perhaps S is also blameworthy for believing that p if some weaker condition holds, e.g., that it would be much less likely that S would have believed that p had S fulfilled her intellectual obligations. Of course, the relation between this and (1) depends on one's account of counterfactuals. For present purposes we need not enter this forbidding swamp. I am shortly going to argue that the concept of epistemic justification that emerges from (1) is inadequate for epistemology; and that argument will not rest on taking the counterfactual to be stronger or weaker.

We can now move on to developing a deontological notion of epistemic justification that is based on the above. One point is obvious: when S is to blame for believing that p, that belief is not justified. But that will presumably cover only a tiny proportion of beliefs. What about the others?

One possibility would be to treat being justified as the mirror image of being unjustified. To justifiably believe that p, then, is for one's belief that p to be to one's credit. That is, one is justified in believing that p *iff* one wouldn't have believed that p unless one had fulfilled one's intellectual obligations in some way: by doing what is intellectually required of one or by refraining from doing what one is intellectually forbidden to do.

This might seem to leave us with precious few justified beliefs. How many of our beliefs have intellectually dutiful deeds as an essential part of their ancestry? But before embracing that conclusion we should remember that part of the formulation that has to do with refraining from doing what is forbidden. The formulation does not imply that we are justified only where some positive act of duty is in the causal ancestry. One might argue that it is always open to us to engage in attempts to build up disreputable belief forming tendencies, e.g., wishful thinking; and that often we wouldn't have the perfectly respectable beliefs we do have if we had engaged in that enterprise with sufficient vigor. But even so it still remains that no such counterfactual would hold for beliefs that are beyond the reach of voluntary endeavors, like typical perceptual, memory, and introspective beliefs. No amount of striving after wishful thinking would dislodge most of these. Hence they would fall outside the scope of justified belief on this construal.

There is a simple way to set up the justified-unjustified distinction on the basis of (1) without coming into so violent a conflict with our ordinary judgments. We can take any belief that is not unjustified by the above criterion to be justified. On this construal, 'unjustified' would be the term that "wears the trousers" (Austin), and 'justified' would simply be its negation. A belief is justified *iff* the subject is not intellectually to blame for holding it. This brings us back to the deontological conception of justification advocated by Ginet and others. Remember that we quoted Ginet as saying that one is justified provided that "one could not be justly reproached for being confident that p". The only difference is that whereas Ginet was thinking of blame as attaching to belief as something that is itself under voluntary control, we are thinking of it in the more complex, derivative way developed in this section.

VII. Critique of This New Conception

The upshot of the paper thus far is that the only viable deontological conception of justification is the one that identifies being justified in believing that p with not being intellectually to blame for believing that p, in a sense of 'to blame for' explicated in (1). To put this into a canonical formula:

> (2) S is justified in believing that p *iff* it is not the case that if S had fulfilled all her intellectual obligations, then S's belief forming habits would have changed, or S's access to relevant adverse considerations would have changed, in such a way that S would not have believed that p.

What follows the *iff* is, of course, the denial of the account of being to blame for a belief given by (1). "Of course", since on this conception, being justified in believing that p is just not being to blame for believing that p.

In the remainder of the paper I shall present reasons for denying that (2) gives us a concept of justification that is what we are, or should be, looking for in epistemology. I shall point out ways in which one can be justified according to (2), and yet not justified in any way that is crucial for epistemological concerns; and, conversely, that one can be justified in an epistemologically crucial way and yet not deontologically justified, as spelled out by (2). But first a terminological disclaimer. My linguistic intuitions tell me that 'justified' and its cognates are properly used only in a deontological sense. To be justified in doing or believing something just *is* to not have violated any relevant rules, norms, or principles in so doing, believing . If, as I believe, most epistemologists use 'justified' for some quite different notion, they are speaking infelicitously. However, this way of talking is so firmly entrenched that I shall go along with it, albeit with an uneasy linguistic conscience.

If I am to argue that (2) does not amount to real epistemic justification, I must proceed on the basis of some assumption as to what epistemic justification really is. I have no time to argue for any such assumption at the tag end of this paper.[32] Hence I shall argue the point separately for two different conceptions, one more externalist, the other more internalist.[33] I shall devote most of the time to my favorite conception, which is basically externalist with an internalist twist. Let me begin by briefly explaining that.

Start from the idea of forming a belief in such a way as to be in a good position to get a true belief. Call this, if you like, a "favorable position" conception of justification. One is justified in believing that p only if that belief was formed in such a way as to make it at least very likely that the belief is true, or, as is sometimes said, only if it was formed in a "truth-conducive" way.[34] Reliability theory is a natural way of further developing the notion: The belief is justified only if it was formed in a *reliable* fashion, one that can generally be *relied* on to produce true beliefs. Note that there is no guarantee that the subject will be aware of the crucial aspects of the mode of formation, much less of the fact that that mode is truth conducive; that is what makes this conception externalist. My internalist twist consists in also requiring that the belief be based on a "ground" that the subject can be aware of fairly readily. This twist does not negate the externalism. I do not also require that the subject be aware, or have the capacity to be aware, that the ground is an adequate one or that the belief was formed in a reliable or a truth conducive way. My internalist qualification will play no role in what follows. The argument will depend solely on the requirement that the ground be in fact an adequate one (sufficiently indicative of the truth of the belief). I mention my internalist twist only to point out that the ensuing argument against (2) does not depend on embracing the most extreme form of externalism.

The first point to mention about (2) is that the concept does not apply at all to subjects that lack sufficient sophistication, reflectiveness, or freedom to be subject to intellectual requirements, prohibitions, and the like. This includes lower animals and very young children as well as the mentally defective. But I don't want to stress this consideration, since it can be plausibly argued that the notion of epistemic justification has no significant application to such subjects either. If I went along with the popular view that justification is necessary for knowledge, I would resist this claim, for it is clear to me that lower animals and very young children often know what is going on in their environment. But since I am prepared to recognize knowledge without justification, I am free to acknowledge that the notion of epistemic justification gets a foothold only where subjects are capable of evaluating their own doxastic states and those of others and responding to those evaluations appropriately. Hence the discussion will be restricted to normal adult humans, to whom deontological concepts are applicable.

Next I shall explore ways in which one may be deontologically justified in a belief without forming the belief in a truth conducive way. But first, how we are to tell when one is free of blame in forming a belief? That depends on whether the belief stemmed, in the specified way, from any failure of obligations. But how are we to think of those obligations? I am not now asking about the content of our intellectual obligations. As for that, I shall simply draw on the illustrations given earlier. I am asking rather: How much is a person obliged to do along these lines in a particular situation? And the main point is that we must distinguish between "counsels of perfection" and what it is reasonable to expect of a person. With world enough and time we could require people to carry out an exhaustive investigation of each witness, search through all the relevant literature for considerations pertinent to each candidate for belief, check each calculation ten times, and so on. But we simply do not have time for all that. Even if we were exclusively devoted to the search for truth we would not be able to do that for all the matters on which we need to form beliefs. And given that we have various other commitments and obligations, it is doubly impossible. Hence, abandoning counsels of perfection, let us say that one can properly be blamed for a belief only if that belief stems, in the specified way, from failures to do what could reasonably be expected of one; simply failing to do what would be ideally adequate is not enough.

In Alston (1985) I presented two putative examples of subjects who are deontologically justified but in a poor position to get the truth. One is a case of cultural isolation. S has lived all his life in an isolated primitive community where everyone unhesitatingly accepts the traditions of the tribe as authoritative. These have to do with alleged events distant in time and space, about which S and his fellows have no chance to gather independent evidence. S has never encountered anyone who questions the traditions, and these traditions play a key role in the communal life of the tribe. Under these conditions it seems clear to me that S is in no way to blame for forming beliefs on the basis of the traditions. He has not failed to do anything he could reasonably be expected to do. His beliefs about, e.g., the origins of the tribe, stem from what, so far as he can see, are the best grounds one could have for such beliefs. And yet, let us suppose, the traditions have not been formed in such a way as to be a reliable indication of their own truth. S is deontologically justified, but he is not believing in a truth conducive way.

The first half of this judgment has been challenged by Matthias Steup (forthcoming), who takes a hard line with my tribesman:

> No matter how grim the circumstances are, if an agent holds a belief contrary to evidence, it is within his power, given that he is a rational agent, to reflect upon his belief and thereby to find out that he had better withhold it, or even assent to its negation. Being a rational agent, I would say, involves the capacity to find out, with respect to any belief, whether or not it is being held on good grounds. (pp. 19-20).

Hence, contrary to my judgment, S is not free of intellectual blame and so is not deontologically justified.

I think that Steup is displaying an insensitivity to cultural differences. He supposes that there are standards recognized in all cultures that determine what is adequate evidence, or good enough grounds, for one or another kind of belief. That does not seem to me to be the case. There may very well be trans-cultural epistemic standards, such as consistency and reliability, but I see no reason to suppose that they are sufficient to settle all issues as to what counts as adequate reasons or grounds. On the contrary, the criteria for this vary significantly from one culture to another. The judgments of adequacy of grounds that are transmitted across generations will differ across cultures. Hence what can reasonably be expected of a subject with respect to, e.g., critical examination of beliefs and their bases will differ across cultures. We require adults in our culture to be critical of "tradition", but this is a relatively recent phenomenon, given the time humans have been on earth; it cannot be reasonably required of everyone in every society. Note that I am not saying that what *is* adequate evidence varies with the culture. I am no cultural relativist. On the contrary. My judgment that S's belief lacks adequate grounds was based on the supposition that there are objective standards for adequacy of grounds that hold whatever is accepted in one or another culture. But that is just the point. Deontological justification is sensitive to cultural differences because it depends on what can reasonably be expected of one, and that in turn depends on one's social inheritance and the influences to which one is exposed. But truth conducivity does not so depend. Hence they can diverge.

The other case I presented was a "cognitive deficiency" case. It concerned a college student who doesn't have what it takes to follow abstract philosophical exposition or reasoning. Having read parts of

Book IV of Locke's Essay, he takes it that Locke's view is that everything is a matter of opinion. He is simply incapable of distinguishing between that view and Locke's view that one's knowledge is restricted to one's own ideas. There is nothing he could do, at least nothing that could reasonably be expected of him, given his other commitments and obligations, that would lead him to appreciate that difference. Hence he cannot be blamed for interpreting Locke as he does; he is doing he best he can. But surely this belief is outrageously ill grounded, based as it is on the student's dim witted impressions of Locke.

Steup challenges this case by claiming that even if the student is incapable of attaining a better understanding of Locke, he could have done something that would have led him to withold acceptance of the interpretation in question, viz., ask himself "Do I understand Locke's Essay well enough to be justified in assenting to this interpretation?". (p. 22) Now, as Steup intimates, I certainly don't want to depict the case in such a way that the student is incapable of asking himself this question. However I do want to construe it in such a way that asking the question would not lead him to withold assent. The case I have in mind is one in which the student feels quite confident of his reading; this is definitely the way it strikes him, and he has no tendency to doubt it (at least not prior to seeing the grade he gets on the final exam). Certainly that scenario is a possible one and it, too, illustrates the possibility of a gap between deontological justification and truth conducive justification.

However it may have been poor strategy to trot out this hapless student as one of only two cases, for it undoubtedly raises too many controversial issues. (Not to mention the fact that some of my readers may think that the student has Locke straight!) Moreover it may give the impression that counterexamples based on cognitive deficiency are limited to such extreme and, we may hope, such unusual cases as this. Whereas in fact they are all too common. We have such a case whenever one forms a belief, on poor grounds, on something beyond one's intellectual capacity; and this is surely a common occurrence. Just consider a person who forms the belief that socialism is contrary to Christianity, for the reasons that are often given for this view by the New Right, and who is intellectually incapable of figuring out how bad these reasons are.

However, cultural isolation and cognitive deficiency cases only scratch the surface. We have so far been considering cases that are either rather extreme in our culture or come from a very different culture. But there are other sorts of cases that are around us every day. I am thinking particularly of those in which we lack the time or resources to look into a matter in an epistemically ideal fashion. Consider the innumerable beliefs each of us form on testimony or authority. Most of what we believe, beyond what we experience personally, comes from this source. Ideally we would check out each source to make sure that it is reliable before accepting the testimony. But who has time for that? We can do it in special cases where the matter is of particular importance; but no one could do it for even a small percentage of the items proferred by others for our belief. Nor is it a real option to withold belief save where we do run a check. That would leave our doxastic structure so impoverished we would not be able to function in our society. Practically everything we believe about science, history, geography, and current affairs is taken on authority. Moreover, even if we had the time to check up on each authority, in most cases we lack the resources for making an informed judgment. For the same reason that I cannot engage in astrophysics on my own, I am in no position to determine who is a competent authority in the field, except by taking the word of other alleged authorities. Thus in most cases in which I uncritically accept testimony I have done as much as could reasonably be expected of me. And now let us consider those cases in which the authority is incompetent or the witness is unreliable. There we are forming a belief on an objectively unreliable basis, though deontologically justified in doing so. One could hardly deny that this happens significantly often.

This same pattern is found outside the sphere of testimony. Consider perception. Sometimes peoples' eyes deceive them because of physiological or psychological malfunctioning, or because of abnormalities in the environment (cleverly constructed imitations, unusual conditions of the medium, etc.). Should we check for such abnormalities each time we are on the verge of forming a perceptual belief? Obviously we have no time for this, even if our perceptual belief forming mechanisms were sufficiently under voluntary control. Hence, except where there are definite indications that things are off, we will not have failed in our intellectual obligations if we simply form perceptual beliefs unselfconsciously and uncritically; and hence we are deontologically justified in doing so. But now consider cases in which our visual impressions are misleading, even though we are not aware of any indications of this. There one is forming beliefs on an unreliable basis, though deontologically justified in doing so.

Next consider irresistible beliefs and belief tendencies. If it is strictly impossible for me to alter a certain belief or tendency, then I can hardly be expected to do so. But some of these irresistible beliefs may be formed in an unreliable fashion. The most obvious examples concern strong emotional attachments that are, in practice, unshakeable. For many people their religious, or irreligious, beliefs have this status, as do beliefs concerning one's country, one's close relations, or one's political party. Such beliefs are often not formed in a truth-conducive fashion. But the person cannot be blamed for having something she can't help having, and so we get our discrepancy once more.

Finally, consider timing problems. Suppose that I come to realize that it is incumbent on me to look more fully into matters relevant to basic religious issues: the existence of God, the conditions of salvation, the authority of Scripture, and so on. I have deeply rooted beliefs on these matters; I am not going to throw them over just because I am reopening the questions, nor am I obliged to do so. And even if suspension of belief would be ideally required, it is not a real possibility for me until I see conclusive negative evidence. In any event, I enter onto my investigation. Let's say that the investigation reveals that my beliefs were ill founded all along. As soon as I see that, I cease to believe, either immediately or after some period of readjustment. But while the investigation is proceeding, something that might occupy many years, I am deontologically justified in continuing to hold the beliefs, for I am not obliged to give them up, even if I could, just because questions have been raised; and yet they are not held on truth-conducive grounds. Again our discrepancy. And again it would seem that such cases are quite frequent.

This completes my case for the possibility, and the actuality, of deontological justification without truth conducive justification. Even if I am mistaken about the possibility or actuality of some of the above cases, I can safely ignore the possibility that I am mistaken about all. We may take it that our deontological formula, (2), fails to capture what we are looking for in epistemology under the rubric of 'justification', when we are looking for something in the neighborhood of "being in a favorable position in believing that p", favorable from the standpoint of the aim at believing the true and avoiding believing the false.

But we can have discrepancies in the opposite direction as well: believing on an adequately truth conducive ground while not deontologically justified. This possibility will be realised where: (1) I form a belief that p on ground G; (2) G is in fact an adequate ground for that belief; (3) if I had reflected critically on this belief forming proclivity, as I should have done, I would have found sufficient reasons to doubt its adequacy, and as a result this belief would not have been formed. Here is an example. Let's suppose that it is incumbent on me to look into the credentials of anyone on whose word I believe something of practical importance. An acquaintance, Broom, tells me that Robinson, whom we are considering for a position in my department, has just been made an offer by Princeton. The press of affairs and my instinctive confidence in Broom lead me to neglect my duty and accept Broom's report uncritically. If I had looked into the matter I would have found strong evidence that Broom is untrustworthy in such matters. However this evidence would have been misleading, and in fact Broom is extremely scrupulous and reliable in reporting such things. Thus I formed the belief on an objectively adequate ground, but had I done my intellectual duty I would have mistrusted the ground and hence not formed the belief. I was justified on truth-conducivity standards but not according to (2).

I have been seeking to show that the deontological conception of justification, the only one of that ilk we have found to be internally viable, fails to deliver what is expected of justification if those expectations include truth conducivity. But not all contemporary epistemologists go along with this; in particular, the most extreme internalists do not. Not that they sever justification altogether from the aim at attaining the true and avoiding the false. They hold, to put it into my terms, that for a belief to be justified it is necessary, not that its ground be in fact such as to render it likely that the belief is true, but that the subject be justified in supposing this, that the belief appear to be truth-conducive "from the subject's own perspective on the world".[35] Although this kind of internalism is developed in various ways, by no means all of which exactly fit this formula given in the last sentence, we cannot go into all that in this paper. I shall work with the characterization just given.

I believe this view to be subject to an infinite regress of requirements of justification, and to other fatal difficulties.[36] However my present concern is to point out divergencies between it and (2), and hence to show that the deontological conception runs afoul of both externalism and internalism. After the lengthy discussion just completed I can be briefer here. The general point is that even after one has done everything that is reasonably expected of one intellectually, it is by no means guaranteed that one is justified in supposing that the ground of one's belief is an adequate one. Let's take a brief glance at a few of the cases just presented in connection with my moderate externalism. First, the point with respect to irresistible beliefs is precisely the same. If a belief is irresistible, then no matter how intellectually virtuous I am, I will form that belief whether or not I am justified in supposing its ground to be an adequate one. Turning to resistible beliefs, let's note first that we often do not have time to look into whether the ground of the belief is an adequate one. In such cases (assuming the belief doesn't stem from some other failure to carry out intellectual obligations) one would be deontologically justified; but, assuming that a failure to consider the matter would prevent one from being justified in supposing one's ground to be adequate, one would not satisfy internalist requirements. Again, consider another version of lack of cognitive powers. It seems plausible to suppose that many cognitive subjects are simply incapable of engaging in a rational consideration of whether the grounds of their beliefs (at least many sorts of beliefs, e.g., those involving complex inductive grounds) are adequate ones. Even if they raise the question they are not capable of coming to well grounded conclusions. These people might have done everything that could be reasonably be expected of them in an intellectual way, and yet, because of their inability to effectively submit the grounds of their beliefs to a critical assessment, would not be justified in supposing the ground of a certain belief to be sufficient. Again, deontological justification without internalist justification.

The internalist might reply that we have set our standards for higher level justification too high. To be justified in supposing the ground of a certain belief to be adequate, it is not necessary to have actively considered the matter. But even if this is so, one obvious requirement for being justified in believing that p is that one does believe that p.[37] And it seems clear that one could have done everything that could be expected of one intellectually and never have formed the belief that the ground of a certain normal and veridical perceptual belief is an adequate one; in which case one would be deontologically justified but not internalistically justified. If the internalist retorts that any failure to form such a belief is intellectually culpable and hence that the combination just alleged is impossible, I would reply that it would be intolerable to require such belief formation for all one's beliefs. If it is required for all levels, one is requiring an infinite hierarchy of belief. But even if we cut off the requirement at the second level, it would still be totally unrealistic to require that one have such a higher level belief for every first level belief one has.

Moreover, here too we get the possibility of internalist justification without deontological justification. Consider one who is justified in supposing the ground of her belief that the hostages are in Iran to be an adequate one. That is, the information and general principles at her disposal indicate her evidence to be sufficient. She is internalistically justified in this belief about the hostages. Yet had she engaged in further investigation, as she should have done, her internal perspective would have been enlarged and corrected in such a way that she would no longer be justified in this higher level belief. Her total set of knowledge and justified belief would then have indicated that her evidence for this proposition is not sufficient. Here we have internalist justification without deontological justification.

Thus the deontological conception embodied in (2) matches an internalist conception of justification no better than it matches an externalist one. I conclude that there is nothing to be said for the deontological conception, the only one that is not vitiated by internal flaws, as a fundamental concept for epistemology. This is not to deny that it is an interesting and important concept. There are, no doubt, contexts in which it is highly relevant to consider whether a person has failed in any intellectual duty and what bearing this has on the fact that he now believes that p. We would want to consider this if, e.g., we were engaged in training the person to be more intellectually responsible or to improve his belief forming tendencies. But we have seen that these deontological issues are not central to the basic concerns of epistemology with truth and falsity, whether this is conceived externalistically as the formation of propositional attitudes in such a way as to maximize truth and minimize falsity, or internalistically as the formation of propositional attitudes in accordance with what is indicated by the subject's perspective as to the chances for maximizing truth and minimizing falsity. Deontological justification is not epistemic justification.

VIII. Conclusion

Let's draw the threads of this paper together. We have examined several forms of a deontological conception of epistemic justification in terms of freedom from blame in taking up a certain propositional attitude. All of these but one was seen to be untenable by reason of requiring a degree of control over our propositional attitudes that we do not enjoy. The only version that escapes this fate was seen to be not the sort of concept we need to play a central role in epistemology. Therefore, despite the connotations of the term, we are ill advised to think of epistemic justification in terms of freedom from blame for believing.[38]

Notes

1. Robert Audi has suggested that for me to *have justifiably done A* it is also necessary that I did it *because* it was permitted by the relevant system of principles (though this is not required, he says, for *A's having been justified for me*). This would be on the analogy of the distinction between S's *being justified in believing that p*, and *the proposition that p's being justified for S*. This may be right, but I am unable to go into the matter more fully here. The point I need for this paper is that *permission*, rather than *requirement*, by the relevant principles is *necessary* for the justification of action.
2. Principles having to do with the way a belief is formed is not the only possibility here. A deontologist might prefer to make the permissibility of a belief depend on what evidence or grounds the subject *has* for the belief, rather than on the grounds that were actually used as a basis in the formation of the belief. Since this difference is not germane to the issues of this paper, I have chosen to state the matter in terms of my position, according to which the basis on which a belief was formed is crucial for its justificatory status.
3. This formulation is itself subject to both internalist and externalist versions (in fact to several varieties of each), depending on whether the "likelihood" is objective or "within the subject's perspective". Moreover, as foreshadowed in the last sentence in the text, this version of a deontological conception is only the one that is closest to the usual concept of the justification of actions; in the course of the paper it will be found not to be viable and will be replaced by a deontological conception that is further from the action case.
4. See Chisholm (1968), (1977), (1982).
5. Ginet (1975), p. 28. Other epistemologists who explicitly endorse a deontological conception are Bonjour (1985), Ch. 1; Moser (1985), Chs. 1, 4; Wolterstorff (1983); Plantinga (1983); Pollock (1986), pp. 7-8. It should be noted that Plantinga makes it explicit that he would be just as happy

with a conception in terms of "excellence" rather than in terms of freedom from blame. This indifference has since shifted to a definite preference for the latter. See, e.g., Plantinga (1988). Goldman (1986), though a reliabilist, also advocates a deontological conception.

6. Various exceptions to the principle have been noted recently. See, e.g., Stocker (1971). However, none of the exceptions involve kinds of actions that are not normally under voluntary control. Hence they have no tendency to show that one could be required or forbidden to believe while one lacks voluntary control over beliefs. The formulations in this paragraph should be taken as requiring that one normally have voluntary control over one's beliefs, not that one has voluntary control over a particular belief in a particular situation.

7. This last claim will be modified in the course of the paper, when we see that there is a way in which one might be responsible and blameworthy for beliefs, without *their* being under voluntary control, and hence without beliefs themselves being subject to requirement, prohibition, and permission. But we must await that development. For now, we will treat the family of deontological terms as an indivisible package.

8. See, e.g., Chisholm (1977), pp. 14-15.

9. This qualification is needed because something that we are capable of bringing about not by voluntarily doing something else, e.g., a movement of one's arm, one can bring about by doing something else, e.g., lifting one arm by moving the other arm.

10. I will often omit the modifier 'voluntary' in speaking of control. In this paper it is always to be tacitly understood.

11. Most of these people limit their voluntarism to cases in which it is not clear to the subject whether the belief is true or false. For an excellent account of the history of thought on this subject, with many specific references, see Pojman (1986).

12. See, e.g., Ginet (1985) and Meiland (1980). Neither of these maintains that belief is always under basic voluntary control.

13. (1977), Ch. 1.

14. To be sure, one might lack the power to determine which of a number of incompatible alternatives is realised; but one could not have the power to choose A at will without also having the power to determine at will that some contrary of A (at least not-A) is realized.

15. I understand "accepting" a proposition as an activity that gives rise to a belief. Therefore, unlike Lehrer (1979) and others, I am not using the term in such a sense that one could accept a proposition without believing it; though, of course, the belief engendered by an acceptance may be more or less long lived. I also recognize processes of belief formation that do not involve any activity of acceptance.

16. The best known defence of the logical impossibility claim is by Williams (1972). It has been criticized by, inter alia, Govier (1976) and Winters (1979).

17. It may also stem from misdiagnoses of a sort to be presented shortly.

18. Ginet disagrees. He holds that "we can interpret an ascription of unjustifiedness to a belief that the subject cannot help having as saying

that, if the subject were able to help it, she ought not to hold the belief" (1985), p. 183. Thus we can extend a deontological concept of justification to irresistible beliefs by invoking a counterfactual. I have two comments to make on this move. (1) This renders epistemic justification quite different from the justification of action, where 'justified' and other deontological terms are withheld from actions the subject couldn't help performing. (2) Insofar as we can make a judgment as to what would be permitted or forbidden were a certain range of involuntary states within our voluntary control, it will turn out that the deontological evaluation is simply a misleading way of making evaluations that could be stated more straightfowardly and more candidly in other terms. Suppose that we judge that if we had voluntary control over the secretion of gastric juices, then we ought to secrete them in such a way as to be maximally conducive to health and a feeling of well being; e.g., we should not secrete them so as to produce hyperacidity. But since gastric juices are not within our voluntary control, this would seem to be just a misleading way of saying that a certain pattern of secretion is desirable or worthwhile. The deontological formulation is a wheel that moves nothing else in the machine.

19. Cf. Pojman (1986), Ch. 13, for excellent diagnoses of putative cases of basic control of beliefs.

20. In maintaining that one cannot believe that p without its at least seeming to one that p is more probable than any envisaged alternative, I am not joining, e.g., Richard Swinburne (1981, Ch. 1), in supposing that to believe that p is just to take p to be more probable than some alternative(s).

21. See, e.g., Goldman (1980), Plantinga (1983), Wolterstorff (1983), Moser (1985), Ch. IV, Steup, forthcoming.

22. Even the extended treatment in Pojman (1986) fails to make any distinctions within "indirect control".

23. When the 'non-basic' qualifier is omitted, 'immediate' is hardly a felicitous term for something that contrasts with basic control. Nevertheless, I shall, for the sake of concision, mostly speak in terms of 'immediate control'. The 'non-basic' qualifier is to be understood.

24. This notion of doing something "right away" will serve to distinguish the present form of direct control from the next category.

25. Chisholm (1968), p. 224.

26. I should make it explicit that I do not suppose that an intention must be conscious, much less focally conscious, during all the time it is playing a role in guiding behavior.

27. I am not saying that S could be held responsible for taking attitude A toward p only if S himself had in fact been successful in intentionally bringing about that attitude. The requirement is rather that p be the sort of proposition toward which people generally are usually successful in bringing about a certain attitude when they try hard enough to do so. If the more stringent requirement were adopted, for actions generally, it would prevent us from holding S reponsible for an habitual action where he could have successfully carried out an intention to refrain from

that action if he had had such an intention.

28. See Wolterstorff (1983) for an excellent discussion of these modes of influence.

29. Note that the activities in this second category are even further removed from the intentional formation of a certain belief than those in the first, which themselves are clearly distinct from any such thing. The activities in the first category are concerned with a small number of alternatives for attitude formation. Though the activities are not undertaken with the aim of taking up one particular attitude from this field, they are directed to seeking out influences that will resolve *this* indeterminacy in some way or other. While the activities in the second group are directed much more generally to our tendencies of attitude formation on a wide variety of topics and in a wide variety of situations. But the most important point is that in neither case do the activities in question involve the carrying out of an intention to take up a particular propositional attitude.

30. Thus the closest we get to the principle mentioned above would be something like: "One should do what one can to see to it that one is so disposed as to believe that p only when that belief is based on adequate evidence". Hence the power to do things that influence belief formation can be thought of as, inter alia, a higher level capacity to get ourselves into, or make it more likely that we will be in, a condition that would be required of us if we had sufficient voluntary control over belief.

31. I am indebted to Emily Robertson for calling my attention to this problem.

32. For a defence of a conception of epistemic justification see Alston (forthcoming). For an account of some differences in concepts of epistemic justification, together with a brief defence of a chosen alternative, see Alston (1985).

33. For an account of the varieties of internalism and externalism see Alston (1986).

34. A more detailed account would look into the epistemic status of the belief at times subsequent to its formation as well. We must forego that in this brief discussion.

35. See, e.g., Foley (1987); Bonjour (1985), Ch. 1; Fumerton (1985), Ch. 2; Lehrer(1986).

36. For details see Alston (1986).

37. Some epistemologist understand 'S is justified in believing that p' to mean something like 'If S were to believe that p, in S's present situation, that belief would be justified'. On this understanding the above requirement does not hold. However I have throughout the paper been understanding 'S is justified in believing that p' as 'S justifiably believes that p'.

38. Thanks are due to Robert Audi and Jonathan Bennett for very useful comments on this paper. I have greatly profited from discussions with Carl Ginet about these issues.

References

Alston, William P.
> (1985) "Concepts of Epistemic Justification", *The Monist*, 68, no. 2. (1986) "Internalism and Externalism in Epistemology", *Phil. Top.*, 14, no. 1. (forthcoming) "An Internalist Externalism", *Synthese*.

Bonjour, Laurence
> (1985) *The Structure of Empirical Knowledge* (Cambridge, MA: Harvard U. Press).

Chisholm, Roderick
> (1968) "Lewis' Ethics of Belief", in *The Philosophy of C. I. Lewis*, ed. P. A. Schilpp (La Salle, IL: Open Court Pub. Co.).
> (1977) *Theory of Knowledge*, 2nd. ed. (Englewood Cliffs, NJ: Prentice-Hall, Inc.).
> (1982) "A Version of Foundationalism", in *The Foundations of Knowing* (Minneapolis: U. of Minn. Press).

Foley, Richard
> (1987) *The Theory of Epistemic Rationality* (Cambridge, MA: Harvard U. Press).

Fumerton, Richard A.
> (1985) *Metaphysical and Epistemological Problems of Perception* (Lincoln, NE: U. of Nebraska Press).

Ginet, Carl
> (1975) *Knowledge, Perception, and Memory* (Dordrecht:D. Reidel Pub. Co.).
> (1985) "Contra Reliabilism", *The Monist*, 68, no. 2.

Goldman, A. I.
> (1980) "The Internalist Conception of Justification", *Midwest Stud. Phil., Vol. 5.*
> (1986) *Epistemology and Cognition* (Cambridge, MA:Harvard U. Press).

Govier, Trudy
> (1976) "Belief, Values, and the Will", *Dialogue*, 15.

Lehrer, Keith
> (1979) "The Gettier Problem and the Analysis of Knowledge" in *Justification and Knowledge*, ed. G. S. Pappas (Dordrecht: D. Reidel Pub. Co.).
> (1986) "The Coherence Theory of Knowledge", *Phil. Top.*, 14, #no.1).

Meiland, Jack
> (1980) "What Ought We to Believe? or the Ethics of Belief Revisited", *Amer. Phil. Quart.*, 17.

Moser, Paul
> (1985) *Empirical Justification* (Dordrecht: D. Reidel Pub. Co.).

Plantinga, Alvin
> (1983) "Reason and Belief in God", in *Faith and Rationality*, ed. A. Plantinga & N. Wolterstorff (Notre Dame: U. of Notre Dame Press)
> (1988) "Positive Epistemic Status and Proper Function", *Philosophical Perspectives*, this volume.

Pojman, Louis
> (1986) *Religious Belief and the Will* (London: Routledge & Kegan Paul).

Pollock, John
(1986) *Contemporary Theories of Knowledge* (Totowa, NJ: Rowman & Littlefield).
Steup, Matthia
(forthcoming) "The Deontic Conception of Epistemic Justification", *Phil. Stud.*
Stocker, Michael
(1971) "'Ought' and 'Can'" *Australasian Journ. Philos.*, 49.
Swinburne, Richard
(1981) *Faith and Reason* (Oxford: Clarendon Press).
Williams, Bernard
(1972) "Deciding to Believe", in *Problems of the Self* (Cambridge: Cambridge U. Press).
Winters, Barbara
(1979) "Believing at Will", *Journ. Philos.*, 76.
Wolterstorff, Nicholas
(1983) "Can Belief in God Be Rational If It Has No Foundations?", in *Faith and Rationality*, ed., A. Plantinga & N. Wolterstorff (Notre Dame: U. of Notre Dame Press).

Philosophical Perspectives, 2, Epistemology, 1988

ON ACCEPTING FIRST PRINCIPLES

Wilfrid Sellars
University of Pittsburgh

My purpose in this essay is to examine the authority of first principles. The first principles I shall discuss may not have the full stature, the all-around primacy usually associated with this term. Indeed some of them would be taken by many to belong to a much lower order, if they are accepted as 'principles' at all. But principles they are, I shall argue, and, in a legitimate sense, 'first.'

It is clear that a first principle does not gain its authority by having been derived from premises for the simple reason that, if it did, they and not it would be 'first.' On the other hand, a first principle must have authority. It is as rational beings that we accept them; it is *reasonable* to accept them. But what *kind* of reasonableness might first principles have? And how can they be shown to have it?

Now the idea of showing or establishing that it is reasonable to accept a first principle suggests that there is such a thing as reasoning of the following kind

> [premises]
> Therefore, it is reasonable to accept P,

even when there is no corresponding argument

> [premises]
> Therefore, P.

Where there is a good argument of the latter kind, there must be a good argument of the former kind. It is the vice versa that doesn't hold.

Let us consider this in more detail. Suppose we have an argument

P
If P, then Q
Therefore, Q

For example: If it is day it is light; it is day; therefore it is light. Here we have a good argument. In the first place it is logically valid. It is also a good argument in that the premises are true so that, since it is valid, the conclusion must also be true. Furthermore, it is a good argument as it stands. No additional premise needs to be "understood."

On the other hand, intimately related to the above is another argument; something like the following:

Q follows logically from P and if P, then Q
P and if P, then Q are true
Therefore, it is reasonable to accept Q

This time there may well be "understood" premises, or at least definitions. But the major premise is powerful, and surely takes as a long way towards the conclusion.

The first of the preceding arguments is a good, explicitly valid, argument of which Q is the conclusion. The second argument, though closely related, doesn't have as its conclusion Q by itself, but rather "It is reasonable to accept Q." Nor does its content seem to be quite as explicit. That there *are* good arguments of the second kind is clear. But what is their significance? Should we look them in the face and then walk on? I want to suggest that a careful study of such arguments provides the key to the problem with which we began.

Notice, to begin with, that the conclusion of the second argument says something about the conclusion of the first. It pats Q on the back, so to speak, by telling us that it is reasonable to accept it. The conclusion of the first argument, on the other hand, doesn't *say* that it is reasonable to accept Q. It simply says Q, though by preceding it by a "therefore" it *implies*, in some sense, that it is reasonable to accept Q.

Now accepting a proposition is, in a broad sense, a *doing*.[1] It is not a physical doing, but rather a mental doing, but it is a doing, none the less, and, like all doings, is something that can be correctly or incorrectly done. It is, so to speak, subject to a kind of ethics or morality, as are all doings. Let us, therefore, consider briefly the general idea of its being reasonable and proper to do something. Perhaps, by turning our attention to the ethics of doing in general, we gain some insight into the ethics of this very special king of doing which is accepting a proposition.

"It is reasonable and proper to do A." What does this mean? Surely something like the following: There is a good and sufficient argument for doing A. What kind of argument? Arguments for doing something are classically called 'practical' arguments. So, in effect, we have led to the topic of the practical syllogism. This topic is of great importance not only for ethics but for a theory of action or conduct generally. I have no time on the present occasion even to articulate this topic, let alone touch on the many exciting issues it involves. I shall therefore select a simple paradigm and elaborate it just enough to mobilize your logical and philosophical intuitions for the use to which I am going to put the concept of a practical syllogism.

Consider the following piece of reasoning:

> Bringing about E implies doing A.
> I shall bring about E.
> Therefore, I shall do A.

The argument has the ring of validity. Can it be a *good* argument? In our earlier discussion we characterized a good argument as one which is valid and has true premises. In the present case, the major premise is the sort of thing which can be true. But what of "I shall bring about E?" If this were a mere prediction, it, too, could be true. But in the present context it expresses an intention, and it is not clear that intentions are properly characterized as true or false. I shall, for the moment at least, simply dodge this issue and assume that an argument of the above form can be good as well as valid, and that what makes it good (though not necessarily, of course, *morally* good) as opposed to *merely* valid (as a valid argument with a false premise is *merely* valid) is a matter of my actually having the intention to bring about E. There might be a stronger sense of 'good' which requires that I not only intend to bring about E, but that the bringing about of E has some kind of objective or natural claim on me. But whether this might be so and if so, in what sense, is not my problem on the present occasion.

Let me call the conclusion of the above argument—"I shall do A"— its *logical* outcome. But "I shall do A" expresses an intention. Thus, if I am persuaded by the argument, I will acquire the intention to do A. Let me call the acquisition of this intention the *practical* outcome of the argument. Finally, there will be what I call its *terminal* outcome, namely a doing of A.[2] Other things being equal we do what we intend to do. We may fail, but, unless we change our minds, we try to do what we intend to do.

Let us now return to our original example of a logically valid or deductive argument.

(α) P
if P, then Q
Therefore, Q

Clearly, if this argument presents our grounds for accepting Q, then latter is not a first principle, because P, as its ground would be prior or, so to speak, more first. Consider, now, the argument which we found to be correlated with it:

(β) Q follows logically from P and if P, then Q.
P and if P, then Q are true.
Therefore it is reasonable to accept Q.

Argument (β) ends up with a conclusion which surely amounts to the idea that there is a good and sufficient practical argument for accepting Q. In a sense argument schema (β) is the schema of a proof that there is a good and sufficient practical argument for accepting Q. What would that practical argument be?

Notice that (β) itself is not a practical argument. It does not have a conclusion of the form 'I shall do A.' We are looking for an argument of the form,

[premises]
Therefore, I shall accept Q.

Argument (β) not only tells us *that* there is such an argument, it tells us *something* about its nature. If we follow its clues, we arrive at something like,

(γ) Accepting the logical implications of true beliefs is conducive to E.
Q is logically implied by P and if P, then Q.
I shall bring about E.
I believe P and if P, then Q.

P and if P, then Q are true.
Therefore, I shall accept Q.

What exactly the end-in-view, E, might be, is by no means easy to spell out. Clearly it is some advantageous epistemic state involving the making explicit of our beliefs so that inconsistent beliefs can be confronted with one another and questions pinpointed for subsequent investigation. However this may be, I shall say nothing more about argument (γ) on the present occasion. My aim has been to highlight the distinction between three closely related kinds of argument:

(1) the ground floor argument (α) which culminates in the assertion of Q;

(2) the third level argument (β) which culminates in the assertion that there is a good and sufficient argument for accepting Q;

(3) the second floor argument (γ) which has as its conclusion "I shall accept Q."

The above distinction present a framework in terms of which, I believe, some light can be thrown on the problem of first principles. And the first first principles which I shall examine are the first principles of a scientific theory. Consider, for example, the hackneyed example of the kinetic theory of gases developed as a deductive system. One distinguishes between its postulates and the theorems which are derived from them by logical means, thus:

[Postulates]
Therefore, [Theorems].

The theory isn't a mere, or 'uninterpreted,' deductive system. Its point is to be so correlated with empirical generalizations that it can be said to explain them. These empirical generalizations are based on observations and experiments, and constitute what many contemporary philosophers of science call 'confirmed law-like statements.' They can, for our present purposes, be called empirical laws. In our present example these laws pertain to temperature, volume, pressure, etc. as empirical constructs, definable in terms of observable and measurable quantities. The correlation of empirical laws with theorems in the deductive system is made by correlating the empirical concepts which occur in the empirical laws with theoretical expressions defined in terms of the basic vocabulary of the theory. This correlation of the vocabulary of the empirical laws with the vocabulary of the theory was compared by Norman Campbell to a dictionary. The dictionary is such as to correlate each confirmed empirical generalization or law with a theorem in the theory, and no theorem in the theory with an empirical generalization which has been falsified in the laboratory. The theory, if it is a good one, will have 'surplus value' in at least the following sense. There will be indefinitely many theorems which the dictionary 'translates' into empirical law-like statements which have not yet been tested, indeed may not yet have been thought of, or entertained. Thus the theory suggests hypotheses some of which, given the current state of experimental technique, can be put to the test. If they survive, this is a feather in the cap of the theory; if not something in the theory must be modified.

But my purpose today is not to discuss in detail the correlation of theoretical structures with experimental laws. The reader who is interested in this topic, will find an excellent account in Ernest Nagel's *The Structure of Science*.[3] My aim is rather to call attention to and philosophize about a very simple and obvious point. It is not necessary to support a theory by deriving its postulates or assumptions from other propositions, thus

[prior principles]
Therefore, [postulates of the theory].

If we refer to the postulates of the theory as its first principles, one doesn't, typically, support a theory be deriving its principles from something 'more first.' Yet even without such derivation it is often reasonable to accept a theory. What makes it reasonable? What kind of reasonableness is involved?

If we can solve the problem of the reasonableness of accepting theories, we may get some light on the problem of the reasonableness of first principles generally. For, it will be remembered, the problem with which we began was exactly how it could be reasonable to accept first principles in view of the fact that this reasonableness cannot consist in their being derivable by logical means from prior principles.

Now the general lines of the move I am going to make are obvious. We accept the first principles of a theory because we accept the theory; and we accept the theory because of what it enables us to *do*. This suggests that the *rationale* of accepting the theory is bound up with practical reasoning. In other words we try to show that there is a good and sufficient practical argument of which the conclusion is 'I (or better, we) shall accept the theory.' We have thus established contact with the considerations advanced in the opening section.

In other words, we need something like the following:

[premises]
Therefore, we shall accept the theory.

And our previous discussion suggests that it will be of the form:

We shall bring about E.
Bringing about E implies accepting theories of such and such a character.
T is of this character.
Therefore, we shall accept T.

The logical outcome of this practical syllogism would be our intention to accept the theory. The terminal outcome would be the accepting of it.

Clearly the above is but the bare bones of an argument. I shall attempt shortly to put some flesh on these bones and, in particular, to discuss (albeit briefly) the character a theory must have in order to be worthy of acceptance. But before I do this, let me call attention to the fact that intimately related to the above is another argument schema of decisive importance for our problem.

It will be remembered in the case of the deductive argument

P
If P, then Q
Therefore, Q

we distinguished between three interestingly related arguments. This time we find only two, because *ex hypothesi* there is no relevant argument which has the first principles of the theory as its conclusion.

As we saw, this is exactly the difference between a first principle and derivative principles. In the case of derivative principles there is a relevant deductive argument which ends up with the principle. In the case of a *first* principle, there is no such argument, but there is nevertheless a relevant *practical* argument and a higher order argument which concludes with the assertion that there is such a good and sufficient practical argument. The latter is of the form:

[premises]
Therefore, there is a good and sufficient practical argument
of kind K for accepting T.

But what might the premises of this meta-argument be?

Before attempting to answer this question let me call attention to
the fact that its conclusion seems to be equivalent to "It is *probable*
that-T" (where 'T' abbreviates the principles of the theory). It is
sometimes denied that the concept of probability has any application to theories. Many theories of probability take as their paradigm
a metrical probability which can be manipulated in accordance with
the mathematical calculus of probabilities, for example the probability
which is relevant to statistical contexts. This I regard as a radical
error, which has led to Procrustean theories of probability. I shall
argue that the concept of probability, though in a non-metrical and,
perhaps, comparative form, legitimately applies to theories and that
the way in which it applies illuminates the concept of probability
generally. The suggestion is that probability statements are
statements asserting the existence of a good and sufficient argument
for accepting the proposition which is said to be probable.

What would it be to show that there is a good and sufficient argument of a certain kind for accepting a certain proposition. Consider
the argument schema

(A_1) We shall bring about E.
Bringing about E implies accepting Ts which are ϕ.
T_1 is ϕ.
Therefore, we shall accept T_1.

What would the *probability* argument schema which corresponds
to this *practical* argument schema look like? Its conclusion, according to the above, will be: "Therefore there is a good and sufficient
argument of a certain kind for accepting T_1," (i.e., according to our
analysis, "T_1 is probable"). The higher order argument, itself, will
look something like this:

(MA_1) A_1 is a good and sufficient argument of kind K.
The conclusion of A_1 is 'We shall accept T_1'.
Therefore there is a good and sufficient argument of kind K
for accepting T_1.

But what kind of argument is kind K? It is, in the first place, a practical argument. Furthermore it is an argument of a kind which postulates a certain end E and relates accepting theories of a certain character φ to that end. But what kind of end-in-view might E be? In the essay referred to above[4] I characterize the property φ and the end-in-view E in the case of the probability of theories as follows:

> φ is the character of being the simplest available framework which generates new testable law-like statements, generates acceptable approximations of empirically confirmed law-like statements, and generates no falsified law-like statements.

What, then, is the end-in-view which we might have, so that we would be favorably disposed to accept theories of such a character? It will be remembered that in our discussion of the practical reasoning which has as its outcome the intention to accept the conclusion of a *deductive* argument, we found the end-in-view to be achieving an epistemically advantageous state in which inconsistent beliefs can be explicitly confronted with one another and brought within the scope of systematic investigation. If we suppose that the end-in-view of the latter investigation is the direct ability to produce adequate conceptual pictures of relevant parts of our environment, then epistemic states which contribute to this ability would come within the scope of practical reasoning of the kinds we are considering. How 'good' (fine grained, coarse grained, etc.) a conceptual picture must be to make possible the achieving of specific ends-in-view of a 'practical' character in a narrower sense of this term is a relative matter. A map which is adequate for our purpose may be totally inadequate for another.[5]

Thus, the epistemic end-in-view of *unlimited* accuracy and *openended* relevance is one which appeals to very few, and, of course, to those to whom it has no appeal it cannot provide a major premise for reasoning which culminates in "Therefore, I shall perform such and such an epistemic act." Who, then, has this end-in-view, and what does having it involve?

To one who does have this end-in-view, whatever may be involved in having it, the value of explicit consistency is clear. So, also, is the value of working with theories which, in addition to generating observationally acceptable approximations of established empirical generalizations, provide new empirical hypotheses which can be put to the test as is the value of modifying or laying aside theories which generate disconfirmed law-like statements. But the upshot of this is that while we have filled in some of the details of the family of arguments pertaining to the accepting of theories by bringing in as proximate end-in-view the having of confirmed empirical law-like statements, thus

> We shall have confirmed law-like statements.
> Accepting theories which are φ is conducive to having confirmed law-like statements.
> T₁ is φ.
> Therefore, we shall accept T₁.

(with which is correlated a higher order argument which has as its conclusion

> Therefore, there is a good and sufficient argument of kind K for accepting T₁,

i.e., T₁ is probable in the way in which theories are probable), there is a gap between the abstract end-in-view we were discussing a moment ago, and the end-in-view of having confirmed law-like statements.

To fill this gap I must develop one more line of thought pertaining to the concept of probability. I argued above that those philosophers who work with this concept and take as their paradigm those probabilities which fit neatly into the mathematical equations of the calculus of probability tend to overlook the real conceptual core of probability. It is characterized by some as a logical relation which holds between an hypothesis and its evidence, but which, unlike implication, does not authorize the *acceptance* of the hypothesis on the basis of the evidence. Thus the rationale of accepting probable hypotheses is left obscure—or it is even denied that there is such a rationale. By others, probability statements are classified with descriptive and factual statements about relative frequencies, idealized into statements about the limits of such relative frequencies. Again the connection of such factual statements with the reasonableness of accepting hypotheses concerning a short run to which these ideal frequencies are relevant is left obscure, or even denied.

On the approach I have been defending, however, the connection between probability and reasonable acceptance is analytic. Thus, given that a proposition is probable, no additional step need be taken to show that it is reasonable to accept it. To recommend this view, however, I must take into account more than the probability of theories—for the very significance of this phrase is denied by many of those with whom I am taking issue. I want, therefore, to show how this approach can be extended to the probability of empirical generalizations. It is my conviction that once we get a feeling for what probability amounts to in the case of theories, then the classical problem of induction with respect to empirical generalizations turns out to be much more manageable, and many things fall into place which would otherwise remain a tangled mess.

Let's suppose therefore that to say of a law-like statement, LL_1, that it is probable means something like this:

> There is a good and sufficient argument of a certain kind for accepting LL_1.

This would itself be the conclusion of an argument of the type represented by (β) in our earlier discussion. And the argument which is asserted to exist will be a practical syllogism of the type represented by (γ).

The practical argument in question has the form:

> We shall bring about E.
> Bringing about E involves accepting law-like statements which are ψ.
> LL_1 is ψ.
> Therefore, we shall accept LL_1.

This schema raises the questions,

> What is E?

and

> What is the character, ψ?

To take up the latter question first, it is clear that ψ has something to do with the relation of LL_1 to observation. This relation is a logical relation, R_L. Let us put it by saying that the law-like statement must 'accord' with the observational evidence. To determine what 'according,' R_L, might be, we must first come to some conclusion about the form of a law-like statement. And, curiously enough, to do this we must come to some conclusion about the nature of the end-in-view, E. Is it, perhaps, the state of possessing true beliefs about the limit frequency of a quaesitum property, Q, in an infinite reference class, R? In other words, the relative frequency of cases of Q among cases of R "in the long run?" Is it, limiting ourselves for simplicity to non-statistical law-like statements, the state of having true beliefs of the form:

$$(x)(fx \rightarrow gx),$$

i.e., (roughly) for all values of 'x', if x is f then x is g? Whichever line we take we run into the difficulty that the end is one we could never know ourselves to have reached, and I submit that any end with reference to which the doing of a certain action is to be justified must be the sort of thing that can be known to be realized.

The general point is related to our earlier attempt to distinguish between a *good* practical argument and one which was *merely* valid, i.e., to specify something which would play a role analogous to "having true premises" in the case of good non-practical arguments. There we suggested that it was a matter of the actual existence of the intention to bring about E. But it now appears that the appraisal of a practical argument as good requires that we say not only that the agent had the intention and that he *believed* that the action would realize it, but that it is actually realized. Thus, "Jones' action was justified *because it brought about E*."

Instead of the phantom ends considered above I suggest that the end-in-view, E, in the case of the acceptance of law-like statements is the state of being in a position to draw inferences concerning new cases, in a way which explains the observed cases. In other words, our proximate end-in-view is to have a principle of inference which applies in the same way to 'new' and 'old' cases. And the state of having such a principle *is* the sort of thing that we can know that we are in. And to be in this state requires *accepting* principles of inference which conform to this criterion. This *accepting* is what in our terminology is called the *terminal* outcome of a practical syllogism which has as its *logical* outcome or conclusion, "I shall accept LL_1".

Thus, reflection on the proximate end-in-view of inductive reasoning supports the view, which, as we shall see, has independent support, that law-like statements have the form of principles of inference.

In the case of non-statistical law-like statements, we can suppose that they have the form (roughly):

From 'x is f,' it may be inferred that 'x is g'.

The statistical case is more complex, and its exposition would involve the discussion of still another dimension of probability, that which is represented by the schema

n/m Rs are Q.
This is an R.
Therefore, the probability that this is Q is n/m.

I have discussed this, as well as the above modes of probability, in the essay referred to above[6] and shall omit the topic here.

Now new evidence may well lead us to abandon one inference ticket and accept another. But the point is that as long as we have the evidence we do have, and this evidence is that all observed cases of f are g, we know that we have an inference ticket which accords with evidence and applies to the cases we expect to encounter.

As I see it, then reflection on the probability of law-like statements reinforces a conception which arises independently in the exploration of problems pertaining to counter-factual conditionals, the intuitive distinction between accidental and non-accidental uniformities and the concept of 'natural necessity.' For this exploration has constantly generated the idea (rejected only because it treads on radical empiricist toes) that law-like statements are inference tickets. Unlike the inference tickets of formal logic, they are empirically based in the sense that they are accepted because it is reasonable to accept them, given the evidence and given our proximate end-in-view.

Law-like statements, therefore, are empirically based principles of inference which authorize such inferences as, to use a crude example, 'Lightning now, therefore thunder shortly.' It also authorizes such conditionals as 'If there had been lightning then, there would have been thunder shortly' and such statements as 'There was thunder then *because* there had been lightning shortly before' and 'That there was lightning shortly before made it necessary that there be thunder then.'

It might well be said, "If the character of being a first principle, as you conceive it, is one which can be possessed by "low-level empirical generalizations," it can scarcely be that which makes First Principles First." I would begin my reply with an aside. The process of theoretical explanation is *in a sense* the process of turning low-level first principles into derivative principles. I would then add that there are many varieties (indeed dimensions) of first principles which play into each others hands in the course of inquiring without losing their firstness. But above all I would point out that our problem was not "What is a first principle?" but "How can it be reasonable to accept a first principle?" and it may well be that the strategy outlined above for dealing with the reasonableness of law-like statements and theories may throw some light on the reasonableness of holding those more exalted First Principles with which philosophy must sooner or later come to grips.

Notes

1. It should be clear that here as elsewhere I have been influenced by Herbert Feigl's fruitful distinction between 'validation' and 'vindication' in his important essay "*De Principiis Non est Disputandum...?*" in *Philosophical Analysis*, ed. Max Black, Ithaca: Cornell University Press, 1950.
2. These distinctions, as well as the framework in which they are used, were developed in my "Induction as Vindication," *Philosophy of Science*, Vol. 31, No. 3, July, 1964.
3. Hackett Publishing Co.
4. Footnote 2.
5. For an exploration of the connection between factual truth and conceptual picturing see: "Truth and 'Correspondence'" *Journal of Philosophy*, 59, 1962, reprinted as chapter II in *Science, Perception and Reality*, Routledge and Kegan Paul (London, 1963); chapters IV and V of *Science and Metaphysics*, Routledge and Kegan Paul (London, 1967); and chapter 5 of *Naturalism and Ontology*, Ridgeview Publishing Co. (Atascadero, CA, 1979). For a discussion of the relevance of this connection to the problem of the truth of scientific theories see my "Scientific Realism and Irenic Instrumentalism: A Critique of Nagel and Feyerabend on Theoretical Explanation" in Robert S. Cohen and Marx Wartofshy (eds.) *Boston Studies in the Philosophy of Science* (Vol.II) New York, The Humanities Press.
6. Footnote 2.

Philosophical Perspectives, 2, Epistemology, 1988

THE BUILDING OF OSCAR*

John L. Pollock
University of Arizona

1. Introduction

You all know about the importance of being Ernest. This paper is about the importance of being Oscar. Who, might you ask, is Oscar? Oscar is the little man who lives in my computer and reasons just like we do, or, at least, almost just like we do. Let me tell you about Oscar.

One of the major accomplishments of contemporary epistemology has been the recognition that most reasoning is defeasible, in the sense that reasons may justify a conclusion when taken alone, but no longer justify that conclusion when additional "defeating" information is added to them. This is what computer scientists working in AI call 'non-monotonic reasoning'. Philosophers know a lot about some aspects of defeasible reasoning. We know about prima facie reasons and defeaters, and we know quite a bit about what prima facie reasons there are. But we do not have a good understanding of precisely how these constituents are put together in reasoning to arrive at conclusions. Our situation is analogous to knowing what primitive logical entailments there are, but not knowing the principles for constructing deductive arguments out of those entailments. The purpose of this paper is to investigate the structure of defeasible reasoning. Given an array of defeasible and nondefeasible reasons, how are they to be used in drawing conclusions?

A satisfactory theory of defeasible reasoning ought to be sufficiently precise that we can actually program a computer to reason in that way. This may seem like a pedestrian point, but I have found it to be of overwhelming *practical* importance in getting the theory of defeasible reasoning right. Constructing a computer program to implement a theory of reasoning and then seeing what the program does is an extremely useful tool for coming to understand your own theory. My experience has been that the program almost invariably does unexpected things. We are frequently in a position of knowing what conclusions *should* be obtainable from a certain set of inputs, and if those conclusions are not forthcoming from the program then we know that there is something wrong with the theory. Analyzing why the program yields the wrong result is a powerful technique for discovering flaws in the original philosophical theory. In effect, the computer program is a mechanical aid in the construction of counterexamples. If the philosophical theory is sufficiently complex, this technique can lead to the discovery of counterexamples that would probably never have been found from the comfort of your armchair.

The implementation of theories of reasoning on computers is useful in another way as well. Somewhat paradoxically, it helps in assuring that the theories are psychologically realistic. That a theory can be implemented on a computer does not guarantee that that is the way people work, but if it cannot be implemented on a computer, that pretty much guarantees that people *do not* and *cannot* work that way. Also, in trying to figure out how some feature of reasoning works, it often helps to approach the problem from an "engineering" perspective. If you have at least a rough idea of what a reasoning system should accomplish, ask yourself how you might build something that does that. That tends to yield valuable insights into the way human reasoning works. Frequently, the only obvious solution to a problem of system design turns out upon reflection to be precisely the solution adopted by human beings. So appeal to computers can help both in constructing theories of reasoning and in testing them.

In light of these observations, we can think of AI work on nonmonotonic reasoning and philosophical work on the logical analysis of defeasible reasoning, as addressing the same problem from two different perspectives. So what I am going to do here is construct a theory of defeasible reasoning, describe a computer program called 'OSCAR' that implements the theory, and then say a few words about how well OSCAR performs.

2. A Sketch of Human Rational Architecture

Let me begin with some general remarks about human rational architecture. Reasoning is guided by rules, and when the reasoning is in accordance with the rules the resultant beliefs are said to be *justified*. Epistemic rules are normative, and that suggests that their formulation is independent of psychology. But I have argued (Pollock [1986]) that that is a mistake. We know how to reason. That is, reasoning is governed by internalized rules. The possession of such internalized rules constitutes procedural knowledge. Jointly, these rules comprise what is called "a production system". These rules are the rules for "correct reasoning"—the very rules that are the subject of epistemology. One does not always conform to these rules, but this is because the production system for reasoning is embedded in a larger system that can override it. Reasoning can be fruitfully compared to using language. We have procedural knowledge governing the production of grammatical utterances, but our utterances are not always grammatical. This gives rise to the "competence/performance" distinction in linguistics. Precisely the same distinction needs to be made in connection with reasoning, and it is the existence of this distinction that is responsible for the use of normative language in epistemology. What we "should" do is what the rules of our production system tell us to do, but we do not always conform to those rules because they are embedded in a larger system that can override them.

Crudely put, reasoning proceeds in terms of reasons. Reasons are strung together into arguments and in this way the conclusions of the arguments become justified. As I use the term, the study of reasoning is intended to be the general study of justified change in belief. It should explain both how we acquire new beliefs and how we come to reject old beliefs. As such, reasoning includes the process of belief acquisition through perception, the process of holding beliefs on the basis of memory, the process of acquiring beliefs on the basis of deductive or inductive inference, and so on.

Human reasoning begins from various kinds of input states, the most familiar of which are straightforward perceptual states. These are nondoxastic states. For instance, something can look red to you without your having any belief to that effect. Furthermore, you can reason from the way things look to conclusions about their objective properties without forming intermediate beliefs about your own perceptual states. If you look around, you will form myriad beliefs about your surroundings but few if any beliefs about how things look to you. You do not usually attend to the way things look to you. This is important in the present context because it means that if we are to describe this process in terms of reasoning (and I think that there is good reason to do so), then we must acknowledge that reasons need not be beliefs. At the very least, perceptual states can be reasons. In general, I will call the states from which reasoning begins *foundational states*.

Epistemologists have tended to assume that reasons must be beliefs. This is the *doxastic assumption*. The rationale for the doxastic assumption is the supposition that in deciding what to believe, we can only take account of something insofar as we have beliefs about it, and hence only beliefs can be relevant to reasoning. But this over-intellectualizes the process of belief change. We do not consciously think about what our beliefs are, consider our rules for reasoning, and then overtly decide what to believe. Instead, our rules for reasoning describe internal processes that go on automatically and nondeliberatively. These processes can have access to any of our internal states, not just beliefs, so it is not necessary for the inputs to reasoning to consist exclusively of beliefs.[1]

Reasoning proceeds in terms of reasons. Reasons legitimate conclusions. The general notion of a reason can be defined as follows:

> (2.1) Being in states $M_1,...,M_n$ is a *reason* for S to believe Q iff it is logically possible for S to be justified in believing Q on the basis of being in states $M_1,...,M_n$.

Usually, reasons are beliefs or sets of beliefs, and in that case, rather than talking about *believing P* being a reason for believing Q, I will say more simply that P is a reason for Q.

There are two kinds of reasons—*defeasible* and *non-defeasible*. Non-defeasible reasons are those reasons that logically entail their conclusions. Such reasons are *conclusive reasons*. Focusing upon reasons that are beliefs, P is a defeasible reason for Q just in case P is a reason for Q, but adding additional information may destroy the reason connection. Such reasons are called "prima facie reasons". This notion can be defined more precisely as follows:

> (2.2) P is a *prima facie reason* for S to believe Q iff P is a reason for S to believe Q and there is an R such that R is

logically consistent with P but (P & R) is not a reason for S to believe Q.

(To keep this and subsequent definitions simple, I just formulate them for the case of a reason that is a single proposition rather than a set of propositions, but the general case is analogous.)

The R's that defeat prima facie reasons are called "defeaters". There are two kinds of defeaters for prima facie reasons. "Rebutting defeaters" are reasons for denying the conclusion:

(2.3) R is a *rebutting defeater* for P as a prima facie reason for Q iff R is a defeater and R is a reason for believing $\sim$Q.

Rebutting defeaters are reasonably familiar, but there is another kind of defeater that is often overlooked. *Undercutting defeaters* attack the connection between the reason and the conclusion rather than attacking the conclusion itself. For instance, 'x looks red to me' is a prima facie reason for me to believe that x is red. Suppose I discover that x is illuminated by red lights and illumination by red lights often makes things look red when they are not. This is a defeater, but it is not a reason for denying that x is red (red things look red in red light too). Instead, this is a reason for denying that x wouldn't look red to me unless it were red.

(2.4) R is an *undercutting defeater* for P as a prima facie reason for S to believe Q iff R is a defeater and R is a reason for denying that P wouldn't be true unless Q were true.

Undercutting defeaters have generally been overlooked both in philosophy and in AI.

In (2.4), 'P wouldn't be true unless Q were true' is the *subjunctive conditional* ($\sim$Q > $\sim$P), where '>' is the so-called "simple subjunctive".[2] Contraposition fails for subjunctive conditionals, so this cannot be written more simply as '(P > Q)'. To simplify the notation, I will write '($\sim$Q > $\sim$P)' as '(P == > Q)'. The justification for this notation is that although '== >' is not equivalent to the simple subjunctive '>', it is still "conditional-like" and can be regarded as a kind of conditional.

Defeaters are defeaters by virtue of being reasons for either $\sim$Q or $\sim$(P == > Q). They may be only defeasible reasons for these conclusions, in which case their defeaters are "defeater defeaters". There may similarly be defeater defeater defeaters, and so on.

Conclusive reasons, prima facie reason, rebutting defeaters, and undercutting defeaters, comprise the basic machinery for a theory of defeasible reasoning. Let us turn now to the construction of such a theory.

3. Warrant

In constructing a theory of defeasible reasoning, it is useful to begin by considering the fiction of an ideal reasoner, or if you like, an ideal intelligent machine with no limits on memory or computational capacity. How should such a reasoner employ prima facie reasons and defeaters in deciding what to believe? Let us say that a proposition is *warranted* in an epistemic situation iff an ideal reasoner starting from that situation would be justified in believing the proposition. This section is devoted to a discussion of the set of warranted propositions.

3.1 *Linear Arguments*

Reasoning proceeds by arguments, and arguments are constructed by starting from perceptual and memory states, moving from them to beliefs, from those beliefs to new beliefs, and so on. What arguments can be constructed depends upon what perceptual and memory states one is in. Let us take these to comprise the *epistemic basis*.

In the simplest case, an argument is a finite sequence of propositions each of which either describes the epistemic basis or is such that there is a set of earlier members of the sequence that constitutes a reason for it. We might call such arguments *linear arguments*. A proposition is *supported by* a linear argument just in case it occurs in that argument. Not all arguments are linear arguments. There are more complicated kinds of arguments that involve various kinds of indirect argument (conditionalization, reductio ad absurdum, and so on). Indirect arguments proceed by adopting as premises suppositions that have not been established, using those premises to obtain a conclusion, and then "discharging" the premises by using some rule like conditionalization or reductio ad absurdum. Indirect arguments make the theory much more complicated. For this reason, I am going to confine my attention to linear arguments in this paper. An account of reasoning will be constructed based on the simplifying assumption that all arguments are linear, and then I will say a bit about how to modify the account to accommodate indirect arguments.

3.2 *Ultimately undefeated arguments*

Warrant is always relative to a set of foundational states (the epistemic basis) that provide the starting points for arguments. In the following, by 'argument' I always mean arguments relative to some fixed epistemic basis. Merely having an argument for a proposition does not guarantee that the proposition is warranted, because one might also have arguments for defeaters for some of the steps in the first argument. Iterating the process, one argument might be defeated by a second, but then the second argument could be defeated by a third thus reinstating the first, and so on. A proposition is warranted only if it ultimately emerges from this process undefeated. Given the simplifying assumption that all arguments are linear, we can give a fairly simple characterization of warrant. The defeat of one argument always results from another argument supporting a defeater for some use of a defeasible reason in the first. Let us say that all arguments are *level 0 arguments*. Some level 0 arguments may provide us with defeaters for lines of other level 0 arguments, so let us say that an argument is a *level 1 argument* iff no level 0 argument supports a defeater for it. As there are fewer level 1 arguments than level 0 arguments, fewer propositions will be supported by level 1 arguments than level 0 arguments. In particular, fewer defeaters for level 0 arguments will be supported by level 1 arguments than by level 0 arguments. Thus having moved to level 1 arguments, we may have removed some defeaters and thereby reinstated some level 0 arguments. Let us say that a *level 2 argument* is a level 0 argument having no lines defeated by any level 1 argument. Some level 0 arguments that were defeated at level 1 may be reinstated at level 2. Hence level 2 arguments may support some defeaters that were not supported by level 1 arguments, thus defeating some level 0 arguments that were not defeated by level 1 arguments. Consequently, we take a *level 3 argument* to be any level 0 argument not defeated by level 2 arguments; and so on. In general, a *level n + 1 argument* is any level 0 argument not defeated by level n arguments. More precisely:

(3.1) σ is a *level n+1 argument* iff σ is a level 0 argument and there is no level n argument η that supports a defeater for a defeasible step of σ.

A given level 0 argument may be defeated and reinstated many times by this alternating process. Only if we eventually reach a point where it stays undefeated can we say that it warrants its conclusion. Let us say that an argument is *ultimately undefeated* iff there is some m such that the argument is a level n argument for every n > m. On the simplifying assumption that all arguments are linear arguments, it seems that epistemological warrant can then be characterized in terms of arguments that are ultimately undefeated:

(3.2) P is warranted relative to an epistemic basis iff P is supported by some ultimately undefeated argument proceeding from that epistemic basis.

To illustrate, suppose we have the following three arguments:

α	β	γ
.	.	.
.	.	.
.	.	.
Q	T	~(T ==> U)
R	U	
.	.	
.	.	
.	.	
V	~R	

Here β defeats α, and γ defeats β. It is assumed that nothing defeats γ. Thus γ is ultimately undefeated. Neither α nor β is a level 1 argument, because both are defeated by level 0 arguments. As γ is a level n argument for every n, β is defeated at every level greater than 0, so β is not a level n argument for n > 0. As a result α is reinstated at level 2, and is a level n argument for every n > 1. Hence α is ultimately undefeated, and V is warranted.

3.3 *Collective defeat*

Our analysis of warrant will have to be made slightly more complicated, but in order to appreciate the difficulty we must first note that the analysis entails an important principle of rationality, which

I call *the principle of collective defeat*. The following form of the principle follows from the analysis:

> (3.3) If we are warranted in believing R and there is a set Γ of propositions such that:
> (1) we have equally good defeasible arguments for believing each member of Γ;
> (2) for each P in Γ there is a finite subset Γ_P of Γ such that the conjunction of R with the members of Γ_P provides a deductive argument for $\sim P$ that is as strong as our initial argument is for P; and
> (3) none of these arguments is defeated except possibly by their interactions with one another;
> then none of the propositions in Γ is warranted on the basis of these defeasible arguments.

The proof of this principle is as follows. Suppose we have such a set Γ and proposition R. For each P in Γ, combining the argument supporting R with the arguments supporting the members of Γ_P gives us an argument supporting $\sim P$. Intuitively, we have equally strong support for both P and $\sim P$, and hence we could not reasonably believe either on this basis, i.e., neither is warranted. This holds for each P in Γ, so none of them should be warranted. They "collectively defeat one another". And, indeed, this is forthcoming from our analysis of warrant. We have level 0 arguments supporting each P. But these can be combined to generate level 0 arguments that also support rebutting defeaters for the argument for each P. Thus none of these are level 1 arguments. But this means that none of the defeating arguments are level 1 arguments either. Thus all of the arguments are level 2 arguments. But then they fail to be level 3 arguments. And so on. For each even number n, each P is supported by a level n argument, but that argument is not a level $n+1$ argument. Thus the P's are not supported by ultimately undefeated arguments, and hence are not warranted.

The most common instances of (3.3) occur when Γ is a minimal finite set of propositions deductively inconsistent with R. In that case, for each P in Γ, $\{R\} \cup (\Gamma - \{P\})$ gives us a deductive reason for $\sim P$. Principle (3.3) can be illustrated by an example of this form that has played an important role in the philosophical foundations of probability theory. This is the *lottery paradox* (due to Kyburg [1961]). Suppose we are warranted in believing we have a fair lottery with one million tickets. Let this be R. Then the probability of the ith ticket being drawn in such a lottery is .000001. By statistical syllogism, this gives us a prima facie reason for believing that the ith ticket will not be drawn.[3] Let the latter be P_i. But we have an analogous argument supporting each P_i. Furthermore, by R we are warranted in believing that some ticket will be drawn, so these conclusions conflict with one another. Intuitively, there is no reason to prefer some of the P_i's over others, so we cannot be warranted in believing any of them unless we are warranted in believing all of them. But we cannot be warranted in believing all of them, because the set $\{R, P_1, ..., P_{1000000}\}$ is inconsistent. In fact, it is a minimal inconsistent set. Hence by (3.3), we are not warranted in believing any of the P_i's.

Principle (3.3) is a principle of *collective rebutting defeat*. It only pertains to cases in which we have arguments supporting both P and $\sim$P. But we can obtain a *principle of collective undercutting defeat* in precisely the same way:

> (3.4) If we are warranted in believing R and there is a set Γ of propositions such that:
> (1) we have equally good defeasible arguments for believing each member of Γ;
> (2) for each P in Γ, the supporting argument involves a defeasible step proceeding from some premise S to a conclusion T, and there is a finite subset Γ_P of Γ such that the conjunction of R with the members of Γ_P provides a deductive argument for $\sim(S ==> T)$ that is as strong as our initial argument is for P; and
> (3) none of these arguments is defeated except possibly by their interactions with one another;
> then none of the propositions in Γ is warranted on the basis of these defeasible arguments.

To illustrate this principle, suppose we know that people generally tell the truth. But now suppose Jones says 'Smith is unreliable' and Smith says 'Jones is unreliable'. Each provides an undercutting defeater for the other. What should we believe about Smith and Jones? The intuitive answer is, 'Nothing'. We have no basis for deciding that one rather than the other, or possibly both, is unreliable. Under the circumstances, we should withhold belief regarding their reliability. And that is just what principle (3.4) tells us.

3.4 *Two Paradoxes of Defeasible Reasoning*

The simple account of warrant that I gave above has some unacceptable consequences that will force its modification. This can be illustrated by looking at two apparent paradoxes of reasoning. First, let us look again at the lottery paradox. The lottery paradox is generated by supposing that we are warranted in believing a proposition R describing the lottery (it is a fair lottery, has one million tickets, and so on). Given that R is warranted, we get collective defeat for the proposition that any given ticket will not be drawn. But the present account makes it problematic how R can ever be warranted. Normally, we will believe R on the basis of being told that it is true (orally or in writing). In such a case, our evidence for R is statistical, proceeding in accordance with the statistical syllogism. That is, we know inductively that most things we are told that fall within a certain broad range are true, and that gives us a prima facie reason for believing R. So we have only a defeasible reason for believing R. Let σ be the argument supporting R. Let T_i be the proposition that ticket i will be drawn. In accordance with the standard reasoning involved in the lottery paradox, we can extend σ to generate a longer argument η supporting $\sim R$:

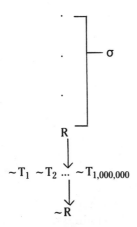

The final step of the argument is justified by the observation that if none of the tickets is drawn then the lottery is not fair.

The difficulty is now that η defeats σ by (3.1). Thus σ and η defeat one another, with the result that neither is ultimately undefeated.

In other words, R and ~R are subject to collective defeat. This result is intuitively wrong. It should be possible for us to become warranted in believing R on the basis described.

Consider a second instance of paradoxical reasoning. Suppose we observe n A's r of which are B's, and then by statistical induction we infer that $prob(Bx/Ax) \approx r/n$.[4] Suppose that r/n is high. Then if we observe a further set of k A's without knowing whether they are B's, we can infer by statistical syllogism that each one is a B. This gives us n+k A's of which r+k are B's. By a second application of statistical induction, this gives us a reason for thinking that $prob(Bx/Ax) \approx (r+k)/(n+k)$. If k is large enough, $(r+k)/(n+k) \not\approx r/n$, and so we can infer that $prob(Bx/Ax) \not\approx r/n$, which contradicts our original conclusion and undermines all of the reasoning. Making this more precise, we have two nested arguments:

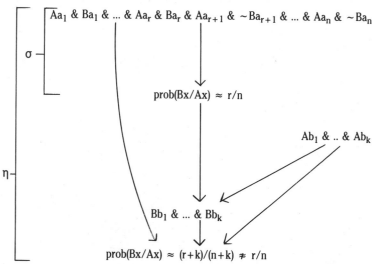

σ and η defeat one another by (3.1), so we have a case of collective defeat. But this is intuitively wrong. All we actually have in this case is a reason for believing that $prob(Bx/Ax) \approx r/n$, and a bunch of A's regarding which we do not know whether they are B's. The latter should have no effect on our warrant for the former. But by (3.1), it does. I will call this *the paradox of statistical induction*.

I believe that these two paradoxes illustrate a single inadequacy in our analysis of warrant. In each case we begin with an argument σ supporting a conclusion P, and then we extend σ to obtain an argument η supporting ~P. By (3.1), this is a case of collective defeat, but intuitively it seems that P should be warranted. What I think is happening here is that argument η is faulty all by itself. It is *self-defeating*, and that removes it from contention in any contest with conflicting arguments. Thus it cannot enter into collective defeat with other arguments, and in particular it cannot enter into collective defeat with σ.

In order to handle the paradoxes, it suffices to modify (3.1) so that it rules that self-defeating arguments are automatically defeated at every level. Let us define more precisely:

> (3.5) σ is *self-defeating* iff σ supports a defeater for one of its own defeasible steps.

We could then achieve our desired results by modifying (3.1) to read as follows:

> (3.1*) σ is a *level n + 1 argument* iff σ is a level 0 argument that is not self-defeating and there is no level n argument η that supports a defeater for a defeasible step of σ.

However, there is a simpler modification that is equivalent to this. The simpler modification retains the earlier formulation of (3.1), but revises the definition of 'level 0 argument' to require that level 0 arguments be non-self-defeating. I will adopt this latter modification.

It is of interest to compare the arguments involved in the paradoxes with reductio ad absurdum arguments. In both cases we have arguments that proceed from R to ~R, but in reductio ad absurdum we take that to warrant the conclusion ~R, whereas in the paradoxes we take that to defeat the whole argument and leave us with no warranted conclusion following from it. The difference is that reductio ad absurdum arguments are nondefeasible and hence cannot be self-defeating. There can be no defeaters for a reductio ad absurdum argument because it has no defeasible steps. The paradoxical arguments, on the other hand, are defeasible arguments and so can be self-defeating.

With this modification to the definition of 'level 0 argument', I believe that our theory of warrant for linear arguments is correct. The principle of collective defeat comes out true as formulated, but the paradoxes of defeasible reasoning are no longer cases of collective defeat because the paradoxical arguments are no longer level 0 arguments.

4. Justified Belief and Rules for Reasoning

I glossed 'warrant' as 'what an ideal reasoner would believe'. An ideal reasoner is one unconstrained by a finite memory or processing capacity. Warrant is an ideal to which "real" epistemic agents aspire. But we cannot expect real epistemic agents to believe only warranted propositions. Warrant is a "global" concept defined in terms of the set of all possible arguments available to an epistemic agent at a single time. No one can actually survey that infinite totality and decide what to believe by applying the definition of 'warrant' to it. That definition involves the comparison of infinitely many arguments and, in cases of collective defeat, the infinite cycling of arguments through defeat and reinstatement. This could not reflect the way we actually reason. Actual rules for reasoning must appeal exclusively to "local" considerations—readily accessible features of the epistemic situation.

Insofar as we reason in accordance with our built-in rules for reasoning, whatever they may be, our beliefs are said to be *justified*, but this does not guarantee that they are warranted. Justification only approximates warrant. We can, for example, be justified in holding deductively inconsistent beliefs if we are unaware that they are inconsistent and we got to them in reasonable ways, but deductively inconsistent beliefs can never be warranted. Warrant is at most an ideal to which justified reasoning aspires. Actual reasoning takes the form of working out arguments and defeating and reinstating them in the same manner as is involved in the definition of warrant, but we are limited in how many arguments and how many steps of defeat and reinstatement we can go through. If we could keep going indefinitely, our rules for reasoning would lead to warranted beliefs, but of course, we cannot. Instead, our rules for justified belief formation involve the presumption that the reasoning we have done at any given time is "all right" unless we have some concrete reason, in the form of a defeating argument, for thinking otherwise. This is a kind of second-order default assumption about the existence of defeating arguments.

Let us try to be more specific about the rules for justified belief formation. In this section I will make some general remarks about the form of the rules for defeasible reasoning, and in the next section I will attempt to construct concrete rules of this form.

The most natural assumption is that rules for reasoning tell us to form certain beliefs if we already have other appropriately related beliefs. Such rules *prescribe* the formation of beliefs whenever we believe the premises from which they can be obtained. But actual rules for reasoning do not take this form. The simplest rules are "permission rules", telling us that it is *all right* to form various kinds of beliefs, but not that we *must* form them. For example, a common mistake is to formulate a rule of *modus ponens* as follows:

(4.1) If one believes both P and (P ⊃ Q) then he should believe Q.

But this is wrong. One does not automatically have an epistemic obligation to believe everything he can infer from his various beliefs. As Gilbert Harman [1986] has observed, such an obligation would lead to unmanageable clutter in one's beliefs. Normally, one only draws conclusions insofar as one is interested in the conclusions or there is reason to believe that the conclusions bear upon matters that interest one. Thus *modus ponens* should be at most a permission rule, *allowing* us to draw a certain conclusion rather than mandating our drawing that conclusion.[5] It is such epistemic permission rules that have been the focus of much work in epistemology.

On the other hand, a production system for belief formation must tell us to adopt particular beliefs under various circumstances. It cannot just tell us to do so if we want. Thus there must be rules prescribing belief formation, but what the above observations indicate is that these rules must appeal not just to what other beliefs we have, but also to what our interests are. This suggests that epistemic rules must incorporate a certain amount of goal directed reasoning. It is only by taking interests into account in addition to beliefs that one can hope to generate rules prescribing belief formation. Such rules must have forms more like the following:

(4.2) If you have beliefs $P_1,...,P_n$ and you are interested in whether Q is true then you should believe Q.

For now, I will not worry about how one becomes interested in various propositions, although this is a matter that must eventually be addressed.

It appears that there must be three kinds of rules for belief formation. First, there are *adoption rules* telling us that we should adopt beliefs if we care about whether they are true and we have arguments supporting them. These rules create a "prima facie obligation" to adopt beliefs. Second, there are *defeat rules* canceling that prima facie obligation when we discover defeating arguments for the initial arguments. This second category of rules consists of obligation rules prescribing the withholding of belief. Again, these rules create only prima facie obligations, because defeating arguments can themselves be defeated. This leads to the third class of rules—the *reinstatement rules*—which concern reinstatement from defeat. Reinstatement occurs when defeaters are themselves defeated.

The defeat rules pertain to the discovery of defeaters for the arguments on the basis of which beliefs are held. A natural hypothesis is that whenever P is a prima facie reason for Q and R is a reason for either $\sim Q$ or $\sim (P = = > Q)$, we must have a rule something like the following:

> (4.3) If you believe Q on the basis of an argument one line of which is obtained by using P as a prima facie reason for Q, then if you adopt R as a new belief, you should cease to believe Q on this basis.

We can make several observations about this rule. First, its implementation requires the cognizer to keep track not only of his beliefs but also of the arguments on the basis of which he holds the beliefs. Human beings are not terribly good at this. They have access to their arguments only insofar as they can remember them, and they generally do not remember them. When that happens, we regard it as reasonable to maintain the belief in Q. Furthermore, if we were designing an intelligent machine, we would not want it to have to store all of its arguments and continually refer back to them. It would expend most of its cognitive resources in book-keeping rather than getting on with the business of belief formation. This suggests that in place of (4.3), what we actually have is a "doxastic" rule more like:

> (4.4) If (1) you believe that you believe Q on the basis of an argument one line of which is obtained by using P as a prima facie reason for Q, and (2) you believe a defeater, then you should cease to believe Q on this basis.

I am, however, uncomfortable with (4.4). (4.4) has the consequence that defeat requires higher-order monitoring of our reasoning processes. It is indisputable that such higher-order monitoring sometimes occurs, but it is a complicated process and I do not think that defeat requires it. Defeat often proceeds in a more automatic fashion. If I believe Q on the basis of a prima facie reason P, and then I adopt a new belief R that is a prima facie reason for ~Q, I just automatically retract Q without having to think about the matter. How to construct rules for defeat that work in such an automatic fashion without higher-order monitoring is one of the problems that I will face in the next section. In a recent book (Pollock [1986]) I argued that this was impossible, but it turns out to be fairly easy.

A major problem that must be faced in the construction of rules for reasoning is that they must avoid infinite cycling. The theory of warrant handles collective defeat in terms of infinite cycling between competing arguments, but actual reasoning must work in some simpler fashion.

With these preliminary remarks as a background, I turn now to the construction of a concrete system of rules for defeasible reasoning. This system, and the computer program implementing it, will be called 'OSCAR'.[6]

5. OSCAR: A Framework for Defeasible Reasoning

The problem of constructing a general framework for defeasible reasoning is a difficult one, and I do not at this time have an entirely general solution to the problem. Instead, my strategy is to adopt some simplifying assumptions and construct a theory of defeasible reasoning based on those assumptions. My strategy for future research will then be to remove the simplifying assumptions one at a time, each time making the theory more sophisticated in order to handle the greater generality. In some cases I already have a version of OSCAR that relaxes the simplifying assumptions, but I have chosen to present the simpler system here because it is easier to understand and the additional complexities are not of great theoretical interest.

I will make the following simplifying assumptions:

(1) The most important simplification will result from confining my attention to linear arguments. I will pretend that all arguments are linear so that we do not have to contend, for example, with conditional arguments.
(2) I will assume that all reasons have the same strength. This has the consequence that whenever we have a reason for P and a reason for ~P, we have a case of collective defeat. Of course, this consequence is not realistic, because

in actual practice we can have a strong reason for P and a weak reason for ~P, and still be at least mildly justified in believing P.

(3)I will assume that there are only finitely many reasons. In reality, there are infinitely many reasons, because reasons come in schemas. For instance, for *any* P and Q, (P & Q) is a conclusive reason for P. The simplifying assumption that there are only finitely many reasons has the consequence that reasoning will stop after finitely many steps, because there will be no further conclusions that can be drawn. In real life, reasoning can always go on.

(4) Given that reasoning will stop after finitely many steps, we can safely ignore goal directedness in reasoning and instruct the system to draw all the conclusions it can rather than just those in which it is interested. Equivalently, we can take the system to be interested in everything. I will adopt this simplifying assumption.

(5) My final simplifying assumption is that reasons are always individual propositions rather than sets of propositions. This is strictly a convenience in the formulation of the system. I already have a version of OSCAR that avoids this assumption, but I have chosen not to present it here in order to keep the system as simple as possible. Allowing reasons to be sets complicates all the constructions, but does not affect the general ideas underlying OSCAR.

I will now discuss a system of rules for defeasible reasoning based upon these assumptions, and then I will discuss briefly how the rules will have to be modified in order to relax these assumptions.

One of the major problems that a system must solve is how to handle defeat and reinstatement without storing all of the arguments on the basis of which beliefs are adopted. What I have discovered is that this can be done by storing only the "immediate bases" for beliefs, and the bases for defeat. More specifically, rather than storing the entire argument, we just store the last step. If we inferred Q from P, we store that fact, but no more of the argument. Of course, human beings do sometimes remember their arguments, but my concern here is to construct a "basic" system of defeasible reasoning that can accomplish its goals with as little higher-order monitoring as possible. Given such a system, we can consider later how it might be streamlined by allowing higher-order monitoring to play a role when it is available.

In addition to keeping track of the reason for holding a belief, we must keep track of whether that reason is defeasible or conclusive. This makes a difference to the way in which defeat works (see particularly rule (BACKTRACK) below). Let us define:

(5.1) S *believes* P *on* Q iff S believes P on the basis of the defeasible reason Q.

(5.2) S *believes* P *con* Q iff S believes P on the basis of the conclusive reason Q.

These are to be understood in such a way that an agent can believe something on or con several different bases at the same time. I will take *beliefs* to be the set of beliefs held at any given time, *onset* will be the set of pairs $<Q,P>$ such that Q is believed on P, and *conset* will be the set of pairs $<Q,P>$ such that Q is believed con P.

We must also keep track of the bases upon which reasons are defeated. In the case of undercutting defeat, that is simple. If P is a prima facie reason for Q, but it is defeated by undercutting, then the agent believes $\sim(P = = > Q)$, and the basis for that is stored in *onset* or *conset*. Reinstatement then results from anything leading the agent to retract belief in $\sim(P = = > Q)$.

Rebutting defeat is more complicated. Consider the following pair of arguments leading to contradictory conclusions:

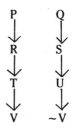

where P is a prima facie reason for R, Q is a prima facie reason for S, and the remaining reasons are conclusive. As this is a case of collective defeat, neither V nor $\sim$V should be believed. But T entails V and U entails $\sim$V, so T and U must be retracted. Similarly for R and S. So the agent is left with P and Q as his only beliefs, and I will say that the pairs $<R,P>$ and $<S,Q>$ *rebut* one another. We will keep track of such rebutting defeat by putting the pair

$\{<R,P>,<S,Q>\}$ in the set *rebut*. Our rules for reinstatement from rebutting defeat will appeal to the set *rebut*. Let us define:

°(5.3) An individual proposition P *is rebutted* iff for some X in *rebut* and for some Q, $<P,Q>\varepsilon X$.

Note that what goes in the set *rebut* is always pairs of prima facie reasons rather than defeasible reasons. In rebutting defeat, we must backtrack to the last defeasible step of reasoning and then take that to be rebutted. As the defeat is collective, this goes in both directions. This is made precise in terms of the notion of a nearest defeasible ancestor, which is defined as follows:

(5.4) Where p is a belief, q is a *nondefeasible ancestor* of p iff there is a sequence $>p_1 ...,p_n>$ $(i > 1)$ of beliefs such that $p = p_n$, $q = p_1$, and for each $i < n$, p_{i+1} is believed con p_i. A pair $<r,s>$ is a *nearest nondefeasible ancestor* of p iff r is a nondefeasible ancestor of p and r is believed on s.

When two chains of reasoning lead to contradictory conclusions, we take the nearest nondefeasible ancestors to rebut one another, and we put the corresponding pairs of pairs in *rebut*.

A distinction must be made between newly adopted beliefs and previously held beliefs. When we adopt a new belief, we then look to see what consequences that has for our other beliefs. It may lead us to adopt further new beliefs, and it may lead us to retract old beliefs. The system keeps track of newly adopted beliefs in a set called *adoptionset*. Similarly, newly retracted propositions are put in the set *retractionset*. When a new belief is adopted, the rules of defeasible reasoning will be applied repeatedly in a certain order until no further adoptions or retractions can be obtained. This requires us to keep track of whether new adoptions or retractions occur at various points in the processing, and this will be done with the *adoptionflag* and the *retractionflag*. These are just functions whose values are initially 0, and they are reset to 1 whenever there is a new adoption or retraction. In deciding what to do at various points, the system will look at the value of these flags. If the flags are both 0 then no new adoptions or retractions have occurred. In that case, *adoptionset* and *retractionset* are cleared and the system is ready to process new inputs.

Let us define:

> (5.5) *Adopting* a belief consists of (1) inserting it into *beliefs* if it is not already there, (2) putting it in *adoptionset*, (3) deleting it from *retractionset*, and (4) setting *adoptionflag* equal to 1. To *adopt P on Q* is insert $<Q,P>$ in *onset* and adopt P. To *adopt P con Q* is to insert $<Q,P>$ in *conset* and adopt P.

Similarly:

> (5.6) *retracting* a belief P consists of (1) deleting it from *beliefs*, (2) inserting it in *retractionset*, (3) deleting it from *adoptionset* if it is there, (4) deleting all pairs of the form $<P,Q>$ from *onset*, and (5) setting *retractionflag* equal to 1. (For technical reasons connected with the rule (BACKTRACK), we do not also delete pairs of the form $<P,Q>$ from *conset*.)

Given these preliminaries, we now formulate our rules for adoption, defeat, and reinstatement precisely as follows:

Adoption:

(ADOPT-ON)

> Where p is a prima facie reason for q:
> If you adopt p then if you do not believe $\sim(p == > q)$ and you do not believe $\sim q$ and neither q nor $\sim q$ is rebutted, then adopt q on p.[7]

(ADOPT-CON)

> Where p is a conclusive reason for q:
> If you adopt p and you do not believe $\sim q$ and neither q nor $\sim q$ is rebutted, then adopt q con p.

Retraction:

(a) By undercutting defeat:

(UNDERCUT)

> Where p is a prima facie reason for q:
> If you believe q on p, but you adopt $\sim(p == > q)$ then

delete <q,p> from *onset*, and retract q if you do not believe it on any other basis:

(b) By rebutting defeat:

(REBUTa)

Where r is a prima facie reason for ~q:
If you believe q and you adopt r and you do not believe ~(r ==> ~q) then find the nearest defeasible ancestors <d,c> of q, and retract q and all the intermediate nondefeasible ancestors, and add the pairs {<d,c>,<~q,r>} to *rebut*.

(REBUTb)

Where r is a conclusive reason for ~q:
If you believe q and you adopt r then (1) find the nearest defeasible ancestors <b,a> of r and retract r and all its intermediate nondefeasible ancestors, (2) find the nearest defeasible ancestors <d,c> of q and retract q and all its intermediate nondefeasible ancestors, and (3) add all the pairs {<d,c>,<b,a>} to *rebut*.

Enlarging collective defeat:

(NEG-COL-DEFa)

Where p is a prima facie reason for q:
If you adopt p and you do not believe ~(p ==> q) and ~q is rebutted, then for each r such that <~q,r>εU*rebut*, add {<q,p>,<~q,r>} to *rebut*.

(NEG-COL-DEFb)

Where p is a conclusive reason for q:
If you adopt p and ~q is rebutted, then find the nearest defeasible ancestors <d,c> of p and retract all the intermediate nondefeasible ancestors, and for each r such that <~q,r> appears in *rebut*, add all the pairs {<d,c>,<~q,r>} to *rebut*.

(POS-COL-DEFa)

> Where p is a prima facie reason for q:
> If you adopt p and do not believe $\sim(p ==> q)$, and q is
> rebutted, then for each r,a,b such that
> $\{<q,r>,<b,a>\}\varepsilon rebut$, add $\{<q,p>,<b,a>\}$ to *rebut*.

(POS-COL-DEFb)

> Where p is a conclusive reason for q:
> If you adopt p, and q is rebutted, then find the nearest
> defeasible ancestors $<d,c>$ of p and retract all the
> intermediate nondefeasible ancestors, and for each $<b,a>$
> such that $\{<q,r>,<b,a>\}\varepsilon rebut$, add $\{<d,c>,<b,a>\}$ to
> *rebut*.

Hereditary retraction:

(H-RETRACT)

> For any p and q, if you believe q on p or q con p, but you
> retract p, then retract q and delete $<q,p>$ from *conset* ∪
> *onset*.

Backtracking for conclusive reasons:

(BACKTRACK)

> For any p and q, if you believe q con p but you retract q,
> then retract p.

Reinstatement:

> Reinstatement is handled by treating propositions as newly
> adopted (even if they have been believed all along) when
> sources of defeat are removed, and then seeing what can be
> inferred from them.

(a) from undercutting defeat:

(U-REINSTATE)

> Where p is a prima facie reason for q:

If you believe p and retract $\sim(p ==> q)$ and neither q nor $\sim q$ is rebutted, then adopt p.

(b) from rebutting defeat:

by undercutting:

(R-REINSTATE/U)

Where p is a prima facie reason for q:
If you adopt $\sim(p ==> q)$ and $\{<q,p>,<d,c>\}\varepsilon rebut$, then delete the latter from *rebut* and adopt c.

by retracting:

(R-REINSTATE/R)

If you retract p but not c, and $\{<q,p>,<d,c>\}\varepsilon rebut$, then delete the latter from *rebut* and adopt c.

———————————————

These rules are combined using the following program architecture:

THE ARCHITECTURE OF OSCAR

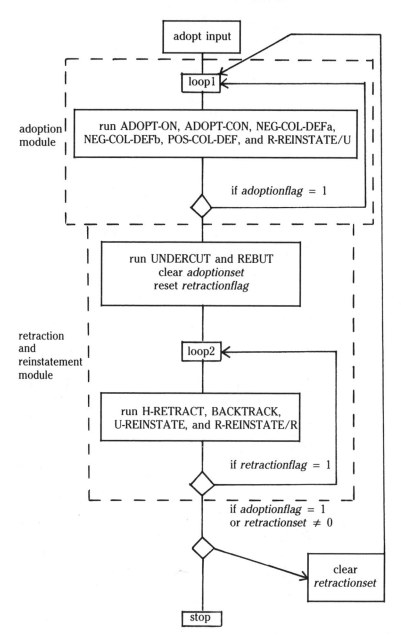

6. Assessment of OSCAR

OSCAR is not an entirely realistic model of human defeasible reasoning, because it is based upon the simplifying assumptions listed at the beginning of the previous section. Nevertheless, OSCAR is a start at developing a realistic theory of defeasible reasoning. OSCAR does most things right, but suffers from some defects connected with those simplifying assumptions. In this concluding section, I will discuss some of these features of OSCAR.

OSCAR has two features that I consider quite important. The first is that he never holds explicitly contradictory beliefs. (ADOPT-ON) and (ADOPT-CON) each preclude the adoption of q if the agent already believes ∼q. Instead, he automatically takes this to be a case of collective defeat. I take it that this is a genuine feature of human defeasible reasoning.

The second feature of OSCAR that I want to emphasize is that the order in which input is given does not make any difference to the ultimate beliefs. This will be particularly important when OSCAR is extended to handle infinite sets of reasons (i.e., reason schemas) and continuous input. In that case the program architecture must be modified, because he cannot be required to draw all possible conclusions from the input before looping back to loop1. He must draw some conclusions and go on, and then later return and draw others. If this is to work, it cannot make a difference which conclusions he draws first.

OSCAR keeps track of 'on' and 'con' relations by storing them automatically whenever a belief is adopted or a new basis for a belief is acquired. The role of these relations in OSCAR is philosophically suggestive. They play a strictly book-keeping role. In particular, they have no epistemology. OSCAR does not need a reason for believing that he believes P on Q before he can store that 'on' relation. On the other hand, the description of OSCAR is mute on the question of whether the 'on' and 'con' relations are stored as beliefs, or stored in some other way. All of this seems to have important bearing on the philosophical problem of the analysis of the basing relation, but I will not pursue it further here.

Another philosophically intriguing feature of OSCAR is that it is absolutely essential for him to distinguish between 'on' and 'con', because he processes them in different ways. But now notice that a system like OSCAR but accommodating conditional reasoning will be able to use conclusive reasons to arrive at a priori truths. If p is a conclusive reason for q, the system can take p as a premise, infer q, and then conditionalize to acquire the belief (p ⊃ q) on the basis of no input at all. I would propose that an analysis of a priori knowledge and necessary truth can be obtained along these lines, and it will take its sole primitive to be the concept of a conclusive reason. Furthermore, the latter concept is indispensable for defeasible reasoning. This, I would propose, is the origin of our concept of necessary truth. It is, in a certain sense, an answer to Quine. Necessary truth is defined in terms of conclusive reasons, and conclusive reasons are characterized by their processing role in a system of defeasible reasoning. This is speculative—the details remain to be worked out—but it is at least suggestive.

How well does the present OSCAR perform? I believe that in cases in which the simplifying assumptions are nonproblematic, he does everything right. There are cases in which his reasoning goes awry, but I believe that these are all connected with the simplifying assumptions. One case worth mentioning is the following. Suppose A is a prima facie reason for P which is a conclusive reason for Q; B is a prima facie reason for R which is a conclusive reason for Q; and C is a prima facie reason for S which is a conclusive reason for ~Q:

$$A \dashrightarrow P \cdots\cdots> Q$$
$$B \dashrightarrow R \cdots\cdots> Q$$
$$C \dashrightarrow S \cdots\cdots> {\sim}Q$$

Given the input {A,C}, rebutting defeat occurs with the result that *beliefs* is just {A,C}, and *rebut* is {{<P,A>,<S,C>}}. So far so good, but now if we give OSCAR the new input {B}, we would like this to add B to *beliefs* (which it does) and add {<R,B>,<S,C>} to *rebut*. The latter fails. Instead, OSCAR adopts R on B and then adopts Q con R. This is because there is no mention of Q itself in *rebut*. Instead, it is the nearest defeasible ancestors of Q that went into *rebut*. There is an *ad hoc* way of handling this in OSCAR. If S is a conclusive reason for ~Q then S entails ~Q, and so Q entails ~S. This suggests that we might require that the set of conclusive reasons be closed under contraposition: whenever a proposition D is a conclusive reason for another proposition E, ~E is also a conclusive reason for ~D. If we impose this constraint on OSCAR then he will reason correctly in this case.

Humans handle this case differently. They use conditional reasoning to get the same result. If S is a conclusive reason for ~Q then by conditional reasoning they can obtain (S ⊃ ~Q) even when S is not believed. Then once they reason (like OSCAR) from B to R to Q, they can go on to ~S, and then the rule (NEG-COL-DEFb) will lead to the retraction of Q, R, and ~S, and the addition of {<R,B>,<S,C>} to *rebut*. But OSCAR cannot reason this way until we give him conditional reasoning.

The main case in which OSCAR goes badly wrong is with collective undercutting defeat. He cannot handle this at all. Recall that a simple example of this occurs when Jones says "Smith is unreliable" and Smith says "Jones is unreliable". In such a case, we should not believe either. Suppose we take P to be a prima facie reason for Q, and Q to be a conclusive reason for ~(R = = > S), and in turn take R to be a prima facie reason for S and S to be a conclusive reason for ~(P = = > Q):

$$P \text{-} \text{-} \text{-} > Q \quad \cdots\cdots\cdots\cdots > \quad \sim(R = = > S)$$
$$R \text{-} \text{-} \text{-} > S \quad \cdots\cdots\cdots\cdots > \quad \sim(P = = > Q)$$

Then giving OSCAR the input {P,R} puts him into an infinite loop. I do not believe that this can be resolved without conditional reasoning. The difficulty can be seen by comparing collective undercutting defeat with collective rebutting defeat. The presence of collective rebutting defeat is signalled by the appearance of an explicit contradiction as the next step a reasoner would otherwise take. This hits the reasoner squarely in the face and cannot be ignored. But collective undercutting defeat can be much more subtle. We might have a long chain of reasoning like the following:

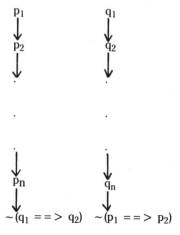

$$p_1 \qquad\qquad q_1$$
$$\downarrow \qquad\qquad \downarrow$$
$$p_2 \qquad\qquad q_2$$
$$\downarrow \qquad\qquad \downarrow$$

$$\downarrow \qquad\qquad \downarrow$$
$$p_n \qquad\qquad q_n$$
$$\downarrow \qquad\qquad \downarrow$$
$$\sim(q_1 = = > q_2) \quad \sim(p_1 = = > p_2)$$

where all the steps are defeasible. This should be a case of collective undercutting defeat, but to discover such collective defeat the reasoner may have to trace his reasoning back arbitrarily far, in this case, all the way back to p_1 and q_1. We do not want to require that OSCAR check for this every time he makes an inference, because the overhead would be immense and his reasoning would be slowed to a crawl.

I suggest that the way this is handled in human beings is that we do not usually worry about collective undercutting defeat, and we only take the inferences involved to be defeated if we happen onto it. We do not automatically check for it. Happening onto it consists of adopting certain conditionals. Specifically, we can use a rule something like the following:

> Where A is a prima facie reason for B and P is a prima facie reason for Q, if you come to believe B on A and Q on P, and also the conditionals $[B ==> \sim(P ==> Q)]$ and $[Q ==> \sim(A ==> B)]$, take $<Q,P>$ and $<B,A>$ to be subject to collective undercutting defeat.

However, such a rule can only be implemented in a system that includes conditional reasoning, so there is no way to build it into the present version of OSCAR.

I have not implemented the "self-defeating" constraint that I used to resolve the paradoxes of defeasible reasoning. Again, we do not want OSCAR to have to continually check whether his arguments are self-defeating, because that requires backtracking arbitrarily far. I suggest that this too is best handled in terms of conditional reasoning, but I will not go into it here.

Notes

*. This paper was first presented at a conference at Brown University, in honor of Roderick Chisholm, held in October, 1986. A more technical account of some of this material can be found in Pollock [1987].
1. See Pollock [1986], chapter five, for a more detailed discussion of all this.
2. See Pollock [1976], chapters one and two, for an informal discussion of the simple subjunctive conditional.
3. Statistical syllogism can be written roughly as follows:

> Most F's are G.
> This is an F
> Therefore (prima facie), this is a G.

A somewhat more accurate formulation is:

> 'prob(Gx/Fx) is high, and Fa' is a prima facie reason for 'Ga', the strength of the reason being determined by how high the probability is.

A rigorous formulation of the principle requires some further qualifications, but they are not relevant here.

4. In statistical induction we reason from the fact that a certain proportion of all the F's we have observed have been G to the conclusion that the probability of an F being a G is approximately the same as that proportion:

> If F and ' ~F' are projectible with respect to G then 'X is a set of F's, and the proportion of members of X that are G is r' is a prima facie reason for 'prob(Gx/Fx) is approximately r'.

5. This is still simplistic, because sometimes what we should do is reject either P or (P ⊃ Q) rather than coming to believe Q.
6. 'Oscar' is the hero in "The Fable of Oscar" (Chapter Five of Pollock [1986]). For the further significance of OSCAR, see my "How to build a person" (*Philosophical Perspectives, 1, Metaphysics, 1987*).
7. In order to avoid complicating the rules throughout, I take ~ ~q to be q. That way we do not have to adopt replicas of our rules throughout for double negations.

References

Gilbert Harman, *Change in View*. Cambridge, MIT Press, 1986.

Henry Kyburg, *Probability and the Logic of Rational Belief*. Middletown: Wesleyan University Press, 1961.

John Pollock, *Subjunctive Reasoning*. Dordrecht: Reidel, 1976.

John Pollock, *Contemporary Theories of Knowledge*. Totowa, NJ: Rowman and Allanheld, 1986.

John Pollock, "Defeasible Reasoning," *Cognitive Science* 11, 1987, 481-518.

James E. Tomberlin, *Philosophical Perspectives, 1, Metaphysics, 1987*. Atascadero, CA: Ridgeview Publishing Co., 1987.

Philosophical Perspectives, 2, Epistemology, 1988

DELIBERATIONAL DYNAMICS AND THE FOUNDATIONS OF BAYESIAN GAME THEORY[1]

Brian Skyrms
University of California, Irvine

1. *Introduction*: There are two rationality concepts at work in separate areas of the theory of rational decision: EQUILIBRIUM, which is the dominant solution concept in the theory of non-cooperative games and MAXIMUM EXPECTED UTILITY which is the central principle in the theory of coherent individual choice under uncertainty. In the development of game theory, the relationship between the two principles, and to a lesser extent the status of the equilibrium principle itself, has been less than crystal clear.[2] This question is put in a new light if we regard deliberation as a dynamical process with informational feedback.

We will take the expected utility principle as basic. One deliberates by calculating expected utility. In the simplest cases deliberation is trivial; one calculates expected utility and maximizes. But in more interesting cases, the very process of deliberation may generate information which is salient to the evaluation of the expected utilities. Then, processing costs permitting, a Bayesian deliberator will feed-back that information and recalculate the expected utilities in light of the new knowledge.[3]

In such an interesting decision problem, deliberation can be modeled as a dynamic system. The decision maker starts in a state of indecision; calculates expected utility; moves in the direction of maximum expected utility; feeds back the information generated and recalculates; etc. In this process, his probabilities of doing the various acts evolve[4] until, at the time of decision, his probabilities of doing the selected act become virtually one.

Dynamic deliberation carries with it an equilibrium principle for individual decision. The decision maker cannot decide to do an act which is not an equilibrium of the deliberational process. If he is about to decide to do it, deliberation carries him away from that decision. This sort of equilibrium requirement for individual decision can be seen to be *a consequence of the expected utility principle*. It is usually neglected only because the process of informational feedback in deliberation is usually neglected. In cases in which there is no salient informational feedback, simple choice of the act with initial maximum expected utility automatically fulfills the equilibrium requirement.

This becomes relevant to game theory if we consider games played by Bayesian deliberators with shared initial subjective probabilities, whose deliberation rules and whose initial subjective probabilities are common knowledge, and who use that common knowledge in the deliberational process to update subjective probabilities by emulation of the other players deliberation. Under these assumptions, we can show that joint deliberational equilibrium on the part of all the players corresponds to a Nash equilibrium point of the game. In this model, choice of a Nash equilibrium is a consequence of the expected utility principle together with these assumptions of common knowledge.

Bayesian analysis provides a foundation for the key solution concept in classical non-cooperative game theory by embedding game theory in the setting of deliberational dynamics. The dynamics provides a straightforward motivation for questions of equilibrium, but it also leads to other questions of qualitative dynamics. After the existence of equilibria is established, questions of stability naturally arise.

In (2) I will give an account of Bayesian deliberation in individual decision making. The dynamic deliberational account is shown to differ from the static Bayesian account in that in certain decision problems, mixed decisions may be the only acceptable ones. The existence of deliberational equilibria under fairly general conditions is established. This account will be applied to non-cooperative games and related to the Nash equilibrium concept in (3). In (4) we will show how questions of stability naturally arise and have consequences of game theoretic interest.

2. *Deliberational Dynamics and Equilibrium Decisions*: Individual decision making does not usually result in informational feedback salient to the decision at hand, but one can contrive examples where it does. In such examples, deliberational dynamics may be non-trivial,

and the requirement for an equilibrium decision may have interesting consequences. In particular, the only decision that a Bayesian deliberator can make may be a *mixed decision*, notwithstanding the often repeated claim to the contrary.[5]

Consider the story of the mean demon.[6] The decision maker must choose to get either the contents of box A or those of box B. A mean demon has predicted her choice, and has already put $1,000,000 under the box he predicts she will choose and nothing under the other. The demon is a very good predictor and she knows this. To simplify the story, she has such strong beliefs in the demon's predictive powers that she maintains rigidly the conditional probabilities of the Million being in box B given that she takes box A and the Million being in box A given that she takes box B virtually equal to one. If she inclines more towards taking B than taking A, then taking A is more attractive, but if this then leads her to favor taking A, that change of mind carries information that gives B higher expected utility. She is in a decision theoretic analogue of the liar paradox, with the only deliberational equilibrium at probability of doing A = probability of doing B = 1/2. If mixed acts are allowed and the demon is no good at predicting the randomizing device, then the best she can do is to decide to flip a coin.

We get much the same story with CHICKEN with a CLONE. Two qualitatively identical bionic teenagers are playing a game of CHICKEN. They drive their Porsches towards one another at high speed and will meet at a point where an enormous sheet of brown paper has been stretched across the road so that they can't see one another. The options are to swerve or not, with the payoffs as follows:

	CHICKEN	
	DON'T	SWERVE
DON'T	$-10, -10$	$5, -5$
SWERVE	$-5, 5$	$0, 0$

ROW knows that her decisions cannot affect those of COL, but nevertheless believes that her deliberations generate compelling evidence about COL, so that she updates her probabilities by the rule: Probability (COL swerves) = Probability (I swerve). Again, her only deliberational equilibrium is at a mixed decision with equal probability of swerving and not swerving.

It is true that upon adopting this mixed equilibrium decision, ROW believing that COL has done the same, will associate the same expected utility with SWERVE, DON'T SWERVE, and all mixtures of the two, as shown in figure 1:

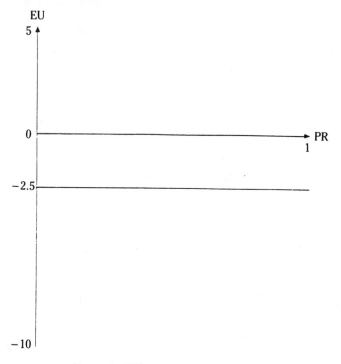

figure 1: EU as seen from (1/2,1/2)

So, although the mixed decision (1/2, 1/2) is no worse in terms of expected utility than the alternatives, it is also no better. It is on these grounds that it has been argued that maximization of expected utility cannot provide an adequate foundation for randomized decisions. But this argument neglects the fact that a different decision can carry with it different degrees of belief and therefore different expected utilities. For the standpoint associated with doing one of the pure acts, every alternative looks better, as shown in figure 2:

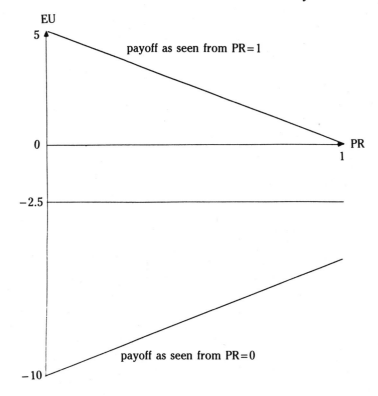

figure 2: EU as seen from pure acts

And any mixed act which deviates in the slightest from (1/2, 1/2) will, from its own perspective, be inferior to (1/2, 1/2), as shown in figure 3:

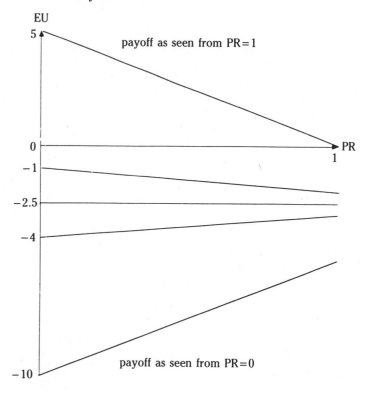

figure 3: EU from five perspectives

The mixed act (1/2, 1/2) considered *statically* appears to be unstable, but when considered *dynamically* is a stable equilibrium.

Are these examples typical? Does the availability of mixed strategies always guarantee an equilibrium decision? To answer these questions, let us model the deliberational situation in an abstract and fairly general way. A Bayesian has to choose between a finite number of acts: $A_1 \ldots A_n$. Calculation takes time for her; although its cost is negligible. We assume that she is certain that deliberation will end and she will choose some act (perhaps a mixed one) at that time. Her *state of indecision* will be a probability vector assigning probabilities to each of the n acts, which sum to one. These are to be interpreted as her probabilities now that she will do the act in question at the end of deliberation. A state of indecision, P, carries with it an expected utility; the expectation according to the probability vector $P = \langle p_1 \ldots p_n \rangle$ of the expected utilities of the acts $A_1 \ldots A_n$. The expected utility of a state of indecision is thus computed just as that of the corresponding mixed act. Indeed, the adoption of a mixed strategy can be thought of as a way to turn the state of indecision for its constituent pure acts to stone. We will call a mixed act corresponding to a state of indecision, its *default mixed act*.

Her state of indecision will evolve during deliberation. In the first place, on completing the calculation of expected utility, she will believe more strongly that she will ultimately do that act (or one of those acts) that are ranked more highly than her current state of indecision. If her calculation yields one act with maximum expected utility, will she not simply become sure that she will do that act? She will not *on pain of incoherence*[7] if she believes that she is in an informational feedback situation and assigns any positive probability at all to the possibility that informational feedback may lead her ultimately to a different decision. So, she will typically in one step of the process move in the direction of the currently perceived good, but not all the way to decision.

We assume that she moves according to some simple dynamical rule, rather than performing an elaborate calculation at each step. One concrete example of such a rule is what I have called the Nash Dynamics [after Nash (1951)]. Define the *Covetability* of an act in a state of indecision, p, as the difference in expected utility between the act and the state of indecision if the act is preferable to the state of indecision, and as zero if the state of indecision is preferable to the act: $COV(A) = MAX[0, U(A) - U(p)]$. Then the Nash dynamics takes the decision maker from state of indecision p to state of indecision p′ where each component p_i of p is changed to:

$$p'_i = [\, k\, p_i + COV(A_i)]/[k + \Sigma_i\, COV(A_i)]$$

Here a bold revision is hedged by averaging with the status quo. The constant k $(k > 0)$ is an index of caution. The higher k is, the more slowly the decision maker moves in the direction of acts which look more attractive than the status quo.

I am not suggesting here that some dynamical rule in this Nash family is optimal. (In fact, a more refined Bayesian analysis would lead elsewhere.) Rather, the Nash dynamics provide simple representatives of a class of dynamical rules, which share a property of special interest. They *seek the good*, in the following modest sense:

1. they raise the probability of an act only if that act has utility greater than that of the status quo;
2. they raise the sum of the probabilities of all acts with utility greater than[9] the status quo (if any).

All dynamical rules which seek the good have the same fixed points; i.e. states in which the expected utility of the status quo is maximal. Here we assume only that the decision maker's rule seeks the good.

In the second place, the decision maker's calculation of expected utility and subsequent application of the dynamical rule constitutes new information which may affect the expected utilities of the pure acts by affecting the probabilities of the states of nature which together with the act determine the payoff. In the mean demon case, the possible states of nature are the possible predictions and actions that the demon has taken; i.e. which box the money is under. In the typical game theoretical contexts they consist of the possible actions of the opposing players. For simplicity, we will assume here a finite number of states of nature.

The decision maker's *personal state* is then, for our purposes, determined by two things: her state of indecision and the probabilities that she assigns to states of nature. Her personal state space is the product space of her space of indecision and her space of states of nature. Deliberation defines a dynamics on this space. We could model the dynamics as either discrete or continuous, but we will discuss only discrete models here. We assume a dynamical function, Φ, which maps a personal state $<x,y>$ into a new personal state $<x',y'>$ in one unit of time. The dynamical function, Φ, has two associated rules: (I) the adaptive dynamical rule, D, which maps $<x,y>$ onto x' and (II) the informational feedback process, I, which maps $<x,y>$ onto y' (where $<x',y'> = \Phi <x,y>$).[8]

A personal state $<x,y>$ is a *deliberational equilibrium* of the dynamics, Φ, iff $\Phi <x,y> = <x,y>$. If D and I are continuous, then Φ is continuous and it follows from the Brower fixed point theorem that a deliberational equilibrium exists. Let N be the Nash dynamics for some $k > 0$. Then if the informational feedback process, I, is continuous, the dynamical function $<N,I>$ is continuous, and has a deliberational equilibrium. Let us say (adapting Jeffrey and Harper) that the mixed act corresponding to a state of indecision, x, is *ratifiable* in a personal state $<x,y>$, iff in that state $U(x) \geq U(A_i)$ for every pure act A_i.[9] Then, since N *seeks the good*, for any continuous informational feedback process, I, $<N,I>$ has a deliberational equilibrium $<x,y>$ whose corresponding mixed act is ratifiable in state $<x,y>$. This is a point from which process I does not move y and process N does not move x. But if process N does not move x, then no other process which seeks the good will either (whether or not it is continuous). So, we have the general result:

> *Theorem I*: If D seeks the good and I is continuous, then there is a deliberational equilibrium, $<x,y>$ for $<D,I>$. If D' also seeks the good then $<x,y>$ is also a deliberational equilibrium for $<D',I>$. Furthermore, the default mixed act corresponding to x is ratifiable at $<x,y>$.

In the examples given in this section, the informational feedback process is especially simple. The probabilities of the states conditional on the acts remain constant, so that the new probabilities of the states follow from the new probabilities of the acts alone. For this sort of informational feedback process, J, $<D,J>$ is continuous if D is; so $<N,J>$ is continuous and the theorem applies.[10] But for deliberational dynamics to be of any real interest, we will have to consider feedback processes that are more complicated than J.

3. *Games played by Bayesian Deliberators:* Suppose that two (or more) Bayesian deliberators are deliberating about what action to take in a non-cooperative non-zero sum game. We assume that here that each player has only one choice to make, and that the choices are causally independent in that there is no way for one player's decision to *influence* the decisions of the other players. Then for each player, the decisions of the other player's constitute the relevant *state* which, together with her decision, determines the *consequence* in accordance with the payoff matrix.

Suppose, in addition, that each player has an adaptive rule, D, which seeks the good (they need not have the same rule) and that what kind of Bayesian deliberator each player is, is common knowledge.[11] Suppose also, that each player's initial state of indecision is common knowledge, and that other player's take a given player's state of indecision as their own best estimate of what that player will ultimately do. Then initially, there is a probability assignment to all the acts for all the players which is shared by all the players and is common knowledge.

In this ideal situation, an interesting informational feedback process becomes available. Starting from the initial position, player 1 calculates expected utility and moves by her adaptive rule to a new state of indecision. She knows that the other players are Bayesian deliberators who have just carried out a similar process. And she knows their initial states of indecision and their updating rules. So she can simply go through their calculations to see their new states of indecision and update her probabilities of their acts accordingly. We will call this sort of informational feedback process *Updating by Emulation*. Suppose that all the players update by emulation. Then, in this ideal case, the new state is common knowledge as well and the process can be repeated.

The joint deliberation of the players can be modeled as a dynamical process in discrete time. Under the foregoing assumptions of common knowledge and updating by emulation, the deliberational state of the system of deliberators can be characterized by an assignment of probabilities to each of the acts of each of the players. Each player interprets the probabilities assigned to his own acts as representing her state of indecision, and the probabilities assigned to the other player's acts as representing her uncertainty about the state of the world. For each player, j, her adaptive dynamical rule maps her old probabilities over her acts to new ones. Taken together, the dynamical rules of the players map the old deliberational state of the whole system into a new one. This dynamical process is continuous if the adaptive dynamical rules of the individual players are (since my adaptive dynamical rule is your informational feedback rule, and conversely). Suppose a finite non-zero sum game is played by n Bayesian deliberators who use the Nash dynamics. Then the dynamics of the system is continuous and a deliberational equilibrium for the whole system exists, which is by definition a deliberational equilibrium for each player.

We say that an assignment of an act (pure or mixed) to each player is a *Nash Equilibrium* if each player, taking the other player's acts as fixed states of nature, is at an act of maximal expected utility. The relation between the concept of the Nash equilibrium of a game played by Bayesian deliberators, and the deliberational equilibria of the individual players is straightforward. An assignment of an mixed act to each player has a corresponding state of system which for each player, gives pure acts the probabilities that the mixed act assigned to her gives them. Each player interprets the state of the system decision theoretically as mirroring her personal state, with the probabilities assigned to her pure acts giving her state of indecision, and the probabilities assigned to other players pure acts giving her probabilities of the states of nature. Then, by definition, an assignment of mixed acts to each player is a Nash Equilibrium iff for each player, her mixed act is ratifiable in the corresponding state of the system.

We can now state the connection between the game theoretic concept of a Nash equilibrium and the decision theoretic concept of a deliberational equilibrium:

> *Theorem II: In a game played by Bayesian deliberators with an adaptive rule which Seeks the Good, and Updating by Emulation, each player is at a deliberational equilibrium at a state of the system if and only if the assignment of the default mixed acts to each player constitutes a Nash equilibrium of the game.*

In a finite N-person non-zero sum game, the availability of mixed strategies guarantees the existence of a Nash equilibrium, because if the game were played by Bayesian players with the Nash dynamics and updating by emulation, deliberation would map the space of states of the system into itself continuously with the Brower fixed point theorem guaranteeing a system state which represents a deliberational equilibrium for each of the players.

This is essentially the way in which Nash himself proved the existence of Nash equilibria, although Nash did not give the Bayesian interpretation to the process that I have supplied. The Bayesian analysis, however, shows in a rather general way how the Nash equilibrium concept can be grounded on Bayesian deliberation and common knowledge.

4. *Stability*: In section 2, we used the examples of the Mean demon and Chicken with a clone to show that it is possible for an equilibrium which appears unstable from a static point of view may be stable with regard to deliberational dynamics. Does this point generalize to the framework developed in the last section for games played by Bayesian deliberators who update by emulation?

Let us reconsider Chicken dropping the Clone assumption and updating by emulation. Then the initial probabilities of the players may be anywhere in the unit square. The dynamical picture for the system of consisting of both players is given in figure 4.

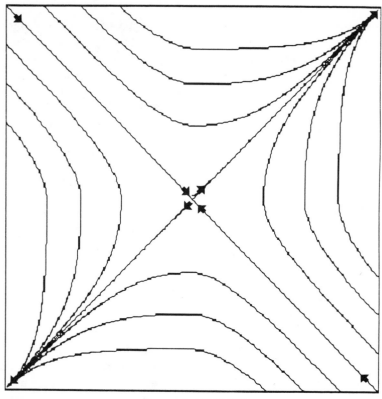

figure 4: CHICKEN

The lower right corner of the graph represents probability one that both swerve; the upper left probability one that neither swerves; the lower left probability one that Row swerves and Column doesn't. The curves plot orbits of points under Nash deliberation. [The questions of concern here are, for the most part, insensitive to the choice of a particular adaptive dynamical rule, as long as it is continuous and seeks the good.] As in Chicken with a Clone, there is an equilibrium at [.5,.5]. But this equilibrium is no longer stable. Any point on the diagonal from [0,1] to [1,0] will converge to it, and indeed Chicken with a Clone lives on this diagonal. But any point in the neighborhood of [.5,.5] which is off the diagonal will converge to one of the pure equilibria at [0,0] and [1,1]. The equilibrium at [.5,.5] is called a *saddle point* equilibrium, and this particular kind of instability will be fairly common.[12] The equilibria in pure strategies at [0,0] and [1,1] on the other hand are *strongly stable*: each has a neighborhood, such that it is an attractor for every orbit in that neighborhood. In fact, every point in the space to the lower left of the diagonal goes to [0,0] and every point to the upper right goes to [1,1]. (The diagonal is a *seperatrix*.) When the assumption of clonehood is relaxed, Chicken loses its paradoxical air. Almost every point in the space converges to a strongly stable pure equilibrium. Which equilibrium depends on which player has a higher initial probability of swerving. If belief is a matter of the will, Chicken is a test of will.

In this game theoretic setting, are pure equilibria always stable and mixed equilibria always unstable? No. Consider the game with the payoff matrix:

[0,0]   [0,0]
[1,1]   [−1,−1]

plotted in figure 5.

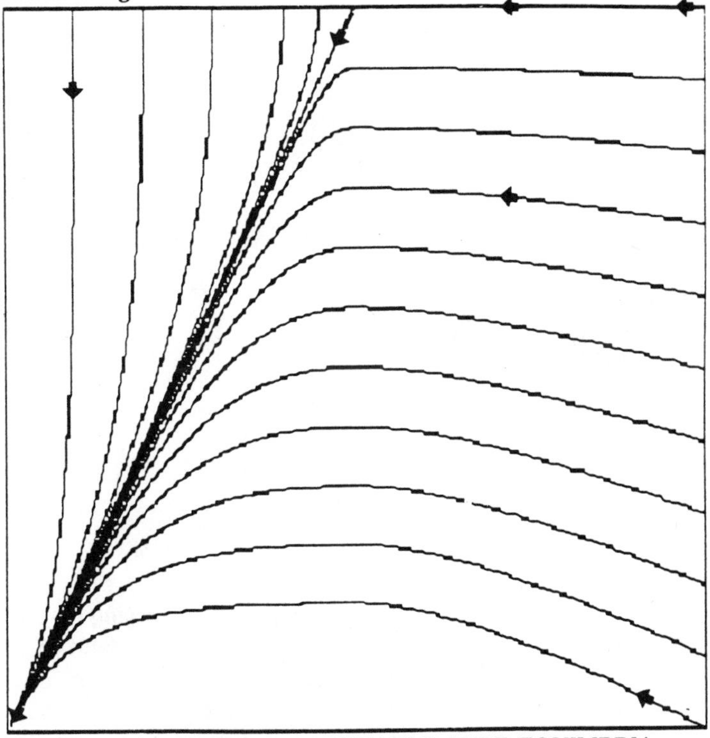

figure 5: STABLE and UNSTABLE PURE EQUILIBRIA

This game has two equilibria: one at [0,0] and one at [1,1]. The equilibrium at [0,0] is strongly stable; that at [1,1] is highly unstable (an "unstable star"). Every point other than itself converges to [1,1].

On the other hand, the game plotted in figure 6 has a unique equilibrium at [.5,.5] which, under Nash dynamics is a strongly stable spiral point. Its payoff matrix is:

[1,0]   [0,1]
[0,1]   [1,0]

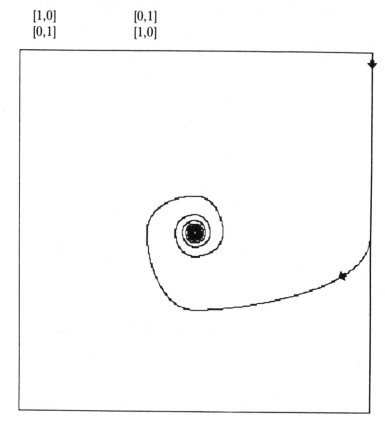

figure 6: STABLE MIXED EQUILIBRIUM

Figure 6 shows the orbit originating at [1,1] and converging to [.5,.5]. It should be noted, however, that this example does depend on the Nash dynamics in a way that the others don't. There are other continuous dynamical rules which seek the good under which [.5,.5] is not strongly stable.[13] The analysis of this game is therefore not

as *robust* over variations in the dynamical adaptive rule as that of
the previous game or of Chicken. Nevertheless, enough has been said
to show that in a setting of deliberational dynamics one can have both
highly stable and highly unstable equilibria in both pure and mixed
acts, and that qualitative dynamics offers resources for the classification of equilibria that are of real game theoretic interest.

There is another kind of dynamical stability that is of interest. That
is stability of the location and type of equilibrium points as the
parameters of the differential (or difference) equations are varied.
This means varying the payoffs of the game, while the adaptive
dynamical rule is kept constant. I will illustrate with game theoretic
models of the arms race. Political Philosophers often model the arms
race as Prisoner's Dilemma, with payoffs:

$$[-5,-5] \qquad [5,-10]$$
$$[-10,5] \qquad [0,0]$$

The Nash dynamics is plotted in figure 7:

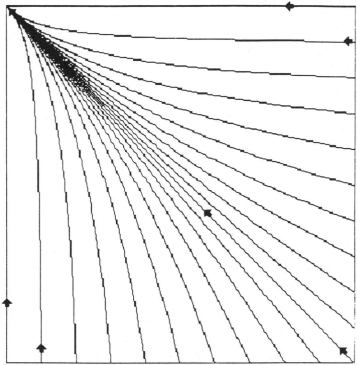

figure 7: PRISONERS' DILEMMA

Deliberational dynamics inexorably carries every point in the space to the tragic strong equilibrium of both sides deciding to arm. But, at least in some arms races, some generals and some politicians may think that the proper model of the arms race is not Prisoner's Dilemma, but rather Chicken. The disagreement is about the relative values of D and R in the payoff matrix:

[D,D]   [5,R]
[R,5]   [0,0]

With $D = -5$, $R = -10$ we have prisoner's dilemma; with $D = -10$ and $R = -5$ we have Chicken. With $D = R = -10$ we have a transition game with payoff matrix:

[-10,-10]   [5,-10]
[-10,5]   [0,0]

which is plotted in figure 8.

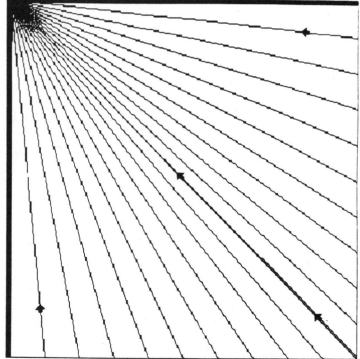

figure 8: TRANSITION from PRISONERS' DILEMMA to CHICKEN

Figure 8 looks much like the portrait of Prisoner's Dilemma in figure 7, but there are some subtle changes. Now there are additional (unstable) equilibria in pure acts at [0,0] and [1,1] and additional (unstable) equilibria in mixed acts at x=0, y<1 and at y=1, x>0. This is indicated in the figure by emboldening these lines. The equilibrium at [0,1] is still stable, but no longer strongly stable for it is not an attractor for orbits of the aforementioned mixed equilibrium points. If D is allowed to creep a little below R, then we have the Birth of Chicken, as depicted in figure 9. The payoff matrix is:

$$[-10.5,-10.5] \qquad [5,-10]$$
$$[-10,5] \qquad\qquad [0,0]$$

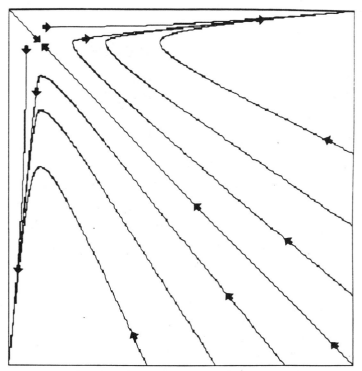

figure 9: The BIRTH of CHICKEN

There is now a dramatic change. The equilibrium point formerly at [0,1] moves down the diagonal and changes from a stable equilibrium to a saddle point. The equilibria at [0,0] and [1,1] change from unstable to strongly stable. They are now attractors for the orbits of almost all points in the space. The former mixed equilibria on $x=0$ and on $y=1$ have vanished. We have passed through the Better R than D Bifurcation.

We plot the equilibrium points as a function of decreasing D, in figure 10.

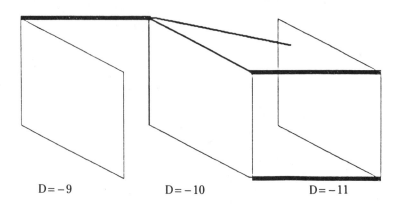

$D=-9$ $D=-10$ $D=-11$

figure 10: The BETTER R than D BIFURCATION

Other transitions are of interest. Consider a Dove's model of the arms race. The dove may well believe that the payoff in the case of mutual disarmament is greater than the payoff in the case in which her country arms and the other doesn't. After all, arming diverts economic resources and may tempt her own country's political leaders into adventures they had best not undertake. Thus, she thinks that in the payoff matrix:

[D,D]	[5,R]
[R,5]	[P,P]

P should be greater than 5. Figure 11 shows the transition from Prisoner's Dilemma to the Dove model with $D=-5$; $R=-10$; $P=5.5$.

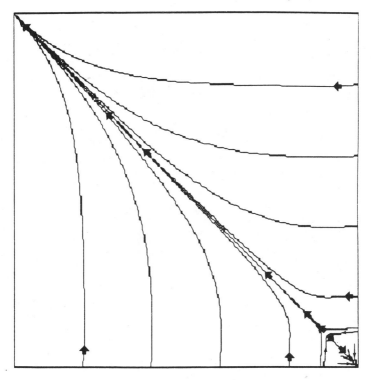

figure 11: The BIRTH of DOVE

A tiny window of hope has opened in the lower right corner. It is bounded by a hyperbolic equilibrium on the [0,1]-[1.0] diagonal. Orbits of points in its interior are attracted to a new stable equilibrium in the lower right corner. If the players come to this game with enough prior good will to put the initial point in the window, they will be carried to this equilibrium. This Dove game is also a test of will.

All of these models (and other variations that may suggest themselves to you) may be reasonable models for arms races in various situations. It is therefore of some real interest to investigate the dramatic changes in deliberational equilibria which can occur as the payoffs are continuously varied.

5. *Conclusion*: If we pay attention to the flow of information during deliberation, rather than idealizing it away, deliberation becomes a dynamic process. A Bayesian theory of deliberation results from

the interplay of considerations of bounded rationality with the expected utility principle. This theory provides a Bayesian foundation for the Nash equilibrium concept, and allows techniques of qualitative dynamics to be applied in the study of equilibria.

There is much more to be said. Deliberational dynamics has a straightforward generalization to games in extensive form, with interesting consequences. And the strongly idealized common knowledge assumptions I have used to derive the connection with the Nash equilibrium concept can be weakened in various ways, again with interesting consequences. If fact, I believe that in the Bayesian scheme of things, classical game theory should have the status of a very special case. These are topics, however, that will have to wait for a more extended exposition.

We have perhaps said enough, however, to indicate that the expected utility principle and the equilibrium principle need not be in conflict, nor need they be relegated to different domains. Rather, the expected utility principle serves as the foundation for the equilibrium principle, under those idealizing assumptions on which the equilibrium principle is justified.

Notes

1. Research partially supported by NSF grant SES-8605122. I wish to thank Michael Teit Nielsen for pointing out a flaw in an earlier version of this paper.
2. So much so that in his comprehensive survey of the subject, Shubik (1982) p. 2 can write:

    The general n-person game postulates a separate "free will" for each of the contending parties and is therefore indeterminate. To be sure, there are limiting cases, which game theorists call "inessential games" in which the indeterminacy can be resolved satisfactorily by applying the familiar principle of self-seeking utility maximization for individual rationality. But there is no principle of societal rationality, of comparable resolving power, that can cope with the "essential game", and none is in sight. Instead, deep seated paradoxes, challenging our intuitive ideas of what kind of behavior should be called "rational" crop up on all sides, as soon as we cross the line from "inessential" to "essential".

3. See the discussion in my "The Value of Knowledge" forthcoming.
4. We are in the realm of what I.J. Good calls "Dynamic Probability".

5. For example, Suppes (1984) writes: "In a competitive environment where we are competing with another intelligent agent, by randomizing and thus making our behavior unpredictable at the level of explicit choice we can guarantee ourselves a best possible result in the sense of minimizing our expected loss.

   It is difficult for Bayesians to accept such results. For a pure Bayesian, in every situation he has an optimal deterministic strategy that will maximize his expected utility-or minimize his expected loss. The weakness of the Bayesian position is that the probability distribution expressing beliefs about an opponent's expected choice of moves often represents very infirm ideas about what the opponent is going to do. In such situations, prudence should rightly overrule purity, and a random minimax strategy should be adopted."

   If I am correct in maintaining that Bayesian first principles motivate Bayesian deliberational dynamics, then there is a sense in which purity entails prudence.

   See also the related discussion in Harper (forthcoming b).
6. From Skyrms (1982).
7. See Goldstein (1983) and Skyrms (1987a,b)(forthcoming a,b).
8. This is more general that the treatment in section VI of my "Deliberational Equilibria" wherein the "autonomy" requirement is that I be a function from x' to y'. It is nevertheless a requirement that one might want to ultimately relax in order to let the next point $<x',y'>$ be a function of the whole previous orbit rather than just the preceding personal state.
9. The relativization to y is required because we do not require y to be a function of x, as it is in the special case of updating by probability kinematics on the acts. It is possible that there may be two personal states with the same x but different y, such the x is ratifiable in $<x,y>$ but not in $<x',y'>$.
10. Thus the theorem and corollary of sections V, VI of Skyrms (1986) are special cases.
11. Each player knows it, and each player knows that the others know it, etc. See Lewis (1969) and Aumann (1976). The treatment here must be procedural rather that model theoretic as in Aumann's version of knowledge conditional on a partition, to allow for the role of computation in generating new knowledge.
12. See Percival and Richards [1982] and, at a more abstract level, Smale [1980] for further discussion on the classification of fixed points of dynamics.
13. For Example, under the "Aristotelian Dynamics" described in Skyrms [1986], orbits are circles centered at [.5,.5] so the equilibrium is stable but not strongly stable.

References

Aumann, R. J. (1976) "Agreeing to Disagree" *The Annals of Statistics* 4, 1236-1239.

Eells. E. (1984) "Metatickles and the Dynamics of Deliberation" *Theory and Decision* 17, 71-95.

Goldstein, M. (1983) "The Prevision of a Prevision" *Journal of the American Statistical Association* 78, 817-819.

Good, I. J. (1967) "On the Principle of Total Evidence" *British Journal for the Philosophy of Science* 17, 319-321.

Good, I. J. (1977) "Dynamic Probability, Computer Chess, and the Measurement of Knowledge" in *Machine Intelligence* 8 ed. E. W. Elcock and D. Michie (John Wiley: New York) 139-150.

Harper, W. (1986) "Mixed Strategies and Ratifiability in Causal Decision Theory" *Erkenntniss* 24, 25-36.

Harper, W. (forthcoming a) "Ratifiability and Causal Decision Theory: Comments on Eells and Seidenfeld" in *PSA 1984* (Philosophy of Science Association: East Lansing, Michigan).

Harper, W. (forthcoming b) "Causal Decision Theory and Game Theory" in *Probability and Causation* ed. W. Harper and B. Skyrms.

Harsanyi, J. C. (1975) "The Tracing Procedure: A Bayesian Approach to Defining a Solution concept for n-person Non-cooperative Games" *International Journal of Game Theory* 4 (1975) 61-94.

Jeffrey, R. C. (1981) "*The Logic of Decision* Defended" *Synthese* 48, 437-492.

Jeffrey, R. C. (1983) *The Logic of Decision* 2nd ed (University of Chicago Press: Chicago).

Lewis, D. (1969) *Convention* (Harvard University Press: Cambridge).

Luce, R. D. and Raiffa, H. (1957) *Games and Decisions* (John Wiley: New York).

Percival, I. and Richards, D. (1982) *Introduction to Dynamics* (Cambridge University Press: Cambridge).

Shubik, M. (1982) *Game Theory in the Social Sciences* (MIT Press: Cambridge, Mass.).

Simon, H. (1957) *Models of Man* (Wiley: New York).

Skyrms, B. (1982) "Causal Decision Theory" *Journal of Philosophy* 79 695-711.

Skyrms, B. (1984) *Pragmatics and Empiricism* (Yale Press: New Haven).

Skyrms, B. (1986) "Deliberational Equilibria" *Topoi* 1 59-67.

Skyrms, B. (1987a) "Coherence" in *Scientific Inquiry in Philosophical Perspective* ed N. Rescher (University of Pittsburgh Press: Pittsburgh) 225-242.

Skyrms, B. (1987b) "Dynamic Coherence" in *Advances in the Statistical Sciences: Vol. II Foundations of Statistical Inference* ed. I.B. MacNeill and G. Umphrey (Reidel: Dordrecht).

Skyrms, B. (forthcoming a) "Dynamic Coherence and Probability Kinematics" *Philosophy of Science.*

Skyrms, B. (forthcoming b) "The Value of Knowledge" in *Justification, Discovery and the Evolution of Scientific Theories* ed. C. W. Savage (University of Minnesota Press: Minneapolis).

Skyrms, B. (forthcoming c) "On the Principle of Total Evidence with and without Observation Sentences" in *Proceedings of the 11th International Wittgenstein Symposium*.

Smale, S. (1980) *The Mathematics of Time* (Springer: New York, Berlin, Heidelberg).

Spohn, W. (1982) "How to Make Sense of Game Theory" in *Studies in Contemporary Economics: vol 2 Philosophy of Economics* ed. W.Stegmuller et. al. (Springer: New York, Heidelberg, Berlin).

Suppes, P. (1984) *Probabilistic Metaphysics* (Basil Blackwell: Oxford).

von Neumann, J. and Morgenstern, O. (1947) *Theory of Games and Economic Behavior* (Princeton University Press: Princeton).

Philosophical Perspectives, 2, Epistemology, 1988

VICIOUS INFINITE REGRESS ARGUMENTS[1]

Romane Clark
Indiana University

Surprisingly, vicious infinite regress arguments seem to be exclusively philosophical arguments. They do not occur in the history or current practice of mathematics, or the law, for instance.[2] They do not occur on editorial pages or in the Sunday Supplements. It seems natural then to conclude that these arguments are not arguments displaying some unique, universally valid pattern of formal inference. This conclusion is reinforced by the practice of logicians. In the way in which, say, Indirect Derivation is separately codified, and semantically justified, in standard logic texts and treatises,[3] we lack in them any discussion, codification, or justification of "derivation by *vicious* infinite regress."

This curious parochialism in turn suggests that regress arguments do not so much constitute a general type of reasoning, whether valid or not, as share some special, philosophical, sort of content. But, thinking about it, that, too, seems implausible. After all, instances of vicious infinite regress arguments range from remote causal, cosmological ones occurring in the history of metaphysics on down to justificatory, foundational ones which occur in contemporary epistemology. Where, we wonder, is the shared, common content to be found in applications as diverse as these?

Given all this, it might be thought that what's special about regress arguments is to be found elsewhere.[4] Showing that some thesis implies a vicious infinite regress shows that there's something wrong with it all right. But what is wrong is not necessarily a matter of logical form or special content. There are after all lots of bad arguments. But not all of these are deductively invalid. Quite to the contrary, some of these are not only deductively valid but even sound. Perhaps theses which imply a vicious infinite regress are like these.

Circular arguments, arguments that beg the question, successions of explanations that deteriorate into trivial repetitions of the same conditional justifications, each of these may involve reasoning which is logically valid. But each of these is nonetheless in other ways quite unacceptable. Each of these flouts one or more of the requirements which govern those underlying acts of informing or persuading which motivate the giving, and are ordinarily discharged in the making, of arguments and explanations. The requirements which are flouted by these arguments are pragmatic or dialectical requirements, not formal or semantical ones.

(Thus, for instance, an argument which assumes what is to be proved goes wrong, but not because the reasoning is not truth-preserving. It goes wrong because whatever need or point there might have been to motivate the production of the proof in the first place is merely transferred to, and so remains undischarged in, the conclusion's pleonastic occurrence as its own premise.)

Theses which imply a vicious infinite regress might be thought to be like these familiar informal fallacies. Valid regress arguments might be thought to show that the thesis which implies its regress also fails for dialectical reasons. Professor Rosenberg, for instance, thought so. Recently, in an introductory text, using as an illustration the thesis that an act is voluntary only if it is the result of an act of will, he wrote this:[5]

> It must, in fact, be a *voluntary* act of will. And if this is so, we haven't been given an answer to our original question. We can only understand *this* answer if we already know what makes an act of will voluntary. But our question is, What makes an act of will voluntary? The only course open to us is to apply the theory again. When we do so, however, all we find is that we need yet another *voluntary* act of will. The question does not go away.
>
> **That is the essence of the criticism. The question does not go away. This is what makes the challenge dialectical rather than logical**. It disqualifies the proposed answer *as an answer* for something qualifies as an answer to

a question only if one can understand it without already knowing the answer to the question. The philosopher who offers this answer, therefore, **violates a canon of rational practice**. [Rosenberg's italics; my boldface.]

The main problem with all this, however, is that while the illustration is meant to have general import, it is not at all clear how to generalize the account.[6] More important, it is not clear that it *can* correctly be generalized.

For one thing, we still lack in the example any explanation or understanding of that puzzling parochialism which initiated our discussion. We don't yet understand why it is that regress arguments seem limited to philosophical theses. After all, arguments that beg the question, and circular explanations, have also been held to violate certain of the dialectical presuppositions which govern the contexts of their production. But these arguments and explanations are not limited in subject matter. Question-begging arguments and circular explanations are not limited to philosophy. Why should it be all that different for vicious infinite regress arguments?

More important is the fact that not all regresses even seem to have dialectical import. In soliloquy I ruminate on a philosophical thesis. I wonder perhaps whether each distinct event must have a distinct prior event as its cause. My silent concern is a metaphysical one. My concern is about the natural order of things. It is about an order which I suppose to be quite independent of my present thought, or of possible later discussions, or of the existence or nature of consciousness at all. Perhaps, rightly or wrongly, I conclude, on pain of a vicious infinite regress, that there must be some initial and initiating uncaused event, a philosophical "big-bang".

If I reason in this way, the implication of my conclusion is not that the original thesis is trivial, or insufficiently persuasive, or in yet some other way dialectically flawed. It is that the original thesis is false. I do not reject the thesis for dialectical reasons. Nor are dialectical constraints flouted, or operative, or even present in my coming to believe what I do. The process I go through, reasoning as I here do, is not a social process.

Evidently, not all occurrences of vicious infinite regress arguments are literally dialectical occurrences. And not all vicious infinite regress arguments involve unending *processes* (as distinct from infinite sequences of elements.[7]) And not all are epistemological, involving justification, or explanation, or the acquisition or exchange of information.

These things being so, it is at the very least not obvious that a dialectical characterization of vicious infinite regress arguments is a sufficiently general characterization of them.

But there is by contrast an obvious, relevant, but absolutely general fact about these arguments. The fact is that they are, all of them, cases of indirect argument. Philosophers who have reasoned in this way have in each instance provisionally adopted some target thesis in order to discredit it. They have in each instance attempted to show that the thesis implies something which could only obtain if the thesis itself were false. Vicious infinite regress arguments are, all of them, instances of a special kind of *reductio ad absurdum*.

It is this obvious but general fact which helps us to understand why it is that there is no need for a special form of derivation, no need for special codification or semantical justification to be separately laid down for vicious infinite regress arguments. None of these in fact exists. But none is separately required, for vicious infinite regress arguments are a special case, a species, of what already exists. They are thus already implicitly characterized by the generic standard formal representation, already at hand, of Indirect Derivation.3

Valid instances of Indirect Derivation, however, are crucially dependent upon a demonstration of a contradiction. But not all (of the often enthymematic) occurrences of vicious infinite regress arguments familiar from the philosophical literature explicitly issue in one. It is true that these familiar philosophical arguments are each evidently a case of *reductio ad absurdum*. Each is aimed at the rejection of some target thesis. But as instances of a species of Indirect Derivation in particular, these rejections must, in full formal representation, be explicitly based upon some demonstration of an overt contradiction. What is special about valid infinite regress arguments as instances of species of *reductio* is the derivation of an infinite regress. But what is not clear is how, if at all, the regress in turn figures in delivering the required contradiction.

The underlying intuition, of course, is that anything whose existence not merely implies but is exclusively dependent upon an infinite succession of similar elements for which there is no independent existence proof does not after all exist. It does not flatly, categorically exist. It only conditionally does so. A foundationalist, for instance, may admit that a proposition which is only inferentially justified has a justi*fication* all right. What he denies, however, is that it is thereby justi*fied*. Justification may only be preserved, may only be conveyed but not conferred, by an inferential process.[8] A proposition which is only inferentially justified is, a foundationalist may say, only conditionally justified. It is not flatly, unconditionally, categorically so. It is possible for a proposition to have a justification without being justified.

One problem in trying to give consistent expression to this underlying intuition is that we lack resources within standard logic for distinguishing implication and dependence. Even so it is possible to capture a bit of the motivating idea without all that. Let us say that something is *conditionally* F just in case there is something to which it stands in an F-preserving relation R which induces a partial order. That is, R must itself be, or imply the existence of, an asymmetrical and transitive relation which orders the entities which R relates.[9] And R must preserve the property F in the sense that if an entity stands in that relation to entities which are F, then it, too, is F. (I.e., R is "upward F-preserving." Things may of course stand in a relation which is F-preserving without being F.)

If this is the only way a thing comes to be F, if something is *only* conditionally F, then, with respect to F, it is *downward dependent* on its R-related heredity.

By contrast, let us say that something is *categorically* F just in case it is F but not only conditionally so.

In these terms, vicious infinite regress arguments from the philosophical literature are (often enthyematic) instances of a special version of Indirect Derivation. This is a version of Indirect Derivation which is special only in exploiting an infinite regress in its derivation of a contradiction.

The typical infinite regress argument is an instance of a schematic pattern which runs like this:

Something in fact has some attribute, F. (This is a line already at hand in the derivation, one which is not at the point of the *reductio* itself in question. We have independent of and serving as a premise for the present Indirect argument that something, **a** perhaps, is F. We have perhaps that a *voluntary* act has occurred; or that a certain proposition is *justified*; or that an individual *has, instances,* a property. **a**'s being F is accordingly a detached, finitely derived line of the derivation; it is an unconditional, categorical assertion. **a**'s being F implies that **a** is categorically F.)

A target thesis, TF, about the nature or presence of F is assumed for the Indirect Derivation. (We assume perhaps that an occurrence of a voluntary act must be preceded by a voluntary act of will; or that a proposition is justified only if it is inferentially justified; or that whatever has a property must exemplify it, where exemplification is itself a relation and relations are multi-termed properties. Assuming things like these, we seek to derive a contradiction; to establish that, after all, the target thesis, TF, is not the case.)

The unique thing about vicious infinite regress arguments, as the special sort of Indirect Derivation which they are, consists we know in the derivation of a certain infinite regress from the thesis TF. The thesis, TF, to complete the proof, must be shown to imply that nothing is F unless there exists an infinite succession of elements, ones which stand in an "upward F-preserving relation," RF, and each of which is downward dependent upon its R-heredity. TF might for instance imply something of this form:

$$(x)[F(x) \text{ only if } (\exists y)(Fy \ \& \ R(x,y)],$$

where R is some suitable asymmetrical and transitive relation. That is, it must be possible to demonstrate that the thesis together with an instance of F would, like the inset formula above, imply the existence of an infinite succession of elements each member of which is only conditionally F. Since the target thesis implies that nothing is F unless a member of this sequence, whatever is F is at most only conditionally so.

This conclusion, by a simple Separation of Cases, is inconsistent with that earlier line, not itself in question, which implies that something is categorically F. Vicious infinite regress arguments of this form are thus special but valid instances of standard Indirect Derivation.

This characterization of vicious infinite regress arguments is capable of some generalization. Not every thesis, TF, which is subject to a valid vicious infinite regress argument, implies a simple linear infinite succession. Some, like those laying down conditions for the justification of belief, may permit or require downward branching. Multiple propositions of higher rank may communally participate in the justification of some given proposition of lower rank; and some of higher rank may even participate in the justification of more than one proposition of lower rank.[10] (Justification may not necessarily consist in a simple tree, but in a possibly tangled hedge of further interlocking, justifications. On the other hand, sometimes even a tree may consist in just a single branch.)

The important thing for the application of the regress argument is just that the target thesis implies there to be embedded in the justificatory tangle an infinite tree which, relative to its initial proposition, can be isolated and explicitly defined, and which is such that any element at any node of higher rank on any arbitrary branch of the tree is RF related to at most one element of the next lower rank *of that branch*. (If there is none such, the element of "higher" rank is in fact an initial element occurring at the origin of the tree.) We know by a theorem due to Beth[11] that an infinite tree must have at least one unending, infinite branch. It is to such a branch that the regress argument can be applied and in terms of which its generalization can be stated.

'a is *conditionally* F' can be redefined "semantically" as stating that a occurs at a node of an infinite "Beth-branch," BF, of an infinite tree.

The argument, now applied to such a tree, runs as before. We have as before an earlier line of the derivation, finitely derived and not itself in question, that **a** is F. This is to say in the present, semantic idiom, that 'a is F' has an occurrence in a finite branch of the tree.

As before, a target thesis, TF, is assumed for a *reductio ad absurdum* argument.

The target thesis, TF, must as before make it demonstrable that nothing is F unless it occurs at a node of the infinite Beth-branch, BF. It entails thus that whatever is F is only conditionally F. But this is inconsistent with **a**'s being categorically F and occurring at some node of some distinct and finite branch.

It is possible, I think, plausibly to construe many of the vicious infinite regress arguments familiar to us from the philosophical literature as enthymematic instances of a species of Indirect Derivation like this. Construed in this way, the reasoning which underlies these arguments is perfectly cogent. But even so, it is not at all clear that these arguments are compelling. Everything turns now on the truth of their premises, and these are themselves often philosophically contentious. Vicious infinite regress arguments, like any argument, may perfectly well be valid but not sound.

This is not to say, however, that such an infinite regress argument is valid but not sound when the regress generated is "benign" rather than "vicious." If an infinite regress which is generated with respect to a target thesis, TF, does not yield an infinite succession ordered by a relation which is upward F-preserving, the members of which are downward-dependent, then the regress is not vicious but benign. And if the regress is not vicious, then the argument is not only not a sound vicious infinite regress argument, it is not even a valid one. It is not a *vicious infinite regress* argument at all. (None of this is to deny that benign regresses may occur in valid arguments, and even in valid instances of (other forms of) Indirect Derivation.)

Philosophical protagonists we know often fail to join issue. A justificatory infinite regress may pull us in two directions. The Mr. Flip inside us may note that each proposition at any stage in an infinite branch of an unending justificatory tree has its justification. Accordingly, since a simple induction establishes that every proposition in the branch has a justi*fication*, an infinite series of them is not, it seems, vicious and so Foundationalism has not been established. But the Mr. Flop within us may in turn point out that at each stage of the infinite justificatory branch there is a proposition which is un-justi*fied*. There is always then some "last," unjustified proposition. But since earlier stages depend for their justification upon later ones, the regress does indeed after all seem to be vicious.

Despite appearances, there is no clash of incompatibilities here. There is no demonstration of the unsoundness of a vicious regress argument. For there are two distinct regresses involved in all this. Each protagonist correctly draws a conclusion appropriate to one of these. One of the regresses is benign; the other is indeed vicious. Flip takes the infinite justificatory branch to be a sequence of propositions each of which has the property of having a justification. It is a sequence generated by the thesis that a proposition has a justification only if there exists a distinct proposition to which it stands in some asymmetrical and transitive relation which preserves justification.

Flop takes the infinite justificatory branch to be a sequence of propositions no one of which has the property being justified. It is a sequence generated by the thesis that a proposition is justified only if there exists a distinct justified proposition to which it stands in some asymmetrical and transitive relation which preserves justification.

Flip generates a benign regress, one in which no element of the sequence is downward dependent upon its heredity. The base case of its justifying induction is finitely and separately provable. It is easy to find or define a suitable justification-preserving relation (perhaps a qualified form of implication) such that for each proposition there provably exists another to which it stands in this relation.[12] All this is quite compatible with the tug we feel to our Flop side. For all of this, a proposition may indeed have, in the Flip sense, a justification and yet also be, in the Flop sense, unjustified. The presence of benign regress like this shows nothing at all about the existence, validity or soundness of a vicious infinite regress.

Flop's regress is, by contrast, both infinite and vicious. Each proposition of the sequence is only conditionally justified; each is downward-dependent upon its unending heredity. One can not establish inductively that the propositions of the sequence are justified. There is, and on Flop's interpretation of the target thesis there can be, no base case demonstration and no demonstration of the inductive step to establish this. There are, on that thesis, only conditionally justified propositions. The thesis is inconsistent with the existence of any categorically justified proposition at all. Flop's argument is a valid infinite regress argument, one quite compatible with Flip's benign but accommodative sense of a proposition's having a justification. The existence of the latter does not show that former is unsound.

Showing that a vicious infinite regress argument is invalid is typically a matter of showing that its target thesis, TF, in conjunction with an instance of F, does not after all imply the existence of an infinite sequence of downward-dependent entities. Showing that a valid vicious infinite regress argument, directed against some target thesis, TF, is unsound is typically a matter of showing that to assert that there is a categorical instance of F is either to assert something false or question-begging.

"No one is a human being unless the biological offspring of humans."[13] Is this true? In these days of exploding biological technologies one may feel a certain prudential tentativeness in the face of a general claim like this. But there are sharper reasons for rejecting the claim as well. The thesis is incompatible with there categorically being any humans like you or me at all. Under natural characterizations of the concept of being a biological offspring of humans, the underlying generating relation preserves the property of being a human and the thesis ensures that human beings are downward-dependent for their humanity upon (the infinite succession of) their ancestors. This is to say that the thesis generates a vicious infinite regress.

One can accept the validity of the argument but maintain the thesis. One can reject the soundness of the argument but at a price. One must deny then that anyone manifests a separate, non-conditional but finitely determinable property of being a human. One must deny that an assertion of our palpable, actual human existence, is when properly understood, really a flat, categorical assertion of our human existence. Properly understood in these rather invidious terms, it will need to be said that we are, all of us, only "conditionally human."

Many of us, accepting as we do both evolutionary theory and the historical record as it comes to us, find the implication of an infinite succession of human generations too costly. The vicious infinite regress argument, we think, is not only valid but sound. The target thesis, naively plausible as it seems, is, we think, false. It would be nice of course to nail things down. It would be nice to pierce the mists of history and date man's emergence from the slime. It is not necessary however that it even be possible to do so. There may always remain a gray area of indeterminacy. But even so, we know enough about life before and after the initial records of human existence to accept the argument and reject the thesis. In actual fact, knowing these things, we reject the thesis even without the formal argument.

All this returns us to our initial puzzle. At the beginning, we were struck by the fact that vicious infinite regress arguments seem to be largely or wholly philosophical arguments. We have since urged that these arguments are a species of a perfectly familiar and quite standard form of inference, Indirect Derivation. What is special about the species is the way in which the contradiction necessary for the *reductio* is achieved. It depends upon the generation of a certain type of infinite succession of elements, one in which the existence of initial elements are dependent upon the unending succession of later ones. So there is after all a certain common, albeit formal, content which is unique to the diverse instances of vicious infinite regress arguments which have come to us. These infinite regresses, whether historical or contemporary, epistemological or metaphysical, silently or socially produced, are each the basis for a special sort of universal negative conclusion. Whatever can only be conditionally thus-and-so is not thus-and-so.

It is not necessary but it is natural that arguments of this sort tend to be philosophical arguments. Dealing in infinite totalities is already a fairly exotic sort of enterprise. (It is not, e.g., the common stuff of politics or the law.) Dealing in infinite sequences without the possibility of establishing a relevant base case for an inductive argument, is a pretty restricted sort of task. (It is not, e.g., the typical mathematical sort of task.) Drawing a universal negative conclusion, where there can be no theory-independent fact of the matter, is not ordinarily a matter of common science, or common sense.

It is understandable then that while there might, logically, be vicious infinite regress arguments which are not philosophical, we do not find them and it remains plausible, I think, to construe the philosophical regress arguments we do know, as common instances of a quite special form of Indirect Derivation.

Notes

1. I have learned the most from, and have been most influenced on this topic by Day [2], Moser [5], and Sanford [8]. Their fine works contain in turn further references to other important discussions of this subject.
2. At least they do not seem to on casual investigation. It would be nice to have some authoritative study to support or discredit this, but I don't know of any.
3. See, e.g., Kalish & Montague [4], pp. 20-25.
4. Rosenberg takes this line in his [7] and John Passmore seems to in his discussion of philosophical arguments. On this, see Day [2].
5. [7], p. 62.
6. Day [2] and other authors have drawn a kind of "process/product" distinction among regresses, contrasting infinite progressions of items with unending tasks.

   In fact, of course, we lack anything like an interesting (let alone complete) list of "the canons of rational practice," or theoretical discussion of their basic properties. That is an important separate problem. Perhaps what can be said here is that it isn't at all obvious that the reason, on Rosenberg's analysis, that "the question doesn't go away" is not based in formal properties of the argument.
7. *Ibid.*
8. See, e.g., Harker [3], Moser [5], Chs. 1 and 4, and Post [6].
9. Sanford [8], p. 110, notes that an ordering relation, like that of being one inch taller, while not itself transitive may imply the presence of one that is, like that of simply being taller.
10. This is a point which Raymundo Morado stressed in an earlier discussion of this characterization of regress arguments.
11. [1], sec. 69, pp. 194-196.
12. Several authors have stressed the triviality of this justification relation, see e.g. Harker, and Post, *op. cit.* Flip does overall go wrong. He goes wrong in providing an account that is too true to be good; one which fails to be sufficiently discriminating in an interesting way. Every con-

tingent proposition has, in his sense, a justification. But he does not go wrong in developing a benign regress. His is not an instance of a valid but, since his regress is benign, unsound vicious infinite regress argument. Rather, his is a valid instance of straightforward inductive argument concerning a rather trivial property.

13. See Sanford's discussion of *"Series that Do Not Terminate because They Trail off Gradually,"* [8], 113-115.

References

[1]   Beth, E. W., *The Foundations of Mathematics*, North-Holland Publishing Co., Amsterdam, 1968.

[2]   Day, Timothy, *Infinite Regress Arguments: Some Metaphysical and Epistemological Problems*, Doctoral Dissertation, Indiana University, 1986.

[3]   Harker, Jay E., "Can There Be an Infinite Regress of Justified Beliefs?," *Australasian Journal of Philosophy*, 62, no. 3, (September 1984) 255-264.

[4]   Kalish & Montague, *Logic: Techniques of Formal Reasoning*, 2nd ed., Harcourt Brace Jovanovich, Inc., New York, 1980.

[5]   Moser, Paul K., *Empirical Justification*, D. Reidel Publishing Co., Dordecht, 1985.

[6]   Post, John F., "Infinite Regresses of Justification and Explanation," *Philosophical Studies*, 38, (1980) 31-52.

[7]   Rosenberg, Jay F., *The Practice of Philosophy*, 2nd ed., Prentice-Hall, Inc., Englewood Cliffs, N.J., 1984.

[8]   Sanford, David, "Infinite Regress Arguments," in Fetzer, Ch. 5, *Principles of Philosophical Reasoning*, 93-117.

Philosophical Perspectives, 2, Epistemology, 1988

WHAT IS "NATURALIZED EPISTEMOLOGY?"

Jaegwon Kim
Brown University

1. Epistemology As a Normative Inquiry

Descartes' epistemological inquiry in the *Meditations* begins with this question: What propositions are worthy of belief? In the *First Meditation* Descartes canvasses beliefs of various kinds he had formerly held as true and finds himself forced to conclude that he ought to reject them, that he ought not to accept them as true. We can view Cartesian epistemology as consisting of the following two projects: to identify the criteria by which we ought to regulate acceptance and rejection of beliefs, and to determine what we may be said to know according to those criteria. Descartes' epistemological agenda has been the agenda of Western epistemology to this day. The twin problems of identifying criteria of justified belief and coming to terms with the skeptical challenge to the possibility of knowledge have defined the central tasks of theory of knowledge since Descartes. This was as true of the empiricists, of Locke and Hume and Mill, as of those who more closely followed Descartes in the rationalist path.[1]

It is no wonder then that modern epistemology has been dominated by a single concept, that of *justification*, and two fundamental questions involving it: What conditions must a belief meet if we are justified in accepting it as true? and What beliefs are we in fact justified in accepting? Note that the first question does not ask for an "analysis" or "meaning" of the term "justified belief". And it is generally assumed, even if not always explicitly stated, that not just any statement of a necessary and sufficient condition for a belief to be justified will do. The implicit requirement has been that the stated conditions must constitute "criteria" of justified belief, and for this it is necessary that the conditions be stated *without the use of epistemic terms*. Thus, formulating conditions of justified belief in such terms as "adequate evidence", "sufficient ground", "good reason", "beyond a reasonable doubt", and so on, would be merely to issue a promissory note redeemable only when these epistemic terms are themselves explained in a way that accords with the requirement.[2]

This requirement, while it points in the right direction, does not go far enough. What is crucial is this: *the criteria of justified belief must be formulated on the basis of descriptive or naturalistic terms alone, without the use of any evaluative or normative ones, whether epistemic or of another kind*.[3] Thus, an analysis of justified belief that makes use of such terms as "intellectual requirement"[4] and "having a right to be sure"[5] would not satisfy this generalized condition; although such an analysis can be informative and enlightening about the inter-relationships of these normative concepts, it will not, on the present conception, count as a statement of *criteria* of justified belief, unless of course these terms are themselves provided with nonnormative criteria. What is problematic, therefore, about the use of epistemic terms in stating criteria of justified belief is not its possible circularity in the usual sense; rather it is the fact that these epistemic terms are themselves essentially normative. We shall later discuss the rationale of this strengthened requirement.

As many philosophers have observed,[6] the two questions we have set forth, one about the criteria of justified belief and the other about what we can be said to know according to those criteria, constrain each other. Although some philosophers have been willing to swallow skepticism just because what we regard as correct criteria of justified belief are seen to lead inexorably to the conclusion that none, or very few, of our beliefs are justified, the usual presumption is that our answer to the first question should leave our epistemic situation largely unchanged. That is to say, it is expected to turn out that according to the criteria of justified belief we come to accept, we know, or are justified in believing, pretty much what we reflectively think we know or are entitled to believe.

Whatever the exact history, it is evident that the concept of justification has come to take center stage in our reflections on the nature of knowledge. And apart from history, there is a simple reason for our preoccupation with justification: it is the only specifically epistemic component in the classic tripartite conception of knowledge. Neither belief nor truth is a specifically epistemic notion: belief is a psychological concept and truth a semantical-metaphysical one. These concepts may have an implicit epistemological dimension, but if they do, it is likely to be through their involvement with essentially normative epistemic notions like justification, evidence, and rationality. Moreover, justification is what makes knowledge itself a normative concept. On surface at least, neither truth nor belief is normative or evaluative (I shall argue below, though, that belief does have an essential normative dimension). But justification manifestly is normative. If a belief is justified for us, then it is *permissible* and *reasonable*, from the epistemic point of view, for us to hold it, and it would be *epistemically irresponsible* to hold beliefs that contradict it. If we consider believing or accepting a proposition to be an "action" in an appropriate sense, belief justification would then be a special case of justification of action, which in its broadest terms is the central concern of normative ethics. Just as it is the business of normative ethics to delineate the conditions under which acts and decisions are justified from the moral point of view, so it is the business of epistemology to identify and analyze the conditions under which beliefs, and perhaps other propositional attitudes, are justified from the epistemological point of view. It probably is only an historical accident that we standardly speak of "normative ethics" but not of "normative epistemology". Epistemology is a normative discipline as much as, and in the same sense as, normative ethics.

We can summarize our discussion thus far in the following points: that justification is a central concept of our epistemological tradition, that justification, as it is understood in this tradition, is a normative concept, and in consequence that epistemology itself is a normative inquiry whose principal aim is a systematic study of the conditions of justified belief. I take it that these points are uncontroversial, although of course there could be disagreement about the details— for example, about what it means to say a concept or theory is "normative" or "evaluative".

2. The Foundationalist Strategy

In order to identify the target of the naturalistic critique—in particular, Quine's—it will be useful to take a brief look at the classic response to the epistemological program set forth by Descartes. Descartes' approach to the problem of justification is a familiar story, at least as the textbook tells it: it takes the form of what is now commonly called "foundationalism". The foundationalist strategy is to divide the task of explaining justification into two stages: first, to identify a set of beliefs that are "directly" justified in that they are justified without deriving their justified status from that of any other belief, and then to explain how other beliefs may be "indirectly" or "inferentially" justified by standing in an appropriate relation to those already justified. Directly justified beliefs, or "basic beliefs", are to constitute the foundation upon which the superstructure of "nonbasic" or "derived" beliefs is to rest. What beliefs then are directly justified, according to Descartes? Subtleties aside, he claimed that beliefs about our own present conscious states are among them. In what does their justification consist? What is it about these beliefs that make them directly justified? Somewhat simplistically again, Descartes' answer is that they are justified because they are *indubitable*, that the attentive and reflective mind *cannot but assent* to them. How are nonbasic beliefs justified? By "deduction"—that is, by a series of inferential steps, or "intuitions", each of which is indubitable. If, therefore, we take Cartesian indubitability as a psychological notion, Descartes' epistemological theory can be said to meet the desideratum of providing nonepistemic, naturalistic criteria of justified belief.

Descartes' foundationalist program was inherited, in its essential outlines, by the empiricists. In particular, his "mentalism", that beliefs about one's own current mental state are epistemologically basic, went essentially unchallenged by the empiricists and positivists, until this century. Epistemologists have differed from one another chiefly in regard to two questions: first, what else belonged in our corpus of basic beliefs, and second, how the derivation of the nonbasic part of our knowledge was to proceed. Even the Logical Positivists were, by and large, foundationalists, although some of them came to renounce Cartesian mentalism in favor of a "physicalistic basis".[7] In fact, the Positivists were foundationalists twice over: for them "observation", whether phenomenological or physical, served not only as the foundation of knowledge but as the foundation of all "cognitive meaning"—that is, as both an epistemological and a semantic foundation.

3. Quine's Arguments

It has become customary for epistemologists who profess allegiance to a "naturalistic" conception of knowledge to pay homage to Quine as the chief contemporary provenance of their inspiration—especially to his influential paper "Epistemology Naturalized".[8] Quine's principal argument in this paper against traditional epistemology is based on the claim that the Cartesian foundationalist program has failed—that the Cartesian "quest for certainty" is "a lost cause". While this claim about the hopelessness of the Cartesian "quest for certainty" is nothing new, using it to discredit the very conception of normative epistemology is new, something that any serious student of epistemology must contend with.

Quine divides the classic epistemological program into two parts: *conceptual reduction* whereby physical terms, including those of theoretical science, are reduced, via definition, to terms referring to phenomenal features of sensory experience, and *doctrinal reduction* whereby truths about the physical world are appropriately obtained from truths about sensory experience. The "appropriateness" just alluded to refers to the requirement that the favored epistemic status ("certainty" for classic epistemologists, according to Quine) of our basic beliefs be transferred, essentially undiminished, to derived beliefs, a necessary requirement if the derivational process is to yield knowledge from knowledge. What derivational methods have this property of preserving epistemic status? Perhaps there are none, given our proneness to err in framing derivations as in anything else, not to mention the possibility of lapses of attention and memory in following lengthy proofs. But logical deduction comes as close to being one as any; it can at least be relied on to transmit truth, if not epistemic status. It could perhaps be argued that no method can preserve certainty unless it preserves (or is known to preserve) truth; and if this is so, logical deduction is the only method worth considering. I do not know whether this was the attitude of most classic epistemologists; but Quine assumes that if deduction doesn't fill their bill, nothing will.

Quine sees the project of conceptual reduction as culminating in Carnap's *Der Logische Aufbau der Welt*. As Quine sees it, Carnap "came nearest to executing" the conceptual half of the classic epistemological project. But coming close is not good enough. Because of the holistic manner in which empirical meaning is generated by experience, no reduction of the sort Carnap and others so eagerly sought could in principle be completed. For definitional reduction requires point-to-point meaning relations[9] between physical terms and phenomenal terms, something that Quine's holism tells us cannot be had. The second half of the program, doctrinal reduction, is in no better shape; in fact, it was the one to stumble first, for, according to Quine, its impossibility was decisively demonstrated long before the *Aufbau*, by Hume in his celebrated discussion of induction. The "Humean predicament" shows that theory cannot be logically deduced from observation; there simply is no way of deriving theory from observation that will transmit the latter's epistemic status intact to the former.

I don't think anyone wants to disagree with Quine in these claims. It is not possible to "validate" science on the basis of sensory experience, if "validation" means justification through logical deduction. Quine of course does not deny that our theories depend on observation for evidential support; he has said that sensory evidence is the only evidence there is. To be sure, Quine's argument against the possibility of conceptual reduction has a new twist: the application of his "holism". But his conclusion is no surprise; "translational phenomenalism" has been moribund for many years.[10] And, as Quine himself notes, his argument against the doctrinal reduction, the "quest for certainty", is only a restatement of Hume's "skeptical" conclusions concerning induction: induction after all is not deduction. Most of us are inclined, I think, to view the situation Quine describes with no great alarm, and I rather doubt that these conclusions of Quine's came as news to most epistemologists when "Epistemology Naturalized" was first published. We are tempted to respond: of course we can't define physical concepts in terms of sense-data; of course observation "underdetermines" theory. That is why observation is observation and not theory.

So it is agreed on all hands that the classical epistemological project, conceived as one of deductively validating physical knowledge from indubitable sensory data, cannot succeed. But what is the moral of this failure? What should be its philosophical lesson to us? Having noted the failure of the Cartesian program, Quine goes on:[11]

> The stimulation of his sensory receptors is all the evidence anybody has had to go on, ultimately, in arriving at his picture of the world. Why not just see how this construction

really proceeds? Why not settle for psychology? Such a surrender of the epistemological burden to psychology is a move that was disallowed in earlier times as circular reasoning. If the epistemologist's goal is validation of the grounds of empirical science, he defeats his purpose by using psychology or other empirical science in the validation. However, such scruples against circularity have little point once we have stopped dreaming of deducing science from observation. If we are out simply to understand the link between observation and science, we are well advised to use any available information, including that provided by the very science whose link with observation we are seeking to understand.

And Quine has the following to say about the failure of Carnap's reductive program in the *Aufbau*:[12]

To relax the demand for definition, and settle for a kind of reduction that does not eliminate, is to renounce the last remaining advantage that we supposed rational reconstruction to have over straight psychology; namely, the advantage of translational reduction. If all we hope for is a reconstruction that links science to experience in explicit ways short of translation, then it would seem more sensible to settle for psychology. Better to discover how science is in fact developed and learned than to fabricate a fictitious structure to a similar effect.

If a task is entirely hopeless, if we know it cannot be executed, no doubt it is rational to abandon it; we would be better off doing something else that has some hope of success. We can agree with Quine that the "validation"—that is, logical deduction—of science on the basis of observation cannot be had; so it is rational to abandon this particular epistemological program, if indeed it ever was a program that anyone seriously undertook. But Quine's recommendations go further. In particular, there are two aspects of Quine's proposals that are of special interest to us: first, he is not only advising us to quit the program of "validating science", but urging us to take up another specific project, an empirical psychological study of our cognitive processes; second, he is also claiming that this new program replaces the old, that both programs are part of something appropriately called "epistemology". Naturalized epistemology is to be a kind of epistemology after all, a "successor subject"[13] to classical epistemology.

How should we react to Quine's urgings? What should be our response? The Cartesian project of validating science starting from the indubitable foundation of first-person psychological reports (perhaps with the help of certain indubitable first principles) is not the whole of classical epistemology—or so it would seem at first blush. In our characterization of classical epistemology, the Cartesian program was seen as one possible response to the problem of epistemic justification, the two-part project of identifying the criteria of epistemic justification and determining what beliefs are in fact justified according to those criteria. In urging "naturalized epistemology" on us, Quine is not suggesting that we give up the Cartesian foundationalist solution and explore others within the same framework[14]—perhaps, to adopt some sort of "coherentist" strategy, or to require of our basic beliefs only some degree of "initial credibility" rather than Cartesian certainty, or to permit some sort of probabilistic derivation in addition to deductive derivation of non-basic knowledge, or to consider the use of special rules of evidence, like Chisholm's "principles of evidence",[15] or to give up the search for a derivational process that transmits undiminished certainty in favor of one that can transmit diminished but still useful degrees of justification. Quine's proposal is more radical than that. He is asking us to set aside the entire framework of justification-centered epistemology. That is what is new in Quine's proposals. Quine is asking us to put in its place a purely descriptive, causal-nomological science of human cognition.[16]

How should we characterize in general terms the difference between traditional epistemological programs, such as foundationalism and coherence theory, on the one hand and Quine's program of naturalized epistemology on the other? Quine's stress is on the *factual* and *descriptive* character of his program; he says, "Why not see how [the construction of theory from observation] *actually proceeds? Why not settle for psychology?*";[17] again, "Better to *discover how science is in fact developed and learned than* ..."[18] We are given to understand that in contrast traditional epistemology is not a descriptive, factual inquiry. Rather, it is an attempt at a "validation" or "rational reconstruction" of science. Validation, according to Quine, proceeds via deduction, and rational reconstruction via definition.

However, their *point* is justificatory—that is, to rationalize our sundry knowledge claims. So Quine is asking us to set aside what is "rational" in rational reconstruction.

Thus, it is normativity that Quine is asking us to repudiate. Although Quine does not explicitly characterize traditional epistemology as "normative" or "prescriptive", his meaning is unmistakable. Epistemology is to be "a chapter of psychology", a law-based predictive-explanatory theory, like any other theory within empirical science; its principal job is to see how human cognizers develop theories (their "picture of the world") from observation ("the stimulation of their sensory receptors"). Epistemology is to go out of the business of justification. We earlier characterized traditional epistemology as essentially normative; we see why Quine wants us to reject it. Quine is urging us to replace a normative theory of cognition with a descriptive science.

4. Losing Knowledge from Epistemology

If justification drops out of epistemology, knowledge itself drops out of epistemology. For our concept of knowledge is inseparably tied to that of justification. As earlier noted, knowledge itself is a normative notion. Quine's nonnormative, naturalized epistemology has no room for our concept of knowledge. It is not surprising that, in describing naturalized epistemology, Quine seldom talks about knowledge; instead, he talks about "science" and "theories" and "representations". Quine would have us investigate how sensory stimulation "leads" to "theories" and "representation" of the world. I take it that within the traditional scheme these "theories" and "representations" correspond to beliefs, or systems of beliefs; thus, what Quine would have us do is to investigate how sensory stimulation leads to the formation of beliefs about the world.

But in what sense of "lead"? I take it that Quine has in mind a causal or nomological sense. He is urging us to develop a theory, an empirical theory, that uncovers lawful regularities governing the processes through which organisms come to develop beliefs about their environment as a causal result of having their sensory receptors stimulated in certain ways. Quine says:[19]

> [Naturalized epistemology] studies a natural phenomenon, viz., a physical human subject. This human subject is

accorded experimentally controlled input—certain patterns of
irradiation in assorted frequencies, for instance—and in the
fullness of time the subject delivers as output a description
of the three-dimensional external world and its history. *The
relation between the meager input and torrential output* is a
relation that we are prompted to study for somewhat the
same reasons that always prompted epistemology; namely,
in order to see *how evidence relates to theory*, and in what
ways one's theory of nature transcends any available
evidence.

The relation Quine speaks of between "meager input" and "torrential output" is a causal relation; at least it is qua causal relation that
the naturalized epistemologist investigates it. It is none of the
naturalized epistemologist's business to assess whether, and to what
degree, the input "justifies" the output, how a given irradiation of
the subject's retinas makes it "reasonable" or "rational" for the subject to emit certain representational output. His interest is strictly
causal and nomological: he wants us to look for patterns of lawlike
dependencies characterizing the input-output relations for this particular organism and others of a like physical structure.

If this is right, it makes Quine's attempt to relate his naturalized
epistemology to traditional epistemology look at best lame. For in
what sense is the study of causal relationships between physical
stimulation of sensory receptors and the resulting cognitive output
a way of "seeing how evidence relates to theory" in an
epistemologically relevant sense? The causal relation between sensory input and cognitive output is a relation between "evidence" and
"theory"; however, it is not an *evidential relation*. This can be seen
from the following consideration: the nomological patterns that Quine
urges us to look for are certain to vary from species to species,
depending on the particular way each biological (and possibly non-
biological) species processes information, but the evidential relation
in its proper normative sense must abstract from such factors and
concern itself only with the degree to which evidence supports
hypothesis.

In any event, the concept of evidence is inseparable from that of
justification. When we talk of "evidence" in an epistemological sense
we are talking about justification: one thing is "evidence" for another
just in case the first tends to enhance the reasonableness or justifica-

tion of the second. And such evidential relations hold in part because of the "contents" of the items involved, not merely because of the causal or nomological connections between them. A strictly nonnormative concept of evidence is not our concept of evidence; it is something that we do not understand.[20]

None of us, I think, would want to quarrel with Quine about the interest or importance of the psychological study of how our sensory input causes our epistemic output. This is only to say that the study of human (or other kinds of) cognition is of interest. That isn't our difficulty; our difficulty is whether, and in what sense, pursuing Quine's "epistemology" is a way of doing epistemology—that is, a way of studying "how evidence relates to theory". Perhaps, Quine's recommendation that we discard justification-centered epistemology is worth pondering; and his exhortation to take up the study of psychology perhaps deserves to be heeded also. What is mysterious is why this recommendation has to be coupled with the rejection of normative epistemology (if normative epistemology is not a possible inquiry, why shouldn't the would-be epistemologist turn to, say, hydrodynamics or ornithology rather than psychology?). But of course Quine is saying more; he is saying that an understandable, if misguided, motivation (that is, seeing "how evidence relates to theory") does underlie our proclivities for indulgence in normative epistemology, but that we would be better served by a scientific study of human cognition than normative epistemology.

But it is difficult to see how an "epistemology" that has been purged of normativity, one that lacks an appropriate normative concept of justification or evidence, can have anything to do with the concerns of traditional epistemology. And unless naturalized epistemology and classical epistemology share some of their central concerns, it's difficult to see how one could *replace* the other, or be a way (a better way) of doing the other.[21] To be sure, they both investigate "how evidence relates to theory". But putting the matter this way can be misleading, and has perhaps misled Quine: the two disciplines do not investigate the same relation. As lately noted, normative epistemology is concerned with the evidential relation properly so-called—that is, the relation of justification—and Quine's naturalized epistemology is meant to study the causal-nomological relation. For epistemology to go out of the business of justification is for it to go out of business.

5. Belief Attribution and Rationality

Perhaps we have said enough to persuade ourselves that Quine's naturalized epistemology, while it may be a legitimate scientific inquiry, is not a kind of epistemology, and, therefore, that the question whether it is a better kind of epistemology cannot arise. In reply, however, it might be said that there was a sense in which Quine's epistemology and traditional epistemology could be viewed as sharing a common subject matter, namely this: they both concern beliefs or "representations". The only difference is that the former investigates their causal histories and connections whereas the latter is concerned with their evidential or justificatory properties and relations. This difference, if Quine is right, leads to another (so continues the reply): the former is a feasible inquiry, the latter is not.

I now want to take my argument a step further: I shall argue that the concept of belief is itself an essentially normative one, and in consequence that if normativity is wholly excluded from naturalized epistemology it cannot even be thought of as being about beliefs. That is, if naturalized epistemology is to be a science of beliefs properly so called, it must presuppose a normative concept of belief.

Briefly, the argument is this. In order to implement Quine's program of naturalized epistemology, we shall need to identify, and individuate, the input and output of cognizers. The input, for Quine, consists of physical events ("the stimulation of sensory receptors") and the output is said to be a "theory" or "picture of the world"—that is, a set of "representations" of the cognizer's environment. Let us focus on the output. In order to study the sensory input-cognitive output relations for the given cognizer, therefore, we must find out what "representations" he has formed as a result of the particular stimulations that have been applied to his sensory transducers. Setting aside the jargon, what we need to be able to do is to attribute *beliefs*, and other contentful intentional states, to the cognizer. But belief attribution ultimately requires a "radical interpretation" of the cognizer, of his speech and intentional states; that is, we must construct an "interpretive theory" that simultaneously assigns meanings to his utterances and attributes to him beliefs and other propositional attitudes.[22]

Even a cursory consideration indicates that such an interpretation cannot begin—we cannot get a foothold in our subject's realm of meanings and intentional states—unless we assume his total system of beliefs and other propositional attitudes to be largely and essentially rational and coherent. As Davidson has emphasized, a given belief has the content it has in part because of its location in a network of other beliefs and propositional attitudes; and what at bottom grounds this network is the evidential relation, a relation that regulates what is reasonable to believe given other beliefs one holds. That is, unless our cognizer is a "rational being", a being whose cognitive "output" is regulated and constrained by norms of rationality—typically, these norms holistically constrain his propositional attitudes in virtue of their contents—we cannot intelligibly interpret his "output" as consisting of beliefs. Conversely, if we are unable to interpret our subject's meanings and propositional attitudes in a way that satisfies a minimal standard of rationality, there is little reason to regard him as a "cognizer", a being that forms representations and constructs theories. This means that there is a sense of "rational" in which the expression "rational belief" is redundant; every belief must be rational in certain minimal ways. It is not important for the purposes of the present argument what these minimal standards of rationality are; the only point that matters is that unless the output of our cognizer is subject to evaluation in accordance with norms of rationality, that output cannot be considered as consisting of beliefs and hence cannot be the object of an epistemological inquiry, whether plain or naturalized.

We can separate the core of these considerations from controversial issues involving the so-called "principle of charity", minimal rationality, and other matters in the theory of radical interpretation. What is crucial is this: for the interpretation and attribution of beliefs to be possible, not only must we assume the overall rationality of cognizers, but also we must continually evaluate and re-evaluate the putative beliefs of a cognizer in their evidential relationship to one another and other propositional attitudes. It is not merely that belief attribution requires the umbrella assumption about the overall rationality of cognizers. Rather, the point is that *belief attribution requires belief evaluation*, in accordance with normative standards of evidence and justification. If this is correct, rationality in its broad and fundamental sense is not an optional property of beliefs, a virtue that some beliefs may enjoy and others lack; it is a precondition of the attribution and individuation of belief—that is, a property without which the concept of belief would be unintelligible and pointless.

Two objections might be raised to counter these considerations. First, one might argue that at best they show only that the normativity of belief is an epistemological assumption—that we need to assume the rationality and coherence of belief systems when we are trying to *find out* what beliefs to attribute to a cognizer. It does not follow from this epistemological point, the objection continues, that the concept of belief is itself normative.[23] In replying to this objection, we can by-pass the entire issue of whether the rationality assumption concerns only the epistemology of belief attribution. Even if this premise (which I think is incorrect) is granted, the point has already been made. For it is an essential part of the business of naturalized epistemology, as a theory of how beliefs are formed as a result of sensory stimulation, to *find out* what particular beliefs the given cognizers have formed. But this is precisely what cannot be done, if our considerations show anything at all, unless the would-be naturalized epistemologist continually evaluates the putative beliefs of his subjects in regard to their rationality and coherence, subject to the overall constraint of the assumption that the cognizers are largely rational. The naturalized epistemologist cannot dispense with normative concepts or disengage himself from valuational activities.

Second, it might be thought that we could simply avoid these considerations stemming from belief attribution by refusing to think of cognitive output as consisting of "beliefs", namely as states having propositional contents. The "representations" Quine speaks of should be taken as appropriate neural states, and this means that all we need is to be able to discern neural states of organisms. This requires only neurophysiology and the like, not the normative theory of rational belief. My reply takes the form of a dilemma: either the "appropriate" neural states are identified by seeing how they correlate with beliefs,[24] in which case we still need to contend with the problem of radical interpretation, or beliefs are entirely by-passed. In the latter case, belief, along with justification, drops out of Quinean epistemology, and it is unclear in what sense we are left with an inquiry that has anything to do with knowledge.[25]

6. The "Psychologistic" Approach to Epistemology

Many philosophers now working in theory of knowledge have stressed the importance of systematic psychology to philosophical epistemology. Reasons proffered for this are various, and so are the conceptions of the proper relationship between psychology and epistemology.[26] But they are virtually unanimous in their rejection of what they take to be the epistemological tradition of Descartes and its modern embodiments in philosophers like Russell, C. I. Lewis, Roderick Chisholm, and A. J. Ayer; and they are united in their endorsement the naturalistic approach of Quine we have been considering. Traditional epistemology is often condemned as "aprioristic", and as having lost sight of human knowledge as a product of natural causal processes and its function in the survival of the organism and the species. Sometimes, the adherents of the traditional approach are taken to task for their implicit antiscientific bias or indifference to the new developments in psychology and related disciplines. Their own approach in contrast is hailed as "naturalistic" and "scientific", better attuned to significant advances in the relevant scientific fields such as "cognitive science" and "neuroscience", promising philosophical returns far richer than what the aprioristic method of traditional epistemology has been able to deliver. We shall here briefly consider how this new naturalism in epistemology is to be understood in relation to the classic epistemological program and Quine's naturalized epistemology.

Let us see how one articulate proponent of the new approach explains the distinctiveness of his position vis-à-vis that of the traditional epistemologists. According to Philip Kitcher, the approach he rejects is characterized by an "apsychologistic" attitude that takes the difference between knowledge and true belief—that is, justification—to consist in "ways which are independent of the causal antecedents of a subject's states".[27] Kitcher writes:[28]

> ...we can present the heart of [the apsychologistic approach] by considering the way in which it would tackle the question of whether a person's true belief that *p* counts as knowledge that *p*. The idea would be to disregard the psychological life of the subject, looking just at the various propositions she believes. If *p* is 'connected in the right way' to other propositions which are believed, then we count the subject as knowing that *p*. Of course, apsychologisitc epistemology will have to supply a criterion for propositions to be 'connected in the right way' ... but proponents of this view of knowledge will emphasize that the criterion is to be

given in *logical* terms. We are concerned with logical
relations among propositions, not with psychological
relations among mental states.

On the other hand, the psychologistic approach considers the crucial
difference between knowledge and true belief—that is, epistemic
justification—to turn on "the factors which produced the belief", focusing on "processes which produce belief, processes which will always
contain, at their latter end, psychological events".[29]
It is not entirely clear from this characterization whether a
psychologistic theory of justification is to be *prohibited* from making *any* reference to logical relations among belief contents (it is difficult to believe how a theory of justification respecting such a blanket
prohibition could succeed); nor is it clear whether, conversely, an
apsychologistic theory will be permitted to refer at all to beliefs qua
psychological states, or exactly what it is for a theory to do so. But
such points of detail are unimportant here; it is clear enough, for
example, that Goldman's proposal to explicate justified belief as belief
generated by a reliable belief-forming process[30] nicely fits Kitcher's
characterization of the psychologistic approach. This account, one
form of the so-called "reliability theory" of justification, probably was
what Kitcher had in mind when he was formulating his general
characterization of epistemological naturalism. However, another influential form of the reliability theory does not qualify under Kitcher's
characterization. This is Armstrong's proposal to explain the difference between knowledge and true belief, at least for non-
inferential knowledge, in terms of "a *law-like connection* between
the state of affairs [of a subject's believing that *p*] and the state of
affairs that makes '*p*' true such that, given the state of affairs [of the
subject's believing that *p*], it must be the case that *p*."[31] There is here
no reference to the causal *antecedents* of beliefs, something that
Kitcher requires of apsychologistic theories.
Perhaps, Kitcher's preliminary characterization needs to be
broadened and sharpened. However, a salient characteristic of the
naturalistic approach has already emerged, which we can put as
follows: justification is to be characterized in terms of *causal* or
nomological connections involving beliefs as *psychological states* or
processes, and not in terms of the *logical* properties or relations pertaining to the *contents* of these beliefs.[32]
If we understand current epistemological naturalism in this way,

how closely is it related to Quine's conception of naturalized epistemology? The answer, I think, is obvious: not very closely at all. In fact, it seems a good deal closer to the Cartesian tradition than to Quine. For, as we saw, the difference that matters between Quine's epistemological program and the traditional program is the former's total renouncement of the latter's normativity, its rejection of epistemology as a normative inquiry. The talk of "replacing" epistemology with psychology is irrelevant and at best misleading, though it could give us a momentary relief from a sense of deprivation. When one abandons justification and other valuational concepts, one abandons the entire framework of normative epistemology. What remains is a descriptive empirical theory of human cognition which, if Quine has his way, will be entirely devoid of the notion of justification or any other evaluative concept.

As I take it, this is not what most advocates of epistemological naturalism are aiming at. By and large they are not Quinean eliminativists in regard to justification, and justification in its full-fledged normative sense continues to play a central role in their epistemological reflections. Where they differ from their nonnaturalist adversaries is the specific way in which criteria of justification are to be formulated. Naturalists and nonnaturalists ("apsychologists") can agree that these criteria must be stated in descriptive terms— that is, without the use of epistemic or any other kind of normative terms. According to Kitcher, an apsychologistic theory of justification would state them primarily in terms of *logical* properties and relations holding for propositional contents of beliefs, whereas the psychologistic approach advocates the exclusive use of *causal* properties and relations holding for beliefs as events or states. Many traditional epistemologists may prefer criteria that confer upon a cognizer a position of special privilege and responsibility with regard to the epistemic status of his beliefs, whereas most self-avowed naturalists prefer "objective" or "externalist" criteria with no such special privileges for the cognizer. But these differences are among those that arise within the familiar normative framework, and are consistent with the exclusion of normative terms in the statement of the criteria of justification.

Normative ethics can serve as a useful model here. To claim that basic ethical terms, like "good" and "right", are *definable* on the basis of descriptive or naturalistic terms is one thing; to insist that it is the business of normative ethics to provide *conditions* or *criteria* for "good" and "right" in descriptive or naturalistic terms is another. One may properly reject the former, the so-called "ethical naturalism", as many moral philosophers have done, and hold the latter; there is no obvious inconsistency here. G. E. Moore is a philosopher who did just that. As is well known, he was a powerful critic of ethical naturalism, holding that goodness is a "simple" and "nonnatural" property. At the same time, he held that a thing's being good "follows" from its possessing certain naturalistic properties. He wrote:[33]

> I should never have thought of suggesting that goodness was 'non-natural', unless I had supposed that it was 'derivative' in the sense that, whenever a thing is good (in the sense in question) its goodness ...'depends on the presence of certain non-ethical characteristics' possessed by the thing in question: I have always supposed that it did so 'depend', in the sense that, if a thing is good (in my sense), then that it is so *follows* from the fact that it possesses certain natural intrinsic properties ...

It makes sense to think of these "natural intrinsic properties" from which a thing's being good is thought to follow as constituting naturalistic criteria of goodness, or at least pointing to the existence of such criteria. One can reject ethical naturalism, the doctrine that ethical concepts are definitionally eliminable in favor of naturalistic terms, and at the same time hold that ethical properties, or the ascription of ethical terms, must be governed by naturalistic criteria. It is clear, then, that we are here using "naturalism" ambiguously in "epistemological naturalism" and "ethical naturalism". In our present usage, epistemological naturalism does not include (nor does it necessarily exclude) the claim that epistemic terms are definitionally reducible to naturalistic terms. (Quine's naturalism is eliminative, though it is not a definitional eliminativism.)

If, therefore, we locate the split between Quine and traditional epistemology at the descriptive vs. normative divide, then currently influential naturalism in epistemology is not likely to fall on Quine's side. On this descriptive vs. normative issue, one can side with Quine in one of two ways: first, one rejects, with Quine, the entire justification-based epistemological program; or second, like ethical naturalists but unlike Quine, one believes that epistemic concepts are naturalistically definable. I doubt that very many epistemological naturalists will embrace either of these alternatives.[34]

7. Epistemic Supervenience—Or Why Normative Epistemology Is Possible

But why should we think that there *must be* naturalistic criteria of justified belief and other terms of epistemic appraisal? If we take the discovery and systematization of such criteria to be the central task of normative epistemology, is there any reason to think that this task can be fruitfully pursued, that normative epistemology is a possible field of inquiry? Quine's point is that it is not. We have already noted the limitation of Quine's negative arguments in "Epistemology Naturalized", but is there a positive reason for thinking that normative epistemology is a viable program? One could consider a similar question about the possibility of normative ethics.

I think there is a short and plausible initial answer, although a detailed defense of it would involve complex general issues about norms and values. The short answer is this: we believe in the supervenience of epistemic properties on naturalistic ones, and more generally, in the supervenience of all valuational and normative properties on naturalistic conditions. This comes out in various ways. We think, with R.M. Hare,[35] that if two persons or acts coincide in all descriptive or naturalistic details, they cannot differ in respect of being good or right, or any other valuational aspects. We also think that if something is "good"—a "good car", "good drop shot", "good argument"—then that must be so "in virtue of" its being a "certain way", that is, its having certain "factual properties". Being a good car, say, cannot be a brute and ultimate fact: a car is good *because* it has a certain contextually indicated set of properties having to do with performance, reliability, comfort, styling, economy, etc. The same goes for justified belief: if a belief is justified, that must be so *because* it has certain factual, nonepistemic properties, such as perhaps that it is "indubitable", that it is seen to be entailed by another belief that is independently justified, that it is appropriately caused by perceptual experience, or whatever. That it is a justified belief cannot be a brute fundamental fact unrelated to the kind of belief it is. There must be a *reason* for it, and this reason must be grounded in the factual descriptive properties of that particular belief. Something like this, I think, is what we believe.

Two important themes underlie these convictions: first, values, though perhaps not reducible to facts, must be "consistent" with them in that objects that are indiscernible in regard to fact must be indiscernible in regard to value; second, there must be nonvaluational "reasons" or "grounds" for the attribution of values, and these "reasons" or "grounds" must be *generalizable*—that is, they are covered by *rules* or *norms*. These two ideas correspond to "weak supervenience" and "strong supervenience" that I have discussed elsewhere.[36] Belief in the supervenience of value upon fact, arguably, is fundamental to the very concepts of value and valuation.[37] Any valuational concept, to be significant, must be governed by a set of criteria, and these criteria must ultimately rest on factual characteristics and relationships of objects and events being evaluated. There is something deeply incoherent about the idea of an infinitely descending series of valuational concepts, each depending on the one below it as its criterion of application.[38]

It seems to me, therefore, that epistemological supervenience is what underlies our belief in the possibility of normative epistemology, and that we do not need new inspirations from the sciences to acknowledge the existence of naturalistic criteria for epistemic and other valuational concepts. The case of normative ethics is entirely parallel: belief in the possibility of normative ethics is rooted in the belief that moral properties and relations are supervenient upon non-moral ones. Unless we are prepared to disown normative ethics as a viable philosophical inquiry, we had better recognize normative epistemology as one, too.[39] We should note, too, that epistemology is likely to parallel normative ethics in regard to the degree to which scientific results are relevant or useful to its development.[40] Saying this of course leaves large room for disagreement concerning how relevant and useful, if at all, empirical psychology of human motivation and action can be to the development and confirmation of normative ethical theories.[41] In any event, once the normativity of epistemology is clearly taken note of, it is no surprise that epistemology and normative ethics share the same metaphilosophical fate. Naturalized epistemology makes no more, and no less, sense than naturalized normative ethics.[42]

Notes

1. In making these remarks I am only repeating the familiar textbook

history of philosophy; however, what *our* textbooks say about the history of a philosophical concept has much to do with *our* understanding of that concept.

2. Alvin Goldman explicitly states this requirement as a desideratum of his own analysis of justified belief in "What is Justified Belief?", in George S. Pappas (ed.), *Justification and Knowledge* (Dordrecht: Reidel, 1979), p. 1. Roderick M. Chisholm's definition of "being evident" in his *Theory of Knowledge*, 2nd ed. (Englewood Cliffs, N.J.: Prentice-Hall, 1977) does not satisfy this requirement as it rests ultimately on an unanalyzed epistemic concept of one belief being *more reasonable than* another. What does the real "criteriological" work for Chisholm is his "principles of evidence". See especially (A) on p. 73 of *Theory of Knowledge*, which can usefully be regarded as an attempt to provide nonnormative, descriptive conditions for certain types of justified beliefs.

3. The basic idea of this stronger requirement seems implicit in Roderick Firth's notion of "warrant-increasing property" in his "Coherence, Certainty, and Epistemic Priority", *Journal of Philosophy* 61 (1964): 545-57. It seems that William P. Alston has something similar in mind when he says, "... like any evaluative property, epistemic justification is a supervenient property, the application of which is based on more fundamental properties" (at this point Alston refers to Firth's paper cited above), in "Two Types of Foundationalism", *Journal of Philosophy* 73 (1976): 165-85 (the quoted remark occurs on p. 170). Although Alston doesn't further explain what he means by "more fundamental properties", the context makes it plausible to suppose that he has in mind nonnormative, descriptive properties. See Section 7 below for further discussion.

4. See Chisholm, ibid., p. 14. Here Chisholm refers to a "person's responsibility or duty *qua* intellectual being".

5. This term was used by A.J. Ayer to characterize the difference between lucky guessing and knowing; see *The Problem of Knowledge* (New York & London: Penguin Books, 1956), p. 33.

6. Notably by Chisholm in *Theory of Knowledge*, 1st ed., ch. 4.

7. See Rudolf Carnap, "Testability and Meaning", *Philosophy of Science* 3 (1936), and 4 (1937). We should also note the presence of a strong coherentist streak among some positivists; see, e.g., Carl G. Hempel, "On the Logical Positivists' Theory of Truth", *Analysis* 2 (1935): 49-59, and "Some Remarks on 'Facts' and Propositions", *Analysis* 2 (1935): 93-96.

8. In W.V. Quine, *Ontological Relativity and Other Essays* (New York: Columbia University Press, 1969). Also see his *Word and Object* (Cambridge: MIT Press, 1960); *The Roots of Reference* (La Salle, Ill.: Open Court, 1973); (with Joseph Ullian) *The Web of Belief* (New York: Random House, 1970); and especially "The Nature of Natural Knowledge" in Samuel Guttenplan (ed.), *Mind and Language* (Oxford: Clarendon Press, 1975). See Frederick F. Schmitt's excellent bibliography on naturalistic epistemology in Hilary Kornblith (ed.), *Naturalizing Epistemology* (Cambridge: MIT/Bradford, 1985).

9. Or confirmational relations, given the Positivists' verificationist theory of meaning.

10. I know of no serious defense of it since Ayer's *The Foundations of Empirical Knowledge* (London: Macmillan, 1940).

11. "Epistemology Naturalized", pp. 75-76.

12. Ibid., p. 78.

13. To use an expression of Richard Rorty's in *Philosophy and the Mirror of Nature* (Princeton: Princeton University Press, 1979), p. 11.

14. Elliott Sober makes a similar point: "And on the question of whether the failure of a foundationalist programme shows that questions of justification cannot be answered, it is worth noting that Quine's advice 'Since Carnap's foundationalism failed, why not settle for psychology' carries weight only to the degree that Carnapian epistemology exhausts the possibilities of epistemology", in "Psychologism", *Journal of Theory of Social Behaviour* 8 (1978): 165-191.

15, See Chisholm, *Theory of Knowledge*, 2nd ed., ch. 4.

16. "If we are seeking only the causal mechanism of our knowledge of the external world, and not a justification of that knowledge in terms prior to science ...", Quine, "Grades of Theoreticity", in L. Foster and J.W. Swanson (eds.), *Experience and Theory* (Amherst: University of Massachusetts Press, 1970), p. 2.

17. Ibid., p. 75. Emphasis added.

18. Ibid., p. 78. Emphasis added.

19. Ibid., p. 83. Emphasis added.

20. But aren't there those who advocate a "causal theory" of evidence or justification? I want to make two brief points about this. First, the nomological or causal input/output relations are not in themselves evidential relations, whether these latter are understood causally or otherwise. Second, a causal theory of evidence attempts to state *criteria* for "e is evidence for h" in causal terms; even if this is successful, it does not necessarily give us a causal "definition" or "reduction" of the concept of evidence. For more details see section 6 below.

21. I am not saying that Quine is under any illusion on this point. My remarks are directed rather at those who endorse Quine without, it seems, a clear appreciation of what is involved.

22. Here I am drawing chiefly on Donald Davidson's writings on radical interpretation. See Essays 9, 10, and 11 in his *Inquiries into Truth and Interpretation* (Oxford: Clarendon Press, 1984). See also David Lewis, "Radical Interpretation", *Synthese* 27 (1974): 331-44.

23. Robert Audi suggested this as a possible objection.

24. For some considerations tending to show that these correlations cannot be lawlike see my "Psychophysical Laws", in Ernest LePore and Brian McLaughlin (eds.), *Actions and Events: Perspectives on the Philosophy of Donald Davidson* (Oxford: Blackwell, 1985).

25. For a more sympathetic account of Quine than mine, see Hilary Kornblith's introductory essay, "What is Naturalistic Epistemology?", in Kornblith (ed.), *Naturalizing Epistemology*.

26. See for more details Alvin I. Goldman, *Epistemology and Cognition* (Cambridge: Harvard University Press, 1986).

27. *The Nature of Mathematical Knowledge* (New York: Oxford University

Press, 1983), p. 14.

28. Ibid.
29. Ibid., p. 13. I should note that Kitcher considers the apsychologistic approach to be an aberration of the twentieth century epistemology, as represented by philosophers like Russell, Moore, C.I. Lewis, and Chisholm, rather than an historical characteristic of the Cartesian tradition. In "The Psychological Turn", *Australasian Journal of Philosophy* 60 (1982): 238-253, Hilary Kornblith gives an analogous characterization of the two approaches to justification; he associates "justification-conferring processes" with the psychologistic approach and "epistemic rules" with the apsychologistic approach.
30. See Goldman, "What is Justified Belief?".
31. David M. Armstrong, *Truth, Belief and Knowledge* (London: Cambridge University Press, 1973), p. 166.
32. The aptness of this characterization of the "apsychologistic" approach for philosophers like Russell, Chisholm, Keith Lehrer, John Pollock, etc. can be debated. Also, there is the issue of "internalism" vs. "externalism" concerning justification, which I believe must be distinguished from the psychologistic vs. apsychologistic division.
33. Moore, "A Reply to My Critics", in P.A. Schilpp (ed.), *The Philosophy of G.E. Moore* (Chicago & Evanston: Open Court, 1942), p. 588.
34. Richard Rorty's claim, which plays a prominent role in his arguments against traditional epistemology in *Philosophy and the Mirror of Nature*, that Locke and other modern epistemologists conflated the normative concept of justification with causal-mechanical concepts is itself based, I believe, on a conflation of just the kind I am describing here. See Rorty, ibid., pp. 139ff. Again, the critical conflation consists in not seeing that the view, which I believe is correct, that epistemic justification, like any other normative concept, must have factual, naturalistic criteria, is entirely consistent with the rejection of the doctrine, which I think is incorrect, that justification itself *is*, or is *reducible* to, a naturalistic-nonnormative concept.
35. *The Language of Morals* (London: Oxford University Press, 1952), p.145.
36. See "Concepts of Supervenience", *Philosophy and Phenomenological Research* 65 (1984): 153-176.
37. Ernest Sosa, too, considers epistemological supervenience as a special case of the supervenience of valuational properties on naturalistic conditions, in "The Foundation of Foundationalism", *Nous* 14 (1980): 547-64; especially p. 551. See also James Van Cleve's instructive discussion in his "Epistemic Supervenience and the Circle of Belief", The *Monist* 68 (1985): 90-104; especially, pp. 97-99.
38. Perhaps one could avoid this kind of criteriological regress by embracing directly apprehended valuational properties (as in ethical intuitionism) on the basis of which criteria for other valuational properties could be formulated. The denial of the supervenience of valuational concepts on factual characteristics, however, would sever the essential connection between value and fact on which, it seems, the whole point of our valuational activities depends. In the absence of such supervenience, the very

notion of valuation would lose its significance and relevance. The elaboration of these points, however, would have to wait for another occasion; but see Van Cleve's paper cited in the preceding note for more details.

39. Quine will not disagree with this: he will "naturalize" them both. For his views on values see "The Nature of Moral Values" in Alvin I. Goldman and Jaegwon Kim (eds.), *Values and Morals* (Dordrecht: Reidel, 1978). For a discussion of the relationship between epistemic and ethical concepts see Roderick Firth, "Are Epistemic Concepts Reducible to Ethical Concepts?" in the same volume.

40. For discussions of this and related issues see Goldman, *Epistemology and Cognition.*

41. For a detailed development of a normative ethical theory that exemplifies the view that it is crucially relevant, see Richard B. Brandt, *A Theory of the Good and the Right* (Oxford: The Clarendon Press, 1979).

42. An early version of this paper was read at a meeting of the Korean Society for Analytic Philosophy in 1984 in Seoul. An expanded version was presented at a symposium at the Western Division meetings of the American Philosophical Association in April, 1985, and at the epistemology conference at Brown University in honor of Roderick Chisholm in 1986. I am grateful to Richard Foley and Robert Audi who presented helpful comments at the APA session and the Chisholm Conference respectively. I am also indebted to Terence Horgan and Robert Meyers for helpful comments and suggestions.

References

Alston, William P., "Two Types of Foundationalism" *Journal of Philosophy* 73 (1976): 165-85.

Armstrong, David M., *Truth, Belief and Knowledge* (London: Cambridge University Press, 1973).

Ayer, A.J., *The Foundations of Empirical Knowledge* (London: Macmillan, 1940).

Ayer, A.J., *The Problem of Knowledge* (New York & London: Penguin Books, 1956).

Brandt, Richard B., *A Theory of the Good and the Right* (Oxford: The Clarendon Press, 1979).

Carnap, Rudolf, "Testability and Meaning", *Philosophy of Science* 3 (1936), and 4 (1937).

Chisholm, Roderick M., *Theory of Knowledge*, 2nd ed. (Englewood Cliffs, N.J.: Prentice-Hall, 1977).

Davidson, Donald, *Inquiries into Truth and Interpretation* (Oxford: Clarendon Press, 1984).

Firth, Roderick, "Coherehce, Certainty, and Epistemic Priority", *Journal of Philosophy* 61 (1964): 545-57.

Firth, Roderick, "Are Epistemic Concepts Reducible to Ethical Concepts?" in Goldman, Alvin I. and Jaegwon Kim (eds.), *Values and Morals*

(Dordrecht: Reidel, 1978).

Goldman, Alvin I., "What is Justified Belief?", in George S. Pappas (ed.), *Justification and Knowledge* (Dordrecht: Reidel, 1979).

Goldman, Alvin I., *Epistemology and Cognition* (Cambridge: Harvard University Press, 1986).

Hare, R.M., *The Language of Morals* (London: Oxford University Press, 1952).

Hempel, Carl G., "On the Logical Positivists' Theory of Truth", *Analysis* 2 (1935): 49-59.

Hempel, Carl G., "Some Remarks on 'Facts' and Propositions", *Analysis* 2 (1935): 93-96.

Kim, Jaegwon, "Concepts of Supervenience", *Philosophy and Phenomenological Research* 65 (1984): 153-176.

Kim, Jaegwon, "Psychophysical Laws", in Ernest LePore and Brian McLaughlin (eds.), *Actions and Events: Perspecties on the Philosophy of Donald Davidson* (Oxford: Blackwell, 1985).

Kitcher, Phillip, *The Nature of Mathematical Knowledge* (New York: Oxford University Press, 1983).

Kornblith, Hilary, "The Psychological Turn", *Australasian Journal of Philosophy* 60 (1982): 238-253.

Kornblith, Hilary, (ed.), *Naturalizing Epistemology* (Cambridge: MIT/ Bradford, 1985).

Kornblith, Hilary, "What is Naturalistic Epistemology?", in Kornblith (ed.), *Naturalizing Epistemology*.

Lewis, David, "Radical Interpretation", *Synthese* 27 (1974): 331-44.

Moore, G.E., "A Reply to My Critics", in P.A. Schilpp (ed.), *The Philosophy of G. E. Moore* (Chicago & Evanston: Open Court, 1942).

Quine, W.V., *Word and Object* (Cambridge: MIT Press, 1960).

Quine, W.V., *Ontological Relativity and Other Essays* (New York: Columbia University Press, 1969).

Quine, W.V., (with Joseph Ullian), *The Web of Belief* (New York: Random House, 1970).

Quine, W.V., "Grades of Theoreticity", in L. Foster and J. W. Swanson (eds.), *Experience and Theory* (Amherst: University of Massachusetts Press, 1970).

Quine, W.V., *The Roots of Reference* (La Salle, IL,: Open Court, 1973); Quine, W.V., "The Nature of Natural Knowledge" in Samuel Guttenplan (ed.), *Mind and Language* (Oxford: Clarendon Press, 1975).

Quine, W.V., "The Nature of Moral Values" in Alvin I. Goldman and Jaegwon Kim (eds.), *Values and Morals* (Dordrecht: Reidel, 1978).

Rorty, Richard, *Philosophy and the Mirror of Nature* (Princeton: Princeton University Press, 1979).

Sober, Elliott, "Psychologism", *Journal of Theory of Social Behavior* 8 (1978): 165-191.

Sosa, Ernest, "The Foundation of Foundationalism", *Nous* 14 (1980): 547-64.

Van Cleve, James, "Epistemic Supervenience and the Circle of Belief", *The Monist* 68 (1985)" 90-104.

Philosophical Perspectives, 2, Epistemology, 1988

FOUNDATIONALISM, COHERENTISM, AND EPISTEMOLOGICAL DOGMATISM

Robert Audi
University of Nebraska, Lincoln

Foundationalism and coherentism each contain significant epistemological truths. Both positions are, moreover, intellectually influential even outside epistemology: even when neither position is mentioned, one or the other of them often affects philosophical discussion of other topics. It is doubtful that any thesis in either spectrum can be cogently defended unless it captures important points associated with the opposing side. But the construction and defense of such a balanced thesis is difficult, and most philosophers defending either tradition have been mainly concerned to argue for their view and against the other tradition, which they have often interpreted through just one leading proponent. It is not surprising, then, that although the foundationalism-coherentism controversy remains a focus of epistemological attention, philosophers in each tradition often feel misunderstood by those in the other. Indeed, while both foundationalism and coherentism have often been set out and discussed,[1] there remains much unclarity about them: about their basic concepts, their central claims, and the main arguments supporting them.

The unclarity goes beyond what one would expect from terminological and philosophical diversity: there are genuine obscurities and misconceptions to be dispelled. Many objections to foundationalism and various criticisms of coherentism rest on unclarity or misunderstanding. My aim in Sections I through III is to clarify both types of position. I hope thereby to advance our understanding of the controversy. If my interpretations of foundationalism and coherentism are sound, it will be clear that epistemologists on each side have unjustly criticized the other. A special concern of the paper is to bring my interpretations to bear on an issue which needs clarification nearly as much as the foundationalism-coherentism controversy itself: the bearing of dogmatism on both positions. It is widely thought that foundationalism, by comparison with coherentism, is dogmatic; and for many philosophers, including many who are not epistemologists, this is a major reason for rejecting foundationalism. Section IV will discuss the nature of dogmatism and its possible applications to both positions.

I. The Epistemic Regress Problem

One approach to my task would be to consider important formulations of both foundationalism and coherentism, try to extract their unifying elements, and connect the resulting formulations with the issue of dogmatism. This approach would require an extended study and even then might yield at best compromise formulations acceptable to few. A better procedure is to take the epistemic regress problem, together with the associated regress argument, as a point of departure. It is widely agreed that some version of this argument is crucial as support for foundationalism, and even coherentists grant that the regress problem is important in motivating their views.[2] I begin, then, with a brief statement of that problem.

There are at least two major contexts (often not distinguished) in which the regress problem arises. Central to one context is pursuit of the question of how one knows a particular thing, most typically a proposition about the external world, or the question what justifies one in believing some particular thing, or both. As one would expect, this context is often colored by the imagined reply to such questions in answering skeptical challenges. Central to the other context are the questions of what it is that grounds (or, in what I shall take to be equivalent terms, is the basis of) one's knowledge, or grounds one's justification. Let us consider the regress problem raised in both ways.

Suppose I am asked how I know that p, where p is either something I have asserted or something I would commonly be taken to know, say that there are books in my study. A natural answer is to offer a ground, say *q*. After all, if I do know, I surely have a ground; and if I have one, it is natural to think that I should be able (at least on reflection) to produce it. But if the query is motivated by an epistemological interest in knowledge, the question how I know is likely to be reiterated, at least if *q* is not self-evident or somehow beyond doubt; for unless it is, the questioner—particularly if skeptically inclined—will accept my citing *q* as answering the question how I know that p, only on the assumption that I also know that *q*. For most epistemologists, the problem here, as in trying to specify what justifies me in believing *p*, is to answer such questions without making one or another apparently inevitable move that ultimately undermines the possibility of knowledge and hence plays into the skeptic's hands. Prima facie, one must choose between falling into vicious circularity or vicious regress or, on the other hand, stopping at a purported ground that either does not constitute knowledge (or at least justified belief), or, if it is knowledge, is only capriciously taken to be, in which case *citing* it as a final answer to the chain of queries seems dogmatic. Call this the *dialectical form of the regress problem*.[3]

Imagine, by contrast, that we simply consider either the entire body of a person's apparent knowledge, as Aristotle seems to have done,[4] or a representative item of apparent knowledge, say my belief that there are over 1,000 books in my study, and ask on what this apparent knowledge is grounded (or based) and whether, if it is grounded on some further belief, *all* our knowledge or justified belief could be so grounded. We are now asking a structural question, not requesting a verbal response. Again we get a regress problem: how to specify my grounds without vicious circularity or regress or, on the other hand, stopping with the specification (or expression) of a belief that does not constitute knowledge (or is not justified), or seems only capriciously regarded as knowledge. Call this the *structural form of the regress problem*.

While one might think that the structural form of the problem is somehow prior, it is easy to suppose, as I believe some philosophers have, that it makes little difference in which of these ways we formulate the problem. I am convinced that it *does* matter, for at least these reasons. The dialectical form invites us to think that we are adequately answering the question *how* we know something only if we are *showing* that we do. This is particularly so if the problem is dialectically formulated, as it often has been, *in* the context of a concern to reply to skepticism. But it is far from self-evident that an adequate answer to the how-question must be an adequate answer to the show-question, especially if the standards for showing that one knows are set by the needs of dealing with a skeptic. Connected with this is a second point: when the problem is dialectically formulated, any fully explicit non-skeptical answer to 'How do you know that *p*?' will itself tend to be a second-order ascription, say 'I know that *q*'; thus, the answer is admissible only if I both have the *concept* of knowledge *and* am at least dialectically warranted in asserting that I do know that *q*. Third, when the problem is so formulated, its solution tends to be conceived as *propositional*, in the sense that the solution is a matter of displaying propositions which, whether or not I believe them prior to being questioned, are both warranted for me and, taken together, justify the proposition originally in question. And fourth, a dialectical formulation, at least as applied to justification, tends to focus our attention on the *process* of justification, though the initial question concerns whether the relevant belief has the *property* of justification.

Using the structural formulation, we find that the criteria for solutions differ on all four counts. Let us consider these in turn, noting the dual use of 'solution' as designating both appropriate truths that can be discovered in studying a problem and statements of those truths, such as we try to offer in articles.

First, structurally conceived, the regress problem is taken to *have* a solution provided there simply *exists* an appropriate sequence of knowings; it is not essential that anyone *say* or *show* anything by way of answer. Perhaps our *knowing* that it is solved requires showing that we know something; but its simply being soluble does not. Dialectically conceived, however, the problem's having a solution tends to be identified with someone's *giving* one in an appropriate context.

Second, on the structural conception neither second-order concepts nor second-order ascriptions are required for the existence, as opposed to the expression, of a solution; it is enough (assuming the belief in question, that *p*, is itself first order) that our subject, *S*, simply *have* an appropriate sequence of first-order knowings.

Third, solving the problem tends to be conceived as *psychological*, and more specifically as *cognitive*, in the sense that it consists in citing both appropriate cognitions (above all beliefs and perhaps only beliefs if knowledge is constituted by beliefs) and psychological facts about

S's cognitive system, such as genetic facts about their grounding in perception. One would, e.g., cite either *S*'s having a sequence of beliefs constituting adequate grounds for believing *p*, the belief whose status as knowledge (or as justified) was originally in question, or such facts as that the belief is grounded in a visual experience.

Fourth, because the structural conception of the problem tends to focus our attention on the property of justification (or the nature of knowledge), on what it *is* for a belief to be justified (or to constitute knowledge), a correct solution is understood largely in terms of an account of the nature of these properties. On the dialectical conception, a correct solution, even if it is taken to require such an account, tends to have a further constraint: that the account make it possible for someone, *S*, who knows or justifiably believes *p* to *give* a dialectically adequate response to the question of how *S* knows, or of what justifies *S* in believing, that *p*. To be sure, one *can* interpret a dialectical solution cognitively or a structural one propositionally. But neither move is entirely natural. The dialectical framework invites one to take grounds of knowledge as propositions warrantedly citable as premises, weapons usable in fending off the skeptic, whether or not one's beliefs of these premises play any causal role in sustaining the belief whose justification is queried at the start of the regress. The structural framework, by contrast, invites one to take grounds of knowledge as what the belief whose status is in question is actually based on—the soil from which the cognitive tree actually grows— and this is not strictly a proposition but another set of beliefs or some other causally sustaining psychological state.

It is important, then, not to conflate these two formulations of the regress problem. How should we decide which formulation is preferable in appraising the foundationalism-coherentism controversy? One consideration is neutrality. The dialectical formulation favors coherentism, or at least non-foundationalism. Let me explain.

Foundationalists typically posit beliefs grounded on experience or reason and thereby both *psychologically direct* (non-inferential in a common sense of that term) and also *epistemically direct*, in the sense that they do not depend (inferentially) for their status as knowledge, or for any justification they have, on other belief, justification, or knowledge. Roughly, such beliefs are not inferentially *based on* other beliefs or knowledge, and this point holds whether or not there is any actual *process* of inference.[5] Now clearly it is far less plausible to suppose that my *second-order* belief that I know I see books in my study is epistemically direct, than to suppose that my *perceptual* belief that there *are* books in it is, since the latter seems non-inferentially based on my seeing them. Thus, foundationalists are less likely to seem to have a good answer to the dialectical formulation of the problem, since that requires them to posit direct second-order knowledge.

A second point emerges if we note that 'How do you know?' can be repeated, and in some fashion answered, indefinitely. Since this question (or a similar one) is central to the dialectical formulation, that formulation tends to be inimical to a foundationalist solution, which posits at least one kind of natural stopping place. It might seem, however, that the structural formulation is not neutral toward coherentism. For on the associated cognitive conception of the problem, it is difficult to see how a normal person might actually *have* anything approaching an infinitely long chain of beliefs constituting knowings, so at least an actual infinite chain of answers to 'How do you know?' seems out of the question. But this only cuts against an infinite regress "solution," not against any finitistic coherentism, which seems the only kind ever plausibly defended. Indeed, even assuming—as coherentists may grant—that much of our knowledge in fact arises, non-inferentially, from experiential states like visual or auditory ones, the structural formulation of the problem allows *both* that, as foundationalists typically claim, there is non-inferential knowledge and that, as coherentists typically claim, non-inferential beliefs are dialectically defensible indefinitely and capable of constituting knowledge only by virtue of coherence.

I believe, then, that the structural formulation is not significantly biased against coherentism, at least not against what seem its most plausible forms. Nor is it biased in favor of internalism over externalism. The dialectical formulation, by contrast, tends to favor internalism, since it invites us to see the regress problem as solved in terms of what propositions warranted for S are also *accessible to* S in answering 'How do you know that p?' and successor queries. If the structural formulation is biased, I am certainly not aware of good reasons to think so. I thus propose to work with it here.

We are now in a position to formulate the regress problem more sharply and to proceed to state the regress argument. Again supposing we have some knowledge, let us ask whether a person's knowledge could all be indirect (for the time being I shall speak only of knowledge, though justification also generates a similar regress problem and will be considered later). This may seem possible by virtue of an infinite *epistemic regress*—roughly, an infinite series of knowings, each based (inferentially) on the next. Just imagine that a belief constituting indirect knowledge is based on knowledge of something else, or at least on a further belief; the further knowledge or belief might be based on knowledge of, or belief about, something still further, and so on. I'll call this an *epistemic chain*; it is simply a chain of beliefs, with at least the first constituting knowledge, and each belief linked to the previous one by being based on it. A standard view has been that there are just four possible kinds of epistemic chain. An epistemic chain might be infinite or circular, hence in either case unending; third, it might terminate with a belief that is not knowledge; and fourth, it might terminate with a belief that constitutes direct knowledge. The epistemic regress problem, as I am conceiving it, is to assess these chains as possible sources of knowledge or justification.

II. A Version of The Epistemic Regress Argument

The most common response to the epistemic regress problem is to offer one or another epistemic regress argument in favor of the fourth possibility as the only genuine one. As I conceive the argument, it is best formulated along these lines:

(1) If one has any knowledge, it occurs in an epistemic chain (possibly including the special case of a single link, such as a perceptual or a priori belief, which constitutes knowledge by virtue of being anchored directly in experience or reason);

(2) the only possible kinds of epistemic chains are the four mutually exclusive kinds just sketched;

(3) knowledge can occur only in the last kind of chain; hence,

(4) if one has any knowledge, one has some direct knowledge.[6]

Some preliminary clarification is in order before we consider the plausibility of this argument.

Note first that it is conditionally formulated. This is to preserve neutrality with respect to skepticism, as is appropriate given that the issue concerns conceptual requirements for the existence of knowledge. Moreover, assuming that knowledge requires a knower, the argument would have existential import if it presupposed that there *is* knowledge. Second, I take (1) to imply that any given instance of indirect knowledge depends on at least one epistemic chain for its status *as* knowledge. So understood, the argument clearly implies the further conclusion that any indirect knowledge *S* has exhibits (inferential) *epistemic dependence* on, in the broad sense that it cannot be knowledge apart from, an appropriate inferential connection, via some epistemic chain, to some direct knowledge *S* has. Thus, the argument would show not only that if there is indirect knowledge, there *is* direct knowledge, but also that if there is indirect knowledge, that very knowledge is *traceable* to some direct knowledge as its foundation. This suggests a third point: if two epistemic chains should *intersect*, as where a belief that *p* is both foundationally grounded in experience and part of a circular chain, then (as I understand the argument), if the belief is knowledge, that *knowledge* should be said to *occur* only in the former chain, though the knowledge qua *belief* belongs to both. Knowledge, then, does not occur in a chain merely because the belief constituting it does. Fourth, the argument concerns the structure, not the content, of a body of knowledge and of its constituent epistemic chains. The argument may thus be used regardless of the purported items of knowledge to which one applies it in the case of a particular person.

A similar argument applies to justification. We simply speak of *justificatory chains* and proceed in a parallel way, substituting justification for knowledge. The conclusion would be that if there are any justified beliefs, there are some directly justified beliefs, and that if one has any indirectly justified belief, it exhibits (inferential) *justificatory dependence* on an epistemic chain appropriately linking it to some directly justified belief one has, that is, to a foundational belief. In discussing foundationalism and coherentism, and in exploring how the question of dogmatism bears on both, I shall often focus on justification.

A detailed assessment of the regress argument is impossible here. I simply want to comment on some important aspects of it to prepare the way for a better understanding of foundationalism and coherentism and of some major objections to each.

The possibility of an infinite epistemic chain has seldom seemed to philosophers likely to solve the regress problem. Indeed, I have elsewhere argued that it is at best doubtful that human beings are psychologically capable of having infinite sets of beliefs.[7] It might seem that we can at least have an infinite set of arithmetical beliefs, say that 2 is twice 1, that 4 is twice 2, and so on. But surely for a finite mind there will be some point or other at which the relevant proposition cannot be grasped. The required formulation (or entertaining of the proposition) would at some point become too lengthy to permit one's understanding it, so that, even if one could read (or entertain) it part by part, when one gets to the end one would be unable to remember enough of the first part to grasp and thereby believe what the formulation expresses. Granted one could believe that *the formulation* expresses a truth; but this is not sufficient for believing *the truth* it expresses. I doubt that there are other lines of argument which show that we in fact can have infinite sets of beliefs; nor, if we can, is it clear how infinite epistemic chains can account for any of our knowledge. I thus propose to leave them aside and consider the other kinds of chain.

The possibility of a circular epistemic chain as a basis of knowledge has been taken much more seriously. The standard objection has been that the circularity would be vicious, since one would ultimately have to know something on the basis of itself; and a standard reply has been that if the circle is wide enough and its content sufficiently rich and coherent, the circularity is innocuous. This is a difficult matter which I intend to bypass, since I shall argue that when coherentism is most plausibly formulated it does not depend on possibility of circular chains.

The third alternative, namely that an epistemic chain terminates in a belief which is not knowledge, has been at best rarely affirmed; and there is little plausibility in the hypothesis that knowledge can originate through a belief of a proposition S does not know. If there are exceptions, it is where, although S does not know that p, S is justified, to *some* extent, in believing p, as in making a reasonable estimate. Suppose it vaguely seems to me that I hear strains of music. If, on the basis of the resulting somewhat justified belief that there is music playing, I believe that my daughter has come home, and she has, do I know this? The answer is not clear. But that would not help anyone who claims knowledge can arise from belief which does not constitute knowledge. For it is equally unclear, and for the same sort of reason, whether my belief that there is music playing is *sufficiently* reasonable—say, in terms of how good my perceptual grounds are—to give me knowledge that it is. Notice something else. In the only cases in which the third kind of chain is likely to ground knowledge (or justification), there *is* a degree— apparently a substantial degree—of justification. If there can be an epistemic chain which ends with belief that is not knowledge only because the chain ends, in this way, with justification, then we are apparently at least least in the general vicinity of knowledge. We seem to be at most a few degrees of justification away. We are not getting knowledge from nothing, as it were, but from something that is characteristically much like it— justified true belief. There would thus be a foundation after all: not bedrock, but perhaps ground firm enough to build on.

The fourth possibility is that epistemic chains end in direct knowledge. That knowledge, in turn, is apparently grounded in experience or in reason, and this non-inferential grounding explains how it is (epistemically) direct: it arises, non-inferentially, from (I shall assume) perception, memory, introspection, or reason. Such grounding also seems to explain why a belief so grounded may be expected to be *true*; for experience and reason seem to connect beliefs grounded in them with the reality constituting their object, in such a way that what is believed about that reality tends to be the case. This, at least, seems our best explanation of why we have the beliefs. In any event, the ground-level knowledge could not be inferential; otherwise the chain would not end without a further link. To illustrate, normally I know that there is music just because I hear it. Hence, the chain grounding my knowledge that my daughter has come home is anchored in my perception. Such non-inferentially grounded epistemic chains may differ in many ways. They differ *compositionally*, in the sorts of beliefs constituting them, and *causally*, in the kind of causal relation holding between one belief and its successor, which, for instance, may or may not be taken to involve the predecessor belief's being necessary or sufficient for its successor. They differ *structurally*, in the kind of *epistemic transmission* they exhibit; it may be deductive, inductive, or combine both deductive and inductive links. They also differ *foundationally*, in their ultimate *grounds*, the anchors of the chains, which may be experiential or rational, and may vary in justificational strength.

Different proponents of the fourth possibility have held various views about the character of the *foundational knowledge*, that is, of the beliefs constituting the knowledge that makes up the final link of the chain and anchors it in experience or reason. Some, including

Descartes, have thought that the appropriate beliefs must be infallible, or at least indefeasibly justified.[8] But this is not implied by anything said here: all that the fourth possibility requires is direct knowledge, knowledge not (inferentially) based on other knowledge (or other justified belief). Direct knowledge need not be of self-evident (thus in a sense "self-justified") propositions, nor constituted by indefeasibly justified belief. The case of introspective beliefs, which are paradigms of those that are directly justified, supports this view,[9] and we shall see other reasons to hold it.

III. Modest Foundationalism and Holistic Coherentism

If the regress argument is as important as I think, both as support for epistemological foundationalism and in constraining its content, then we can now formulate some foundationalist theses. Let us start with two versions of what I shall call *generic foundationalism*. The first concerns knowledge:

> I. For any S and any time, t, the structure of S's knowledge, at t, is foundational, and (thus) any indirect (hence non-foundational) knowledge S has depends on direct (thus in a sense foundational) knowledge of S's.

The second position, regarding justification, is the thesis that

> II. For any S and any t, the structure of S's body of justified beliefs is, at t, foundational, and therefore any indirectly (hence non-foundationally) justified beliefs S has depend on directly (thus in a sense foundationally) justified beliefs of S's.

Different foundationalist theories may diverge in the kind and degree of dependence they assert. I especially want to contrast modest and strong foundationalist theses, particularly in the case of justification.

I take *modest foundationalism*, as applied to justification, to be the fallibilistic, non-deductivist thesis that

> III. For any S and any t, (1) the structure of S's body of justified beliefs is, at t, foundational in the sense indicated by II; (2) the justification of S's foundational beliefs is at least typically defeasible; (3) the inferential transmission of justification need not be deductive; and (4) non-foundationally justified beliefs need not derive *all* their

> justification from foundational ones, but only enough so that
> they would remain justified if any other justification they
> have (say, from coherence) were eliminated.[10]

Weaker versions can be constructed; but I am not seeking a minimal
formulation, and, properly clarified, III will serve here. What most
needs explication is the notion of coherence and how it might figure
in III.

It turns out to be very difficult to explain what coherence is. It is
not mere consistency, though *in*consistency is the clearest case of
incoherence. Whatever coherence is, it is a doxastically *internal* relation, in the sense that it is a matter of how one's beliefs (or other
cognitive items to which it may apply) are related *to one another*—
even if by virtue of their *content* alone rather than, say, causally—
and not to anything outside one's system of beliefs (or other cognitions), such as one's perceptual experience. Coherence is sometimes
connected with explanation; it is widely believed that propositions
that stand in an explanatory relation cohere with one another and
that this coherence counts toward that of a person's beliefs of the
propositions in question. Probability (certainly inductive probability)
is also relevant to coherence. If the probability of one proposition
I believe is raised by that of a second I believe, this at least counts
toward the coherence of the first of the beliefs with the second. The
relevant notions of explanation and probability are themselves
philosophically problematic, but our intuitive grasp of them is perhaps
sufficient to help us understand coherence.

Since I am particularly concerned to clarify the contrast between
foundationalism and coherentism, I want to focus on the role modest
foundationalism allows for coherence in relation to justification. The
first role it allows for coherence, or at least for incoherence, is
negative: *in*coherence may defeat justification or knowledge, even
justification of a directly justified (foundational) belief, as where my
justification for believing I may be hallucinating prevents me from
knowing, or remaining justified in believing, that the books in my
study are before me. (If this is not ultimately a role for coherence
itself— which is the contrary and not merely the contradictory of
incoherence—it *is* a role crucial for explaining points stressed by
coherentism, such as the defeasibility of the justification of a memorial
belief owing to its incoherence with perceptual beliefs.) Second,
modest foundationalism can employ an *independence principle* com-

monly emphasized by coherentists, though foundationalists need not grant that its truth is based on coherence. This principle says that the larger the number of independent mutually coherent factors one believes to support the truth of a proposition, the better one's justification for believing it (other things being equal). The principle can explain, for instance, why my justification for believing that my daughter has come home increases as I acquire new beliefs supporting that conclusion, say that there is a smell of grilled cheese rising from the kitchen. Similar principles consistent with foundationalism can accommodate other cases in which coherence enhances justification, say those in which a proposition's explaining, and thereby cohering with, something one justifiably believes tends to confer some justification on that proposition.

Let us now try to formulate a plausible version of coherentism as applied to justification. The central idea underlying coherentism is that the justification of a belief emerges from its coherence with other beliefs one holds. The unit of coherence may be as large as one's entire set of beliefs (though of course some may be more significant in producing the coherence than others, say because of differing degrees of their closeness in subject matter to the belief in question). This idea would be accepted by a proponent of the circular view, but the thesis I want to explore differs from that view in not being *linear*: it does not construe justification or knowledge as emerging from an inferential line running from premises for that conclusion to it, and from other premises to the first set of premises, and so on until we return to the original proposition as a premise. On the circular view, no matter how wide the circle, and no matter how rich its constituent beliefs, there is a *line* from any one belief in a circular epistemic chain to any other. In practice I may never trace the entire line, as by inferring one thing I know from a second, the second from a third, and so on until I reinfer the first. Still, on this view there is such a line for every belief constituting knowledge.

Coherentism need not, however, be linear, and I believe that the most plausible versions are instead holistic.[11] In a broad form, a modest version of *holistic coherentism* might be expressed as follows:

> IV. For any S and any t, if S has any justified beliefs at t,
> then, at t, (1) they are each justified by virtue of their
> coherence with one or more others of S's beliefs, and (2)
> they would remain justified even if any justification they

may derive from sources other than coherence were eliminated.

To illustrate, consider a question that evokes a justification. Ken wonders how, from my closed study, I know (or why I believe) that my daughter is home. I say that there is music playing in the house. He next wants to know how I can recognize my daughter's music from behind my closed doors. I reply that what I hear is the wrong sort of thing to come from any nearby house. He then asks how I know that it is not from a passing car. I say that the volume is too steady for that. He now wonders whether I can distinguish, with my door closed, music playing from the singing of a neighbor working in her yard. I reply that what I hear has an accompaniment. In giving each justification I apparently go only one step along the inferential line: initially, for instance, just to my belief that there is music playing in the house. For my belief that my daughter is home *is* based on this belief about the music. After that, I do not even mention anything that this belief, in turn, is based on; rather, I defend my beliefs as appropriate, in terms of an entire pattern of beliefs I hold. And I may appeal to many different parts of the pattern. For coherentism, then, beliefs representing knowledge do not lie at one end of a grounded chain; they fit a coherent pattern, and their justification emerges from their fitting it in an appropriate way.

Consider a variant of the case. Suppose I had seemed to hear music of *neither* the kind my daughter plays nor the kind the neighbors play nor the sort I expect from passing cars. The proposition that this is what I hear does not cohere well with my belief that the music is played by my daughter. Suddenly I recall that she was bringing a friend today, and I then remember that her friend likes such music. I might now be justified in believing my daughter is home. When I finally hear her voice, I know that she is. The crucial things here are how, initially, a kind of *incoherence* prevents justification of my belief that she is home, and how, as relevant pieces of the pattern develop, I become justified in believing, and (presumably) come to know, that she is. Arriving at a justified belief, on this view, is more like answering a question by looking up diverse information that suggests an answer than like deducing a desired theorem from axioms.

Examples like this one suggest that holistic coherentism can respond to the regress argument *without* embracing the possibility of an epistemic circle (though its proponents need not reject that either).

It may deny that there are only the four kinds of possible epistemic chains I have specified. There is apparently another, not generally noted: that the chain terminates with belief which is *psychologically direct* and *epistemically indirect* or, if we are talking of coherentism about justification, *justificationally indirect*. Hence, the last link is, as belief, direct, but, as knowledge, *in*direct, not in the usual sense that it is inferential, but rather in the broad sense that the belief constitutes knowledge only by virtue of receiving support from other knowledge or belief. Thus, my belief that there is music playing is psychologically direct because it is simply grounded, causally, in my hearing and is not (inferentially) based on any other belief; yet my *knowledge* that there is music is not epistemically direct. It is epistemically, but not inferentially, based on the coherence of my belief that there is music with my other beliefs, presumably including many that constitute knowledge themselves. It is thus knowledge *through*, though not by inference from, other knowledge—or at least through justified beliefs; hence it is epistemically indirect. It is therefore misleading to call the *knowledge* direct at all. Granted, the belief element *in* my knowledge is non-inferentially grounded in perception and is in that sense direct; but the belief constitutes knowledge only by virtue of coherence with my other beliefs.

The kind of example I have sketched can be used to make a further distinction important in assessing coherentist and other theories. In the example *S*'s justification is manifested in a capacity to exhibit the justificatory elements in explaining or defending the belief in question. Let us call a theory of knowledge or justification which makes such a capacity crucial for knowledge or justification a *capacity theory*. By contrast, I propose to call a theory which requires that knowledge or justified belief actually *arise* from a justificatory process—presumably a conscious process and at least typically taken to be one of inference—a *process theory*. A holistic theory can be of either sort. BonJour seems to hold a capacity theory (see, e.g., 1985, esp. pp. 154-155), while Lehrer apparently holds a process theory (see Lehrer, forthcoming, e.g. the abstract, which speaks of the kind of knowledge that interests him as involving "evaluation of information in terms of a background system").

Capacity theories seem to me by and large more plausible than process theories. They are, for instance, more psychologically realistic regarding the genesis and background of justified belief. Foundationalists, however, need not hold either kind of theory, since they can countenance knowledge and justified beliefs which S (e.g., a child who has just learned to speak) simply cannot (at least in fact) justify. But coherentists apparently must hold one or the other kind *if* they are not simply taking coherence itself to function like a foundation in the way sensory experience does: non-inferentially conferring justification whether S has the capacity to justify the belief in question or not. Certainly the best known coherentist views have tended to fall into one of the two categories (and at times to waver between them). Indeed, suppose one makes coherence itself, independently of the capacity to draw on it in justification and of a process by which its cohering elements justify the belief that p, the ground of justification. This is, as Plantinga has suggested (1986, pp. 125-126), to construe coherentism as a kind of foundationalism without the usual foundations.

Apparently, then, the circularity objection to coherentism, often considered one of the most serious, can be met by taking the thesis to be best construed as holistic and as countenancing psychologically direct beliefs. One could insist that if a non-inferential, thus psychologically direct, belief constitutes knowledge, it *must* be direct knowledge. But the coherentist would reply that in that case there will be two kinds of direct knowledge: the kind the foundationalist posits, which derives from grounding in a basic experiential or rational source, and the kind the coherentist posits, which derives from coherence with other beliefs and not from being based on those sources. This is surely a plausible response.

Is the holistic coherentist trying to have it both ways? Not necessarily. Holistic coherentism can grant that a variant of the regress argument holds for belief, since the only kind of belief chain that it is psychologically realistic to attribute to us is the kind terminating in direct (non-inferential) belief. But even on the assumption that knowledge is constituted by (certain kinds of) beliefs, it does not follow that direct belief which is knowledge is also direct *knowledge*. Epistemic dependence does not imply inferential dependence; hence, a non-inferential belief can depend for its status as knowledge on other beliefs. Thus, the coherentist may grant a kind of *psychological foundationalism*, which says (in part) that if we have any beliefs at all, we have some direct (non-inferential) ones, yet deny epistemological foundationalism, which requires that there be knowledge which is epistemically (and normally also psychologically) direct, if there is any knowledge at all. Holistic coherentism may grant experience and reason the status of psychological foundations of our belief systems. But it denies that they are the basic sources of justification or knowledge.

The circularity problem and the difficulty of explicating the notion of coherence itself are not the only serious problems for coherentism, but I do not want to discuss all the others, since my interest is more in simply clarifying the foundationalism-coherentism controversy and only secondarily in assessing either position, except with respect to the charge of dogmatism. My aim in the remainder of this section, then, is to consider how modest foundationalism and holistic coherentism differ and, related to that, how the controversy is sometimes obscured by failure to take account of the differences.

To begin with, there is one kind of case that seems both to favor foundationalism decisively and to show something about justification which coherentism in any form misses. It might seem that coherence theories of justification are decisively refuted by the possibility of *S*'s having only a single belief, say that there is music playing, which is nevertheless justified. For then there would be a justified belief that coheres with no other beliefs one has. But could one have just a single belief? Could I, for instance, believe that there is music playing yet not believe, say, that there are (or could be) musical instruments, melodies and chords? It is not clear that I could; and foundationalism does not assume this possibility, though the theory may easily be wrongly criticized for implying it. Foundationalism is in fact consistent with *one* kind of coherentism, namely, a *coherence theory of the acquisition of concepts*, according to which a person acquires concepts, say of musical pieces, only in relation to one another and must acquire an entire set of related concepts in order to acquire any concept.

It is a further question, however, whether my justification for believing that there is music playing ultimately *derives* from the coherence of the belief with others, i.e., whether coherence is, or is even part of, the basis of my justification in holding this belief.[12] Let us first grant an important point. Suppose the belief turns out to be *in*coherent with a second, such as my belief that I am standing before the phonograph I seem to hear yet *see* no movement of its turntable; now the belief may *cease* to be justified. But this only shows that the belief's justification is *defeasible*—liable to being either overridden (roughly, outweighed) or undermined—should sufficiently serious incoherence *arise*. It does not show that the justification derives from coherence in the first place. In this case the justification of my belief grounded in hearing may be overridden: my better justified beliefs, including the conviction that a phonograph with a motionless turntable cannot play, may make it more reasonable for me to believe that there is *not* music playing in the house.

The case raises another question regarding the possibility that coherence is the source of my justification, as opposed to a constraint on it. Could incoherence override the justification of my belief in the first place if I were not *independently* justified in believing that a proposition incoherent with certain other ones is, or probably is, false, e.g. in believing that if I do not see the turntable moving, then I am not hearing music from the phonograph? For if I lacked such independent justification, should I not suspend judgment on or reject the other propositions and retain my original belief? And aren't the relevant other beliefs or propositions—those that can override or defeat my justification—precisely the kind for which, directly or inferentially, we have some degree of justification through the experiential and rational sources, such as visual perception of a stockstill turntable?

There is also a second case, in which one's justification is simply undermined: one ceases to be justified in believing the proposition in question, though one does not become justified in believing it false. Suppose I seem to see a black cat, yet it no longer appears to me that there is one there if I move five feet to my left. This experience could justify my believing, and lead me to believe, that I might be hallucinating. This belief in turn is to a degree incoherent with, and undermines the justification of, my visual belief that the cat is there, though it does not by itself justify my believing that there is no cat there. Again, however, I am apparently justified, independently of coherence, in believing a proposition highly relevant to my overall justification for an apparently foundational perceptual belief: namely, the proposition that my seeing the cat there is incoherent with my merely hallucinating it there. The same seems to hold for the proposition that my seeing the cat there coheres with my feeling fur if I extend my hand to the feline focal point of my visual field. Considerations like these suggest that coherence has the role it does in justification only because some beliefs are justified independently of it.

Both examples illustrate an important distinction that is often missed.[13] It is between defeasibility and epistemic dependence or, alternatively, between *negative epistemic dependence*—which is a form of defeasibility—and *positive epistemic dependence*—the kind beliefs bear to the source(s) from which they *derive* any justification they have or, if they represent knowledge, their status as knowledge. The defeasibility of a belief's justification by incoherence does not imply that, as coherentists must hold, its justification positively depends on coherence. If my garden is my source of food, I (positively) depend on it. The fact that people could poison the garden does not make their non-malevolence part of my food source, or imply a (positive) dependence on them, such as I have on the sunshine. Moreover, it is the sunshine which (with rainfall and other conditions) explains both my having the food and the amount that I have. So it is with perceptual experience as a source of justification. Foundationalists need not deny that a belief's justification negatively depends on something else, for as we have seen they need not claim that justification must be indefeasible. But negative dependence does not imply positive dependence. Justification can be defeasible by incoherence, and thus overridden or undermined should incoherence arise, without owing its existence to coherence in the first place. Modest foundationalism does not, then, turn out to be a blend of coherentism, and it remains open just what positive role, if any, it must assign to coherence in explicating justification.

There is a further point which modest foundationalism should grant to coherentism, and in assessing this point we can learn more about both coherentism and justification. *If* I set out to *show* that my belief is justified—as the dialectical formulation of the regress problem invites one to think solving the regress problem requires—I *do* have to cite propositions that cohere with the one to be shown to be justified for me, say that there is music in my house. In some cases, these are not even propositions one already believes. Often, in defending the original belief, one forms new beliefs, such as the belief one acquires, in moving one's head, that one can vividly see the changes in perspective that go with seeing a black cat. More important, *these* beliefs are especially appropriate to the *process of justifying* one's belief; and the result of that process is *showing* that the original belief is justified, together with one's forming the second-order belief that the belief is justified. Thus, coherence is important in showing that a belief is justified. In *that* sense coherence is a pervasive element in justification: it is pervasive in the process of justification.

The moment we reflect on this point, however, we are likely to question whether the second-order beliefs appropriate to showing that a belief is justified must be involved in its *being* justified in the first place. There is no good reason to think they need be. Indeed, why should one's simply having a justified belief imply even that one is justified *in* holding the second-order beliefs appropriate to showing that it is justified? It would seem that just as a little child can be of good character even if unable to defend its character against attack, one can have a justified belief even if, in response to someone who doubts this, one could not show that one does. Supposing *S* has the sophistication to form a second-order belief that his belief that there is a cat before him is justified, the latter can be justified so long as the former is *true*: *S* need not be justified in holding it or be able to show it true.

Justifying a second-order belief is a sophisticated process. The process is particularly sophisticated if the second-order belief concerns a special property like the justification of the original belief. Simply being justified in a belief about, say, the sounds around one, is a much simpler matter. But confusion is easy here, particularly if the governing context is an imagined dialectic with a skeptic. Take, for instance, the question how a simple perceptual belief "is justified." The very phrase is ambiguous. For all it tells us, the question could be 'By what process, say of reasoning, has the belief been (or might it be) justified?' or, on the other hand, 'In virtue of what is the belief justified?' These are two very different questions. The first invites us to think of justification as a process of which the belief is a beneficiary, the second to conceive it as a property that a belief has, whether in virtue of its content, genesis, or other characteristics. Both aspects of the notion are important, but unfortunately much of our talk about justification makes it easy to run them together. A justified belief could be one that *has* justification or one that *has been* justified; and a request for someone's justification could be a request for a list of justifying factors *or* for a recounting of the process by which the person justified the belief.

Once we forswear the mistakes just pointed out, what argument is left to show the (positive) dependence of perceptual justification on coherence? I do not see that any plausible one remains, though given how hard it is to discern what specifically coherence *is*, we cannot be confident that no plausible argument is forthcoming. Granted, one could point to the oddity of saying things like, 'I am justified in believing that there is music playing, but I cannot justify this belief'. Why is this odd if not because, if I have a justified belief,

I can give a justification for it by appeal to beliefs that cohere with it? But consider this. Typically, in asserting something I imply that I *can* justify it in some way or other, especially if the belief I express is not grounded in a basic source such as perception; yet here I deny that very suggestion. It is apparently my *asserting* that my belief is justified, rather than its being so, that gives the appearance that I must here be able to give a justification of the belief.

To be sure, when I say that there is music playing, I can give a justification: for instance, that I hear it. But I need not *believe* that I hear it, *before* the question of justification arises. That question leads me to focus on my circumstances, in which I first had a belief solely about the *music*. I did also have a *disposition*, based on my auditory experience, to form the belief that *I hear* the music, and this is largely why, in the course of justifying that belief, I then *form* the further belief that I *do* hear it. But a disposition to believe something does not imply a dispositional belief of it. Here I tend to form the belief that I hear the music if, as I hear it, the question whether I hear it arises; yet I need not have subliminally believed this already (as a process theorist might hold). The justification I offer, then, is not by appeal to coherence with other beliefs I already had—such as that I saw the turntable moving—but by reference to what has traditionally been considered a basic source of both justification and knowledge: perception. It is thus precisely the kind of justification which foundationalists are likely to consider appropriate for a non-inferential belief. Indeed, one consideration favoring foundationalism about both justification and knowledge, at least as an account of our everyday epistemic practices, including much scientific practice, is that typically we cease to offer justification or to defend a knowledge claim precisely when we reach a basic source.

IV. Coherence, Foundations, and Justification

There is far more to say in clarifying both foundationalism and coherentism. But if what I have said so far is correct, then we can at least understand their basic thrusts and can see how coherentism may respond to the regress argument and foundationalism may reply to the charge that, if modest enough to be plausible, it depends on coherence criteria rather than on grounding in experience and reason, both construed as sources of justification. One may still wonder, however, if modest foundationalism concedes enough to coherentism. Granted that it need not restrict the role of coherence any more than is required by the regress argument, it still denies, as is implicit in formulation III, that coherence is (independently) a necessary condition for justification. It also denies that coherence is a *basic* (non-derivative) source of justification—or at least that if it is, the degree of justification it can produce is sufficient for a belief possessing it to be unqualifiedly justified or (given truth and certain other conditions) to constitute knowledge. The moderate version of holistic coherentism formulated above is parallel in this: while it may grant to foundationalism its typical psychological picture of how our belief systems are structured, it denies that foundational justification is (independently) necessary for justification and that it is a basic source of justification, except possibly of degrees of justification insufficient for knowledge or for unqualifiedly justified belief.

The issue here is the difference in the conceptions of justification appropriate to the two views. Broadly, foundationalists tend to hold that justification supervenes on a belief, whether inferentially or directly, by virtue of its grounding in experience or reason; whereas coherentists tend to hold that justification supervenes on a belief by virtue of its coherence with one or more others of S's beliefs. This is apparently a difference concerning basic sources. To be sure, my formulation may make coherentism sound foundationalistic, since justification is grounded not in an inferential relation to premises but in coherence itself, which sounds parallel to experience or reason. But note three contrasts with foundationalism as I conceive it. First, the source is *doxastic*, since the coherence is an internal property of the belief system; second, the coherence is *inferential*, whereas experiential and rational sources are non-inferential generators of belief; and third, S has *inferential access* to the coherence-making relations: on a capacity theory, S can wield them in inferentially justifying the belief that p, and on a process view that belief emerges from an accessible (at least normally inferential) process involving them. Still, I want to pursue just how deep the difference between foundationalism and coherentism is; for as we have seen, once foundationalism is modestly expressed and grants a coherence theory of the acquisition of concepts, and once coherentism is plausibly stated in a way consistent with psychological foundationalism, it may appear that the views differ far less than usually supposed.

It should help to start by contrasting modest foundationalism with *strong foundationalism* and comparing their relation to coherentism. The latter, if we use, e.g., Descartes' version as a model, is deductivist, takes foundational beliefs as indefeasibly justified, and allows coherence at most a highly limited generative role. To meet these conditions, it may reduce the basic sources of justification to reason and some form of introspection. Moreover, since it is committed to the indefeasibility of foundational justification, it would not grant that incoherence can defeat such justification. It would also concede to coherentists, and hence to any independence principle they countenance, only a minimal positive role, say by insisting that if a belief is supported by two or more independent cohering sources, its justification is increased only "additively," that is, only by bringing together the justification transmitted separately from each relevant basic source.

By contrast, what modest foundationalism denies regarding coherence is only that it is a basic source of justification. Thus, coherence by itself is not sufficient to ground justification, and hence the independence principle does not apply to sources that have *no* justification; at most, the principle allows coherence to raise the level of justification originally drawn from other sources to a level *higher* than it would be if those sources did not mutually cohere. Similarly, if inference is a basic source of coherence (as some coherentists seem to believe), it is not a basic source of justification. It may enhance justification, as where one strengthens one's justification for believing someone's testimony by inferring the same point from someone else's. But inference *alone* does not generate justification: I might infer any number of propositions from several I already believe merely through wishful thinking; yet even if I thereby arrive at a highly coherent set of beliefs, I have not increased my justification for believing any of them.

A natural reply from the coherentist side is that when we consider examples of justified belief not only do we always find some coherence, we also apparently find enough of it to account for the justification. This reply is especially plausible if—as I suggest—coherentism as usually formulated is modified to include, in the coherence base, *dispositions to believe*. Consider my belief that music is playing. It coheres both with my beliefs about what records are in the house, what music my daughter prefers, my auditory capacities, etc., *and* with many of my dispositions to believe, say to form the belief that no one else likely to be in the house would play that music.

Since such dispositions admit of justification and, when realized, can generate inference, they are appropriate items to put in the coherence base, and including them is particularly useful in defending a capacity theory, which is thereby freed from implausibly positing all the beliefs needed for the justificational capacities it takes to underlie justified belief. Given this broad conception of coherence, it is surely plausible to take coherence as at least necessary to the justification of my belief. Perhaps, indeed, its justification supervenes on (and hence is based on) coherence, not on grounding in my auditory experience.

Let us grant both that the case does exhibit a high degree of coherence among my beliefs and dispositions to believe, and even that the coherence is necessary for the justification of my belief. It does not in the least follow that the justification supervenes on the coherence. It could be that coherence is at best a *consequential necessary condition* for justification, one that holds in virtue of the justification itself or what it supervenes on, as opposed to a *constitutive necessary condition*, one that expresses part of what it *is* for a belief to be justified or at least a supervenience base property of it. The relation of coherence to the base properties might be analogous to that of heat to friction: a necessary product of it, but not part of what constitutes it. (The relevant kind of supervenience and necessity in the epistemological case are presumably metaphysical, not causal, but most of my points are neutral regarding the modality of the supervenience relation).

If coherence is a constitutive necessary condition for justification, we should be able to construct cases in which the experiential and rational sources are absent, yet there is sufficient coherence for justified belief. But this is precisely what we do not easily find, if we can find it at all: if I discover a set of my beliefs that intuitively cohere very well yet receive no support from what I believe (or at least am disposed to believe) on the basis of experience or reason, I am not inclined to attribute justification to any of them. To be sure, once the unit of coherence is made large enough, as it typically is, to *include* my actual beliefs, then because I have so many that *are* grounded in experience or reason (indeed, few that are not), I will almost certainly not *in fact* have any intuitively justified beliefs not coherent with some of my beliefs so grounded. This complicates assessment of the role of coherence in justification. But we *can* certainly imagine beings (or ourselves) artificially endowed with coherent sets of beliefs not grounded in experience or reason; and when we do, it appears that coherence does not automatically confer justification.

One might conclude, then, that it is more nearly true that coherence supervenes on justification than that the latter supervenes on the former. Further, the data we have so far considered can be explained on the hypothesis that *both* coherence among beliefs and their justification supervene on the beliefs' being grounded (in an appropriate way) in the basic sources. For particularly if a coherence theory of the acquisition concepts is true, one perhaps cannot have a belief justified by a basic source without having beliefs—or at least dispositions to believe— related in an intimate (and intuitively coherence-generating) way to it. One certainly cannot have a justified belief unless no incoherence defeats the justification. Given these two points, it is to be expected that, on a modest foundationalism, justification will, in normal persons, imply coherence, both in the positive sense involving some sort of mutual support or harmony and in the weak sense of the absence of potential incoherence. There is some reason to think, then, that coherence is not a basic source of justification and is at most a consequentially necessary condition for it.

There is at least one more possibility to be considered, however: that *given* justification from foundational sources, coherence can generate more justification than S would have from those sources alone. If so, we might call coherence a *conditionally basic* source, in that, given some justification from other sources, it can produce new justification. This bears on the interpretation of the independence principle. It is widely agreed that our justification increases markedly when we take into account independent sources of evidence for the proposition in question, as where I confirm that there is music playing by going closer to enhance my auditory impression and by using visual perception to confirm that a phonograph is playing. It is arguable that what explains the dramatic increment in my overall justification here is not just "additivity" of foundational justification, but coherence as a further source of justification.

There is plausibility in this reasoning, but it is not cogent. For one thing, there really are no additive quantities of justification. Perhaps we simply combine degrees of justification, so far as we can, on analogy with combinations of independent probabilities. The relevant probability rules do not seem to depend on coherence; they seem in fact to be justifiable by a priori reasoning in the way beliefs grounded in reason are commonly thought to be justifiable. There remains a contrast between, say, having six independent credible

witnesses tell me that p on separate occasions which I do not connect with one another, and having them do so on a single occasion
when I can note the coherence of their stories. But this is not, say,
a case of six increments of isolated foundational justification versus
a case of six cohering items of evidence. The coherence is present
in both cases; but in the second there is an additional belief (or justified
disposition to believe): *that* six independent witnesses agree. Foundationalists as well as coherentists can offer plausible accounts of
how this additional belief increases the justification one has in the
first case. It would be premature, then, to take cases like this to show
that coherence is even a conditionally basic source of justification.

There is no hope of settling the foundationalism-coherentism controversy in a single paper, if indeed it can be resolved in any single
work (or at all). But we can now see some dimensions of the issue
that have often been neglected, and we have raised some of the questions crucial for sharpening the controversy and strengthening both
positions. One dimension is the formulation of the regress problem
itself; another is the distinction between defeasibility and epistemic
dependence; still another is that between consequential and constitutive necessary conditions; and yet another is between an unqualifiedly and a conditionally basic source. Even if it turns out that
coherence is neither a constitutive necessary condition for justification nor even a conditionally basic source of it, we have still seen
reason to take it to be important for justification. It may even be
a kind of *mark* of justification, a common effect of the same causes
as it were, or a virtue based on the same foundations. It is certainly
significant for justification as indicating a negative constraint; for incoherence is a paradigm of what defeats justification.

V. Epistemological Dogmatism and the Sources of Justification

Given the conception of the foundationalism-coherentism controversy developed above, we can perhaps throw some new light
on how the charge of dogmatism may be relevant to both. First,
however, we must specify what dogmatism is. The notion is not easy
to characterize, and there have apparently been few detailed discussions of it in recent epistemological literature.[14] My focus will be
dogmatism as an epistemological attitude or stance, not as a trait
of personality. Indeed, I shall not even be mainly interested in the

notion of a dogmatic attitude, whether in general or toward a range of propositions, but in what it is to hold a *belief* dogmatically. This is presumably the basic notion in any case: the general attitude is in some way a matter of dogmatically holding beliefs, and the personality trait of dogmatism is in some way a matter of having dogmatic attitudes.

It will be useful to start with some contrasts. Dogmatism in relation to a belief is not equivalent to stubbornness in holding it; for even if a dogmatically held belief cannot be easily given up, one could be stubborn in holding a belief simply from attachment to it, and without the required disposition to defend it or regard it as better grounded than alternatives. For similar reasons, psychological certainty in holding a belief does not entail dogmatism. Indeed, if one is both psychologically certain of a simple logical truth *and* disposed to reject denials of it with confidence and to suspect even well-developed arguments against it as sophistical, one does not qualify as dogmatic. *Content matters.* An attitude that would be dogmatic in holding one belief may not be so in holding another.

Dogmatic people are often closed-minded, and dogmatically held beliefs are often closed-mindedly maintained; but a belief held closed-mindedly need not be held dogmatically: it may be maintained with a guilty realization that emotionally one simply cannot afford to listen to challenges of it, and with an awareness that it might be mistaken. Moreover, although people who hold beliefs dogmatically are often intellectually pugnacious in defending them, or even in trying to win converts, such pugnacity is not sufficient for dogmatism. Intellectual pugnacity is consistent with a keen awareness that one might be mistaken and may be accompanied by openminded argumentation for one's view. Nor need a dogmatically held belief generate such pugnacity; one might be indisposed to argue, and one's dogmatism might surface only when one is challenged.

One thing all of these possible conceptions of dogmatism have in common is lack of a second-order component. But that seems necessary for a dogmatic attitude. It is not that believing, even firmly, that one is right in believing *p* is necessary for dogmatically believing *p*. This is not so, as is shown by certain cases of believing simple logical truths. But typically a dogmatically held belief is maintained with the conviction (often unjustified) that one is right. It may be enough, however, that one be *disposed* to have a certain belief, usually an unwarrantedly positive one, about the status of one's belief that

p. Imagine that Tom thinks that Mozart is a far greater composer than Hayden, asserts it without giving any argument, and sloughs off arguments to the contrary. If he does not believe, but is disposed to believe on considering the matter, that his belief is, say, obviously correct, then he may qualify as dogmatically holding it.

There may be no simple, illuminating way to characterize dogmatism with respect to a belief that p, but if there is, the following elements should be reflected at least as typical conditions: (1) confidence that p, and significantly greater confidence than one's evidence or grounds warrant; (2) unjustified resistance to taking plausible objections seriously when they are intelligibly posed to one; (3) a willingness, or at least a tendency, to assert the proposition flat-out even in the presence of presumptive reasons to question it, including simply the conflicting views of one or more persons whom S sees or should see to be competent concerning the subject matter; and (4) a (second-order) belief, or disposition to believe, that one's belief is clearly true (or certainly true). Note, however, that (i) excessive confidence can come from mere foolhardiness and can be quite unstable; (ii) resistance to plausible objections may be due to intellectual laziness; (iii) a tendency to assert something flat-out can derive from mere downrightness of personality; and (iv) a belief that one is right might arise not from dogmatism but from conceit, intellectual mistake (such as a facile anti-skepticism), or sheer error.

Of the four elements highly characteristic of dogmatism, the last may have the best claim to be an unqualifiedly necessary condition, and perhaps one or more of the others is necessary. The four are probably jointly sufficient; but this is not self-evident, and I certainly doubt that we can find any simple condition that is non-trivially sufficient, such as believing that one knows, or is justified in believing, p (which one does believe), while also believing one has no reasons for p.[15] This condition is not sufficient because it could stem from a certain view of knowledge and reasons, say a view on which one never has reasons (as opposed to a basis) for believing simple self-evident propositions. The condition also seems insufficient because it could be satisfied by a person who lacks the first three of the typical conditions just specified.

Let us work with the full-blooded conception of a dogmatically held belief summarized by conditions (1)-(4). What, then, may we say about the standard charge that foundationalism is dogmatic, in a sense implying that it invites proponents to hold certain beliefs dogmatically? This charge has been leveled on a number of occasions,[16] and some plausible replies have been made.[17] Given the earlier sections of this paper, it should be plain that the charge is more likely to seem cogent if foundationalism is conceived as answering the *dialectical* regress problem, as it has apparently been taken to do by, e.g., Chisholm.[18] For in this case a (doxastic) stopping place in the regress generated by 'How do you know that *p*?' will coincide with the assertion of a second-order belief, such as that I know that q, e.g. that there is white before me; and since knowledge claims are commonly justifiable by evidence, flatly stopping the regress in this way will seem dogmatic. Even if such a claim is itself justified by citing a non-doxastic state of affairs, such as my visual experience of white, one is still *asserting* the existence of this state of affairs and hence apparently *expressing* knowledge: making a what seems a tacit claim *to it*, though not actually claiming *to have* it.

We *can* formulate various second-order foundationalisms, for instance one which says that if *S* knows anything, then there is something that *S* directly knows *S* knows. But a foundationalist need not hold such a view, nor would one who does be committed to maintaining that *many* kinds of belief constitute such knowable foundations or that every epistemic chain terminates in them. In any event, modest foundationalists will be disinclined to hold a second-order foundationalism, even if they think that we do in fact have some second-order knowledge. For one thing, if foundational beliefs are only defeasibly justified, it is likely to be quite difficult to know that they *are* justified, e.g. because this requires warrant for attributing certain grounds to the belief and may also require justification for believing that certain defeaters are absent. This is not to deny that there are kinds of knowledge which one may, without having evidence for this, warrantedly and non-dogmatically say one has, for instance where the first-order knowledge is of a simple self-evident proposition. My point is that foundationalism as such, at least in modest versions, need not make any such second-order knowledge (or justification) a condition for the existence of knowledge (or justification) in general.[19]

If we raise the regress problem in the structural form, there is much less temptation to consider foundationalism dogmatic. For there is no presumption that, with respect to anything I know, I non-inferentially know that I know it (and similarly for justification). Granted, on the assumption that by and large I am entitled, without offering evidence, to assert what I directly know, it may seem that even modest foundationalism justifies me in holding—and expressing—beliefs dogmatically. But this is a mistake: there is considerable difference between what I know or justifiably believe and what I may warrantedly assert without evidence. It is, for example, apparently consistent with knowing that p, say that there is music playing, that I have *some* reason to doubt that p; I might certainly have reason to think others doubt it and that they should not be spoken to as if their objections could not matter. Thus, I might know, through my own good hearing, that p, yet be unwarranted in saying that I know it, and warranted, with only moderate confidence, even in saying that I believe it. Here 'I believe it' would *express*, but not *claim*, my knowledge; 'I know it' explicitly claims knowledge and normally implies that I have justification for beliefs about my objective grounds, not just about my own cognitive and perceptual state.

Furthermore, once the defeasibility of foundational beliefs is appreciated, then even if one does think that one may assert the propositions in question without offering evidence, one will not take the attitudes or other stances required for holding a belief dogmatically. As the example of my belief about the music illustrates, most of the time one is likely to be open to counterargument and may indeed tend to be no more confident than one's grounds warrant. To be sure, fallibilism alone, even when grounded in a proper appreciation of defeasibility, does not preclude dogmatism regarding many of one's beliefs. But it helps toward this end, and it is a natural for modest foundationalists to hold a fallibilistic outlook on their beliefs, especially their empirical beliefs, and to bear it in mind in framing an overall conception of human experience.

If foundationalism has been uncritically thought to encourage dogmatism, coherentism has often been taken to foster intellectual openness. But this second stereotypic conception may be no better justified than the first. Much depends, of course, on the kind of coherentism and on the temperament of its proponent. Let us consider these points in turn.

What makes coherentism seem to foster tolerance is precisely what leads us to wonder how it can account for knowledge (at least without a coherence theory of truth). For as coherentists widely grant, there are indefinitely many coherent systems of beliefs people might in principle have; hence, to suppose that mine embodies knowledge and thus truth, or even justification and thus a presumption of truth, while yours does not, is prima facie unwarranted. But the moment the view is modified so as to seem capable of accounting for knowledge, say by requiring a role for observation beliefs and other cognitively spontaneous beliefs, as BonJour does, or by requiring beliefs accepted on the basis of a desire to believe truth and avoid error, as Lehrer does, it becomes easy to think—and one can be warranted in thinking—that one's beliefs are more likely to constitute knowledge, or to be justified, than someone else's, especially if the other person(s) hold views incompatible with one's own. Indeed, while coherentism makes it easy to see how counterargument can be coherently launched from a wide range of opposing viewpoints, it also provides less in the way of foundational appeals by which debates may be settled—and pretensions quashed. Is one likely to be less dogmatic where one thinks one can always encounter reasoned opposition from someone with a different coherent belief system, right or wrong, than where one believes one can be decisively shown to be mistaken by appeal to foundational sources of knowledge and justification? The answer is not clear; in any given case it will depend on a number of variables, including the temperament of the subject and the propositions in question. And cannot one's conviction that, using one or another coherent resource, one can always continue to argue for one's view generate overconfidence just as much as one's thinking one (defeasibly) knows something through experience or reason? It turns out that coherentism can also produce dogmatism, even if its proponents have tended to be less inclined towards it than some foundationalists.

If there has been such a lesser inclination, it may be due to temperament, including perhaps a greater sympathy with skepticism, as much as to theoretical commitments. In any case, whether one dogmatically holds certain of one's beliefs surely does depend significantly on whether one is dogmatic in temperament or in certain segments of one's outlook. It may be that the tendency to seek justification in large patterns runs stronger in coherentists than in foundationalists, and that the latter tend more than the former to seek it instead in chains of argument or of inference. If so, this could explain a systematic difference in the degree of dogmatism found in the two traditions. But these tendencies are only contingently connected with the respective theories: foundationalism can account for the justificatory importance of large patterns, and coherentists commonly conceive argument and inference as prime sources of coherence. One can also wax dogmatic in insisting that a pattern is decisive in justification, as one can dogmatically assert that a single perceptual belief is incontrovertibly veridical.

One source of the charge of dogmatism, at least as advanced by philosophers, is of course the sense that skepticism is being flatly denied. Moreover, the skeptic in us tends to think that any confident assertion of a non-self-evident, non-introspective proposition is dogmatic. On this score, foundationalism is again likely to seem dogmatic if conceived as an answer to the dialectical regress formulation. For it may then seem to beg the question against skepticism. But again, foundationalism is not committed to the existence of any knowledge or justified belief; and even a foundationalist who maintains that there is some, need not hold that we directly know that there is. Granted, foundationalists are more likely to say, at some point or other, that skepticism is just wrong than are coherentists, who (theoretically) can always trace new justificatory paths through the fabric of their beliefs. But if this is true, it has limited force: perhaps in some such cases foundationalists would be warranted in a way that precludes being dogmatic, and perhaps coherentists are in effect repeating themselves in a way consistent with dogmatic reassertion of the point at issue.

I have argued for the importance of the regress problem, and of how it is formulated, for the controversy between foundationalism and coherentism. It matters considerably whether we conceive the problem dialectically or structurally, at least insofar as we cast foundationalism and coherentism in terms of their capacity to solve it. Using a structural formulation of the regress problem as a partial basis for understanding the controversy, I have suggested plausible versions of both foundationalism and coherentism. Neither has been established, but both have been clarified. In clarifying both views and how they differ, I have stressed a number of distinctions: between the process and the property of justification, between dispositional beliefs and dispositions to believe, between capacity and process theories of justification or knowledge, between epistemically and psychologically foundational beliefs, between defeasibility and epistemic dependence, between constitutive and consequential necessary conditions for justification, and between unqualifiedly and conditionally basic sources of it.

We can see, moreover, how modest foundationalism avoids some of the objections commonly thought to refute it, including its alleged failure to account for the defeasibility of most and perhaps all of our justification, and for the role of coherence in justification. Indeed, foundationalism can even account for coherence as a mark of justification; the chief tension between the two theories concerns not whether coherence is crucial for justification, but whether it is a basic (constitutive) source of it. It is equally clear how coherentism can avoid any obviously vicious circularity and how it expresses at least negative constraints on whatever justification may arise from foundational sources. Of the problems that remain for foundationalism and coherentism, the one most readily clarified by the chief work of this paper—and particularly by the distinction between defeasibility and epistemic dependence—is the dogmatism objection. It turns out that foundationalism need not be damaged by it and coherentism is not immune to it. A properly qualified foundationalism is neither intrinsically dogmatic nor unable to account for the main connections between coherence and justification. Indeed, it may provide the basis for a unified account of both.[20]

Notes

1. For recent statements of foundationalism see, e.g., Chisholm (1966 and 1977) and, especially, his "A Version of Foundationalism," in (1982); Alston, (1976); Audi (1978); Moser (1985), and Foley (1987). For recent statements of coherentism see, e.g., Sellars (1973); Lehrer (1974); Harman (1975); and BonJour (1985). For useful discussion of the controversy between foundationalism and coherentism, see Delaney (1976), which defends a kind of foundationalism, and Blanshard (1964), which defends his earlier views against objections by critics quoted in the same chapter.
2. BonJour, e.g., says that the regress problem is "perhaps the most crucial in the entire theory of knowledge" (1985, p. 18); and he considers it the chief motivation for foundationalism (p. 17) and regards the failure of foundationalism as "the main motivation for a coherence theory" (p. 149).
3. Chisholm seems to raise the problem in this way when he says, "If we try Socratically to formulate our justification for any particular claim to know ("My justification for thinking that I know that *A* is the fact that *B*"), and if we are relentless in our inquiry ("and my justification for thinking that I know that *B* is the fact that *C*"), we will arrive, sooner or later, at a kind of stopping place ("but my justification for thinking that I know that *N* is simply the fact that *N*"). An example of *N* might be the fact that I seem to remember having been here before or that

something now looks blue to me" (1966, p. 2); cp. his (1977), esp. pp. 19-20. In these and other passages Chisholm seems to be thinking of the regress problem dialectically and taking a foundational belief to be second order. To be sure, he is talking about justification of any "claim to know"; but this and similar locutions—such as 'knowledge claim', have often been taken to apply to expressions of first-order knowledge, as where one says that it is raining, on the basis of perceptions which one would normally take to yield knowledge that it is.

4. See *Posterior Analytics*, Bk 3. Having opened Bk. 1 with the statement that "All instruction given or received by way of argument proceeds from pre-existent knowledge" (71a1-2), and thereby established a concern with the structure and presuppositions of knowledge, he formulated the regress argument as a response to the question of what is required for the existence of (what he called scientific) knowledge (72b4-24). (The translation is by W. D. Ross.)

5. In Audi (1986) I have developed a detailed account of what it is for one belief to be based on another in the relevant (broadly inferential) sense.

6. The locus classicus of this argument is the *Posterior Analytics*, Bk. II. But while Aristotle's version agrees with the one given here insofar as his main conclusion is that "not all knowledge is demonstrative," he also says that "since the regress must end in immediate truths, those truths must be indemonstrable" (72b19-24), whereas I hold that direct knowledge does *not* require indemonstrability. There might *be* appropriate premises; *S*'s foundational belief is simply not based on them (I also question the validity of the inference in the second quotation, though I suspect Aristotle had independent grounds for its conclusion).

7. See Audi (1982b). For other discussions of the possibility of justification by infinite regress see Harker, (1984); and Clark (this volume).

8. In Meditation I, e.g., Descartes says that "reason already persuades me that I ought no less carefully to withhold my assent from matters which are not entirely certain and indubitable than from those which appear to me manifestly to be false" (from the Haldane and Ross Trans.)

9. In Audi (1974) I have argued that introspective beliefs are not indefeasibly justified.

10. Clause (4) probably needs a *ceteris paribus* clause after 'would'; and the *level* of justification in question I take to be (as in the counterpart formulation of coherentism) approximately that appropriate to knowledge. The formulation should hold, however, for any given level.

11. This applies to Sellars, Lehrer, and BonJour and is evident in the works cited in note 1. Their coherentist positions are not linear. For a statement of an internal difficulty besetting linear coherentism and probably also the most plausible versions of holistic coherentism, see Audi (1982a).

12. With this question in mind, it is interesting to read Davidson (1983). Cp. Kim, "What Is 'Naturalized Epistemology'?" (this volume).

13. This distinction seems to me to have been often missed, e.g. in Kornblith (1980), as I have argued (especially in relation to Kornblith's paper) in Audi (1983). ·

14. One exception is the discussion by Shatz (1983).

15. Shatz (1983) attributes a similar suggestion to me (from correspondence), and it is appropriate to suggest here why I do not mean to endorse it.
16. The dogmatism charge has been brought by, e.g., Aune (1967, pp. 41-43), and, by implication, by Cornman and Lehrer (1974), pp. 60-61. Alston goes so far as to say that "It is the aversion to dogmatism, to the apparent arbitrariness of putative foundations, that leads many philosophers to embrace some form of coherence or contextualist theory . . ." (1976, pp. 182-183).
17. See Alston (1976) for a reply to the dogmatism charge; his reply supports mine.
18. A formulation of the regress problem by Chisholm is cited in note 3. For a contrasting formulation see Quinton (1973, p. 119). Quinton, it is interesting to note, is sympathetic to the kind of modest foundationalism which would serve as an answer to the problem in his formulation.
19. It is natural to read Descartes as holding a second-order foundationalism; but if he did, he was at least not committed to it by even his strong foundationalism: that requires indefeasible foundations, but it is his commitment to vindicating knowledge in the face of skepticism which apparently commits him to his requirement of second-order knowledge. Similar points hold for Aristotle, who indeed may have taken our second-order knowledge to be at least limited; he said, e.g., "It is hard to be sure whether one knows or not; for it is hard to be sure whether one's knowledge is based on the basic truths appropriate to each attribute—the differentia of true knowledge" (*Posterior Analytics* 76a26-28).
20. For helpful comments on an earlier version I thank Dan D. Crawford, Timothy Day, and Matthias Steup. I also benefited from discussing some of the issues with the NEH Seminar (on Reasons, Justification, and Rationality) that I directed in 1987. The final stages of the paper were completed during my tenure as a fellow at the University of Notre Dame Center for the Philosophy of Religion.

References

Alston, William P.: 1976, "Two Types of Foundationalism," *The Journal of Philosophy* LXXXIII, 7.

Audi, Robert: 1974, "The Limits of Self-Knowledge," *Canadian Journal of Philosophy* IV, 2.

Audi, Robert: 1978, "Psychological Foundationalism," *The Monist* 62, 4.

Audi, Robert: 1982a, "Axiological Foundationalism," *Canadian Journal of Philosophy* XII, 1.

Audi, Robert: 1982b, "Believing and Affirming," *Mind* XCI.

Audi, Robert: 1983, "Foundationalism, Epistemic Dependence, and Defeasibility," *Synthese* 55, 1.

Audi, Robert: 1986, "Belief, Reason, and Inference," *Philosophical Topics* XIV, 1.

Aune, Bruce: 1967, *Knowledge, Mind and Nature*, Atascadero, CA.

442 / Robert Audi

Blanshard, Brand: 1964, "Coherence and Correspondence," in *Philosophical Interrogations*, edited by Sydney and Beatrice Rome, New York.

Bonjour, Laurence: 1985, *The Structure of Empirical Knowledge*, Cambridge, Mass.

Chisholm, Roderick M.: 1966 and 1977, *Theory of Knowledge*, Englewood Cliffs.

Chisholm, Roderick M.: 1982, "A Version of Foundationalism," *The Foundations of Knowing*, Minneapolis.

Clark, Romane: "Vicious Infinite Regress Arguments," this volume.

Cornman, James and Keith Lehrer: 1974, *Philosophical Problems and Arguments*, second edition, New York.

Davidson, Donald: 1983, "A Coherence Theory of Truth and Knowledge," in Dieter Hendrich, ed., *Kant oder Hegel*, Stuttgart.

Delaney, C. F.: 1976, "Foundations of Empirical Knowledge-Again," *The New Scholasticism*, L,1.

Foley, Richard: 1987, *The Theory of Epistemic Rationality*, Cambridge, Mass.

Harker, Jay E.: 1984, "Can There Be an Infinite Regress of Justified Beliefs?," *Australasian Journal of Philosophy* 62, 3.

Harman, Gilbert: 1975, *Thought*, Princeton.

Kim, Jaegwon: "What is 'Naturalized Epistemology'?", this volume.

Kornblith, Hilary: 1980, "Beyond Foundationalism and the Coherence Theory," *The Journal of Philosophy* XXV, 11.

Lehrer, Keith: 1974, *Knowledge*, Oxford.

Lehrer, Keith: forthcoming, "Metaknowledge: Undefeated Justification," *Synthese*.

Moser, Paul K.: 1985, *Empirical Justification*, Dordrecht and Boston.

Plantinga, Alvin: 1986, "Coherentism and the Evidentialist Objection to Belief in God," in *Rationality, Religious Belief, and Moral Commitment*, ed. by Robert Audi and William Wainwright, Ithaca and London.

Quinton, Anthony: 1973, *The Nature of Things*, London.

Sellars, Wilfrid: 1973, "Givenness and Explanatory Coherence," *The Journal of Philosophy* LXX.

Shatz, David: 1983, "Foundationalism, Coherentism, and the Levels Gambit," *Synthese* 55, 1.

Philosophical Perspectives, 2, Epistemology, 1988

THE INTERNALISM/EXTERNALISM CONTROVERSY*

Richard Fumerton
University of Iowa

Much of contemporary epistemology takes place in the shadow of the internalism/externalism debate. Its current place on the centre stage of epistemology seems appropriate given the dramatic revolution in our thought about historical and contemporary epistemological inquiry that would seem to be forced by certain paradigm externalist views. But although the controversy seems to strike deep at the heart of fundamental epistemological issues, I am not certain that it has been clearly defined. It seems to me that philosophers are choosing sides without a thorough understanding of what the respective views entail.

In this paper I want to explore a number of different ways of defining the technical distinction between internalist and externalist epistemologies. As is so often the case with technical philosophical distinctions, it is probably foolish to insist that there is only one "correct" way to define the distinction. I am interested in developing a way of understanding the controversy so that it leaves many philosophers already recognized as paradigm internalists and externalists in their respective categories, but this is not my main goal. Indeed, while my ultimate suggestion as to how to understand internalism will include as internalists many in the history of philosophy, it may be harder to find contemporary epistemologists who satisfy my internalist criteria. My primary concerns are to define the controversy in such a way that it a) involves a fundamentally important distinction, and b) articulates the source of the underlying dissatisfaction that internalists feel toward paradigm externalist analyses of epistemic concepts. At the very least, I want to articulate *this* internalist's view as to the critical mistake of externalism. As one who thinks that externalist analyses of epistemic concepts are somehow irrelevant to the traditional and appropriate philosophical interest in knowledge and justified belief, I am obviously interested in converting philosophers to my own brand of internalism, and the extreme version of foundationalism that it involves. My hope is that when philosophers realize the underlying source of their unhappiness with externalist epistemology, they will come home to a version of foundationalism that has been neglected too long. By way of achieving this last goal, I will also examine and object to one of the methodological assumptions underlying externalist epistemologies. But let us begin by trying to define the concepts of internalism and externalism.

Internalism and Internal States

The term "internalism" might suggest the view that S's knowing that P or having a justified belief that P, consists in S being in some *internal* state. We might, then, understand the externalist as one who is committed to the view that two individuals could be in identical "internal" states of mind while one knows, or has evidence, or has a justified belief, while the other does not. This is surely tempting, but everything hinges on how we understand "same internal state" and "same state of mind". If we include among the properties that define a state of mind *relational* properties, then it would seem obvious that an *externalist* can, and would, embrace the thesis that if my state of mind is identical to yours then I'll know what you know, I'll be justified in believing what you are justified in believing. Goldman, Nozick, Armstrong, and Dretske, to consider just a few externalists, are all willing to pick out a complex relational property that my belief has in virtue of which it constitutes knowledge or justified belief.[1] The relational property will typically be a complex nomological property, such as the property of being caused by a process which satisfies a certain description, or being such that it would not have occurred had not certain other conditions obtained. One gets all sorts of variations on externalism depending on how the relevant nomological relations are characterized. If we are trying to define a view that these externalists reject, then, we cannot simply define internalism as maintaining that one knows or has a justified belief in virtue of being in a certain kind of state of mind when we let the relevant kind be determined in part by its relational properties.

Shall we then say that an internalist identifies knowledge and justified belief with internal states of mind, meaning by internal states of mind, *nonrelational* properties of a mind? The externalist, correspondingly, would maintain only that two individuals could exemplify the same nonrelational properties while one knows or has a justified belief and the other does not. We could, but then we are going to be hardpressed to find very many internalists. Certainly, on this understanding of externalism, everyone who holds that a justified true belief can constitute knowledge even when the justification is logically compatible with the belief being false is committed to an externalist account of knowledge.[2] A non-redundant truth condition in the traditional analysis of knowledge clearly introduces a condition that goes beyond the nonrelational properties of the knower. But even if we restrict our attention to the concept of justified belief, there seem to be precious few philosophers who would identify the having of a justified belief with the exemplification of some nonrelational property (properties).

One of the classic foundationalist approaches to understanding noninferential knowledge identifies at least one condition for such knowledge as *direct acquaintance* with facts. I'll have more to say about this view later, but for now I would merely observe that at least some externalists take such positions to be paradigms of the sort of internalist epistemologies they are rejecting.[3] But clearly when someone like Russell talked about being acquainted with a fact, he intended to be referring to a *relation* that a subject bears to a fact. Having a noninferentially justified belief, on such a view, would *not* be identical with exemplifying nonrelational properties, and a Russellean would *not* argue that if two people were in the same nonrelational states they would have the same justified beliefs. It is not even clear that the externalists' favorite internalist, Descartes, would satisfy the above characterization of an internalist. If, for example, Descartes accepted a relational analysis of believing something to be the case, or having an idea of something, the states of mind that for him constitute knowledge and justified belief would not be nonrelational properties of a self. The only philosophers who could be internalists in the above sense are philosophers who embrace an adverbial theory of consciousness and identify some of the nonrelational properties, exemplification of which constitutes consciousness, with knowledge and justified belief. If one must believe all that in order to be an internalist, not very many philosophers, myself included, would want any part of the view.

Philosophers who have tried to ground knowledge and justified belief in acquaintance with facts have sometimes construed the facts with which one *can* be acquainted as themselves "modifications" of the mind. This might in turn suggest that one could usefully define the internalist as someone who is committed to the view that knowledge and justified belief must be identified either with nonrelational properties of the mind *or* with relational properties of the mind where the relata of the relations are the mind and its nonrelational properties. Such a definition would house more analyses of justified belief under the roof of internalism although any analysis of knowledge involving a nonredundant *truth* condition would still be externalist. But it is important to realize that such a definition of internalism would still leave philosophers who ground justified belief in acquaintance with nonmental facts (e.g.'s, the neutral monist's sense data, the epistemological direct realist's surfaces of physical objects, the Platonist's forms and their relations, the realist's universals and their relations) in the externalist's camp. And I don't think the paradigm externalist wants their company. More importantly, it looks as though we are defining the internalism/externalism debate in a *peculiar* way by putting into opposite camps *fundamentally* similar views. It seems to me that if I am trying to ground the concept of justified belief in acquaintance with nonrelational properties of the mind, and you are trying to ground the concept of justified belief in acquaintance with nonmental sense data, our views are fundamentally alike. The internalism/externalism controversy will not be getting at a *significant* issue if one of these views gets described as a form of internalism while the other is described as a form of externalism.

Internalism and Iteration

There is, of course, more than one natural way to understand the suggestion that conditions for knowledge or justification are internal to the cognizer, or are "in the mind" of the cognizer. When philosophers talked about sense data being "in the mind," for example, at least sometimes they seemed to be pointing to a feature of our *knowledge* of them.[4] Sense data are "in the mind" in the sense that one has a kind of privileged access to them. And this analogy suggests another way of trying to understand what is really at issue between the internalist and the externalist. At least some philosophers want to understand the internalist as someone who maintains that the necessary and sufficient conditions for satisfying epistemic concepts are conditions to which one has a privileged and direct access. "Access," of course, it itself an epistemic term. On this analysis of internalism, then, the internalist might be thought of as someone who is committed to the view that knowledge entails knowing (perhaps directly) that one knows; having a justified belief entails justifiably believing that one has a justified belief.

The above involves a very strong interpretation of having access to the conditions of knowledge and justified belief. A weaker conception of access could construe access as *potential* knowledge or justified belief. Thus a weaker version of internalism along these lines might insist that for a person to be justified in believing a proposition P that person must have "available" to him a method for discovering what the nature of that justification is. Let us consider both this strong and weak attempt to understand internalism as the view that having knowledge or justified belief entails having epistemic access to the conditions for knowledge and justified belief.

As someone who has always thought of himself as an internalist, one of my first concerns with the *strong* requirement of access is that it might saddle the internalist with a view that requires the *impossible* of knowledge and justified belief. As I shall make clear in my concluding remarks, I don't care if, on my analysis of epistemic terms, it turns out that dogs, computers, my Aunt Mary, or even the philosophically sophisticated, do not have *philosophically relevant* knowledge of, or justification for believing, what they think they know or are justified in believing. But I do not want to *define* knowledge and justified belief in such a way that having knowledge and justified belief involves a vicious regress. And the requirements that one must know that one knows P in order to know P; justifiably believe that one is justified in believing P in order to justifiably believe P, certainly seem to flirt with the prospect of a vicious regress.

In elaborating this point, one might, however, usefully distinguish inferential justification from noninferential justification. I *have* defended elsewhere (in [6], Chapter 2; and [7]) the very strong principle that if one is to be justified in *inferring* one proposition P from another E one must be 1) justified in believing E *and* 2) justified in believing that E makes epistemically probable P. Foundationalists have traditionally maintained that if one accepts such a principle, the only way to avoid an infinite number of infinite regresses is to recognize the existence of noninferentially justified beliefs (including, of course, noninferentially justified beliefs in propositions of the form 'E makes probable P'). My reservations with the strong requirement of access, then, have to do with the general thesis that *all* justification involves access to the conditions of justification. In his recent book [2], Bonjour seems to defend a version of internalism defined in terms of a requirement of strong access and he argues, quite plausibly, that foundationalists are going to have an exceedingly difficult time ending the regress of justification within the context of this strong internalism.[5] If a belief that P has some feature X in virtue of which it is supposed to be noninferentially justified, Bonjour's internalism requires us to justifiably believe that the feature X is present and that it makes probable the truth of P. The regress we were trying to end with noninferential justification is obviously about to begin again. If one accepts this incredibly strong version of internalism, it seems to me that one will not be able to escape Bonjour's argument. Indeed it is all too evident that Bonjour cannot escape his own argument as it might be applied to his coherentist alternative to foundationalism. To his credit, Bonjour recognizes that his internalism requires that in order to have empirical justification, one must have *access* to what one believes and the relevant relations of coherence. Since the only kind of epistemic access to empirical propositions he recognizes is through coherence, one will have to find beliefs which cohere with beliefs about what one believes. But the problem rearises with respect to getting access to those beliefs and again we encounter a vicious regress. Bonjour tries to save his view with his "doxastic presumption" (101-05) (you just take it for granted that your metabeliefs are by and large right), but it seems to me that if one reads the text closely, Bonjour as much as admits that his view entails the most radical of skepticisms with respect to empirical justification (105).

The only way one can satisfy the requirement of strong access for justification is to allow the possibility of a mind having an infinite number of increasingly complex intentional states. If, for example,

I hold (as I do) that my belief that P is noninferentially justified when I am acquainted with the fact that P, the thought that P, and the relation of correspondence between the thought that P and the fact that P (call these conditions X) I am not, on the above view, an internalist unless I am willing to assert that in order for X to constitute my noninferential justification for believing P, I must be acquainted with the fact that X, the thought that X, and the relation of correspondence between the thought that X and the fact that X (call *these* Y). And I must also hold that I am acquainted with the fact that Y, and so on. Now I am not saying that this view is obviously impossible to hold. One can suppose that people have an infinite number of thoughts (perhaps dispositional) and one can think of the "layers" of acquaintance as being like perfectly transparent sheets laid one on top of another. But do we, as internalists, want to let ourselves be painted into a corner this tight where the only escape is a view that might not even be intelligible?

While it is not precisely the same problem of a formal vicious regress, the possible limitations of the mind when it comes to considering facts of ever expanding complexity might also make a proponent of the acquaintance theory of noninferential justification reluctant to accept even the *weaker* requirement of access. Speaking for myself, I am not sure I can even keep things straight when I try to form the thought that my thought that my thought that my thought that P corresponds to my thinking that P corresponds to P. And this is still only a few levels away from the first order thought that P.

"Internalism" is, to be sure, a technical expression, but do we want to put a view like mine that refuses to accept either the strong or the weak requirement of access, but that defines noninferential justification in part by reference to the concept of direct acquaintance with facts, on the externalist side of the internalist/externalist controversy? My suspicion is that this is not how the issue is being understood. And to further reinforce the idea that we are not getting at the heart of the controversy by considering requirements of "access", we should reflect on how easily a mischievous externalist can "play along" with access requirements of internalism. For purposes of illustration let us take one of the paradigmatic externalist analyses of epistemic terms, the reliabilist analysis of justification offered by Goldman in [8].[6] In that article Goldman initially suggests the following recursive analysis of justification: A belief is justified if it results either from 1) a belief-independent process that is unconditionally reliable, or 2) a belief-dependent process that is conditionally reliable, where the "input" beliefs are themselves justified. Belief-independent processes do not have beliefs as their "input," and what makes them unconditionally reliable is that the "output" beliefs are usually true. Belief-dependent processes have as their "input" at least some beliefs, and what makes them conditionally reliable is that the "output" beliefs are usually true *when* the "input" beliefs are true. Qualifications having to do with the availability of alternative processes and the consequences of their hypothetical use are later suggested, but they need not concern us for the point I presently wish to discuss.

Now it is obviously a feature of Goldman"s paradigmatic externalism that it does not require that a person whose belief is justified by being the result of some process have epistemic access to that process. My beliefs can be reliably produced even if I have no reason whatsoever for supposing that they are reliably produced. And this might seem to suggest that the important feature of externalism is its rejection of access requirements for justified belief. But suppose the externalist gets tired of hearing internalists complaining about allowing the possibility of having a justified belief with no justification for believing that it is justified.[7] It is useful to ask whether a reliabilist could remain within the spirit of reliabilism and at the same time allow that reliable processes yield justified beliefs only when one is justified in believing that the processes are reliable. Certainly, a reliabilist could accept our weak requirement of access—a reliabilist could allow that a reliable process $P1$ generates justified beliefs only if there is *available* a justification for believing that $P1$ is reliable. Interpreting this justification on the relabilist's model would presumably require there being available a process $P2$ which could generate the belief that $P1$ is reliable. Of course, given the requirement of weak access, $P2$ would itself generate justified beliefs only if there were available a reliable process $P3$ which could generate the belief that $P2$ is reliable, and so on. But it is not obvious that all of these reliable processes or methods need be different (a reliabilist, as far as I can see, can allow, for example, the inductive justification of induction, perceptual justification of the reliability of perception, and so on) and in any event since they need only be available (as opposed to actually used) it is not clear that the regress is vicious.

Could a reliabilist accept even a strong requirement of access?

Could a reliabilist even allow that a process $P1$ generates justified beliefs only if the believer actually justifiably believes that the process is reliable? This is clearly more problematic for there would actually have to be some reliable process $P2$ generating the belief that $P1$ is reliable, and some reliable process $P3$ generating the belief that $P2$ is reliable and so on. The coherence of such a view rests on considerations concerning the potential complexity of the mind that we have already discussed in the context of wondering whether classical foundationalism can cope with strong access requirements. But suppose, for the sake of argument, that our hypothetical reliabilist convinces us that the mind has a kind of infinite complexity that renders harmless even this regress. The important question to ask is whether this hypothetical reliabilist paying his externalist lip service to our requirements of access would make the dissatisfied internalist happy. And I think the answer is that he obviously would not. As long as the reliabilist/externalist keeps offering reliabilist/externalist accounts of knowing that one knows or being justified in believing that one has a justified belief, the internalist isn't going to feel that anything has been accomplished by getting this reliabilist to accept the view that knowing entails knowing that one knows; having a justified belief entails being justified in believing that one has a justified belief. The obvious moral to draw is that the fundamental disagreement between internalists and externalists is not really a disagreement over such questions as whether inferential justification entails actual or potential justified belief in the legitimacy of the inference, or more generally whether justification entails actual or potential access to the fact that the conditions of justification are satisfied.

Internalism and Normativity

One of the more nebulous criteria for distinguishing internalist and externalist analyses involves the suggestion that externalists ignore the *normativity* of epistemic judgments. And, certainly, many of the objections levelled at reliabilism, for example, make the claim that unreliability to which one has no actual or potential access cannot decide questions about the rationality or irrationality of beliefs because charges of irrationality are relevant to evaluations of epistemic *praise* and *blame*. If my beliefs are produced by unreliable processes when there is no possible way for me to find that out, in what sense am I to be blamed for having the belief? The inhabitants of demon worlds are no more blameworthy for their demon induced false beliefs than are the inhabitants on non-demon worlds.[8]

Now in one sense I am perfectly prepared to admit, qua internalist, that when one characterizes a belief as irrational one is *criticizing* that belief, and since I think that externalist accounts are radically mistaken analyses of philosophically relevant epistemic concepts, I obviously think they have incorrectly analyzed the nature of this epistemic criticism. But being a kind of criticism is a very broad criterion for being normative. We criticize beliefs for being irrational, but we also criticize knives for being dull, cars for being too expensive, theories for being false. But does that make judgments about the dullness of knives, the cost of cars, and the falsehood of theories, normative judgments? Perhaps in a sense a judgment about the dullness of knives is *relevant* to a normative judgment about the goodness of that knife in that we usually consider dullness to be a property that makes the knife ineffective for achieving certain ends peculiar to the use of knives. But this is grist for the reliabilist's mill. We criticize the processes producing beliefs for being unreliable, the reliabilist might argue, because such processes typically fail to produce what we want from them—true beliefs.

Surely both internalists and externalists will agree that in some sense charges of irrationality can be construed as *criticisms*. But it is important to distinguish this virtual truism, a truism that isn't going to differentiate the two views, from so-called deontic analyses of epistemic terms, where a deontic analyses *defines* epistemic concepts using value terms. Deontic analyses of epistemic terms may well be incompatible with at least paradigm externalist views, but as an internalist I certainly don't want to be stuck with defending a deontic analysis of epistemic concepts. To *criticize* a person's *belief* is not to suggest that the person is morally reprehensible for having that belief. And this is so even if we successfully avoid the standard "conflicting duties" objections to deontic analyses that were raised against the view that Chisholm suggested in [3] (You've got the duty to believe you will get well—it might help—even though your evidence indicates you will probably die). Specifically, I would argue that a person's belief can be epistemically criticized even if we decide that the person is so far gone, is so irrational, that we do not think it even causally possible for him to figure out why his beliefs are irrational. Such a person is presumably not to be *blamed* for believing anything. He may be doing the very best he can with the potential he has, even though his best effort still results in the having of irrational beliefs. Put another way, we do not (should not) ethically criticize an irrational *person* for holding beliefs that we nevertheless *criticize* as irrational. Again, I do not think that the externalist has a plausible understanding of the conditions under which we philosophically criticize a belief as being irrational, but for the reasons I have tried to indicate, I do not think it is useful to try to understand the internalist/externalist debate as one over the normativity of epistemic judgments. In fact, I would argue that pure deontic analyses of epistemic terms involve a mistake very much like the mistake of externalism.

Externalism and What's Really Wrong with it

For someone whose primary interest is in defining the controversy, this section heading might seem unnecessarily contentious. But you will recall that my concern is to understand the internalist/externalist debate in such a way as to make clear what I take to be the source of the internalist's dissatisfaction with the view, and particularly this internalist's dissatisfaction with the view.

Old philosophical views have a way of resurfacing under new labels. And the roots of externalism go back further than the "naturalistic epistemology" encouraged by Quine. Rather, I think they lie with an old controversy concerning the correct analysis of epistemic probability. While the Russell of [15] clearly took epistemic probability to be a *sui generis* concept (see his discussion of the principle of induction) the Russell of [16] was bound and determined to reduce epistemic probability to a frequency conception of probability.[9] A crude attempt to define epistemic probability in terms of frequency might hold that one proposition E makes probable another proposition P when the pair is of a kind e/p such that usually when a proposition of the first kind is true, a proposition of the second kind is true. For our present purposes we can ignore the difficult questions involving the interpretation of the relevant frequencies, questions to which Russell devoted a great deal of attention. There is, it seems to me, an obvious connection between a frequency analysis of epistemic probability and the fundamental claims of such externalist epistemologies as reliabilism. Both are trying to understand fundamental epistemic concepts in terms of *nomological* concepts. The externalist/naturalist in epistemology (like his counterpart in ethics) is trying to define away the concepts fundamental to his discipline; he is trying to analyze fundamental epistemic concepts in terms of other non-epistemic concepts. Goldman's hard core reliabilism wants to explicate justified belief in terms of either a frequency or propensity (if that is any different) concept of probability. Nozick wants to define epistemic concepts in terms of nomological connections between facts and beliefs of the sort expressed by contingent subjunctive conditionals (in [14]). Armstrong appeals to this same concept of nomological necessity in trying to understand knowledge (in [1]). And if externalism involves a fundamental philosophical error, I would suggest that it is analogous to the alleged mistake of naturalism in ethics, or more accurately, the alleged mistake in ethics of trying to define the indefinable. I would urge you to consider the suggestion that it is a defining characteristic of an internalist epistemology that it takes fundamental epistemic concepts to be *sui generis*. No matter how much lip service our hypothetical reliabilist tries to pay to our insistence that justified belief entails being actually or potentially aware of the conditions of justification, he won't satisfy us as long as he continues to define the epistemic terms with which he pays us lip service in his naturalistic (nomological) way. It is the nomological analyses of epistemic concepts that leads us to keep moving up a level to ask the externalist how he knows that he knows, or knows that he knows that he knows. The externalist might be able to give correct answers within the framework of his view, but we, as internalists, will keep asking the questions until his answer invokes a concept of knowledge or justified belief not captured in terms of nomological connection. The real internalist/externalist controversy, I would suggest, concerns the extent to which sui generis epistemic concepts can be analyzed employing, or even be viewed as supervenient upon (where being supervenient upon involves a necessary connection stronger then causation), such nonepistemic nomological concepts as causation, universal and probabilistic law, and contingent subjunctive conditionals. Ironically, I never have been convinced that there is a naturalistic or definist fallacy in ethics. As an internalist, I am convinced that there is something analogous in epistemology and that it is at the heart of the internalism/externalism debate.

What are these sui generis epistemic concepts that defy reduction or analysis? This is obviously a question about which those who reject the externalists' views will themselves disagree. Perhaps the most famous contemporary philosopher associated with internalism today is Roderick Chisholm and despite periodic flirtations with deontic analyses of epistemic terms, I think one must ultimately take seriously his insistence that we take as primitive the concept of one proposition being more reasonable to believe than another (in, for example, [4]). I would myself locate the fundamental sui generis epistemic concepts elsewhere.

In rejecting externalism, I have tried to be clear that I reject it only as an analysis of philosophically relevant epistemic concepts. Knowing, or have a justified belief, in the externalist's sense doesn't satisfy our philosophical curiosity, doesn't answer our philosophical questions, because qua philosophers trying to be rational, we want more than to be automata responding to stimuli with beliefs. I would argue that we want *facts*, including facts about which propositions make probable others, before our consciousness. This notion of a fact being before consciousness is, of course, itself an epistemic concept, and my suggestion is that one of the fundamental sui generis concepts that defy further analysis or reduction is the concept of direct acquaintance with a fact that in part[10] defines the concept of noninferential knowledge. And in the case of inferential knowledge, what one really wants as an internalist is direct acquaintance with the fact that one's evidence makes epistemically probable one's conclusion. Acquaintance with evidential connections would clearly be impossible if evidential connections are to be understood in terms of frequencies or other nomological connections, and that indicates that the other epistemic concept which resists further analysis is the old Keynesean notion of making probable as a sui generis relation between propositions, analogous to, but obviously different from, entailment.[11] I haven't the space to develop this view here—I have done so elsewhere.[12] My only concern is to sketch the *kind* of view, with its reliance on sui generis epistemic concepts, that I would take to be paradigmatically internalist.

A Presupposition of Externalism

I would like to conclude by briefly commenting on what I take to be a primary motivation of externalist analyses of epistemic concepts. I have said that there are a number of different views as to what the sui generis epistemic concepts might be, and the ease with which one can avoid skepticism depends very much on the details of the view one accepts. But certainly if one accepts the extreme version of foundationalism I recommend, complete with its insistence that one must have noninferential justification for believing propositions asserting evidential connections, the externalist is going to think that the task of avoiding skepticism is impossible. The typical externalist is convinced that one simply cannot be acquainted with facts. And even the internalist will undoubtedly admit that the kinds of facts with which we can be directly acquainted constitute a tiny fraction of what we think we know. When it comes to inferential knowledge, one must take seriously Humean complaints about the phenomenological inaccessibility of the relevant probability connection even if one ultimately rejects those complaints. If one cannot find in thought sui generis probability relations holding between propositions, one may well despair of resolving skeptical problems within the framework of radical foundationalism. On the problem of justifying belief in propositions describing the external world, for example, one might begin to suspect that Hume was right when he suggested with respect to what man ends up believing that

> Nature has not left this to his choice, and has doubtless esteem'd it an affair of too great importance to be trusted to our uncertain reasonings and speculations. ([11], p. 187).

Hume's hypothesis, I suspect, is accepted by externalists, but they do not want its truth to cheat us out of knowledge and justified belief. One of the most attractive features of most versions of externalism is that is makes it easy for us to know what we think we know. As long as nature (we now prefer to talk about evolution) has ensured that we respond to certain stimuli with correct representations of the world, we will know and have justified belief. Indeed, given externalist epistemologies, there is no difficulty in any creature or machine capable of representing reality achieving knowledge and justified belief.

It seems to me, however, that contemporary epistemology has too long let its philosophical analyses of epistemic terms be *driven* by the desire to avoid skepticism, by the desire to accommodate "commonsense intuitions" about what we know or are justified in believing. It is true that we describe ourselves as knowing a great many things. We also say that the dog knows that its master is home, the rat knows that it will get water when it hears the bell, and the salmon knows that it must get upstream to lay its eggs. But it seems clear to me that one need not take seriously our love of anthropomorphizing when analyzing the concepts of knowledge and justified belief that concern philosophers. If Wittgenstein and his followers did nothing else they surely have successfully argued that terms like "know" are used in a wide variety of ways in a wide variety of contexts. As philosophers, however, we can and should try to focus on the philosophically relevant use of epistemic terms. And the philosophically relevant epistemic concepts are those, satisfaction of which, resolves philosophical curiosity and doubt. I remain convinced that the kind of knowledge a philosopher wants, the kind of knowledge that will resolve philosophical doubt, involves the kind of direct confrontation with reality captured by the concept of direct acquaintance. While this is not the place to argue the issue, Hume *may* have been right—it may not be possible to justify in a philosophically satisfying way much of what we unreflectively believe. If this should be true, we may still satisfy, of course, the externalist's criteria for knowledge and justified belief, and these criteria may even mark a perfectly clear and useful distinction between beliefs and kind of relations they bear to the world. Internalists will continue to feel, however, that the externalist has *redefined* fundamental epistemic questions so as to make them irrelevant to traditional philosophical concerns.

Notes

*I would like to thank Richard Foley and Scott Macdonald for their helpful comments on a rough draft of this paper.
  1. Goldman in [8], [9], and [10]; Nozick in [14]; Armstrong in [1]; and Dretske in (among others) [5].
  2. This point is made by Luper-Foy in [13].
  3. See Nozick in [14], p. 281.
  4. Not always. Sometimes "in the mind" meant logically dependent on the mind—the mind was thought of as a necessary condition for their existence.
  5. The argument is presented on p. 32 but is discussed in a number of places throughout the book.
  6. I realize that Goldman has presented a more sophisticated view in his recent book [10]. But it is a view which strays rather far from his reliabilist

intuitions. The idea that justification is a function of reliability in normal worlds where normal worlds are defined in terms of *beliefs* about this world is equivalent to abandoning the idea that justification involves beliefs which are (actually) reliably produced. Indeed the view seems to me to come closer to a version of coherentism than reliabilism. In any event, I gather from a paper he read at a conference in honor of Roderick Chisholm, [9], that he is now more inclined to go back to "hard core" reliabilism for at least one fundamental concept of justification.

7. It is interesting to note that in [9] and [10] Goldman comes very close to accepting something at least analogous. He allows that the use of a method can generate a strongly justified belief only if the method has been acquired in a suitable fashion, acquired by other methods, or ultimately processes, that are either reliable or meta-reliable. He does *not* impose the requirement on *all* processes, however, and in any event his requirement seems to concern the reliable generation of methods, not *beliefs* about methods.

8. In [10], Goldman himself seems to be more concerned with hooking up *one* sense of justification, what he calls weak justification, to considerations of blameworthiness and praiseworthiness. The aforementioned retreat from pure reliabilism in [9] was presumably aimed at achieving this same end.

9. See particularly [16], Part V, Chapters V and VI.

10. Notice that I have nowhere argued that an internalist cannot make reference to concepts other than the *sui generis* epistemic concepts in analyses of epistemic terms.

11. See Keynes's discussion of this issue in [12], Chapter 1.

12. See particularly Chapter 2 of [6].

References

[1]   D. M. Armstrong, *Belief, Truth, and Knowledge* (London: Routledge and Kegan Paul, 1968).

[2]   Laurence BonJour, *The Structure of Empirical Knowledge* (Cambridge: Harvard University Press, 1985).

[3]   R. M. Chisholm, *Perceiving* (Ithaca: Cornell University Press, 1957).

[4]   R. M. Chisholm, *Theory of Knowledge*, 2nd Edition, (Englewood Cliffs, N.J.: Prentice-Hall, 1977).

[5]   Fred Dretske, *Seeing and Knowing* (London: Routledge and Kegan Paul, 1969).

[6]   Richard Fumerton, *Metaphysical and Epistemological Problems of Perception* (Lincoln and London: University of Nebraska Press, 1985).

[7]   Richard Fumerton, "Inferential Justification and Empiricism," *Journal of Philosophy*, 73 (1976), 557-69.

[8]   Alvin Goldman, "What is Justified Belief," in Pappas, ed., *Justification and Knowledge* (Dordrecht: Reidel, 1979), 1-23.

[9]   Alvin Goldman, "Strong and Weak Justification," a paper read at Brown University, Fall, 1986, at a conference in honor of R. M. Chisholm.

A version is reprinted in this volume.
[10] Alvin Goldman, *Epistemology and Cognition* (Cambridge: Harvard University Press, 1986).
[11] David Hume, *A Treatise of Human Nature*, ed. by L. A. Selby-Bigge (London: Oxford University Press, 1888).
[12] John M. Keynes, *Treatise on Probability* (London, Macmillan, 1921).
[13] Steven Luper-Foy, "The Reliabilist Theory of Rational Belief," *The Monist*, April, 1985, 203-25.
[14] Robert Nozick, *Philosophical Explanations* (Cambridge: Harvard University Press, 1981).
[15] Bertrand Russell, *The Problems of Philosophy* (Oxford; Oxford University Press, 1959).
[16] Bertrand Russell, *Human Knowledge: Its Scope and Limits* (New York: Simon and Schuster, 1948).

Philosophical Perspectives, 2, Epistemology, 1988

ALSTON'S INTERNALISTIC EXTERNALISM

Marshall Swain
The Ohio State University

During the last decade the terms "Externalism" and "Internalism" have become common in Epistemology. When first introduced, Externalism was associated primarily with the work of causal and reliability theorists, also known as "naturalistic" epistemologists. Internalism, on the other hand, was primarily associated with more "traditional" theories of knowledge and justification, such as Cartesian and Chisholmian epistemologies. It was thought, by some, that these kinds of theories are wholly disjoint with one another. If you would be an externalist, then you must eschew all internalistic claims, and vice-versa.

Others have always been convinced, however, that these bold claims of incompatibility between the traditional and the new theories are based upon a false dichotomy. In my own efforts to develop causal and reliability theories,[1] I have always operated on the assumption that some of the internalistic tenets of "traditional" epistemology could not be abandoned. For example, I have assumed that the reasons upon which one's belief is based must be internally accessible if that belief is to be epistemically justified, and this is an internalist assumption. But I have also assumed that a necessary condition for a belief's being an instance of empirical knowledge is the presence of an appropriate causal ancestry of that belief, and that the believer be a reliable indicator of the truth of the believed proposition. These are externalist constraints on knowledge and justification.

There are recent signs of recognition among epistemologists that internalistic and externalistic elements can coexist in a theory. The issue of the relationship between these kinds of theoretical constraints is becoming a topic of discussion, and this is a development which I welcome. There are, to be sure, some epistemologists who still maintain that you cannot live in both worlds. But even here, I find, the arguments given are directed more at the inadequacy either of externalism or internalism than at the incompatibility of the two.[2]

In a recent paper,[3] William P. Alston has proposed a theory of justification which explicitly combines both internalistic and externalistic requirements. Alston endeavors to provide a motivation for embracing such a hybrid theory. I find the type of theory suggested by Alston to be congenial, for it bears a clear family resemblance to the account of justification I have myself argued for in other places. In this discussion, I will raise some questions and counterexamples concerning Alston's proposal, and provide what I hope are some constructive suggestions for improvement to his theory. Even if Alston's specific proposal should ultimately prove to be untenable, this discussion should contribute to the larger goal of establishing the respects in which traditional and contemporary epistemologies can complement one another.

Section 1: Alston's Proposal

Let me begin by attempting a concise formulation of Alston's proposed view of epistemic justification. Alston does not provide a schematic definition of justification anywhere in the paper, so the following is an amalgamation of suggestions he makes in various places:

S's belief that p is epistemically justified if and only if:
(1) S's belief that p is based upon some set of grounds, G, such that
  (a) the members of G are the sorts of things which are, typically, accessible to normal human subjects (experiences, beliefs, and perhaps other psychological states); and
  (b) the members of G are fairly directly accessible to S upon reflection; and

(c) *G* is a reliable indicator of the truth of *S*'s belief that
p; and

(2) there are no additional beliefs of *S* such that the union
of these beliefs with *G* fails to be a reliable indicator of
the truth of *S*'s belief that *p*.

In this definition, a number of auxiliary concepts are employed,
but given only a minimal explication. The *basing relation*, which is
employed in condition (1), is intended to be a form of causal
dependence. If a belief that *p* is based upon some grounds, *G*, then
G must at least be part of the causal explanation of that belief's being held. However, as Alston is careful to note, not just any instance
of causal dependence will count as basing. Only when we can also
say that a belief is "guided by" (p. 2ms) the causal factor *G* is it appropriate to say that it is based upon *G*. Alston does not attempt a
precise characterization of this difficult concept in the paper under
discussion.

Of equal difficulty is the concept of *grounds* employed in Alston's
definition. The grounds of a belief are, of course, those things that
the belief is based upon. (p. 4ms) Given that the basing relation is
causal, we know antecedently that the grounds of a belief must be
things that can enter into causal transactions. This narrows the field
of candidates somewhat, but still allows many possible events or
states of affairs to be grounds. A natural way of distinguishing those
causal antecedents which are grounds from those which are not is
by restricting the grounds to psychological states. This is the strategy
Alston adopts when he identifies beliefs and experiences as the most
likely candidates for the grounds of a belief. (pp. 4-7ms) Alston does
not provide any precise argument or justification for his identifica-
tion of grounds with beliefs and experiences. As will be seen later,
his account faces some serious problems in this area.

In the informal characterization of his view, Alston says that a
justified belief is one that is "...based on an adequate ground." (p.
1ms) He explicates the notion of adequacy, as in condition (c) above,
in terms of reliable indication.[4] The grounds of a belief that *p* are
a reliable indication of the truth of that belief provided that the probability of *p*, given those grounds, is high. In speaking of probabilities
here, Alston has in mind some form of "objective" probability—he
mentions the "tendency", or "propensity" account as a possible interpretation. (p.8ms) Although there is much to be discussed in con-

nection with the auxiliary concepts employed by Alston, I will forego the temptation to do so (except that I will return to consider the concept of grounds later). Rather, I move directly to a discussion of the internalistic and externalistic features of Alston's proposal.

Section 2: Externalist and Internalist Features

This view is externalistic, Alston suggests, because of the reliable indicator requirement expressed in (1c). It is internalistic because of the other requirements, which together indicate that the grounds of a justified belief must be psychological states or experiences accessible to the believer and other normal human subjects.

The specific feature of Alston's view which most obviously makes it an internalistic one is the accessibility requirement. As he points out (p. 9ms), restricting the grounds for a belief to psychological states and experiences will not alone make a view internalistic. In arguing for his accessibility requirements, Alston refers to the strong shared intuition that one cannot be justified in believing something "...while totally lacking any capacity to determine what is responsible for that justification." (p.12ms) He endeavors to explain this intuition by reference to the relation between *providing a justification* and *being justified*. (pp. 12-15ms) This explanatory suggestion is not put forth as a proof that accessibility of reasons is required for justification, and no other arguments are offered for this claim.

Although I largely agree with Alston that some kind of accessibility condition is appropriate, I find his stated requirements to be too strong. Alston hedges a little on this himself when he allows that special circumstances might make one's grounds for a justified belief inaccessible. (p. 16ms) Even so, he wants to require that the grounds of a justified belief must be of a sort whose members are *accessible to normal human subjects* and *fairly directly accessible to the believer*. Alston is well aware that the terms "normal" and "fairly directly" render his proposal vague, and he indicates that further work will be required to clarify them.

But even these qualified requirements, if intended to apply universally, seem too strong. Consider the requirement that the subject's grounds must be of a kind that is, typically, accessible to normal human subjects. This might be acceptable if we restrict the scope of justified believing to entities which *are* normal human subjects.

But why should we do that? It is not difficult to imagine a race of beings who have beliefs of the kind we do but whose cognitive resources are vastly superior to ours. I can also imagine beings whose experiences, perceptual and otherwise, are much more finely tuned to the way the world is than ours (we are told that dogs, bats, and dolphins are like this in some respects). For such beings, the grounds for a belief may be utterly unlike anything that normal human subjects can access, but surely we would not deny them the privilege of justification on those grounds!

If such possibilities were the only problem with the requirement under consideration, then it might be solved by adding a restriction having to do with the *kind* of entity whose beliefs are being judged for justifiability. We might say that an X's reasons must be of a kind typically accessible to normal X's, where human beings would be one instantiation of 'X'. Such a solution would cohere well with Alston's sociological explanation of why we have the intuition that reasons should be accessible. However, it would fail to account for a human being who is quite normal except for some very special ability. Perhaps there really are clairvoyants, mind-readers, and the like, whose beliefs are sometimes based upon grounds that are, typically, not accessible to *normal* human subjects. The abnormality of their grounds should not be a formal barrier to justification. Do we then allow 'clairvoyant' as a substituend for 'X'?

I am not sure how far to carry this line of argument. A person whose internal, accessible states are radically unlike our own might still have beliefs based upon such states. At what point do we ostracize such an abnormal cognizer from the fraternity of epistemic privilege? And on what grounds? Is it because such a person could not convey the grounds of justification, could not describe them, etc.? If these are the reasons for ostracism, then I think we would be taking the connection between *being able to provide a justification* and *being justified* too seriously. From the point of view of justification, it does not matter, so far as I can see, whether one's grounds for a belief are, typically, accessible to anyone, or any kind of entity, besides oneself.

A related point concerns the other major part of Alston's accessibility requirement, which says that one must have *fairly direct access* to one's grounds if one is to be justified. This requirement can be satisfied even if one's grounds are uniquely inaccessible to everyone else, as in the case of an abnormal cognizer imagined above. Suppose we have such an a cognizer, S, who has adequate grounds for the belief that p but whose grounds are so unlike any normal human psychological states that even if we asked S to provide the grounds, S would not be able to communicate this to us. Then, what difference does it make whether S has access ("fairly direct" or otherwise) to the grounds or not? Is it somehow of importance to justification that S be able to *provide* a justification, if only for his own benefit? I am inclined to agree with Alston that it is important, but I cannot find a good reason, other than the avoidance of certain examples.

I turn now to another, somewhat different, kind of observation. Although Alston is concerned to require accessibility of the grounds for one's belief, he is equally concerned to avoid imposing a condition on justified belief which requires the subject to be cognizant of the *adequacy* of those grounds. The grounds must be accessible, but not their adequacy. If we were to impose the requirement that the adequacy of grounds must be accessible, then we will have the consequence that every justified belief will require an infinite hierarchy of justified beliefs, actual or potential. Alston provides detailed arguments against this consequence, and this is the basis of his rejection of the requirement (pp. 18-23ms).

I agree that a requirement which entails an infinite hierarchy of either actual or potential beliefs is highly suspect, at best. However, when the accessibility-of-adequacy requirement is *not* included in an account of justification, then the account appears to face other undesirable consequences. For example, it is possible for a subject to satisfy all of Alston's conditions for justification but fail to be justified precisely because the adequacy of the subject's grounds is hopelessly inaccessible. Let me suggest some scenarios which will illustrate this possibility.

Mystics and others who have religious experiences often claim that some of their experiences provide direct access to the nature of reality and/or a supreme being. While they speak of such experiences as "ineffable," they also take them as strong evidence for belief in the existence of a god, evidence which is akin to direct perceptual evidence. Many a heathen has become an instant believer on the basis of these kinds of mystical experiences (the conversion of Saul is a particularly well-known example of this). Investigation of mystical experiences by psychologists reveals that there is good reason to think that some form of unique experience is, in fact, involved on such occasions. It is also thought that such experiences can be explained as well by physical hypotheses as by any hypotheses which entail the existence of a god (these experiences can be induced by drugs, for example).

But, just suppose that mystical experiences are, in fact, precisely what the mystics think they are. Then, when one has such an experience, and comes to believe that there is a supreme being on the basis of this experience, one's belief will be reliable in exactly the way Alston intends. The ground will be such that, "...the *probability* of the belief's being true, given that ground, is very high...[that is,] the world is such that...the ground is a reliable indication of the fact believed." (p. 7ms) Moreover, I see no reason to suppose that the rest of Alston's conditions could not be satisfied by our imagined mystic. The grounds consist of experiences (perhaps even beliefs), they are fairly directly accessible to the subject, they are of a type that a normal human being could have, and the subject need have no other overriding beliefs. But, I submit, the mystic is *not justified* in the belief that there is a supreme being. I suggest, too, that the mystic is not justified precisely because the (objective) adequacy of the grounds is completely obscure and hidden. Even though the mystic has an experience which provides incontrovertible grounds (in Alston's reliabilist sense) for the existence of a deity, the resulting belief is neither justified nor an instance of knowledge.

The example just provided is controversial, and will not be intuitive to everyone.[5] But other, more mundane, examples come to mind. Suppose our subject, an inept detective, has evidence which entails that Smith killed Jones. Each individual piece of evidence is justified for this detective. The entailment, as in a good detective novel, is extremely complicated, the kind that could be unraveled only by Sherlock Holmes. The detective comes to believe that Smith killed Jones on the basis of the evidence, but not because she has worked out the entailment. She had a prior disposition to believe the conclusion, and the evidence just serves as a convenient rationalization. Moreover, working out the entailment would be beyond her capabilities. In such a case, it seems to me, Alston's conditions are satisfied. The detective has a reliable belief, based upon adequate grounds (they do, after all, entail the conclusion), the *grounds* are accessible, and she has no overriding beliefs. But, the detective is not justified in the belief that Smith killed Jones. Not only is she too lazy to try working out the entailment, she would not be able to if she tried. The adequacy of her grounds is beyond her, for all practical purposes.

Examples of this sort convince me that *some* sort of requirement beyond those Alston has proposed must be imposed on an acceptable account of justified belief. I am strongly inclined to agree with Alston, however, that any requirement which leads to an actual or potential infinite hierarchy of justifications would be unacceptable. In the remaining section of this paper, I want to suggest considerations that may hold some promise for solving the problems just raised. Even if they do not, I believe they point to another respect in which Alston's view must be modified.

Section 3: Relevant Characteristics

As I have already noted, Alston adopts a reliable-indicator view of the adequacy of one's grounds for a belief. On his version of this, it is the subject's *grounds* which are a reliable indication of the truth of the grounded belief. So far as I can tell (Alston's discussion of this is rather brief), the reliable-indicator relation between grounds and believed proposition is one that holds independently of the subject who happens to have those grounds. Another subject who has the same grounds, and no other relevant additional beliefs or experiences, would also have adequate grounds for belief that p.

Alston's version of a reliable indicator view differs from my own in an important way. It does not take into account relevant characteristics of the cognizer, specifically, those characteristics which determine how reliable the subject is as an information-processing mechanism. Such characteristics are, I have argued elsewhere,[6] relevant to ascriptions of justification and knowledge. Examples make this clear.

Suppose two subjects, Smith and Jones, who have the same evidence (grounds) for the belief that p, where the evidence consists of justified belief in the proposition $p \vee (p \& q)$. Both subjects come to believe that p on the basis of this evidence (and no other evidence). In the case of Smith, the mechanism for generating the belief is an inference which instantiates a tendency to invalidly infer p from any sentence of the form '$p \vee q$'. In the case of Jones, the mechanism is an inference which is based on an internalized valid inference schema (of which several are possible). It seems clear to me that only Jones has a justified belief that p, even though they have the same grounds. And it is obvious why this is so. Smith is a defective inference mechanism, Jones is not.[7]

Goldman-style discrimination examples[8] also provide support for the suggestion that characteristics of the believer are relevant to epistemic appraisal. If Jones can discriminate A's from B's, and Smith cannot, then Jones may be justified in believing x to be an A when Smith is not, even though both are perceiving an A (and, thus, have the same perceptual grounds). Again, the explanation of the difference lies in relevant characteristics of the cognizer (in this case, discriminatory abilities).

In such examples, it appears that Alston's conditions for justified belief are met for both subjects, even though only one is justified. Both Smith and Jones, in that example, have beliefs based upon the relevant kinds of grounds (beliefs), these grounds are of a type accessible to normal human subjects, are fairly directly accessible to Smith and Jones, and the proposition believed is highly probable, given those grounds. Similar things can be said about the perceptual discrimination example, except that the grounds in that case are experiential.

Alston's view could be revised to include reference to relevant characteristics of the subject. Instead of having the *grounds* for a belief be a reliable indicator of the truth of that belief, it would be the *subject* who is a reliable indicator. More precisely, the subject's believing, on the basis of the grounds, and given the subject's relevant cognitive characteristics, would be the reliable indicator in a revised definition. Such a definition would be very similar to the one I proposed in *Reasons and Knowledge*.[9]

In the revised version of the paper under consideration, Alston addresses the examples raised above. He agrees that they present a problem for his definition, but rejects the suggestion that these examples indicate the need for a relevant characteristics requirement. Instead, he suggests that "...unwanted applications like these can be excluded just by giving a sufficiently discriminating specification of grounds." (p. 6ms) To back this up, Alston provides some additional specification of the notion of grounds, as he is using it:

> As I am using the term, the "ground" for a belief is not what we might call the total concrete input to the belief forming mechanism, but rather those features of that input that are actually taken account of in forming the belief. (p. 6ms)

In the cases that I suggested, the individuals involved would thus have different grounds for their beliefs, and this explains why one is justified and the other is not. In the inferential case, Jones' belief that p is based upon the fully specified proposition '$p \vee (p \,\&\, q)$', while Smith's is based upon some other grounds. Alston characterizes these other grounds, in the case of Smith, by saying that "...the only feature of the belief input taken account of by Smith was that its propositional object was of the form '$p \vee q$'." (p. 6ms) Since Jones' grounds are reliable, while Smith's are not, we get the correct result in the example.

In perceptual cases, a similar analysis is suggested by Alston. He fills in my schematic suggestion with the following concrete example.

> ...consider two persons, A and B, who come to believe that a collie is in the room on the basis of qualitatively identical visual experiences. But A recognizes the dog as a collie on the basis of distinctively collie features, whereas B would take any largish dog to be a collie. (p. 6ms)

As in the inferential case, the two subjects will turn out to have different grounds for their beliefs, even though both are perceiving the same dog and are, presumably, having the same perceptual experience.

I do not find Alston's alternative explanation of such examples to be convincing. Whether in the inferential case or the perceptual one, both subjects are experiencing the same "raw input." What distinguishes them in each case is the manner in which they *interpret*, or *process* that input. It is true that in both cases one of the cognizers is a more discriminating processor of the information being received, but the input is the same. It seems to me that this is most accurately characterized by saying that one of the cognizers has superior, and the other inferior, discriminative capabilities in each case, and not by saying that the grounds are different for the individuals involved.

In "Discrimination and Perceptual Knowledge," Goldman suggests an analysis which would support my interpretation of these examples.[10] He discusses several kinds of cases in which the same (or very similar) perceptual inputs might be processed in a different manner depending upon the discriminative abilities of the cognizer. These discriminative abilities can be characterized, in part, by reference to iconic schemata possessed by the individual. When an incoming percept matches a schema, such as that for a collie, the appropriate belief is formed. Someone who is deficient in relevant schemata might be caused to form a collie-belief when perceiving any large dog, whereas the discriminating cognizer will have a schema for every dog-perceiving occasion. Without going into all the details, it is important to note that the difference between the discriminate and the indiscriminate believer depends on the schemata present and the causal mechanisms which are triggered by input. It would, I believe, not be appropriate to say that the inputs (grounds) are different in the kind of case that I have suggested. Rather, it is the schemata and their attendant causal propensities which are different, and these are relevant characteristics of the believer.

Alston, of course, may not be any more willing to accept Goldman's account of such situations than mine. I am not sure what would settle this particular dispute between us. The discovery of an example in which Alston's explanation of differences in justification does not work and mine does (or vice-versa) would be helpful in this regard, but I have not been able to think of a clear one.

Independently of these cases, the addition of a relevant characteristics requirement might help to provide a solution to the other problems raised above in connection with the accessibility of adequacy.

Consider the example involving the mystic. Why are we inclined to deny justification for the mystic's belief even though (as we have imagined) the grounds are objectively reliable? A plausible explanation is that the mystic is defective in an important way as a belief-forming mechanism. The mystic is unable to provide even the slightest proof, or any shred of evidence, of the adequacy of his grounds for belief in a supreme being. And yet, the mystic is prepared to believe on the basis of those grounds. A subject who is so disposed is (I submit) defective as a cognizer. If consistently followed, the strategy of believing on the basis of grounds for which you have no indication of reliability would not be truth-conducive. The objective reliability of the mystic's grounds is overridden by his tendency to believe on the basis of evidence whose truth-conduciveness is completely unestablished.

In the example concerning the detective, the explanation of our being disinclined to grant justification is clearly related to characteristics of the subject. The detective is unable to complete the demonstration of conclusion from premises, and has not bothered to try in any case. Even though the evidence in fact entails that Smith killed Jones, the detective's characteristics as a cognizer render this fact inaccessible to him (at least, in the circumstances described). The detective is defective in relevant ways as a cognizer.

Alston's reasons for rejecting an accessibility of adequacy requirement have to do with his legitimate desire to avoid an infinite hierarchy of justified beliefs. I do not think that my suggested way of dealing with the examples generates any such problems with infinite hierarchies. We can require a person to be free from cognitive defects if a grounded belief is to count as justified without requiring that this fact be accessible, justified, or known. Hence Alston's desire to avoid requiring second-level justifications in his account of justified belief (and elsewhere in his epistemology) is well served by the addition of a relevant characteristics requirement.

Notes

1. See my book, *Reasons and Knowledge*, Cornell University Press, 1981, for a sustained discussion of these matters.
2. An example, I believe, is Laurence Bonjour, in his excellent book *The Structure of Empirical Knowledge*, Harvard University Press, 1985. Bonjour argues forcefully in favor of very strong internalistic requirements for epistemic justification. A major part of his argument consists of a rejection of all forms of externalism. Nowhere does he argue, however, that the two are incompatible. I discuss Bonjour's views in "Bonjour's Coherence Theory of Knowledge," forthcoming in a volume to be edited by Jack Bender.
3. W. P. Alston, "An Internalist Externalism," forthcoming in a special issue of *Synthese*, devoted to Externalism and Internalism, edited by Stephen Luper-Foy. Alston's paper was originally presented at a Conference on Epistemic Justification, in honor of Roderick M. Chisholm, at Brown University, November, 1986. I was the commentator on Alston's paper, and the present paper is an outgrowth of my commentary. The published version of Alston's paper addresses some of the problems raised in my original commentary, as I will indicate later.
4. See my *Reasons and Knowledge*, *op. cit.*, Chapter Three, for a detailed development of the reliable indication theory.
5. Least of all to Alston! After writing this commentary, I discovered that he has written a paper, "Perceiving God," *The Journal of Philosophy*, 1986, 655-666, in which he defends the claim that religious experiences can provide epistemic justification for beliefs about God in a manner analogous to ordinary modes of perception. Although I do not agree with Alston's arguments in that paper, I cannot address them here.
6. See *Reasons and Knowledge*, *op. cit.*, pp. 104-115.

7. This example is similar to one suggested to me by Larry Powers.
8. I have in mind examples of the kind introduced by Alvin Goldman in his important paper, "Discrimination and Perceptual Knowledge, *The Journal of Philosophy*, 73 (1976), 771-791.
9. *op. cit.*, pp. 99 and 133.
10. *Ibid.*, especially section II.

James E. Tomberlin is a Professor of Philosophy at California State University, Northridge, where he has taught since completing graduate study at Wayne State University in 1969. He has published more than fifty essays and reviews in action theory, deontic logic, metaphysics, philosophy of language, mind, religion, and the theory of knowledge. Besides editorship of the present series, he has edited *Agent, Language, and the Structure of the World* (Hackett, 1983), *Hector-Neri Castaneda, Profiles* (D. Reidel, 1986) and he co-edited *Alvin Plantinga, Profiles* (D. Reidel, 1985).